Lecture Notes in Artificial Intelligence 3359

Edited by J. G. Carbonell and J. Siekmann

Subseries of Lecture Notes in Computer Science

Foreword

This book is about knowledge, it is about the externalization of human knowledge and about all the attempts we are undertaking to access what we have externalized before. Thus, the book should be of interest to a wide audience.

On the other hand, there are books about knowledge, knowledge management and the like galore. There is an even larger flood of journal articles, conference papers and technical reports, but it is rumored that most are not read by anyone at all. So, why read the present book or, at least, some of its papers?

In my opinion, it is the idea of *memetics* which makes these proceedings special. Not every contribution deals with memetics, but Tanaka's work and his current projects are carving out the profile of what you find in the book. Let's have a closer look.

Richard Dawkins in his book *The Selfish Gene*, 1976 coined the term *meme*; the term is established now. The *Oxford English Dictionary* says: '**meme** (mi:m), *n*. Biol. (shortened from *mimeme* ... that which is imitated, after GENE *n*.) An element of a culture that may be considered to be passed on by non-genetic means, esp. imitation'.

Yuzuru Tanaka has seized upon Dawkin's suggestion and extended it towards concepts and implementations that set the stage for non-genetic evolution in computer and network environments. He has coined the term *meme media*. His comprehensive book *Meme Media and Meme Market Architectures*, 2003 summarizes the current state of affairs from the perspecive of information and communication technologies.

Susan Blackmore's book *The Meme Machine*, 1999 is my favorite introduction into memetics, exhibiting the appealing theory's reach toward psychology, philosophy and religion. This book is nicely complemented by Chris Fields' recent article entitled *Why do we talk to ourselves?*, JETAI 14 (2002) 4, pp. 255–272. Based on results from cognitive sciences, neurosciences and evolutionary psychology, he offers very good reasons for why the human brain has a place in breeding memes.

As an intermediate summary I would say: Read Dawkins' seminal book to know where everything comes from, read Blackmore's book to understand how much it affects all of us, and read Tanaka's book to learn how to exploit memetics for the benefit of computer-supported knowledge evolution – a term that goes intentionally far beyond knowledge management. To keep it simple, you might start by reading some of the contributions collected in this volume.

The 'knowledge society' we are living in brings with it a trend toward a greater role of knowledge in almost every area of our society. Managing knowledge is of growing importance to industry, it is crucial to economic competition, and it is a requirement for enterprises who want to treat their customers appropriately. From the thousands of arguments explaining and illustrating the growing value of knowledge just one might be sufficient: the urgent need for security in information technologies and, in particular, in IT-based communication.

I am not going to risk a discussion on the terms *knowledge, information* and *data*, including their mutual relationships. Many readers will know from their university studies that this involves endless discussions with no proper outcome.

Knowledge is understood quite differently in different areas. Some people are very much convinced that they are able to encode knowledge into data and to transmit those data through networks like the Internet to certain addressees such that the addressees are able to decode the knowledge from the data they receive. In simple cases this may really work well. You may send to somebody your address, and in most situations this may succeed such that postings arrive at your home or your office and visitors come to your party on time.

In more complex situations of interest to us, knowledge is not only wrapped into data packages so that it can be unwrapped suitably by somebody else, frequently knowledge turns out to be the result of a more or less complex process of knowledge construction. This phenomenon is currently under in-depth investigations for the purpose of technology-enhanced learning (slightly differing variants also named e-learning, computer-based training, Web-based training, . . .). In the technology-enhanced learning area, by its very nature you need to ponder about setting up IT systems filled with bits and bytes such that learners when dealing with the systems and the bytes prepared for them may acquire knowledge according to the learners' needs and according to your intentions. Knowledge externalization and knowledge (re-)construction are certainly key issues of technology-enhanced learning.

Though there have already been a few decades of computer-based instruction and there is currently a flood of research and development projects, as well as topical journals and conferences galore, the area seems still to be in its infancy. The crux is that different learners may acquire different knowledge from one and the same data.

When knowledge is externalized, there may be a variety of motivations. In the most simple case, one may externalize knowledge to store it for later use. Knowledge may be externalized with the intention of making it available to other humans. The addressees may be very well-known to us, like, for example, a single communication partner. There may be also a group of addressees more or less well-known to us like, for instance, co-operation partners in some CSCW environment. In the extreme case, addressees may be completely unknown to the authors, like in certain technology-enhanced learning settings. Another intention of knowledge externalization is to make the knowledge subject to computer processing. In the currently most far reaching approach, knowledge may be externalized with the aim of launching knowledge evolution.

When knowledge has been externalized, it may be accessed afterwards by a few individuals, by large communities of varying users, or by computer systems.

The papers collected in this volume were presented at an international workshop held at Dagstuhl Castle, Germany. The main concerns of the workshop participants were concepts, methods, principles, tools, and problems of mutually related knowledge externalization and access.

When humans are interested in accessing appropriately what has been externalized before, the key question is *what* it is that has been externalized. Memetics may provide the right basis for a systematic approach, because *everything that is passed from person to person in this way is a meme. This includes all the words in your vocabulary, the stories you know, the skills and habits you have picked up from others and the games you like to play. It includes the songs you sing and the rules you obey.* [S. Blackmore, *The Meme Machine*, p. 7].

But why should we adopt the perspective of memetics? What does it buy us to see the knowledge world from a meme's viewpoint?

Memes have lives of their own. Memes spread themselves around indiscriminately without regard to whether they are useful, neutral, or positively harmful to us. We can draw advantage from our insights into memetics, and we should be warned to be careful when releasing memes.

To illustrate that, let me cite Susan Blackmore again: *Take the song 'Happy Birthday to You'. Millions of people – probably thousands of millions of people the world over – know this tune. Indeed, I only have to write down those four words to have a pretty good idea that you may soon start humming it to yourself. Those words affect you, probably quite without any conscious intention on your part, by stirring up a memory you already possess. And where did that come from? Like millions of other people you have acquired it by imitation. Something, some kind of information, some kind of instruction, has become lodged in all those brains so that now we all do the same thing at birthday parties. That something is what we call a meme.*

The perspective of memetics is not yet widespread in the scientific community when dealing with issues like knowledge externalization, access to knowledge sources and the like. This perspective may widen our horizons remarkably.

The memes took a great step forward when they got into books, as Blackmore says. But memes are taking enormously greater steps forward when getting into computers and, in particular, into the Internet.

When designing our systems, when externalizing our ideas, we may benefit from the living power of memes when shaping the meme media objects we are launching appropriately. We have to make them fit for lives in the Internet.

In contrast, when accessing what we consider to be knowledge on our computers or in the Internet, we have to ask ourselves what the gist might be in the series of bytes we are receiving. We should also be careful: It is easy to get infected by unwelcome memes.

But do not worry too much. Which memes easily nest into your brain depends very much on the memplexes that are already there. Memes come and go, and most of them do not reside for a long time. They are not fit enough.

The latter perspective, by the way, provides an important guideline for much of our work on knowledge externalization. It is particularly relevant to the technology-enhanced learning endeavor. Whenever we are planning to launch meme media objects via the Internet, we should think about the memetic environment which they may find at their destinations. It is necessary to tailor our meme media objects to fit their target environments.

Let me conclude with a hint possibly not surprising to you: If you have not been infected before, you have caught it now – the meme meme.

Forio d'Ischia, Italy   Klaus P. Jantke
September 2004

Preface

Over the next 10 to 15 years, all kinds of intellectual resources ranging from science and technology through to everyday information will be expressed using electronic media, and we expect these resources not just to be available for browsing, as with current Web-based publication, but to be redistributed and reedited over networks to form large-scale accumulations at the levels of individuals and societies. Like today's markets brimming with commodities, there will be a flood of intellectual resources in society.

To handle this, we need to change from information organization and access based on rational, logical consideration and inference, as used up to now, to organization and access techniques that make maximum use of human intuitive sensibilities. By intuition humans can instantly grasp holistic ideas, instantly narrow or broaden their focus of attention, instantly change the viewpoint or way of looking at something, and recognize and make judgments about higher-order structures. There are many cases in which the goal of a search can only be stipulated in vague terms, but by repeatedly changing one's viewpoint or focus one can gradually clarify what the required target object is. This too is a feature of intuition-based access. In existing rational, logic-based access methods we have pursued management and search techniques that use categorization and arrangement of target objects on the basis of their attributes. By contrast, we believe that for an intuition-based access method it will become effective to pursue management and search not just by focusing on the objects themselves but also on the process and context of the search that leads to an object. We call the system approach based on this standpoint an 'access architecture.' Organization and access techniques for intellectual resources are intimately related to the design and production of distribution spaces for such resources. In this approach we aim to integrate theories of information design, media structure, and basic knowledge engineering, pursuing access-architecture-based research and development of human interfaces whose presentation and manipulation mechanisms are suited to human intuitive abilities. Hence we aim to research how best to design and organize spaces supporting distribution, exchange and access for intellectual resources, and to establish the fundamental technologies needed for access to the intellectual assets that will flood the society of tomorrow.

To discuss these issues, to exchange about new theories and technologies the series of annual international workshops on *Intuitive Human Interface for Organizing and Accessing Intellectual Assets* was initiated. This volume contains selected papers of the 2004 workshop which was held during March 1–5, 2004 at Dagstuhl Castle, Germany.

To achieve the above goals, research and development are needed in the areas of construction methods for media spaces supporting organization and access activities, the process by which vaguely specified requests are gradually made concrete, design and production methods for media spaces, theories and simulations of intuitive sensibility as well as for mechanisms for augmenting receptivity to information. These lead to the following six research topics on which the workshop focused.

R&D into visual design and construction methods for media spaces
> The media spaces that will act as markets for the distribution, organization and access to intellectual resources can define the resources available and the means for making accesses to them. R&D on visual design and construction methods for media spaces will proceed by research into management and search methods focused on the process and context of access.

Intuitive interfaces for data science
> To address the rapid accumulation of high-volume data in the domain of science and technology, we will require information visualization techniques aimed at supporting analysis, synthesis and understanding through providing display and manipulation mechanisms that fit the mental models and intuition of the scientists involved.

Research into the information-access formulation process and a system to support it
> Based on concept-formulation techniques, we need to investigate techniques for handling access requests specified in vague form, and gradually clarifying such requests during the course of the access process.

Research into design and production of media spaces, and narrative databases
> To design and produce distribution spaces with appeal to human intuition, we will need to elucidate the reasoning used since olden times in storytelling, establishing theories regarding the special elements of stories such as archetypal patterns and arbitrary degrees of semantic compressiveness. As well as applying these to the design and production of distribution spaces for intellectual resources, research should be carried out into a 'narrative database' that could be searched using archetypes and summaries.

Theories and simulation of intuition
> This theme involves research based on non-monotonic reasoning to provide theories for the intuitive information access mechanisms that allow humans instantaneous grasping of gestalts, narrowing of focus, changing of viewpoint, and recognition and inferences involving higher-order structures.

R&D into mechanisms for augmentation of information reception ability
> This is the research into interfaces that will utilize and enhance the information-gathering aspects of the human sensory system.

The papers in this volume cover all these research topics. For the sake of clarity and since some papers deal with more than one topic they are grouped into four categories. Within these categories the papers are ordered alphabetically.

The editors want to thank many people who contributed to the success of the workshop. First of all, we thank the participants for submitting papers, giving talks and discussing till late in the night. The program committee did a good job in reviewing and selecting the papers. Finally, we thank the Dagstuhl crew who (as always) provided a stimulating atmosphere and Springer for making this volume possible.

July 2004   Gunter Grieser
                                                         Yuzuru Tanaka

Organization

Program Committee

Gunter Grieser (Co-chair)	Technical University Darmstadt, Germany
Yuzuru Tanaka (Co-chair)	Hokkaido University, Japan
Mina Akaishi	Tokyo University, Japan
Matthew Chalmers	Glasgow University, UK
Koichi Hori	Tokyo University, Japan
Klaus P. Jantke	DFKI Saarbrücken, Germany
Robert Kowalski	Imperial College London, UK
Steffen Lange	DFKI Saarbrücken, Germany
Aran Lunzer	University of Copenhagen, Denmark
Ken Satoh	National Institute of Informatics, Japan
Nicolas Spyratos	Université de Paris, France
Takeshi Sunaga	Tama Art University, Japan
Akihiro Yamamoto	Kyoto University, Japan

Organisation

Program Committee

Table of Contents

Semantic and Narrative Organization and Access of Knowledge

Do Knowledge Assets Really Exist in the World and Can We Access Such Knowledge?

Knowledge Evolves Through a Cycle of Knowledge Liquidization and Crystallization

Koichi Hori

RCAST, University of Tokyo, 4-6-1 Komaba Meguro-ku Tokyo 153-8904, Japan

Abstract. This paper describes a new view of knowledge and how computer systems can support knowledge evolution. In the classic view of knowledge, knowledge should be well articulated and universal. In reality, knowledge evolves dynamically depending on context. Computer systems should support not only the access to the knowledge but also the knowledge evolution.

1 Introduction

This paper reports the overview of the results of the studies done by the author's group in the Japanese research project carried out since 1999 until 2003 led by Yuzuru Tanaka under the title 'Intuitive Human Interface for Organizing and Accessing Intellectual Assets'. The author's group was assigned the topic of 'Supporting the Formation of Access' in the research project. In the project, we have also used a term 'knowledge asset' in the place of 'intellectual asset'.

The aim of the research entitled 'supporting the formation of access' was to build a system to support humans to form the requirement to access the knowledge asset. Tanaka and the author considered that we need a system to support the requirement formation because most of the existing systems – knowledge base, database, and web applications – can only work when the user's requirement is articulated in advance; for example, we cannot search information using the web search engines if we cannot express what we want to search by keywords. Actually, the users often cannot express their requirements by keywords or sometimes they even do not know clearly what they want to search. We need a system that can help the users to articulate their requirement. The author's group has investigated the real communication between sales clerks and customers in shops and have found the problem of requirement articulation is more complicated than we had expected. That is, not only the requirement but also the knowledge evolves dynamically during the communication. In the following sections, we introduce a new view of what is knowledge and how we can access the knowledge. And, we propose concept of knowledge liquidization and crystallization as a model of knowledge evolution process. Finally, we propose the idea of knowledge nebula crystallizers which are the systems to support the knowl-

G. Grieser and Y. Tanaka (Eds.): Intuitive Human Interface 2004, LNAI 3359, pp. 1–13, 2004.

edge liquidization and crystallization, and show an example of the implemented system.

2   A Classic View of Knowledge

The classic view of knowledge is that the knowledge by its definition should be well articulated, objective and universal. However, the researchers in the field of artificial intelligence have known through the experience of the struggle to acquire knowledge for building expert systems that the classic view of knowledge does not necessarily hold in the real world[1]; the experts cannot always verbalize their knowledge, much part of the knowledge is tacit, and the knowledge is very often not universal but context dependent. Nevertheless, most of the current application of the database, knowledge base, and the world wide web still seem to rely on the classic view of knowledge. We show this situation in Fig. 1. In the current application systems that aim at providing knowledge or information to the users, the users are expected to express their requirement in some forms and access and reach the required knowledge. This situation applies only to some limited cases such as purchasing music CDs or books where the users know at least some parts of the indexing data to reach the goal. In our analysis of the real communication protocols, we have found this classic view does not hold at all[2]. The difference between the classic view and the real situation is described in the following sections.

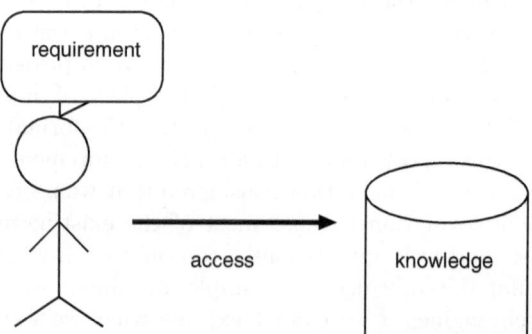

Fig. 1. A classic view of knowledge and access to the knowledge

3   Goal Change of the Users

In the classic view of knowledge and access to the knowledge, the goal or the requirement of the access should be articulated and fixed in advance. Let's see what happens in the real situation. We have found interesting cases in our recorded protocol of the conversation between customers and sales clerks. We can assume here that the sales clerk is knowledgeable about the products and the customer is accessing the knowledge. In one case of shopping, the customer was looking for a jacket. She thought the jacket she picked up was too short and asked the sales clerk if the shop had a longer jacket. If we adopt the classic view of knowledge, this is a very easy case. The customer's requirement is to know if there is a longer jacket and the sales clerk who has knowledge on the product sold in the shop can simply answer yes or no. This actually happened in one case of the real shopping. One sales clerk answered yes and brought the customer a longer jacket, but in this case, the customer did not buy the longer jacket. In another case where the sales clerk seemed to be more expert, she did not answer yes or no but said the problem was not the length of the jacket but the balance between the jacket and the skirt, and succeeded in selling both the short jacket and a long skirt. In the latter case, we can say that the goal of the customer changed; i.e. the goal of looking for a longer jacket changed into the goal of looking for a well balanced jacket and skirt as shown in Fig 2.

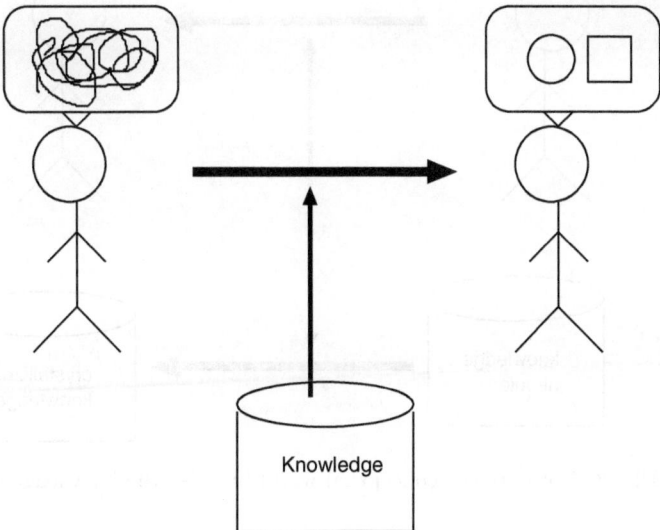

Fig. 2. The requirement or goal changes through the interaction with knowledge

This case may suggest that the expert sales clerk had not only the knowledge on the products but also the meta knowledge or the strategic knowledge on how the knowledge of the products should be applied in the sales. This suggestion may lead to an idea of the system that has some meta knowledge and can provide intelligent advice to the user on how the user can access and use the knowledge stored in the system. Such system may be able to help the user change the user's goal appropriately. This idea may be effective and actually there have been studies on intelligent advisory systems, but we have extended the idea further to the area of creativity as described in the following sections.

4   Dynamic Evolution of Knowledge

If the knowledge in this world is fixed and universal, the problem of building systems to support the user's requirement formation may be simple. However, the real problem is not so simple. The case of real shopping conversation shown in the previous section has suggested that the expert sales clerks have both the object level knowledge and the meta level knowledge. Further analysis of the protocol suggests that those knowledge is not fixed but evolves as shown in Fig. 3.

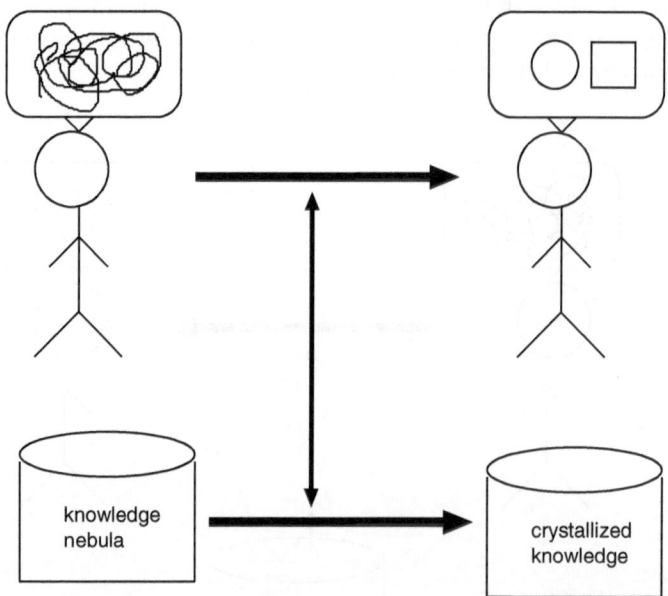

Fig. 3. Not only the conceptual world but also the knowledge evolves

We have found many cases that the expert sales clerks and the customers developed new stories of the customer wearing the clothes to be purchased, e.g. how the customer may look and can behave in certain situations such as wedding parties. We can say that the expert sales clerks sell not just the products but the value or the meaning of the products. The value or the meaning emerges during the communication between the customer and the sales clerk developing the story or the expected experience. We can say that this new value can be new knowledge on the products. The new story cannot be built just relying on the knowledge stored in the sales clerk but should be built depending on the customer's goals. This means that there should be an evolving circle between the customer's goal and the knowledge; neither the goal nor the knowledge is fixed.

What we have found in the analysis of shopping conversation is same as what happens when professional designers design new artifacts. The designers do not design just relying on their knowledge but reflect in action[3]. The conceptual space is not fixed but sometimes jumps into another new space. This phenomenon fits the definition of creativity. Gero classified design into 1) routine design, 2) innovative design, and 3) creative design [4]. Routine design was defined as that design activity which occurs when all the necessary knowledge is available. Innovative design was defined as that design activity which occurs when the context which constrains the available ranges of the values for the variables is jettisoned so that unexpected values become possible. Creative design was defined as that design activity which occurs when a new variable is introduced into the design. Boden says an idea is P-creative if the person in whose mind it arises could not have had it before, and, by contrast, an idea is H-creative if it is P-creative and no-one else has ever had it before [5].

We can say that creativity takes place even in such daily activity of shopping and that the systems which are intended to provide knowledge asset should take this aspect of creativity into consideration.

5   Knowledge Evolution

If it is true that both the user's goal and the knowledge which was sought by the user evolve dynamically, what can the computer systems do?

Our basic idea is that knowledge is not a static chunk of information but dynamically evolves depending on contexts. In this sense, we share Fischer's claim that knowledge is not an existing commodity but a work product[6]. Even though knowledge dynamically evolves, it is obvious that nothing evolves out of the empty. Then where does knowledge come from? Our answer to this question is that knowledge evolves as new relations among the conceptual world, representational world, and the real world as shown in Fig. 4.

In the real world, real objects including humans exist and certain relations hold among them. In the representational world, there exist words and texts in natural language and other forms of representation such as diagrams, graphs and pictures. The conceptual world exists in the human mind and concepts are formed there.

Let's reconsider the example of knowledge evolution in shopping. In the real world, a short jacket existed and the customer picked it up. The customer thought it was too short for her. The concept of length was focused in the customer's conceptual world and it was conveyed to the sales clerk using the word 'length' in the representational world. But at the same time, though the customer did not represent it explicitly, the concept of, say, good looking must have existed in the customer's conceptual world. The sales clerk who was not expert brought a longer jacket in the real world and showed it to the customer. The expert sales clerk guessed what existed in the customer's conceptual world, and moved the customer's attention from the concept of length to the concept of balance by using the word 'balance' and by showing the real relation held between

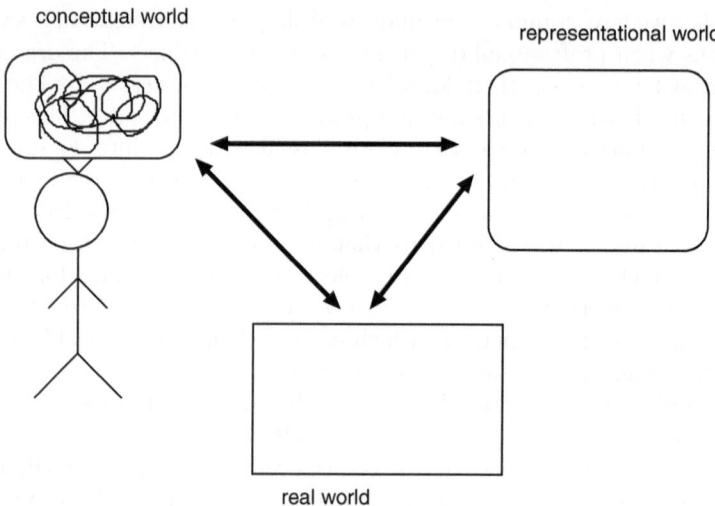

Fig. 4. Knowledge appears in the triangular relation among the conceptual world, representational world, and the real world

the short jacket and a long skirt. Then a story of attending at a wedding party was formed in the representational world. The story evoked other concepts in the conceptual world. The evoked concepts were represented in some words and they evoked the search of the corresponding objects or relations in the real world. The knowledge around the jacket (for example, the value or the meaning of the jacket) emerged in this spiral evolution of the relations among the conceptual world, the representational world, and the real world as shown in Fig. 5. We find that new knowledge emerges even in the experts and this evolution never stops. We give a model of this evolution process in the next section.

6   Knowledge Liquidization and Crystallization

Let's try to model the knowledge evolution process in more details.

The knowledge that exists in the triangular relation shown in Fig. 4 is usually represented in the representational world, which often takes the form of natural language text such as textbooks and manuals. When one expert sales clerk has found new knowledge on the balance of jacket and skirt, she may convey it to novice sales clerks in the textbook of sales. If the novice keeps using the text as it is, she should remain novice. To make her own knowledge, she should apply some parts of the knowledge represented in the text to the new real situation and discover new relations among the representational world, conceptual world, and the real world. When applying some parts of the knowledge to the new real situation, she cannot use the existing knowledge as a whole but she should divide the existing knowledge into smaller parts and restructure the combinations of the parts incorporating new parts of representations, concepts,

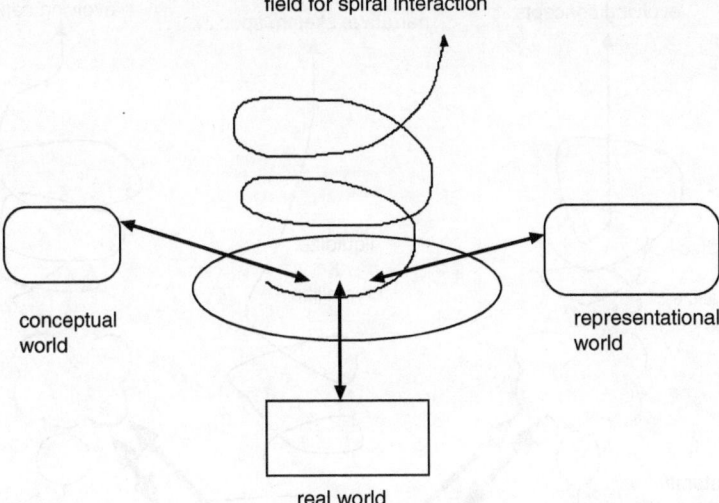

field for spiral interaction

conceptual
world

representational
world

real world

Fig. 5. New knowledge emerges through the spiral interaction among the conceptual world, representational world, and the real world

and real world objects. We name the dividing process of knowledge as knowledge liquidization, and the recombining process of knowledge as knowledge crystallization. We show this model in Fig. 6. As shown in the figure, the liquidization and the crystallization is visibly reflected on the liquidization and crystallization of representation, meanwhile the conceptual world in the human mental worlds are invisibly liquidized and crystallized at the same time.

Here we encounter the answer to the question of the existence of knowledge in the world and the possibility of access to the knowledge. The answer is that knowledge exists not as static chunk but as the evolving relations among representations, concepts, and the real world. People do not just access and use the knowledge but collaboratively build new knowledge at the same time of using the knowledge.

7   Knowledge Nebula Crystallizer to Enable the Knowledge Liquidization and Crystallization

Let's consider what computers can do to promote the process of knowledge liquidization and crystallization shown in Fig. 6.

Our answer in this paper is to replace one person with a computer system. At the beginning of our research project, the authors thought of some extension of existing thinking support tools such as the ones the authors and other researchers have built since ten years ago[7][8], which were the systems to give the users fields and stimuli to reconsider the user's mental world. The previous systems have been basically passive, that is, only the users could build new knowledge.

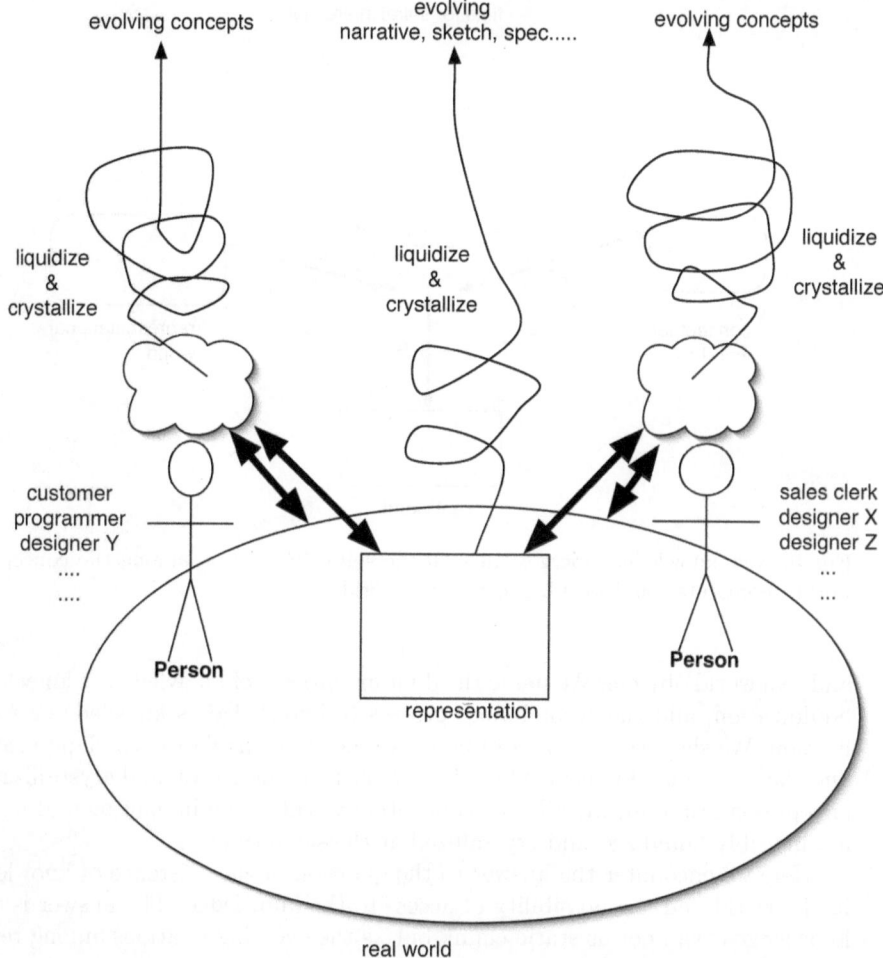

Fig. 6. Knowledge evolves through liquidization and crystallization

In contrast to the previous systems, the Knowledge Nebula Crystallizers the authors are now building and testing are more active systems, that is, the system itself liquidizes and crystallizes knowledge. Looking at and interacting with the process of liquidization and crystallization done by the system, the users also liquidize and crystallize their knowledge. This is shown in Fig. 7.

The liquidization process is formalized as follows.

1. A chunk of representation designated as T1 is given. The most usual form of the representation is a natural language text. T1 consists of unit representations u11, u12, ,,,u1n, where the size of each unit should be determined depending on the application domain. For example, T1 may be a narrative story written in natural language and each u1i may be a sentence in the story.

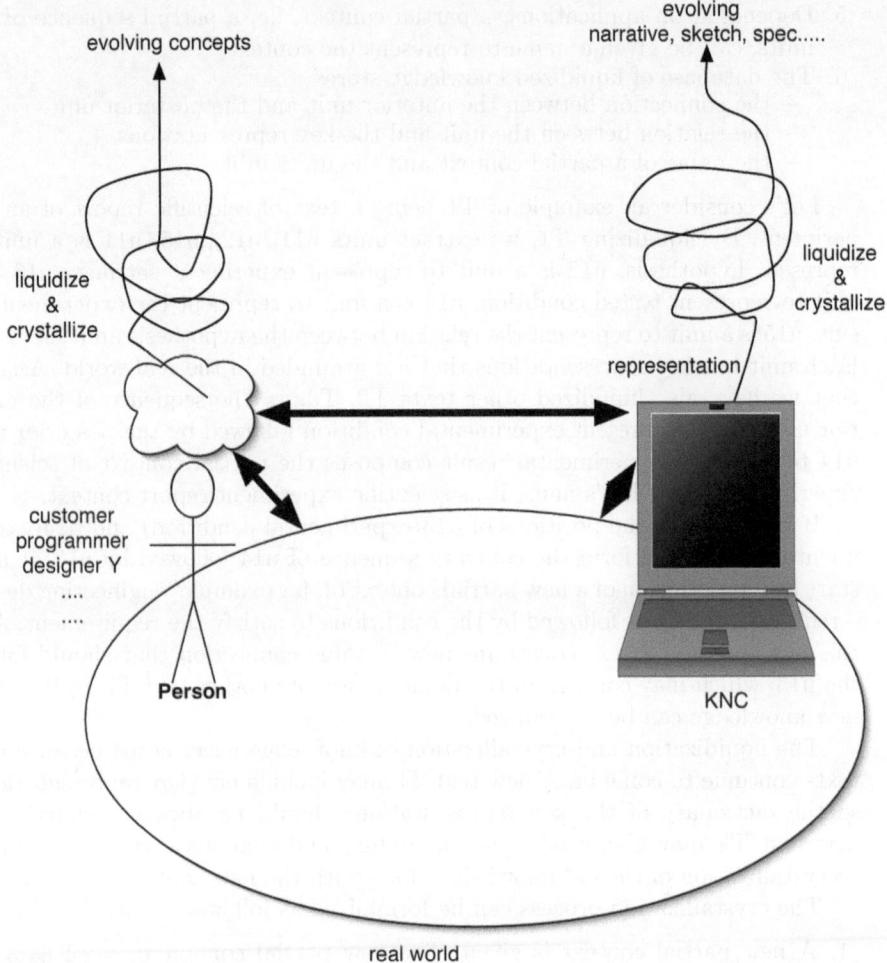

Fig. 7. A computer system named Knowledge Nebula Crystallizer (KNC) liquidizes and crystallizes knowledge

2. Each u1i may or may not include key representations which can be grounded on real world objects or connected to firmly fixed key concepts. Such key representations are given in an application-dependent dictionary and extracted from the representation units u1i.
3. The original connection between u1i and u1i+1 is often achieved by cohesive relation (i.e. surface structure connection such as using pronouns). The cohesive relation should be replaced by the representation which represents coherent connection(i.e. connection in the real world or conceptual world).
4. The anterior unit u1i is connected to the posterior unit u1i+1 under the context of T1. The context emerged from the sequence of the units and the context constrained the sequence of the units; a circular relation held between the context and the units.

5. Depending on applications, a partial context, i.e. a partial sequence of the units, can be given a name to represent the context.
6. The database of liquidized knowledge stores
   - the connection between the anterior unit and the posterior unit.
   - the relation between the unit and the key representations.
   - the name of a partial context and the units in it.

Let's consider an example of T1 being a text of scientific report of an experiment. By liquidizing T1, we extract units u11, u12,,,u15. u11 is a unit to represent hypothesis. u12 is a unit to represent experiment settings. u13 is a unit to represent tested condition. u14 is a unit to represent the experiment result. u15 is a unit to represent the relation between the hypothesis and the result. Each unit has key representations that are grounded in the real world. Assume that we have also liquidized other texts T2, T3,,,,. The sequence of the anterior unit u13 to represent experimental condition followed by the posterior unit u14 to represent experimental result composes the partial context of scientific experiment report. Let's name it as scientific experiment report context.

If we exchange the positions of u13(experimental condition) and u14(experimental result) and form the contrary sequence of u14 followed by u13, it may start the composition of a new partial context of, for example, engineering design – required properties followed by the conditions to satisfy the requirement. And this new partial context constrains new possible connection that should follow the u13, which may come from the liquidization of another text Tj. In this way, new knowledge can be crystallized.

The liquidization and crystallization of knowledge never stops because new texts continue to come in. A new text Tk may include new key representations, so the dictionary of the key representations should be always updated. The new text Tk may give a new partial context and that may trigger the whole recrystallization of the old knowledge along with the new context.

The crystallization process can be formalized as follows.

1. A new partial context is given. The new partial context is given as a sequence of some key representations and this works as the kernels to start the crystallization.
2. Units which are connected to the kernels are retrieved from the liquidized knowledge base. They are called kernel units.
3. Other units which can be connected to the kernel units are retrieved from the liquidized knowledge base. The connection possibility is calculated by application-dependent rules.
4. Partial connections between the units are selected from the candidate connections. This partial connection composes a partial context.
5. The composed partial context is checked against the liquidized knowledge base. If it has some match, the further possible connection growth is biased by the context; since the knowledge base has the relation between the context and the units, the units that matches the context has more priority than other units.
6. The selection of possible connections and the composition of partial context is iterated.

We are now trying several types of automatic and manual liquidization and crystallization. The next section shows one type of knowledge nebula crystallizer we have implemented and tested.

8   An Example of a Knowledge Nebula Crystallizer

In this section, we show one type of knowledge nebula crystallizer we have implemented and tested. Amitani in the author's group has built a system named KNC4ED (Knowledge Nebula Crystallizer for Exhibition Design)[9]. Fig. 8 shows a screen shot of KNC4ED.

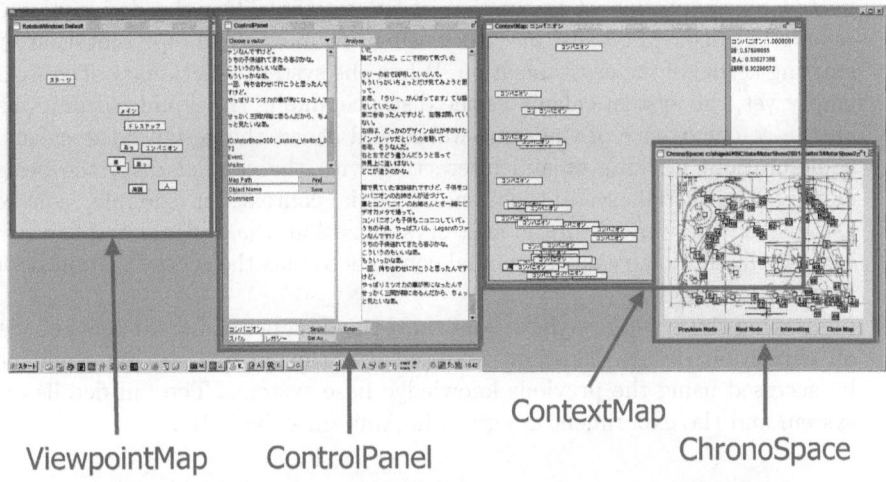

Fig. 8. Knowledge Nebula Crystallizer (KNC) for exhibition design

The system liquidizes and crystallizes knowledge on exhibition design. We have tested the system in the actual design of Tokyo Motor Show in collaboration with Dentsu corporation. At first, we interviewed designers of one booth of an automobile company in the Tokyo Motor Show 2001. In the interview, we asked the designers the design rationale of the booth design – what was the concept to be conveyed to the visitors and which configuration of which objects in the booth was how designed to convey which concept. The results of the interview were transcribed as natural language texts. We can say that the text is a sort of narrative story the designers wanted to share with the visitors. Then during the period of the actual Tokyo Motor Show, we employed subjects and asked to visit the exhibition wearing a wearable apparatus which recorded all the behavior of the subject. After each visit, we carried out retrospective report analysis by showing the subjects the recorded behavior video and asking the mental process of the subjects. We transcribed the retrospective report protocols, and they formed the stories of the user's experience.

The window named ChronoSpace in Fig. 8 shows one story of one visitor along with the behavior trace in the map of the exhibition booth. The story was liquidized using the exhibition object in the booth to determine the unit size of liquidized knowledge representation. The story (the retrospective protocols of the visitors or the design intention talked by the designers) was divided into units based on the objects in the booth. The key representations of the objects and the key concepts of the designers were provided in the dictionary. Clicking each object in the booth shown in the chronospace, the system shows what the visitor thought or the designer intended around the object. In the chronospace, each context of each visit to the booth is preserved.

The context map in Fig. 8 shows possible crystallizations of the liquidized knowledge. Looking at the chronospace, the designer sometimes finds unexpected representation of impression of the visitor. Then the designer can try re-crystallization of the visitors' story using the unexpected representation as the starting kernel of the crystallization. When the system's dictionary of contexts is empty yet, the system calculates the distance among the liquidized units based on the co-occurrence of the same words and shows the designer the calculated configuration. Looking at and interacting with the context map, the designer can give the partial crystal the name of partial context, for example, 'context of astonishing the visitor'. In the next crystallization, the designer and the system can use the dictionary on the partial contexts to bias the crystallization starting from other kernels.

Testing the system, we have confirmed the designer can build new knowledge on exhibition design. The new knowledge is the knowledge that could never be accessed using the previous knowledge base systems. The full details of the system and the experiment are given in Amitani's thesis[10].

9   Conclusions

The author's group was assigned the research topic of 'Supporting the formation of access to knowledge asset' and we have studied what can be knowledge asset and what should be the access to the knowledge asset. We have found that neither the access requirement nor the knowledge is fixed in advance but that both of them evolve dynamically. We have built a system to enable the dynamic evolution process of knowledge. The system liquidizes existing knowledge and shows new possible crystallization. We are now building and testing several types of knowledge liquidization and crystallization systems. This paper described basic concepts of those systems.

References

1. Göranzon, B., Josefson, I., eds.:   Knowledge, Skill and Artificial Intelligence. Springer-Verlag, London (1988)
2. Shoji, H., Hori, K.: Creative communication for chance discovery in shopping. New Generation Computing **21** (2003) 73–86

3. Schön, D.A.: The Reflective Practitioner – How Professionals Think in Action –. Basic Books, New York (1983)
4. Gero, J.S.: Computational models of creative design processes. In Dartnall, T., ed.: Artificial Intelligence and Creativity. Volume 17 of Studies in Cognitive Systems. Kluwer Academic Publishers, Dordrecht (1994) 269–281
5. Boden, M.: The Creative Mind: Myths and Mechanisms. Basic Books, New York (1991)
6. Fischer, G., Ostwald, J.: Knowledge management: Problems, promises, realities, and challenges. IEEE Intelligent Systems **16** (2001) 60–72
7. Hori, K.: A system for aiding creative concept formation. IEEE Transactions on Systems, Man, and Cybernetics **24** (1994) 882–894
8. Hori, K.: Concept space connected to knowledge processing for supporting creative design. Knowledge-Based Systems **10** (1997) 29–35
9. Amitani, S., Mori, M., Hori, K.: An approach to a knowledge reconstruction engine for supporting event planning. In et al., E.D., ed.: Proc. of KES2002, IOS Press (2002) 1281–1285
10. Amitani, S.: A Method and a System for Supporting the Process of Knowledge Creation. PhD thesis, School of Engineering, University of Tokyo (2004)

Benefits of Subjunctive Interface Support for Exploratory Access to Online Resources

Aran Lunzer

Meme Media Laboratory*, Hokkaido University, Sapporo 060-8628, Japan
`aran@meme.hokudai.ac.jp`

Abstract. When exploring online resources, users often make many separate retrievals – specifying in turn various parameter values to make up a request, and examining the corresponding results. Any interface that supports only one retrieval at a time, i.e., one set of parameter values and the corresponding results, places a heavy burden on a user who wants to compare available results, or simply to try a range of retrievals. A subjunctive-interface approach may reduce this burden. Subjunctive interfaces support the setting up, viewing and adjustment of multiple scenarios in parallel, leading to more efficient iteration through related scenarios, and the opportunity for side-by-side instead of temporally separated viewing. We examine how these facilities can be applied in a range of information-access applications, and the benefits that can be obtained.

1 Introduction

People explore online resources in a wide variety of domains – notionally as wide as the variety of databases, or of Web applications. However, many resource-access applications only deliver results in response to explicit, pinpoint requests. For example, interfaces for flight enquiries typically require the user to specify exactly one destination city; while this is convenient for users with precisely formulated travel plans, someone who wants to compare the deals and schedules available for a range of destinations must embark on an exploration: submitting various requests and analysing their respective results. Depending on the applications available, such explorations can present the following kinds of challenge:

Poor support for covering a range of requests. When a user wants to submit a range of requests, the details of those requests often follow some pattern. For example, when searching for flights, a user might request information for several routes on a given date, or for a single route over many dates, or combinations of a few routes and dates.

> If the interface only supports the handling of a single request at a time, this burdens the user not only with a potentially high number of interface actions to specify and submit the requests, but also mental effort in planning the requests, remembering which requests have been made so far, and remembering where interesting results were found.

---

* Since May 2004. The work reported here was partly carried out during earlier employment at the same laboratory (1997–2001), and partly at the Natural Sciences ICT Competence Centre, University of Copenhagen, 2200 Copenhagen Ø, Denmark.

G. Grieser and Y. Tanaka (Eds.): Intuitive Human Interface 2004, LNAI 3359, pp. 14–32, 2004.

Poor support for comparing results. Few things in life can be evaluated in
isolation. In many kinds of information exploration, comparing the results
of alternative requests is what gives meaning to those results – for example,
in judging whether a given flight is good or bad value for money.

However, many application interfaces only display the results from the latest
request; each request replaces the previous one. Therefore comparing results
requires the user to remember – or to have written down, or to request again
– the details of those that are currently out of sight. This again can constitute
both a physical and a mental burden.

Poor support for ambiguous retrievals. A well known challenge in the field
of Information Retrieval is sense disambiguation. For example, because the
word 'bank' might refer to a financial institution or the edge of a river, results
retrieved for one sense may be completely unhelpful for a user interested in
the other. Similarly, in the burgeoning field of context-sensitive information
delivery, the provided information can be tailored in accordance with details
of the user's current context. But context is subject to interpretation, so
again the results may not be what the user expects.

A common tendency is for application designers to invoke some form of
heuristics in deciding on a single way to interpret the situation. In some cases,
inevitably, users will feel that they have been offered irrelevant information.
The situation is even worse if there is no way to remove the heuristic bias,
in order to access the information that was intended.

This paper reviews how applications equipped with 'subjunctive interface'
facilities [1–3] may help to relieve these problems. The idea of a subjunctive
interface is to let the user of a computer application set up multiple scenarios
that can then be viewed and adjusted in parallel; the concept was inspired by
Hofstadter's [4] playful notion of a Subjunc-TV – a magical television whose
tuning knobs would provide access to alternative versions of a given broadcast,
based on arbitrarily different circumstances chosen by the viewer.

Before going any further, we should clarify our use of the term 'scenario'.
Taking an abstract view of an application, as a program that computes some
outcome on the basis of user-specified inputs, a scenario comprises a combination
of inputs and the corresponding outcome. In some applications time is also significant – in the timing of input specifications, evolution of the outcome, or both.
Typically scenarios that have different inputs will also have different outcomes;
in addition, if a computation depends on factors other than the user's inputs,
such as some randomisation within a simulation, scenarios may have different
outcomes even if their inputs are identical.

The key features of an application with a subjunctive interface are as follows:

Multiple scenarios can co-exist. At any given time, the application can support multiple independent scenarios. Typically these are created by a user
(though exceptions will be shown later). For example, when choosing a value
for some application input, the user may be equally interested in several alternative values, such as alternative destination cities; creating a separate
scenario to cater for each value allows all those interests to be captured.

The user can view scenarios side by side. The application can display all its currently existing scenarios side by side, in a way that lets the user compare them, or read the values (inputs and outcomes) for each scenario individually.

The user can adjust scenarios in parallel. The user can control scenarios in parallel, for example by adjusting an input parameter that is shared by many scenarios and seeing simultaneously how this adjustment affects each scenario.

How might such facilities help in addressing the three information-exploration challenges outlined above?

– For a start we can expect that covering a range of retrievals will become less laborious, at least if there is some repeating pattern in the retrievals. For example, consider a user who is interested in several possible dates of travel, and wants to enquire about several possible destinations for each of those dates. This can be achieved by setting up a scenario for each city, then successively working through the various dates in all the scenarios in parallel (or the converse: setting up a scenario for each date, then changing the city in all those scenarios). In either case, the number of interface actions needed will be reduced, as will the burden of remembering which retrievals have been run so far.

– Comparison is supported, because of the ability to see multiple scenarios (i.e., multiple retrievals) side by side rather than having to remember their contents or revisit them repeatedly.

– In a situation where the specified retrieval is ambiguous, the ability to establish multiple scenarios can be used to deliver alternative results reflecting the various available interpretations. Seeing those scenarios, the user can evaluate which of them reflect(s) the most relevant interpretation for the current occasion – especially if each scenario is annotated with the reasoning used by the system in offering it.

In the following section we introduce five applications that demonstrate multiple-scenario support applied to information exploration. These applications have been implemented primarily to test out concepts and interface approaches, rather than to stand as generally useful tools; that said, the census browser described in Sect. 2.1 has undergone several design iterations in response to user trials, and even the prototype Web-application clipping tool described in Sect. 2.2 turns out to be capable of addressing a wide range of situations.

After the application descriptions, in Sect. 3 we outline related work, while Sect. 4 looks to a generalisation of the findings reported here.

2   Sample Applications

In this section we introduce five applications that illustrate how the use of multiple scenarios, as supported by subjunctive interfaces, can provide benefits to users pursuing explorations among online resources. The applications are as follows:

1. A browser for census records, in which the use of multiple scenarios helps the user to view and compare trends among the records.
2. C3W: a framework that lets users extract and reuse elements of Web applications, for which multiple scenarios allow for efficient execution and viewing of multiple Web retrievals.
3. TopicaBrush: an interface for highlighting subsets of data in a multi-faceted repository, where linked scenarios help the user to compare data subsets based on subtly differing criteria.
4. HIBench: a simple framework for setting up queries against a database of multi-attribute data items; scenarios are used to represent parallel searches requested by the user, or implied by ambiguity in such requests.
5. ScheduleBlender: a prototype of a calendar that would support experimentation with alternative placements of events – or, as shown here, could use tailoring information to calculate and deliver event-related data.

The applications can be broadly categorised according to whether the creation of scenarios is entirely on the user's initiative (1–3), or can also be triggered by the system (4, 5). The demonstrations of the latter, mixed-initiative systems address situations in which a user's request turns out to be ambiguous.

2.1 Browsing Census Records

First we describe a simple browser for census data, that we extended with a subjunctive interface. We have evaluated the relative performance of the browser with and without this extension.

Figure 1 shows a browser based on the 'simultaneous menus' interface created by Hochheiser and Shneiderman [5], for browsing census data on commercial activities in the state of Maryland. The data set contains 828 records, holding statistics for nine industry areas in each of twenty-three counties over four successive years. Each record specifies the number of employees, the number of establishments, and the total annual payroll. The user specifies a record by selecting a county, industry and year in the three menus in the upper part of the browser; the statistics appear in the result displays below those menus.

However, this browser does not provide good support for iterative retrievals, or for comparisons. For example, a user who wants to compare the statistics for a given county and industry over several years must click each year in turn, read off the statistics for that year, and remember them (or write them down) for comparison with the other years. To make the equivalent comparison for the same county but a different industry, the user must change the industry selection and again work through the years.

Establishing Multiple Scenarios. In this application a scenario comprises a selection in each menu, and the corresponding statistics. Figure 2 shows a subjunctive-interface version of the application, in which the user has established four scenarios – for two years' records in each of two counties. Therefore the three result displays are each showing four values, and instead of the one-marker-per-menu style of the simple interface, the menus' markers can now show

Fig. 1. A 'simultaneous menus' style of exploration interface for census data, after [5]. For each combination of County, Industry and Year specified on the three 'menus' of links, the dataset contains the three statistics that are retrieved and displayed across the lower part of the browser.

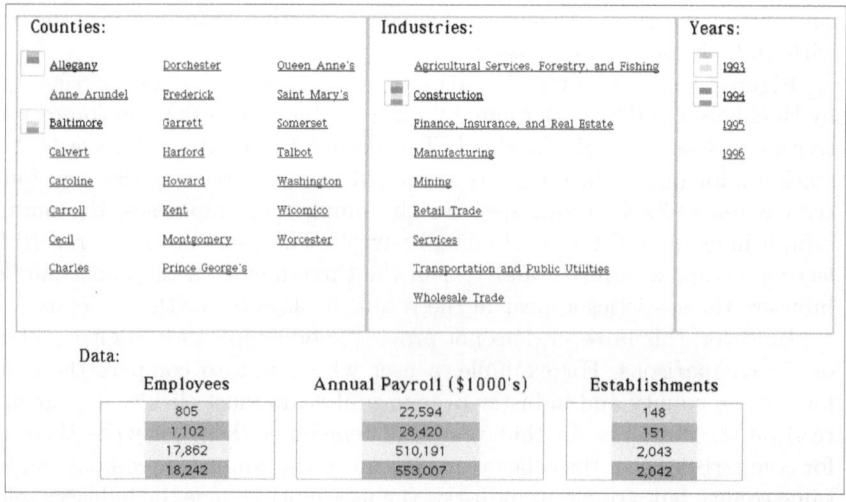

Fig. 2. A subjunctive-interface version of the browser in Fig. 1. The browser is showing four scenarios corresponding to the Construction statistics for both Allegany and Baltimore, in 1993 and 1994. Correspondence between menu selections and result values is indicated with position and colour cues in the result displays and in the markers next to menu items; for example, the values 805, 22594 and 148 at the top of the result displays are for Allegany in 1993.

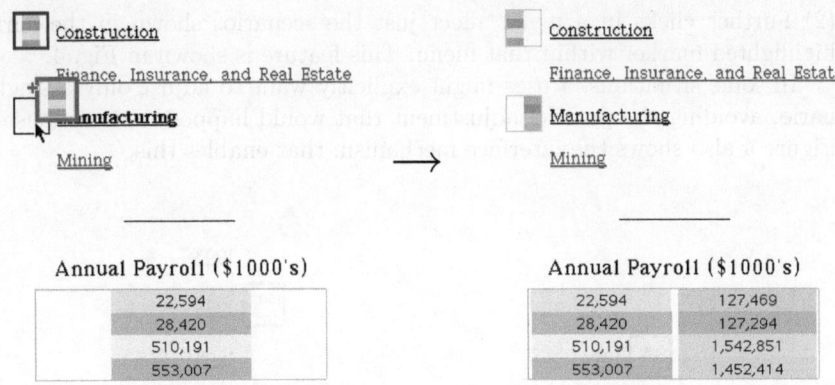

Fig. 3. A user cloning four scenarios that relate to Construction, giving the new scenarios the value Manufacturing. At top left, the user has picked up the menu marker for Construction while holding the Ctrl key, and is about to drop it onto Manufacturing; at top right is the menu state after this operation. Below are corresponding snapshots of one of the result displays, showing the increase in the number of scenarios.

when several scenarios have the same setting. As shown in Fig. 3, a user creates new scenarios by cloning existing ones, through interaction with these markers. Picking up a marker while holding the Ctrl key, and dropping it on some other item within the same menu, will clone the scenarios shown in the dragged marker. The new scenarios are identical to the originals, except for having the setting of the menu item where the marker was dropped.

Side-by-Side Viewing. The interface in Fig. 2 is based on a refinement of our 'widget multiplexer' approach [2], that allows an application to show multiple scenarios without wastefully replicating the parts of its interface that are identical in all cases. Each multiplexer handles the presentation of and interaction with a single input or output widget, and provides side-by-side display of the widget's various states in the existing scenarios. In this application, multiplexers are used for the menus and the result displays. All multiplexers within an application use correlated geometrical layout and colouring for the scenarios' values, to help the user locate the values that constitute each scenario; here the menu markers are designed to be correlated easily with the values in the statistics displays.

Parallel Adjustment. The only kind of 'adjustment' supported in the original application is changing which census record is retrieved, by changing the selection within some menu. For example, having requested the statistics for Allegany Construction in 1994, as shown in Fig. 1, the user might click on Dorchester to retrieve that county's corresponding statistics instead.

In the subjunctive interface, clicking within a menu can affect more than one scenario at a time, according to the following two rules: (1) When none of a menu's items is selected, a click on any item sets that value in all scenarios;

(2) Further clicks in a menu affect just the scenarios shown in the currently highlighted marker within that menu. This feature is shown in Fig. 4.

In some situations, a user might explicitly want to adjust only a single scenario, avoiding the parallel adjustment that would happen with a mouse click. Figure 4 also shows the interface mechanism that enables this.

Fig. 4. Left: By default, a mouse click in a menu updates the scenarios shown in the menus's currently highlighted marker. Here the marker for 1994 is highlighted (shown by its dark blue outline, and replicated in the mouse pointer), so a click on 1995 would switch the two 1994 scenarios to that value. The user can highlight a different marker by clicking on it. **Right:** Clicking and holding the mouse button on a menu item creates a pop-up that lets the user choose a single scenario to receive the clicked value. Here the user has clicked on 1996; releasing the mouse in its present position would set the year to 1996 in just the second scenario.

Benefits. We briefly describe two experiments that we ran to compare the usability and performance of the original and subjunctive-interface census browsers.

The experimental tasks used by Hochheiser and Shneiderman to evaluate the simultaneous-menus browser [5] were all simple two-case comparisons. For this experiment we defined more complex retrieval and comparison tasks, of the following three types:

Intra-set comparison. These tasks require pairwise comparisons between many combinations of the records in some set. For example, one task asks: 'Considering Wholesale Trade in [five named counties] in 1993, find how the counties are ordered in terms of number of Employees. In order from fewest Employees to most, what are the Payroll values for these counties?'

Iterative examination. These tasks call for examination of records that lie in a repeating pattern. For example, 'In 1996, for which of the industries do [three named counties] all have 1000 or more Employees?'

Iterative comparison. These tasks are similar to iterative examination, but call for comparison between the records rather than merely checking whether each record satisfies some criterion. For example, 'In which counties does the Payroll for Wholesale Trade fall in every year from 1993 to 1996?'

We expected that, for each task type, appropriate use of the subjunctive interface would provide some benefit over using the simple interface. For intra-set comparisons the benefit is merely in being able to keep values on view rather than having to remember them or write them down. For iterative examinations and comparisons, the iteration can be performed more efficiently if the user first sets up scenarios that express the repeating pattern required by the task.

In the first experiment, twenty subjects were each given sets of tasks to complete with each interface. The subjects significantly preferred the subjunctive interface, and rated it as being more satisfying to use. When using the subjunctive interface they depended less on writing down or remembering data, as suggested by fewer interim marks made on paper and by reports of lower mental workload. They also used fewer interface actions to complete the tasks. However, we found no corresponding reduction in task completion time, mainly because some subjects encountered problems in using the facilities for setting up and controlling scenarios.

By examining the subjects' interface logs, we found a number of commonly made mistakes and difficulties that seemed to stem from the interface design. In addition, many subjects commented that they would probably become more effective at using the subjunctive interface if they had more practice. We therefore ran a second experiment, using an interface that was modified to address the most common difficulties, and incorporating a considerably longer period of use. Our main hypothesis was that, after extended practice with both the simple and subjunctive interfaces, the subjunctive interface would become significantly faster than the simple interface.

In the second experiment, seven subjects performed tasks using the simple interface and the modified subjunctive interface, over five sessions each lasting approximately one hour. In the final session, the tasks were completed 27% more quickly when tackled with the subjunctive rather than with the simple interface – and for some of the iterative comparison tasks, the subjunctive interface was more than twice as fast. Our hypothesis was thus confirmed.

2.2   C3W: Capturing and Reusing Web-Application Behaviour

In this section we describe C3W (Clip, Connect and Clone for the Web) [6], a prototype that enhances access to resources provided by Web applications. C3W is being developed by Hokkaido University Ph.D. student Jun Fujima.

Part of the motivation for developing C3W was that Web applications often exhibit the problems outlined in the Introduction – i.e., handling only precisely specified requests, thus making it hard for users to cover a range of requests or to compare results. A further challenge is that the Web pages serving as the interfaces to these applications are often cluttered with elements of no interest to the user; finding the relevant elements among that clutter incurs a cognitive load, especially in repeated use. Finally, we noticed a chance to automate the setting of inputs for one Web application based on results from others.

True to its name, C3W is based on the following three facilities:

Clipping. By drag-and-drop manipulation, a user can select and extract input and result elements from the pages of a Web application. Placing the elements on a substrate called a C3Sheet turns them into cells that work as viewports onto the original Web pages. Clipped input elements continue to support user input, and clipped result elements display the Web application's corresponding results. Thus the user can create compact, customised applications based on processing facilities offered over the Web.

Connecting. A single C3Sheet can hold input and result cells taken from multiple Web applications. For any input cell that takes a text-string value, the user can define a formula to derive its value from the values of other cells – typically, cells that hold results from other applications. This allows independent applications to be connected in user-specified ways.

Cloning. The user can set up multiple scenarios – i.e., different settings for the Web-application inputs, leading to different results – to be shown at the same time. Each cell displays, side by side, its contents in the various scenarios. This provides an efficient way for a user to explore and compare the different results available through a given Web application, or the user's own custom-built application combinations.

Establishing and Using Multiple Scenarios. Cloning, the key to C3W's subjunctive-interface support, is supported as follows:

Creating scenarios. The user creates new scenarios by cloning a cell that represents an input value. All cells downstream of the cloned input – either in terms of captured Web-application behaviour, or through formulas added by the user – are cloned too, so that they can display distinct results for each scenario. Cells that do not depend on the cloned cell's value are not cloned, and maintain their current value in every scenario.

Cloning additional inputs. When multiple scenarios have been created by cloning, the user can ask to clone another input cell that is not currently cloned. That cell is automatically given a clone for each existing scenario, as are any cells downstream of it. The number of scenarios does not change[1].

Adjusting scenarios. Entering a new value in one clone of a cloned cell will only affect the scenario corresponding to that clone. Entering a new value in an uncloned cell will affect all scenarios simultaneously.

Deleting scenarios. The user can delete a scenario. This removes all cell clones associated with that scenario.

Benefits. Figure 5 shows a simple instance of C3W in use. By cloning cells, the user has set up an interface that allows three different Google searches to be run automatically whenever new search keywords are supplied. Even this

---

[1] An alternative approach would be to multiply the number of existing scenarios. However, since Web-based retrieval is still a relatively resource-hungry activity, we are reluctant to lead users down this path.

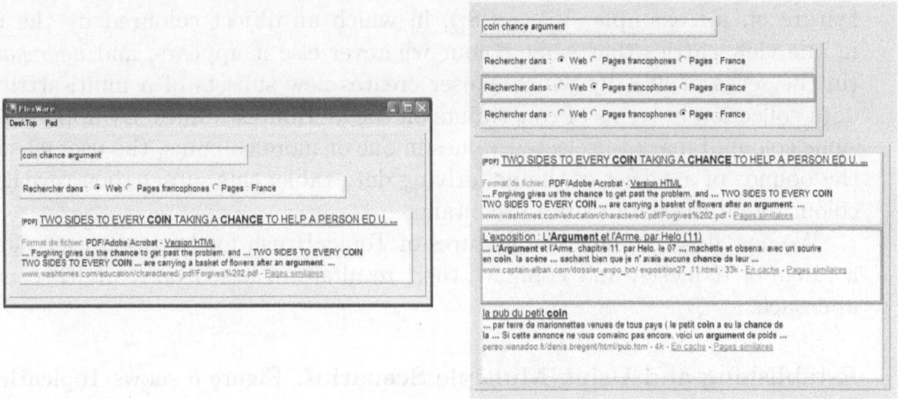

Fig. 5. Use of multiple scenarios in C3W. **Left:** A user has set up three cells containing elements extracted from a search at www.google.fr: the keyword input field; the switch that selects whether the search should cover the whole Web, just pages in French, or just pages in France; and the top result (showing page name and keyword context) from a sample search. **Right:** The user has cloned the switch cell to create three instances, and has given each instance a different setting. Because the state of this switch potentially affects the value for the top result, that cell has automatically been cloned too. Entering new search keywords into the keyword cell will therefore execute three Google queries with different scopes, and display the three respective top results.

simple example shows a clear benefit to the user: no matter how easy it is, in a normal browser, to re-run a given Google search with each position of the search-scope switch, the actions required to do so – adjusting the switch, re-running the search, figuring out whether the results have changed – stand as a barrier. A setup such as the one shown in the figure can, in effect, remove this barrier.

When a user has connected multiple applications using formulas, the labour-saving afforded by processing multiple scenarios in parallel becomes even more significant.

2.3   TopicaBrush: Dynamic Exploration of Relational-Data Subsets

Under the Topica [7] approach, information providers gather diverse resources into a relational table, then combine that table with a Web-page-like presentation object. The resulting assembly is called a Topica Document. Within a Topica Document's presentation, each column of its underlying relational table appears as a 'topos' (plural 'topoi') – an interactive region of the presentation, through which a user gains access to the values in that column. If a user examines the contents of one topos and marks an interest in some subset of the resources shown there, then resources at other topoi, correlated through the underlying table, will automatically be marked too.

TopicaBrush was built to explore Topica-Document interaction; in essence, how to support a user in marking and examining portions of relational tables. TopicaBrush combines two well known data-exploration techniques: *brushing* (a

feature of, for example, Visage [8]), in which an object coloured by the user
in one view carries that same colour wherever else it appears; and *aggregation*
(in the sense of [9]), by which a user creates new subsets of a multi-attribute
data collection in terms of constraints on the attributes' values. By applying the
same coloured mark to selected values in one or more columns, the user specifies
the bounds of a subset of the underlying data table; this subset then reveals its
colour on all the data values it contains.

We now describe how the features of TopicaBrush for letting a user pursue
a range of requests, and compare their results, are based on a multi-scenario
approach.

Establishing and Using Multiple Scenarios. Figure 6 shows TopicaBrush
being used to investigate a dataset describing travel packages. The four lists
across the bottom of the figure are topoi whose contents the user has chosen to
view; these lists support mouse-click selection to indicate values that are of inter-

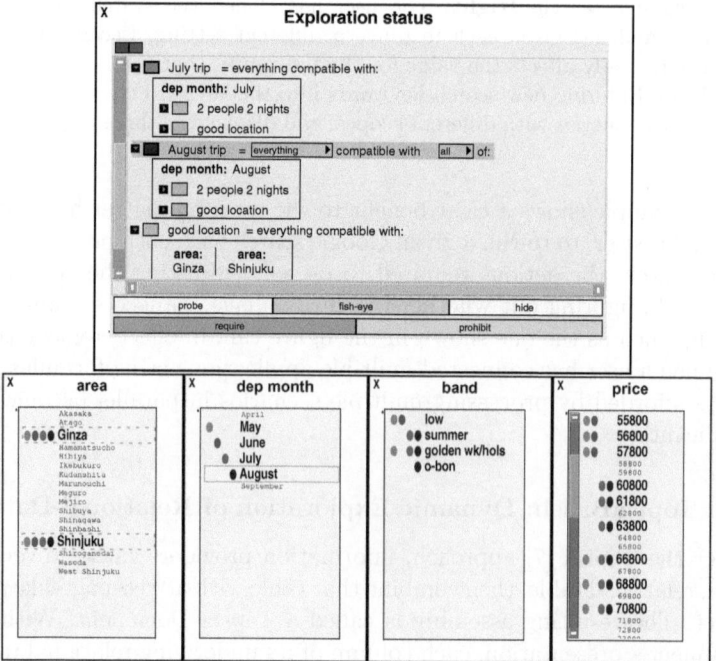

Fig. 6. Highlighting data subsets in TopicaBrush, on a database of travel packages.
The user has set up and marked four main sets, addressing the months May to August
respectively. Their markings are seen in the topos lists; in the price topos, for example,
it is seen that both May and June have deals at the same low prices, while some other
prices in May are high. The criteria defining each of the month sets include both the
'2 person 2 night' set (definition not shown here) and the 'good location' set, currently
defined as a disjunction of Ginza and Shinjuku. If the definition of 'good location' were
changed, all four derived sets and their marking would be updated simultaneously.

est. The 'exploration status' view supports the further operations needed to manipulate and combine the subsets identified in the topoi, and to assign coloured marks to whichever derived sets are of interest. It is these sets, representing potentially complex relational queries, that are the scenarios in TopicaBrush.

The sets are displayed by drawing the user-assigned marks against the appropriate values within the topos lists. Rather than use a widget-multiplexer approach, displaying numerous copies of the lists, TopicaBrush takes advantage of the fact that the lists themselves have static content. Each element within a list is tagged with markers representing all the sets of which that element is a member; as shown in the figure, elements with no marking can be shown at reduced size to save screen space while maintaining context for the other elements.

Allowing the sets to be displayed independently gives more information to the user than if the system could only support a single set at a time. In the case shown in Fig. 6, for example, the user could have specified a single set where the month was 'May OR June OR July OR August' – but this would contain a mass of undifferentiated prices, with no clues as to the seasonal variation.

TopicaBrush supports users in adjusting multiple scenarios in parallel, in that sets can be defined in terms of other sets. If many scenarios include some common set S within their definition, any update to S will simultaneously affect all those scenarios.

Benefits. The concepts explored in TopicaBrush seem promising for the general challenge of retrieval from faceted repositories, where even recent interfaces (such as [10]) embody the dubious assumption that a user is always willing to define his or her interests as a single – albeit complex and evolving – query.

2.4   HIBench: Browsing Relationships in Multi-attribute Data

Whereas the previous examples all involve explicit request of alternative scenarios by the user, this and the next are examples of mixed initiative; the application itself can generate supplementary scenarios to assist the user. The typical pattern of use is that a user makes a request for some information, and the system provides a number of equally appropriate but distinct results, along with information that clarifies how each result has arisen.

Figure 7 shows a display detail from HIBench, a specialised retrieval interface inspired by, and built around, an online historical-event collection that mirrors the contents of [11][2]. The notional goal in building HIBench was to help people understand the context of any event in the repository, by using queries to discover similar events in its chronological vicinity.

Like C3W (Sect. 2.2), HIBench is a spreadsheet-like framework in which users can create cells whose contents are derived from other cells. However, in addition

---

[2] In total there are approximately fifty thousand items; we used just the latter half, covering events in the 20th century. All information in the repository is in Japanese; the English place-name translations seen here were added to assist non-Japanese explanation.

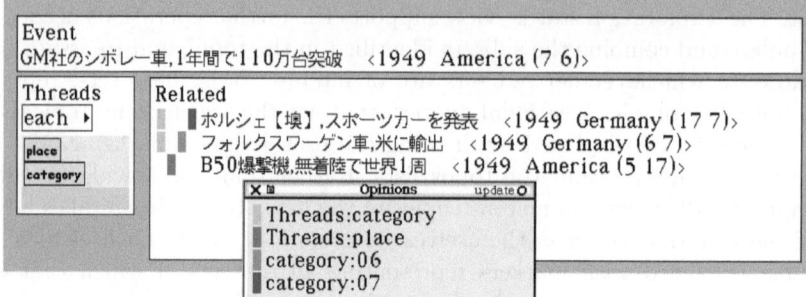

Fig. 7. Matching in HIBench, with ambiguity. The cell called Related is deriving its contents by applying the matchers in the cell Threads to the reference event currently held in Event. Because Threads specifies both 'place' and 'category' matching, and because the current reference event belongs to two categories (7 and 6), matching events are found for each category as well as for the place (America). The three results are marked with coloured tags whose meanings are listed in the 'Opinions' view.

Key/translation: Category 7 covers corporate business, while 6 is international trade. The reference event here comments on Chevrolet production. The top related item (another corporate business item) is an announcement by the Porsche company; the next (matching international trade) tells of the export of Volkswagens; the last (matching America) is a round-the-world flight by an American B50 bomber.

to standard arithmetic and string functions as normally found in spreadsheets, HIBench offers specialised functions for searching against the event repository. One such function takes a reference event and a match condition, specified by the user as a combination of property-specific matchers, and retrieves the next event (in the repository's chronological sequence) that matches the reference event in the specified way. The properties available for matching against an event are its news-headline-like description, a date, one or more locations (typically countries) affected by the event, and one or more categories (denoting fields such as politics, education, various branches of science and technology, literature and so on) assigned by the repository's editors.

Establishing and Using Multiple Scenarios. HIBench supports both user-requested and system-generated creation of scenarios. Figure 7 shows a case involving both. The user has set up matching based on the contents of the cell labelled Threads, into which two matchers ('place' and 'category') have been dropped. At the top of the Threads cell is a menu, in which the value *each* is currently selected. This menu, which also contains the values *any* and *all*, specifies how multiple matchers within the cell are to be combined. The *any* setting is like a relational OR; the compound condition will be satisfied by the first event to satisfy any matcher. *All* is like AND, only matching an event that satisfies all matchers. The setting *each* forces a separate search to be performed for each matcher, in separate scenarios, and the distinct matches (which may coincidentally be the same event) to be collected and displayed together.

In addition, the system has detected that in this case a 'category' match is ambiguous, because the reference event happens to be registered under two categories. Correspondingly, separate scenarios have been created to perform matching for each category. The total number of scenarios is thus three: one for place, and one for each of the two categories. These three scenarios have each delivered a different matching event for display in the Related cell.

HIBench, like TopicaBrush (Sect. 2.3), does not use widget multiplexers to create multi-scenario displays. Cells containing multiple values are presented as lists, with each list element marked to show which scenario(s) it is related to.

HIBench supports parallel adjustment of scenarios in the sense that, when the user has set up compound match conditions using the *each* setting, a replacement of the reference event will automatically cause multiple retrievals to be executed in parallel. This can be applied at nested levels. For example, although not shown in Fig. 7, the 'place' matcher is itself defined as a compound condition involving matchers for city, country and continent; it is up to the user to decide whether those matchers are combined using *any*, *all*, or *each*.

Benefits. We believe that HIBench's transparent, open way of handling ambiguous queries is helpful for users. Rather than silently adopting some default behaviour – resolving the ambiguity in an arbitrary way in order to deliver a 'best guess' result – we believe it is appropriate for systems to highlight and capitalise on ambiguity; offering distinct results that arise from distinct interpretations, and letting the user choose.

2.5   ScheduleBlender: Tailoring in the Face of Ambiguous Context

Finally we show another system that, like HIBench, offers mixed-initiative creation of scenarios to support user exploration. ScheduleBlender is a demonstration of how a tool might support provisional factors in one's personal calendar, such as undecided placement, duration and order of events. It also demonstrates how a system can behave in situations that demand a context-specific, tailored response – but where the system cannot determine, at any given time, which elements of the detected context are most relevant to the user.

Figure 8 shows a user experimenting with a travel itinerary, while the system performs lookups to provide an overall hotel-price estimate for the nights designated as being in foreign cities. However, this lookup involves an ambiguity: the application has access to travel policies set up in the past by this user – relating to business trips, single-person tourism, or tourism as a couple – but the user has not specified which of those policies applies to the current trip. Common approaches to such ambiguity would be to force the user to choose a policy, or for the system to choose one based on some heuristics (such as whichever policy was used most recently) and leave the user to change that choice if wanted. As in the case of HIBench, our belief is that explicitly revealing and working with the ambiguity is more helpful.

Establishing and Using Multiple Scenarios. By creating multiple scenarios, ScheduleBlender can apply all the applicable policies in parallel, dynamically updating them all as the trip details are changed.

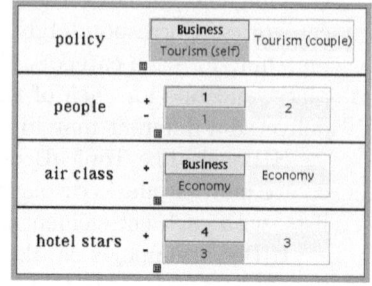

HCI 2003	10 Sep 2003	3 days
Venice	17 Sep 2003	4 days
Munich	21 Sep 2003	2 days
Prague	23 Sep 2003	3 days

overlap check: –

hotel estimate: 778 / 583 / 700

policy	Business / Tourism (self)	Tourism (couple)
people	1 / 1	2
air class	Business / Economy	Economy
hotel stars	4 / 3	3

Fig. 8. A ScheduleBlender display showing a tentative travel plan, where the user has not yet specified who will be travelling. The display on the left shows the user's proposed order and duration of visits on a multi-city trip. Underneath are two pieces of information supplied by the system: a check for overlaps between the dates, and an estimate of the total hotel cost. For the hotel cost, the system is proposing three alternative values. The reason for this is shown in the display on the right: hotel price depends on the requested hotel class and room type, for which the system has three stored policies – and the user has not yet specified which policy to apply for this trip. The system has therefore applied all three in turn, providing the corresponding values for the user to consider.

One difference between ScheduleBlender and the preceding examples is that it shows how multiple scenarios are sometimes relevant in a highly localised way. While a hotel-cost calculation may need to take account of travel policies, other lookups within the same situation may call on other context elements – such as the preferred airlines to use for international flights, or the format to use in displaying dates. We are now in the early days of investigating how such localised scenario-management should best be presented to users.

Benefits. Today's computing environments include many features designed to help users by suggesting parameter values that, according to some designers' heuristics, are believed to be of interest to the user. One common example is the suggestion of which folder to use as the destination for saving a file. When the heuristics match an individual's pattern of use, these suggestions are welcome; when there is a mismatch, the same suggestions can become a great frustration.

Explicit enumeration and offering of alternatives, as demonstrated here, increases the chance that the value wanted on a given occasion is among those offered by the system. There are also cases where the alternatives may remind the user of forgotten options, or lead to serendipitous discoveries – for example, happening to find a trip for which the cost of business-class travel is so near the tourist price that it's worth making the upgrade.

The gathering momentum of context-aware ubiquitous computing brings many new opportunities for such tailored suggestions – and many opportunities for frustration. We believe that subjunctive-interface techniques have an important role to play in helping users to feel in control of the options available to them.

3   Related Work

The origin of the subjunctive interface research theme was the observation that users often want to explore alternatives, and that this is poorly supported by applications that always require the user to commit to unambiguous input values. Terry and Mynatt [12], examining this issue in the domain of open-ended design tasks, characterised existing applications as being tied to a 'single state document model' that works against the legitimate need of designers to work by experimentation, branching, evaluation and iteration. Terry et al. [13] later demonstrated an interface that supports a form of simultaneous development of alternative versions of a graphical design.

Recognising a corresponding need for exploration and experimentation in information access also has a long history: in 1989, Bates [14] argued against the classic model of information retrieval, that posits a user iteratively refining the definition of a query, with the goal of arriving at a single precise expression of his or her information needs. Instead, Bates argued, interfaces should support the less tidy reality of information-seeking in which users may adjust their expectations, try alternative approaches, and benefit from relevant information that they gather ('berrypick') along the way. Facilities for pursuing queries in parallel, as described in this paper, at least free users from having to encapsulate their interests in a monolithic query.

The emphasis on presenting alternatives in parallel can be seen as helping users to place alternatives into context. This concern has been addressed in various fields within HCI, including information visualisation [15] and the development of direct-manipulation interfaces [16]. For viewing and comparing alternatives within tabular data, for example, interfaces such as Polaris [17] provide rich facilities for constructing and reconfiguring tables, while the Table Lens [18] lets a user visualise chosen rows relative to each other and to the full range of values in each column. These tools, however, are limited to data suitable for row-and-column display, while the goal of subjunctive interfaces is that alternatives can be handled for any input or display region in an application.

Tools specifically designed to support interactive experimentation include the Influence Explorer [19] and Spotfire [20], both of which project numerical or ordinal data onto a two-dimensional graphical layout and provide interactive controls allowing a user to highlight data elements or ranges. Comparison is supported by the user's ability to switch the display rapidly and reversibly among different settings for the highlighting. Such dynamic switching is good for drawing attention to subtle distinctions, especially along some continuous range, but in other cases comparison may be better supported by simultaneous, side-by-side presentation of a set of key cases as provided by a subjunctive interface. In particular we believe that the use of widget multiplexers constitutes an instance of the 'small multiples' approach, which Tufte [21] supports with the comment that 'Multiples directly depict comparisons, the essence of statistical thinking' (p.105). Roberts [22] likewise recommends view multiplicity in computer interfaces as a way to encourage users to try out alternatives.

The cell-and-formula approach of C3W and HIBench aims to capitalise on users' familiarity with the spreadsheet model. Other well known spreadsheet-like systems include Forms/3 [23] and the Information Visualization Spreadsheet [24]. In general, such projects selectively adopt or abandon various features of what could be called the traditional spreadsheet. Our use of formulas conforms to the tradition that each formula determines the value of just one cell; on the other hand, our implementations are not alone in breaking free of the restriction that cells should contain only text or numbers, or the idea that cells should be positioned and named according to a tabular grid. And while we do use Microsoft Excel®'s API to support formulas in C3W, our handling of multiple scenarios is quite different from Excel's scenario management facilities – most notably in our insistence that cells' contents always be manipulated and displayed in place, rather than by calling on specialised input dialogues or pivot tables.

4   Future: Recipe-Based Exploration

As was mentioned in the Introduction, the example applications presented here have been developed in a spirit of exploring and illustrating interface concepts. While the studies carried out on the census browser show that users can understand facilities of the kind offered in a subjunctive interface, and that for certain tasks such an interface can give large, statistically significant performance benefits, clearly much remains to be done in delivering this work as a general contribution to HCI research.

Our main efforts are now focussed on the concepts demonstrated in the two spreadsheet-like systems: C3W (Sect. 2.2) and HIBench (Sect. 2.4). We consider these as early examples of tools supporting Recipe-Based Exploration – a specialisation of the subjunctive interface concept, suited to applications that can be characterised as spreadsheet-like acyclic graphs of cells and formulas. This application model, which we believe can subsume a wide range of today's applications (including, not least, spreadsheets), offers opportunities to simplify the handling of knock-on effects of alternative values assigned to cells within the dependency graph.

One goal for recipe-based exploration is to make effective use of mixed-initiative variation – i.e., where the system can take the initiative in creating alternative scenarios to help a user understand the range of possibilities on offer. We believe this will be important in handling the increasing amount of information offered by the systems pervading our working and living environments. When context-sensing computational agents clamour to provide people with information, recommendations, connections and a cornucopia of other services, no heuristics could sensibly boil down all these offers to a single recommended source. Users must be given the opportunity to explore and evaluate the alternatives that are on offer; in doing so, they should be supported by the multiple-scenario capabilities of subjunctive interfaces.

Acknowledgements

The work reported here could not have been carried out without the extensive support, of many kinds, provided by the staff, students and visitors of the Meme Media Laboratory in Hokkaido University and of the Natural Sciences ICT Competence Centre at the University of Copenhagen. Above all I am grateful to Yuzuru Tanaka in Hokkaido and Kasper Hornbæk in Copenhagen, for their continual collaboration, counselling and cajoling.

I also thank the organisers and other attendees of the Dagstuhl workshop – especially Klaus Jantke and Gunter Grieser – for creating an atmosphere so conducive to optimism and inspiration.

References

1. Lunzer, A.: Choice and comparison where the user wants them: Subjunctive interfaces for computer-supported exploration. In: Proceedings of IFIP TC. 13 International Conference on Human-Computer Interaction (INTERACT '99), IOS Press (1999) 474–482
2. Lunzer, A., Hornbæk, K.: Side-by-side display and control of multiple scenarios: Subjunctive interfaces for exploring multi-attribute data. In: Proceedings of the Australian Conference on Computer-Human Interaction (OZCHI 2003), IEEE Computer Society Press, Los Alamitos, CA (2003) 202–210
3. Lunzer, A., Hornbæk, K.: Usability studies on a visualisation for parallel display and control of alternative scenarios. In: Proceedings of the 7th International Working Conference on Advanced Visual Interfaces (AVI 2004), ACM Press, New York, NY (2004) 125–132
4. Hofstadter, D.R.: Gödel, Escher, Bach: an Eternal Golden Braid. Basic Books (1979)
5. Hochheiser, H., Shneiderman, B.: Performance benefits of simultaneous over sequential menus as task complexity increases. International Journal of Human-Computer Interaction 12 (2000) 173–192
6. Fujima, J., Lunzer, A., Hornbæk, K., Tanaka, Y.: Clip, connect, clone: Combining application elements to build custom interfaces for information access. In: Proceedings of the 17th annual ACM symposium on user interface software and technology (UIST 2004), ACM Press, New York, NY (2004) To appear.
7. Tanaka, Y., Fujima, J.: Meme media and topica architectures for editing, distributing, and managing intellectual resources. In: Proceedings of 2000 Kyoto International Conference on Digital Libraries: Research and Practice. (2000) 208–216
8. Kolojejchick, J., Roth, S.F., Lucas, P.: Information appliances and tools in visage. IEEE Computer Graphics and Applications 17 (1997) 32–41
9. Goldstein, J., Roth, S.: Using aggregation and dynamic queries for exploring large data sets. In: Proceedings of the SIGCHI conference on human factors in computing systems (CHI '94), ACM Press, New York, NY (1994) 23–29
10. Yee, K.P., Swearingen, K., Li, K., Hearst, M.: Faceted metadata for image search and browsing. In: Proceedings of the conference on human factors in computing systems (CHI 2003), ACM Press, New York, NY (2003) 401–408
11. Matsuoka, S.: The Longest Chronicle: History Informs. NTT (1996) In Japanese.

12. Terry, M., Mynatt, E.D.: Side views: persistent, on-demand previews for open-ended tasks. In: Proceedings of the 15th annual ACM symposium on user interface software and technology (UIST 2002), ACM Press, New York, NY (2002) 71–80

13. Terry, M., Mynatt, E.D., Nakakoji, K., Yamamoto, Y.: Variation in element and action: Supporting simultaneous development of alternative solutions. In: Proceedings of the SIGCHI conference on human factors in computing systems (CHI 2004), ACM Press, New York, NY (2004) 711–718

14. Bates, M.J.: The design of browsing and berrypicking techniques for the online search interface. Online Review **13** (1989) 407–424

15. Card, S.K., Mackinlay, J.D., Shneiderman, B.: Readings in Information Visualization. Morgan Kaufmann, San Francisco, CA (1999)

16. Shneiderman, B.: Direct manipulation: a step beyond programming languages. IEEE Computer **16** (1983) 57–68

17. Stolte, C., Tang, D., Hanrahan, P.: Polaris: a system for query, analysis and visualization of multidimensional relational databases. IEEE Transactions on Visualization and Computer Graphics **8** (2002) 52–65

18. Rao, R., Card, S.K.: The table lens: Merging graphical and symbolic representations in an interactive focus+context visualization for tabular information. In: Proceedings of the SIGCHI conference on human factors in computing systems (CHI '94), ACM Press, New York, NY (1994) 318–322

19. Tweedie, L., Spence, R., Dawkes, H., Su, H.: Externalising abstract mathematical models. In: Proceedings of the SIGCHI conference on human factors in computing systems (CHI '96), ACM Press, New York, NY (1996) 406–412

20. Ahlberg, C., Shneiderman, B.: Visual information seeking: Tight coupling of dynamic query filters with starfield displays. In: Proceedings of the SIGCHI conference on human factors in computing systems (CHI '94), ACM Press, New York, NY (1994) 313–317

21. Tufte, E.R.: Visual Explanations. Graphic Press, Cheshire, CT (1997)

22. Roberts, J.C.: Multiple-View and Multiform Visualization. In Erbacher, R., Pang, A., Wittenbrink, C., Roberts, J., eds.: Visual Data Exploration and Analysis VII, Proceedings of SPIE. Volume 3960., IS&T and SPIE (2000) 176–185

23. Burnett, M., Atwood, J., Djang, R.W., Gottfried, H., Reichwein, J., Yang, S.: Forms/3: A first-order visual language to explore the boundaries of the spreadsheet paradigm. Journal of Functional Programming **11** (2001) 155–206

24. Chi, E.H., Riedl, J., Barry, P., Konstan, J.: Principles for information visualization spreadsheets. IEEE Computer Graphics and Applications **18** (1998) 30–38

Eye Movement Navigation Interface Supporting Reading

Satoru Morita

Yamaguchi University, 2557 Tokiwadai Ube, Japan

Abstract. To read Japanese document fast, it is important to decrease the time required the understanding and the number that viewpoint moving backward. In this paper, we propose the navigating interface to read Japanese document fast and the eye movement information processing model in reading Japanese document. We show that the reading speed becomes to be fast if human is navigated by using the interface such as the distance between neighbor fixation points become to be long. The result measured for human is similar to the computer simulation. This computer simulation is realized by introducing the mechanisms that the viewpoint moves backward based on the resolution and the short-term memory integrated by using feature matching to the traditional eye movement model. The eye movements according to the 24 kinds of information processing models are realized and evaluated using the navigation interface. Human eye movements for 15 experiments are measured using the navigation interface. We show the effectiveness of the eye movement model from these results. Moreover, it is found that the reading time can be shortened by using the eye movement navigation interface with the colored marker in the text window.

1 Introduction

In order to read quickly, it is necessary to decrease fixation time, fixation frequency, and the number of times the viewpoint moves backward on a line. It may be considered useful for increasing reading speed to place marks at constant intervals along the printed line, with the eye being trained to decrease fixation frequency.

On the other hand, the interface to get viewpoint positions has been studied[1]. And the method how to control the text scrolling using the viewpoint information is proposed[2]. We can click the scrolling bar and the icon displayed in the screen using the viewpoint. We generate an eye movement navigation interface that is composed of a laptop computer, the stand fixing the head, and an eye mark camera. We set the mark position at a constant interval. We introduce a method in which a document cannot be read without looking at colored fonts. Initially, 20 characters are concealed from the viewpoint in the forward direction using an × mark. As soon as the viewpoint is on the mark, the letters can be looked at. Eye movement is navigated using the moving colored font and mask according to the current viewpoint.

G. Grieser and Y. Tanaka (Eds.): Intuitive Human Interface 2004, LNAI 3359, pp. 33–48, 2004.

The relation between the short-term memory[3] and reading is discussed[4, 5]. On the other hand, the relation between the short-term memory and vision is discussed[6]. In this paper, we take the attention to the relation between the short term memory and vision in reading. We regard the image saved in the short-term memory as the image which human looks at[7, 8]. We cannot read the letter due to its low resolution at the periphery of foveated vision. If the resolution of the short-term memory is is under the constant resolution, the viewpoint moves backward along the line because we cannot read the letters. If the resolution of the short-term memory is over the constant resolution, the viewpoint moves forward along the line because we can read the letter. The document is not recovered from the short-term memory image if the document is integrated without considering the movement by scrolling the text. The short-term memory image can be recovered by matching features. It is confirmed that that decreasing the load of the feature-matching task and decreasing the resolution necessary for the understanding of the clauses results in a fast reading speed. We apply for the eye movement model based on the short-term memory to that in reading English [9–12]. In this paper, we extend the eye movement model to that in reading Japanese.

The psychology related to reading speed is studied[13]. The properties of the duration time to read a word is duscussed. The first fixation position on a word resulting in identifying the word most quickly has been called OVP. This phenomenon that OVP appears has been called OVP effect[14–22]. Psychological aspect of eye movement in reading such as the OVP is sumulated[11, 12]. The relation between the reading speed and the factor is analyzed using the eye movements simulated for the several situations. In order to increase reading speed, I found that the average resolution required for the understanding of the clause region should be decreased, the distance between the mark and the viewpoint should be increased, and the saccad distance along the line should be increased. We measure human eye movement navigated by mark and examine features. We show this method's effectiveness by comparing human eye movement to the simulated eye movement.

We explain the navigation mark and scrolling method in section 2, and the eye movement information processing model reading Japanese in section 3. Eye movement is simulated according to the eye movement model based on the navigation interface described in section 4. Human eye movement measured using the eye movement navigation interface is shown in section 5. Finally, we examine a method for shortening reading speed.

2   Scrolling Text and Navigation Interface Using Colored Letter

Scrolling texts are used in such applications as movie credit and as passenger guides in mass transit systems. Scrolled text is commonly used to convey information using a small display and large letters. Generally, the text scrolls in the forward and upward directions.

− Text scrolls in the backward direction in reading.
− Text scrolls in the upward direction.

It is known that the speed of reading normal non-scrolled text is faster than the speed reading a scrolled text. Reading the scrolling text has been studied based on psychological measurement[2]. The average speed for reading normal printing is 278 (*letter/minutes*). The average speed for reading scrolled text is 96 (*letter/minutes*). But we find that the understanding degree between normal non-scrolled text and scrolled text do not differ. It is found that we read the scrolling text slower than the normal text which does not scroll. The speed for reading scrolled text is 20 pixels and 60 pixels per 200ms in the forward reading direction. The speed of scrolled text is 5 pixels per 200ms in the upward direction. Upward-scrolled text is used for movie credits text, and text scrolling forward is used for the passenger guidance on public transportation.

In general, the eye movement in reading is composed of fixations, eye movements in which the viewpoint moves forward and backward along a line and movement of the eye to the next line. As a child develops reading skill, the fixation frequency and backward eye movements decrease as shown in Table 1. The important factors necessary for text to be read quickly are the following.

a. smooth movement to the next line
b. decreasing fixation frequency
c. shortening fixation time
d. decreasing fixation frequency of backward eye movement

The viewpoint is always navigated by putting the mark are constant distance from the viewpoint along the line in consideration of these factors. Human can be trained to reduce the fixation frequency decreases by lengthening the distance between mark and the current viewpoint. We extend this to the method which navigates actively according to the viewpoint derived using an eye mark camera. It is useful to use the navigating mark and scrolling based on the viewpoint shown in this paper. We must know the viewpoint in order to realize the present system. In this paper, we generate an eye movement navigation interface composed of an eye mark camera, a laptop computer and a stand fixing the head. The eye mark

Table 1. Development of eye movement

Grade	Fixation frequency /100letter	Frequency viewpoint moves backward /200letter	Fixation time time	reading letters num/s
1	136.2	21.9	330	2.14
2	97.6	15.2	291	3.45
3	64.6	8.4	267	5.78
4	51.7	5.4	203	8.92
5	44.4	4.1	228	9.41
6	45.7	2.7	198	9.30

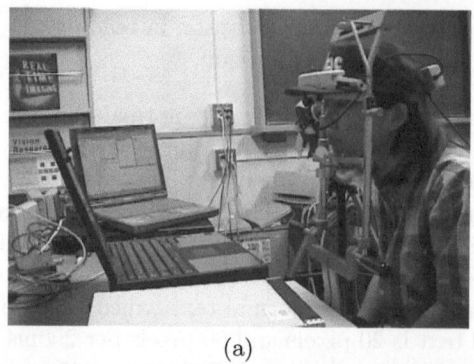

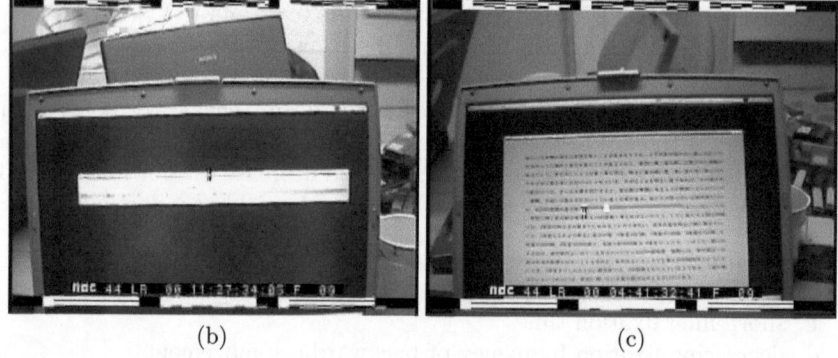

Fig. 1. (a) Eye movement navigation system (b)The navigation display scrolling forward (c)The navigation display scrolling upward and not scrolling

camera used in the experiment is EMR-8 generated by the NAC corporation. Figure 1(a) shows the eye movement navigation interface. The colored fonts are used for the current candidate viewpoint and the next candidate viewpoint. The 20 letters in the forward reading direction from the current candidate viewpoint are concealed using × marks. The background color, the normal font color, and the special font color are black, green, and white, respectively. It is necessary to move the viewpoint according to the current candidate viewpoint shown by the navigation interface. Figure 1(b) shows the display in the case of scrolling text in the forward direction and Figure 1(c) shows the case of scrolling the text in the upward direction. Rayner and Bertera found that when foveal vision was masked, reading was still possible from parafoveal vision but at a rate of only 12 words per minute using the moving-window technique[23]. Similarly, the × mark and the colored font moves actively according the current viewpoint position in our proposed system.

3   Eye Movement Model in Reading Japanese

Reading speed is determined by fixation frequency, fixation time, backward and forward eye movement, and the smoothness with which the viewpoint moves to the next line. In this paper, we simulate human eye movement reading the scrolled text. The information processing model in reading Japanese differs from that in reading English because Japanese does not have spaces between words while English does[11, 12]. We propose an eye movement information model of reading Japanese.

3.1 Foveated Vision

People perceive objects by sensing light via eyesight. The light coming into the eyeball from the pupil is received by photoreceptor cells which exist at the back part of the retina. Then the ionic permeability of the cells's membrane changes and negative potential occurs in the cells. The change of the potential is transferred to ganglion cells, which exist over the surface of the retina, through horizontal cells, bipolar cells, and amacrine cells. A ganglion cell receives the electricity from more than one photoreceptor cell in the receptive field of the ganglion cell. The ganglion cell generates impulses of different frequency according to the potential occurring in the cell. From the eye ball, the impulsed travel to the optic nerve. Photoreceptor cells are classified as cones or rods. Rods work in a dim light and do not exist at the fovea. Cones work in light and many cones exist at the fovea. The density of cones is 150000 cells/mm^2 at the center of the fovea and are reduced to 10000 cells/mm^2 at the periphery of the fovea[24]. Therefore, people can distinguish objects in detail at the fovea only. In this paper, we realize foveated vision based on the following sampling model. We use the ratio of the number of sampled pixels to the number of pixels in an area as the resolution of the area. $Reso(x)$ gives the resolution at a position x pixels away from the center of the fovea. If this value is 0.1, the receptive fields exist at 100 points among 1000 points. We generating the receptive field randomly according to statistics. The resolution is represented using %.

$Reso(x)$ is shown below using the sigmoid function,

$$Reso(x) = \frac{1 + \exp(-ab)}{1 + \exp(a(x - b))}(1.0 - 0.067) + 0.067. \tag{1}$$

The decrease of resolution depends on two parameters a and b. $a = 1.0$, $b = 70.0$. $Reso(x)$ is 1.0 at the center of the fovea and is reduced to $10000/150000{\approx}0.067$ on the periphery due to the decrease of the cone's on the human retina. A fovea image is generated by sampling each pixel on an original image according to the resolution at the pixel. The pixel where the resolution is 0.8 is sampled at 80%. Figure 2 shows the change of $Reso(x)$. The horizontal axis is the distance between the fovea center and the sampling point. The vertical axis is the probability which the receptive field exists. If the probability which the receptive field exist is high, the resolution of the seeing image is high. We explain how to generate the attention region. A 150 × 24 pixels rectangle is situated forward and behind the current viewpoint. The unit of resolution is %. 100% is the highest of all resolutions and the point is on the receptive field. The radius of the viewpoint

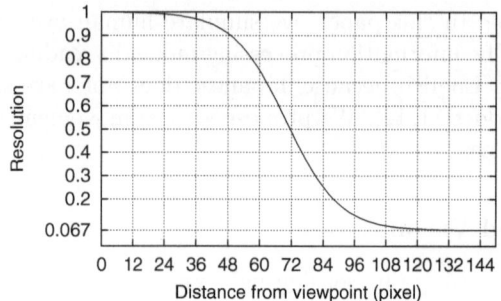

Fig. 2. The resolution change in foveated vision

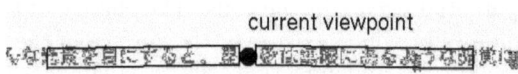

Fig. 3. Calculation of the attention region

field is 250 pixels. The attention region is generated using a rectangle size of 150×24 pixels as shown in Figure 3.

3.2 Short-Term Memory

It is considered that information saved in the short-term memory for adequately 20 seconds plays an important role. Recently, the importance of the relation between vision and the working memory has been investigated[6]. In the present paper, we examine the relation between the short term memory and vision, and regard the image saved in the short-term memory as that image which the human recognizes. A human does not apprehend movement though his or her eye moves quickly. Similarly, a human feel that the image at which he or her looks does not suddenly move though his or her eye moves quickly. The reason is that the image that human looks at is not the instant image, but the image integrated some foveated images in the short-term. Thus, while the instant image changes suddenly, it is difficult to change the integrated image quickly[8]. So we think it adequate that the image which a human recognizes is a integrated image. So we generate the integrated 2D image while the eye moves quickly. We call this a short-term memory image.

First, we generate a short-term memory image. The receptive field is defined using the statistics calculated from the distance between the center of retina and the sample point. The color of each pixel is the same as the color in the neighbor receptive fields. Initially, an image in foveated vision is generated, and it overlaps with the current viewpoint in the short-term memory. If the pixel resolution of the current foveated image is greater than that in the previous short-term memory image, the pixel value is updated. If not, the pixel value is not updated. The size of the short-term memory is limited. We use the time value to give the limit for each pixel. We delete the old pixels in the short-term memory image.

We calculate the geometric distance between the RGB values of neighbor edges. We define $E(x, y)$ as the weight of the edge feature. Resolution $Reso(x)$ is the probability that the sample point is on the receptive field. If the value is 0.0, it is not a receptive field. If the value is 0.5, the receptive fields tend to exist in two positions. We define the eye movement probability so that the eye movement probability becomes to be high for the object which you do not observe carefully. Thus we define a viewpoint using short-term memory image,

$$Sum = \Sigma_{(x,y) \in Fe}(1.0 - Reso(x, y)).$$

Fe is the set of feature points in the short-term memory image. The probability $P(x, y)$ by which the feature point (x, y) is selected as the next viewpoint are defined in the following:

$$P(x, y) = \frac{E(x, y) \cdot (1.0 - Reso(x, y))}{\Sigma_{(x',y') \in Fe}E(x', y')(1.0 - Reso(x', y'))}.$$

We define the next viewpoint according to $P(x, y)$. The next viewpoint tends to exist on an edge in which the color difference between the neighbor points is high and the resolution is low.

3.3 Eye Movement Model in Which the Viewpoint Moves Backward

Subjects were asked to look at a string consisting of 9 letters presented on a monitor for 20ms, and to determine by pressing a response key whether or not a prespecified letter was in the string. Nazir, O'Regan and Jacobs[25] examined the relationship between the frequency of identifying a prespecified letter and the distance between a viewpoint and the letter. The farther away a letter was from a viewpoint, the lower the probability of identifying the letter was. If the distant between the viewpoint and a letter is far, the resolution of the foveated image on the letter is low. We think that the resolution related to identify the letter as well as the distant between the viewpoint and a letter.

We propose a model in which viewpoint moves backward along the line if the average resolution required to understand the content of the clause region is not over the constant value. Generally, backward eye movement is related to understanding; the viewpoint moves backward along the line if a human cannot understand the text content. In this paper, we regard the short-term memory image as the image that human looks at. The reason why the frequency of backward eye movements decreases is that a human can become to understand the letters in the clause even if the resolution is low. As shown Figure 3, human looks at a rectangle with a size of 150 × 24 pixels in the forward and backward directions during reading. If the average resolution is required to understand the content within the rectangle region is over a constant value, the attention region is only right rectangle. If not, the attention region is fixed both the right and left rectangles. Edge number is calculated inside the 150 × 24 pixel rectangle. The edge intensity is the geometrical distance between neighbor colors. We realize the eye movement that the viewpoint moves backward along the line. In this experiment, we use 60% and 90% as the average resolution's required to understand the content of the clause region. If the average resolution is low, we can understand the clause's content. If the average resolution is high, we cannot understand the clause content. In the proposed information processing model, the document can be read quickly by gradually decreasing the average resolution required to understand the clause's content. Figure 4 shows the clauses used in the experiment.

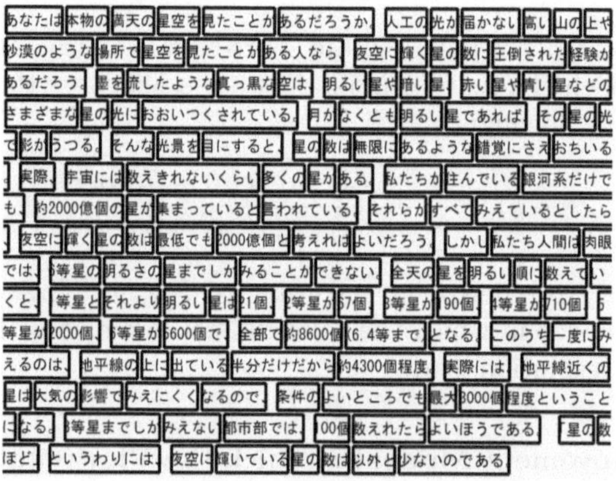

Fig. 4. Clauses of the document used in the experiment

3.4   Memory Integration Using Feature Matching

Human can read scrolled text as easily as they can read non-scrolled text. The letters cannot be adequately recovered in the short-term memory image if the image is integrated without considering the letter movement by scrolling. So it is difficult to read the short-term memory image recovered without matching features. The short-term memory image can be adequately recovered in the case of reading a scrolling text. It is necessary to match features to make up the gap caused by scrolling. Edge densities are compared for all pixels of the two images and the optimal position is calculated. If the short-term memory image is regarded as the understood image, the letter cannot be understood because the short-term memory image is not recovered. It takes the time required for the feature matching to recover the short-term memory. This is a reason why the time necessary to read scrolling text is three times longer than the time necessary to read the normal text.

4   Simulating Eye Movement Based on Navigation

We simulated eye movement for 24 settings in which the distance between the viewpoint and the mark varies from 100 to 125 pixels or from 75 to 100 pixels, and the scrolling speed is ether 20 *pixel/s* or 5 *pixel/s* and the average resolution is

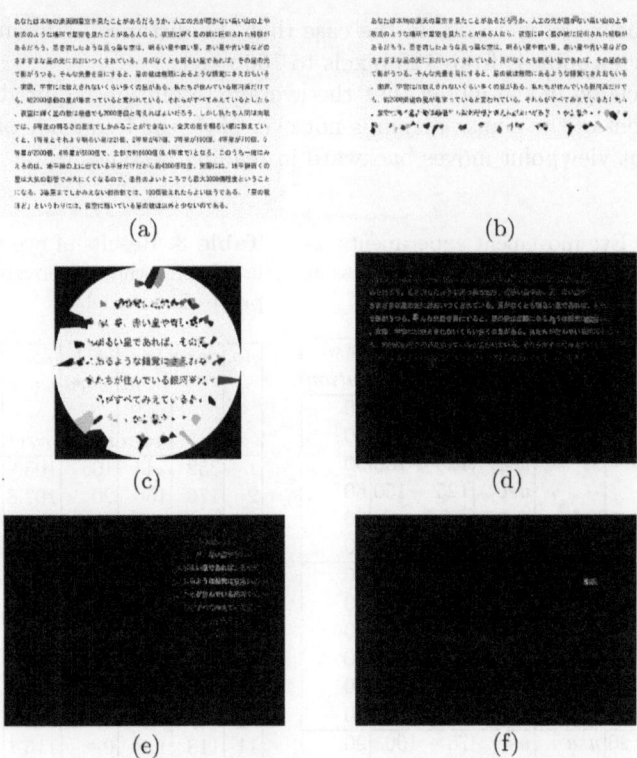

Fig. 5. (a)Display of eye movement navigation system. (b)Short-term memory image.(c)Foveated vision.(d)Short-term memory edge image in which viewpoint moves to the next line.(e)Short-term memory edge image in which viewpoint moves along the line.(f)Short-term memory image of the 100th viewpoint

ether 90% or 60% while feature matching is used to generate images in the short-term memory, as shown in Table 5 and Table 6. Figures 5 (a), (b), (c), (d), (e), and (f) show the image of the eye movement navigation interface, the short-term memory image, the foveated vision image, the short-term memory edge image necessary for the viewpoint to move to the next line, the short-term memory edge image along the line, and the short-term memory image, respectively.

Normal non-nscrolled text is used from *model*1 to *model*6. Upward-scrolling text is used from *model*8 to *model*12. Forward-scrolling text is used for *model*8 and from *model*13 to *model*24 . Fixation frequency, the eye movement frequency that viewpoint moves forward and backward, the saccad distance of eye movement, the average distance, skip frequency, and the time are shown in Table 3. The time units are converted to seconds based on the numbers. The average fixation time in terms of seconds is calculated by multiplying $200ms$ which is the average time in a fixation. The order of the reading speed is *model*6, *model*4, *model*2, *model*1, *model*5 and *model*3. The frequency in which the viewpoint moves backward increases in the case that the distance between mark and the current viewpoint is from 125 pixels to 150 pixels.

Especially, in the model that the average resolution required to understand the content of the clause region is not over 90%, the frequency of the eye movement that viewpoint moves backward in reading becomes to be much.

Table 2. Eye movement experiments using eye movement information processing model

model	scrol	match	guide	region	reso. lution
1	×	−	use	75 − 100	90
2	×	−	use	75 − 100	60
3	×	−	use	125 − 150	90
4	×	−	use	125 − 150	60
5	×	−	×	−	90
6	×	−	×	−	60
7	← 20	−	use	125 − 150	60
8	↑ 5	−	use	125 − 150	60
9	↑ 5	use	use	75 − 100	90
10	↑ 5	use	use	75 − 100	60
11	↑ 5	use	use	125 − 150	60
12	↑ 5	use	use	−	60
13	← 20	use	use	75 − 100	90
14	← 20	use	use	75 − 100	60
15	← 20	use	use	125 − 150	90
16	← 20	use	use	125 − 150	60
17	← 20	use	×	−	90
18	← 20	use	×	−	60
19	←60	use	use	75 − 100	90
20	←60	use	use	75 − 100	60
21	←60	use	use	125 − 150	90
22	←60	use	use	125 − 150	60
23	←60	use	×	−	90
24	←60	use	×	−	60

Table 3. Results of eye movement simulated using the eye movement information processing model

no.	gaze	for num	back word	for word	back word	skip	time
		num	num	pixel	pixel	num	num
1	352	246	106	105.9	107.3	96	355
2	176	156	20	107.8	103.0	40	178
3	367	243	124	118.4	113.3	125	374
4	164	139	25	127.4	117.9	70	165
5	359	250	109	110.5	118.5	119	372
6	167	147	20	112.7	94.3	47	159
7	−	−	−	−	−	−	−
8	−	−	−	−	−	−	−
9	225	182	43	101.3	113.8	64	241
10	136	135	1	99.65	94.00	32	153
11	118	118	0	116.1	−	37	133
12	129	128	1	107.9	64.00	29	145
13	271	179	92	128.2	89.47	99	278
14	141	128	13	124.7	97.00	47	142
15	285	181	104	136.4	95.80	112	287
16	130	118	12	136.6	113.5	55	131
17	321	200	121	132.3	96.64	103	327
18	148	129	19	128.7	98.05	53	150
19	258	140	118	159.0	63.69	98	283
20	109	90	11	159.7	80.55	48	178
21	224	124	100	173.9	67.38	86	254
22	97	89	8	172.8	72.63	52	100
23	259	143	116	159.4	69.82	89	294
24	100	91	9	169.1	69.89	51	103

Figure 7(a), (b), (c), and (d) show the short-term memory image for $model16$, $model7$, $model11$, and $model8$, respectively. We cannot read the short-term memory image without matching features in $model7$ because the short-term memory image moves. In $model7$ and $model8$, we cannot read the short-term memory image without matching features, because the short-term memory image moves by scrolling text. We cannot recognize the letter because the short-term memory image becomes distorted. As the letters are adequately recovered in the short-term memory image by integrating the foveated vision images using feature matching, a human can understand the document's contents. In $model16$ and $model11$, the

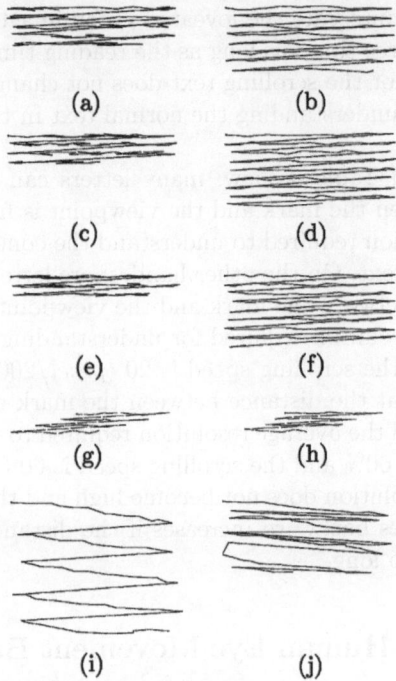

Fig. 6. Tracking results for eye movement generated by eye movement information processing models: (a)*model*1, (b)*model*2, (c)*model*3, (d)*model*4, (e)*model*5, (f)*model*6, (g)*model*16, (h)*model*7, (i)*model*11, (j)*model*8

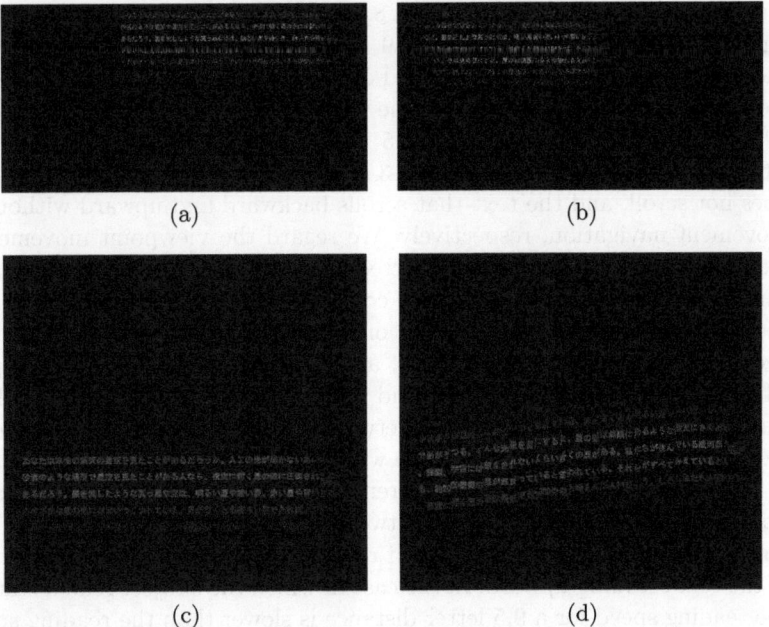

Fig. 7. Short-term memory image for (a)model16, (b)model17, (c)model11, (d)model8

time is required to integrate the foveated vision images using feature matching; this takes about three times as long as the reading time. But the time necessary for understanding for the scrolling text does not change in comparison with the time necessary for understanding the normal text in the case of using matching features.

As Table 2 and Table 3 show, many letters can be read in the case that the distance between the mark and the viewpoint is from 125 to 150 pixels and the average resolution required to understand the content of the clause region is 90% in a scrolling text. On the other hand, more letters can be read in the case that the distance between the mark and the viewpoint is from 125 to 150 pixels and the average resolution required for understanding the content of the clause region is 60% and the scrolling speed is 20 ($pixel/200ms$). More letters can be read in the case that the distance between the mark and the viewpoint is from 75 to 100 pixels and the average resolution required to understand the content of the clause region is 60% and the scrolling speed is 60 ($pixel/200ms$). This is the reason why the resolution does not become high and the eye movement in which the viewpoint moves backward increases if the distance between the viewpoint and the mark is too long.

5   Measuring Human Eye Movement Based on Navigation

We measure a eye movements when the subjects read 580 Japanese. The image size is 1220 × 920 pixels and the letter size is 24 × 24 pixels. We executed the experiments of the 15 settings shown in Table 4.

In no. 1, no. 2, no. 3, and no. 4, the subjects read normal text which does not scroll. In no. 5, no. 6, no. 7, and no. 8, the subjects read text which scrolls in the forward direction in reading. In no. 9, no. 10, no. 11 and no. 12, the subjects read the text which scrolls in the upward direction in reading. The distance between viewpoint and the mark used for the navigation is 9($cell$), 19($cell$),29($cell$), and 39($cell$) which are the same as 4.5 letters, 9.5 letters, 14.5 letters, and 19.5 letters, respectively. In no. 12, no. 13 and no. 14, the subjects read the text that does not scroll, and the text that scrolls backward and upward without the eye movement navigation, respectively. We regard the viewpoint movement as the fixations. The subjects were instructed to look at the mark which is the current candidate viewpoint. 20 letters are concealed using ×. The subjects could read the document, if the viewpoint is on the next mark. We got a result as the averages of the five measurements, after we measure five times a experiment. The background color was black and the font color was green. The colored font was white because the difference between black and white is important for eye movement navigation. The cell size was 24 × 12 pixels which is 0.5 *letters*.

Table 5 shows the result measurements. The reading time in the case of the text scrolling in the left direction is two times as long as the normal reading time. On the other hand, the difference of reading speed is not remarkable in the case of the text scrolling upward. In the case in which the subject read a static image, the reading speed for a 9.5 letter distance is slower than the reading speed for a

Table 4. Experiments measuring human eye movement using a navigation interface

no.	mark	scroll direct	scroll speed (cell)	mark distance (cell)	mask width (cell)
1	o	–	–	9	40
2	o	–	–	19	40
3	o	–	–	29	40
4	o	–	–	39	40
5	o	←	3.0	9	40
6	o	←	3.0	19	40
7	o	←	6.0	29	40
8	o	←	6.0	39	40
9	o	↑	0.2	9	40
10	o	↑	0.2	19	40
11	o	↑	0.2	29	40
12	o	↑	0.2	39	40
13	×	–	–	–	40
14	×	←	6.0	–	40
15	×	↑	0.2	–	40

Table 5. Results of measurement of human eye movement using navigation interface

no.	gaze	for word	back word	for word	back word	skip	time
	num	num	num	pixel	pixel	num	s
1	523	331	192	101.4	70.20	53	75.7
2	433	281	152	133.0	70.47	18	57.4
3	367	224	143	113.5	81.51	7	48.6
4	345	230	115	95.44	94.65	9	42.0
5	841	300	541	282.3	75.08	212	120.8
6	847	374	473	266.7	84.26	113	113.5
7	512	152	360	208.5	48.61	22	58.2
8	508	177	331	211.7	57.24	26	59.1
9	206	147	59	96.26	95.10	37	36.7
10	212	142	70	86.80	90.21	13	32.3
11	241	144	97	84.83	91.65	5	35.4
12	228	131	97	79.02	95.10	3	29.6
13	291	212	79	132.9	67.76	40	50.9
14	809	360	449	179.6	61.05	170	111.5
15	232	170	63	139.2	96.08	35	42.5

4.5 letter distance and faster than the reading speed for a 19.5 letter distance. If the mark position from the viewpoint is distant from 9.5 letter to 19.5 letter, the reading speed is comparatively fast.

The speed required to read the text scrolling forward is twice as slow as the speed required to read the normal text which does not scroll. This is the same as the speed required to read when not using the navigation mark. As the distance between the mark and viewpoint increases, the reading speed increases. The reading speed for upward-scrolling text decreases as the distance between the mark and the viewpoint increases. The reading speed for normal text which does not scroll is the fastest.

We can define the optimal saccad distance required to increase the reading speed. The human reading speed measured without a navigation interface is optimal for a distance between 14.5 and 19.5 letters. The human reading speed measured without a navigation interface is faster for the a 4.5 letter distance for upward-scrolling text.

Eye movement in which the viewpoint moves backward is related to word understanding[5]. Low resolution is required for words used frequently while the high resolution is required for words used occasionally in order to understand a text's contents. We can define the resolution of all words. Thus we can include the properties necessary for the understanding for words in the eye movement information processing model. When human reads a document, the viewpoint sometimes skips frequently used short words because the resolution required for the understanding is low.

6   Training and Reading Speed

Table 6 shows the reading speed and the average resolution required to understand the content of the clause region. If the average resolution required to understand clauses is high, the reading speed is slow. Table 7 shows the average resolution over 180(num) for all distances between the viewpoint and the mark position.

Table 6. Relation between reading speed and the average resolution required for understanding

(re sol uti on) num	$gaze$ num	for $word$ num	$back$ $word$ num	for $word$ $pixel$	$back$ $word$ $pixel$	$skip$ num	$time$ num
0.5	154	140	14	114.1	92.07	50	156
0.6	167	147	20	112.7	94.30	47	169
0.7	190	160	30	111.4	104.0	47	193
0.8	183	153	31	119.3.	118.6	59	187
0.9	359	250	109	110.5	118.5	119	362

Table 7. Resolution between the navigation mark position and the average resolution required for understanding

$pos.$	$0-25$	$25-50$	$50-75$	$75-100$	$100-124$	$125-150$
$res.$	0.6	0.6	0.6	0.7	0.7	0.8

In order to increase reading speed, the average resolution should be decreased, the distance between the mark and the viewpoint should be increased, and the saccad distance along the line should be increased. However a decrease in average resolution cannot be achieved suddenly. In order to do this, we examine the optimal mark positions that allow the document to be read quickly. Next, we gradually lengthen the distance between the viewpoint and the position of the mark. Thus reading speed can be increased.

The fixation point movement in reading the Japanese document include in 580 letters is measured for a university student. The image size is 1220×920 pixels and the letter size is 24 × 24 pixels. The head of the subject with the eye mark camera is fixed to the jaw stand. The some simple questions are requested after the subject read the document. If the result dose not reach to the point required for the understanding the document, the data is rejected. The width between the viewpoint and the mark changes from 3 letters to 10 letters per a half letter. The data is measured 5 times for each width. The data is measured 10 times without supporting the navigation interface before the experiment. Similarly, the data is measured 10 times without supporting reading with the navigation interface after the experiment. Table 8 shows the medium result in 10 data. $no.1$

shows the result before supporting reading with the interface. *no.*2 shows the result after supporting reading with the interface. The reading time change from 59.15 (s) to 33.40 (s), and you can find that the reading time decrease. While the average forward distance become to be long, the number that viewpoint moves backward decreases. As a result, the reading time decreases. Thus, it is found that the reading speed can be increased by training with the viewpoint navigation interface.

Table 8. The results of human eye movement measured without navigation interface and with navigation interface

no.	gaze	for num	back word	for word	back word	skip	time
	num	num	num	pixel	pixel	num	s
1	287	217	70	78.93	118.0	56	59.15
2	133	112	21	112.2	76.71	45	33.40

7 Conclusions

We show that the reading speed becomes to be fast if human is navigated by using the interface such as the distance between neighbor fixation points become to be long. But the reading speed become to be slow if human is navigated using the interface such as the distance between neighbor fixation points is longer than the constant time. The result measured for a human is the same as the computer simulation. This computer simulation is realized by introducing the mechanisms that the viewpoint moves backward based on the resolution and the short-term memory generated by using feature matching to the traditional eye movement model. Moreover, it is found that the reading time can be shortened by using the eye movement navigation interface with the colored marker in the text window.

References

1. R. Jacob, "What you look at is what you get: Eye movement-based interaction techniques," proc. of ACM CHI90 Human Factors in Computing System Conference, pp. 11-18, 1990
2. A. Sekey and J. Tietz, "Text display by Saccadic Scrolling,"' Visible Language, 16(1), pp. 62-77, 1982
3. R. C. Atkinson and R. M. Shiffrin, "Human memory: A proposed system and its control process., The Psychology of Learning and Motivation, Vol. 2, Academic Press, 1968.
4. A. Baddeley and G. Hitch, "Working memory,"The Psychology of Learning and Motivation, pp.47-89,1974.
5. M. Osaka and N. Osaka, "Language-independent working memory: Evidence from and French reading span tests, " Bulletin of the Psychonomic Society, 31, pp. 117-118, 1993.

6. van der Kleji G. and De Kamps M. van der Velde F., "A neural model of binding and capacity in visual working memory," proc. of ICANN/ICONIP2003, LNCS2714, pp. 771-778, 2003.

7. S. Morita and Y. Ishihara, " Control of Foveated Vision based on Short-term Memory," Proc. of IEEE MFI99, pp. 13-18, 1999.

8. S. Morita, "Short-term Memory Optical Flow Image," proc.of ICANN/ICONIP 2003, LNCS2714, pp.409-416, 2003.

9. S. Morita, "Simulating Eye Movement in Reading Using Short-term Memory," IEEE Vision Interface 2002, pp. 206-212, 2002.

10. S. Morita, "Eye Movement in Reading the Document including Several Sized Letter", JCIS2003, 2003.(accepted)

11. Y. Ishihara and S. Morita, "Computation model of eye movement in reading using foveated vision, " BMCV2000, pp. 108–117, 2000.

12. Y. Ishihara and S. Morita, "Reading Speed and Superiority of Right Visiau Field based on Foveated Vision," BMCV2002,pp. 70–79,2002.

13. K. Rayner and A. Pollatsek, "The Psychology of Reading," Lawrence Erlbaum Associates Inc. Publishers, 1989.

14. M. Brysbaert, F. Vitu and W. Schroyens, "The right field visual advantage and the optimal viewing position effect: on the relation between foveal and parafoveal word recognition, " Neuropsychologia, 10(3), pp. 385–395, 1996.

15. G. W. McConkie, P. W. Kerr, M. D. Reddix, , D. Zola and A. M. Jacobs, "Eye movement control during reading: II. Frequency of refixating a word, " Perception and Psychophysics, 46, pp. 245–253, 1989.

16. J. K. O'Regan and A. Lévy-Schoen, "Eye movement strategy and tactics in word recognition and reading, " In M. Coltheart, Attention and performance XII: The psychology of reading (pp. 363–383). Hillsdale, NJ: Erlbaum. 1987.

17. J. K. O'Regan, "Eye movements and reading, " In E. Kowler, Eye movements and their role in visual and cognitive processes (pp. 395–453). Elsevier. 1990.

18. J. K. O'Regan and A. M. Jacobs, "The optimal viewing position effect in word recognition: A challenge to current theory, " Journal of Experimental Psychology: Human Perception and Performance, 18, pp. 185–197, 1992.

19. K. Rayner and M. H. Fischer, "Mindless reading revisited: eye movements during reading and scanning are different, " Perception & Psychophysics, 58(5), pp. 734–747, 1996.

20. K. Rayner, S. C. Seneno and G. E. Raney, "Eye movement control in reading: a comparison of two types of models, " Journal of Experimental Psychology: Human Perception and Performance, 22(5), pp. 1188–1200, 1996.

21. F. Vitu, J. K. O'Regan and M. Mittau, "Optimal landing position in reading isolated words and continuous text, " Perception and Psychophysics, 47, pp. 583–600, 1990.

22. F. Vitu, "The influence of parafoveal preprocessing and linguistic context on the optimal landing position effect, " Perception and Psychophysics, 50, pp. 58–75, 1991.

23. K. Rayner and J. H. Bertera, "Reading without a fovea, " Science, 206, pp. 468-469

24. M. H. Pirenne, "Vision and the eye, " 2nd ed., Chapman and Hall, London. 1967.

25. T. A. Nazir, J. K. O'Regan and A. M. Jacobs, "On words and their letters, " Bulletin of the Psychonomics Society, 29, pp. 171–174, 1991.

Intuitive Interfaces for Motion Generation and Search

Yoshihiro Okada, Hiroaki Etou, and Koichi Niijima

Graduate School of Information Science and Electrical Engineering, Kyushu University,
6-1 Kasuga-koen, Kasuga, Fukuoka, 816-8580, Japan
{okada,h-etou,niijima}@i.kyushu-u.ac.jp

Abstract. This paper treats intuitive interfaces for motion generation and motion search. These are research results on the interactive animation system achieved by the research group of the authors as the part of a research project "Intuitive Human Interface for Organizing and Accessing Intellectual Assets". For CG animation creation, the motion design of CG characters as well as the shape design is very laborious work. For the motion design, the authors have already proposed a component based motion editing environment, a real-time motion generation system using puppet/marionette metaphors and a motion database management system. These allow the user to create motions interactively, intuitively and make it easy to distribute and re-edit motions. In this paper, the authors introduce these motion generation and motion search systems.

1   Introduction

We have been interested in narrative database systems. Traditionally narrative data have been represented by the text media so far. Now narrative data would be possible to be represented by the CG animation because advances of recent computer hardware technologies have made it possible to create CG animations by very lower costs rather than ever. Towards the development of a narrative database system, we have been studying on an interactive animation system. Especially, this paper treats intuitive interfaces for motion generation and motion search. These are research results on the interactive animation system achieved by our research group as the part of a research project "Intuitive Human Interface for Organizing and Accessing Intellectual Assets".

For 3D animation creation, the character design is a very important factor but very hard work. Especially its motion design and shape modeling are very laborious work. For the motion design, we have already proposed a component based motion editing environment [1, 2]. There are many researches on motion generation for computer animation. Witkin and Kass proposed concept of *spacetime* constraints [3]. After that, many research papers based on *spacetime* constraints were published [4, 5]. IK (Inverse Kinematics) is one of the other popular methods for efficient motion generation. The motion path functionality is also a popular technique to intuitively define movement of a character's center of mass. However, most popular and traditional motion design is based on key-frame animation [6]. A motion is represented as a sequence of a number of poses those are automatically generated by interpolation of several key-poses. Each key-pose is defined by specifying the joints angles of an articulated figure model. Our proposed motion editing environment is also based on the key-frame animation technology. This environment displays all sequential key-poses at the same time on a computer screen. Then by looking at those key-poses users can recognize a complete motion those key-poses mean and can edit each key-pose interactively and easily through comparing with its adjoining poses on a computer screen. We have developed such motion editing environment using *IntelligentBox* [7, 8], which is a component based 3D graphics software development system that provides functional components called *boxes*. The proposed motion editing environment is developed as a composite *box*, which includes user-defined motion information itself. Therefore, users can exchange their edited motions with each other through *Internet* by copy-and-transfer operations of such a composite *box*, and create new motions only by modifying the motions already defined by other users.

Besides the above motion editing environment, for motion generations, we have also proposed a real-time motion generation system using puppet/marionette metaphors [9, 10]. The puppet is a children toy and it is easy to manipulate for even children. For this reason, at first, we employed the puppet metaphor for real-time motion generation. We developed such a real-time motion generation system using *IntelligentBox* [9]. This system used the set of a data-glove and a magnetic motion sensor as its interfaces. A puppet motion is controlled using one-hand actions. Our data-glove generates only ten finger-joint angles. This number is not enough to fully control an articulated figure. So the system requested the user to prepare multiple mapping tables that defines association between ten finger-joint angles of a data-glove and 17 joint of an articulated figure. When the user performs his/her hand action to generate the motion of an articulated figure, he/she chooses an adequate mapping-table and changes the current one into the chosen one by additional keyboard manipulation. Indeed this was inconvenient. Therefore we introduced another metaphor, i.e., a marionette metaphor and especially introduced gravity field concept and ground contact constraint [10]. Actually in the real world, a human action is performed in the gravity field and usually on a floor or on the ground. Similarly a marionette action is also performed based on the physics of the gravity and the ground contact constraint. For this reason, we employed a marionette metaphor to generate the motions of an articulated figure in real time by one-hand actions. As related works, there are researches on the use of motion capture systems as a real-time input interface to control CG character interactively [11]. Noser and Thalmann proposed virtual tennis game environment using a full-body motion capture system as a real-time motion input interface [12]. Full-body motion capture systems have become common. However they are still very expensive and they cannot be used on the desktop. Laszlo, et al [13] proposed interactive control technique for physically-based animation using standard input devices, i.e., a mouse device and a keyboard. This technique requests the user to prepare many motion primitives. The use of a mouse device and a keyboard is convenient but they are not intuitive devices. Oore, et al proposed a desktop input device and interface for interactive 3D character animation [14, 15]. Our research system is very similar to theirs. They use two magnetic-based motion sensors while we use the set of a magnetic-based motion sensor and a data-grove. While our system generates motions of an articulated figure in real time by the user's one-hand actions, which are squat and jump, walking motion and so on, Oore's system can not generate a character animation in real time. This means that their system generates motions of some parts of a figure separately and later it has to compose a full body motion of them. Although the quality of motions generated by Oore's system seems better than that of our system, the abstract motions generated by our system are able to be used for various applications, e.g., as initial motions for key-frame animation [1, 2], as query motions to search required motions from motion databases and so on.

The above motion editing environment and real-time motion generation system are main research results for motion generations of our interactive animation system research. Indeed, besides the above two topics, we have been studying motion database systems. The development of motion database management systems poses two main questions: which feature can be assumed to be the best similarity among motions, and what is the best way to specify the query. We employed new similarity feature based on the symbolic representation of motion data by the spatial quantization as the answer of the first question. Motion data is a sequence of several poses, each of which consists of joints angles data of an articulated figure model at a different frame time. To reduce the calculation cost for the motion search, we employ not all the joints but a small number of the joints, those mean semantically important joints called feature joints, of each pose of a complete motion data. Furthermore we employed new similarity measure based on the spatial occurrence probability. We divided the 3D space around a model into a small number of subspaces semantically. At each frame, the position of each feature joint is represented as the symbol value that corresponds one of the subspaces, in which the feature joint exists. This means spatial quantization. In this paper, we show two spatial quantization ways and their experimental results for the evaluation. We have already developed its prototype system using *IntelligentBox*. In this paper, we also propose an intuitive interface as the answer of the second question. This interface provides the facility allows the user to intuitively enter query motions for motion data searches. Researches on motion database systems are very few so far. As for motion generation aspects, Unuma et al. [16] proposed an algorithm for the motion regeneration by composing from several semantic primitive motions based on Fourier transform. Uehara group [17] proposed a method for the extraction of primitive motions represented symbolized values to recognize human motions by matching those symbolized sequential values. Lim et al. [18] also proposed an algorithm for the key-posture extraction out of human motion data based on the curve simplification algorithm. We have never found motion database management systems like our prototype that employs the symbolic representation for motion data to reduce the calculation cost of motion searches and that provides an intuitive interface for entering query motions.

The remainder of this paper is organized as follows: Section 2 describes the component based motion editing environment. Section 3 describes the real-time motion generation system using puppet/marionette metaphors. Section 4 treats the motion database system. Especially we describe symbolic representation of motion data for motion searches. Finally Section 5 concludes the paper.

2 Component Based Motion Editing Environment

This section describes the component based motion editing environment. Especially we explain what kinds of *boxes* of *IntelligentBox* are developed and used.

2.1   Component Structure of a Human-Like Model and Its One Pose Data

Fig. 2.1 shows components of a human-like model. This model is consisted of 17 joints. Each joint is *3DRotationBox*. The bottom *box* is *ArrayBox* that stores xyz-angle data of the all joints. Therefore, this *ArrayBox* keeps one pose data. This composite *box* illustrated in the figure is used as a unit for editing one pose.

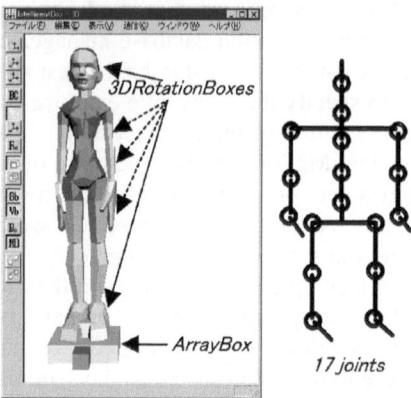

Fig. 2.1. Component structure of a human-like model.

2.2   Editing of Multiple Key-Poses

Fig. 2.2 (left) shows multiple key-poses those mean a walking motion. This motion is consisted of five key-poses. By looking at the five key-poses, it is possible to understand that motion is a walking motion. Figure 2.2 (center) shows another motion. This is a jump motion consisting of six different poses. As for the walking motion, the character's center of mass moves gradually in one direction. So it is not difficult to specify each pose by directly dragging the joints of the corresponding model on a computer screen. However as for the jump motion, the character's center of mass moves up and then down again. So it is difficult to specify each pose by directly dragging the joints of the corresponding model on a computer screen because some poses

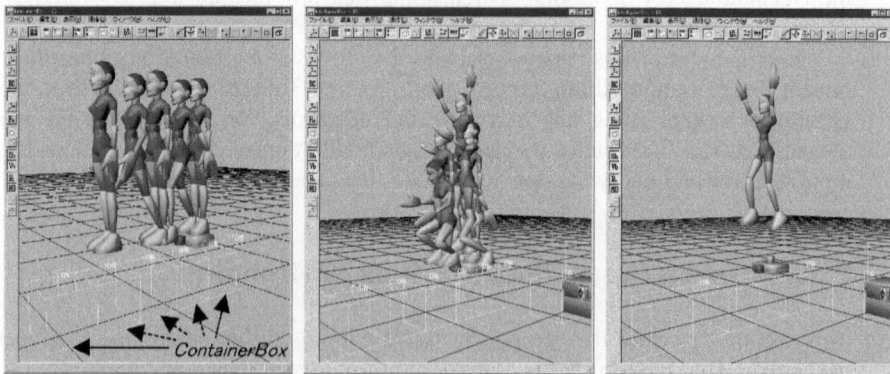

Fig. 2.2. Editing of a walk motion, and editing of a jump motion and its one key-pose.

are occluded. For this case, the system provides functionality to disappear other unnecessary poses except the one pose that the user is currently modifying. There is a
particular *box* called *ContainerBox* to provide such functionality. Several *Container-
Boxes* are located below each model and assigned as its parent *box*. *ContainerBox*
controls visibility of its descendant *boxes*. If a user clicks a mouse button on *ContainerBox*, its descendant *boxes* become invisible, and the user clicks again then its
descendant *boxes* become visible. By interactively controlling their visibility, users
can edit each pose with showing only one corresponding pose as shown in Figure 2.2
(right).

2.3 Mechanism of Motion Generation

Fig. 2.3 (left) shows data flow and component structure for concatenated motion generation. The upper part of the figure is component structure for one motion generation. There is *InterpolationBox*. *InterpolationBox* generates a motion as a complete
sequence of poses generated by interpolation among several key-poses. The motion is
stored in the *slot* of *ArrayBox*. Furthermore the lower part of the figure is component
structure for concatenation of several motions. There is *MotionConcatenationBox*.
MotionConcatenationBox generates one motion as a sequence of several motions. If
there are two difference motions, i.e., a walking motion and a jump motion, and the
walk motion is assigned a value of zero as its ID number and the jump motion is assigned a value of one. After the user specifies a sequence of ID number values like (0,
1, 1, 0) as the parameter of *MotionConcatenationBox*, the *MotionConcatenationBox*
generates one concatenated motion. That motion acts in the order of a walk, a jump, a
jump and a walk. Two sequential motions are concatenated smoothly by a linear
combination of last *n* frames of the first motion and first *n* frames of the second motion. Strictly speaking, concatenation process generates a smooth motion, i.e., the first
motion fades out and the second motion simultaneously fades in.

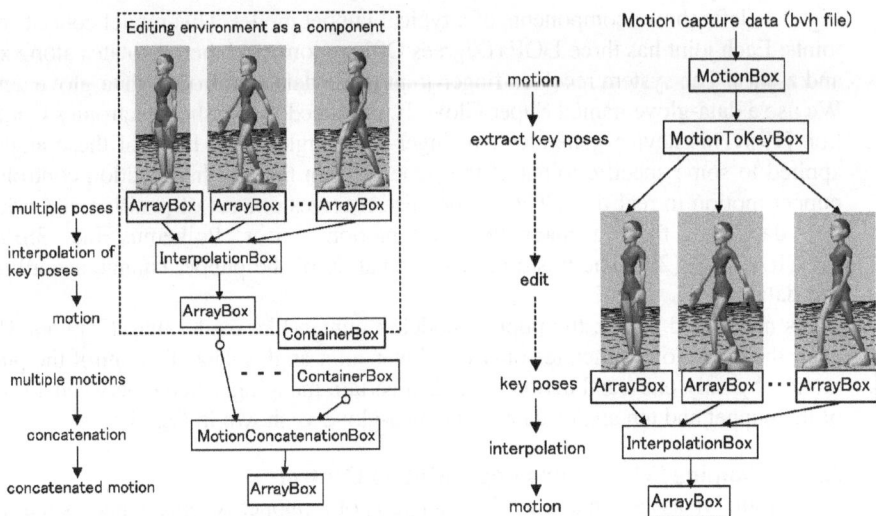

Fig. 2.3. Data flow of concatenated motion generation (left) and data flow to generate new
motion by re-editing a motion capture data (right).

2.4 Motion Capture Data Support

As shown in Fig. 2.3 (right), *IntelligentBox* provides a particular *box* called *Motion-Box*. This *box* reads a motion capture data file and generates a motion as a sequence of several poses. Currently this *box* supports *BioVision* Inc. BVH file format. In the figure, there is another *box* called *MotionToKeyBox* under *MotionBox*. This *box* automatically extracts multiple key-poses from the motion data generated by the *MotionBox*. Once several poses are extracted as key-poses, the user can create new motions by reediting those key-poses.

3 Real-Time Motion Generation Using Puppet/Marionette Metaphors

This section describes the real-time motion generation method proposed in this research project. Especially we explain how the user creates motions interactively by the intuitive interface of the proposed system.

3.1 Motion Generation Using Puppet Metaphor

Before explaining the mechanism of motion generation using marionette metaphor, this subsection explains the mechanism of motion generation based on the puppet metaphor. We use the term of 'puppet' to indicate an articulated figure that is directly controlled by the user hand action. On the other hand, we use the term of 'marionette' to indicate a string hung articulated figure. This 'marionette' case has to simulate physical effects, i.e., gravity field and ground contact constraint besides direct control by the user hand action.

3.1.1 Component Structure of a Puppet Model

Fig. 3.1 (left) shows components of a typical puppet model. This model consists of 17 joints. Each joint has three DOF (Degrees Of Freedom) and then it rotates along x-, y- and z-axes. The system receives finger-joint angle data sent from a data-glove device. We use a data-glove named Super Glove Jr. produced by Nissho Electronics Corporation [19]. This device generates ten finger-joint angles data. Each of these angles is applied to some specific joints of the puppet. Then the real-hand action controls the puppet motion in real time. The system also receives one set of position and orientation data sent from a magnetic-based motion sensor, Polhemus Inc. 3SPACE ISOTRACK II [20]. The position and orientation of the puppet change according to this data.

As mentioned above, the puppet model, a human-like model, has 17 joints. However, the data-glove generates only ten finger-joint angles data. To control the puppet motion by only one-hand action it needs a certain mapping scheme between 17 joints of the puppet and ten angles data of the data-glove as shown in Fig. 3.1.

3.1.2 Mapping Scheme for Puppet Motion Control

First of all, we assume that each joint angle p_i of a puppet is represented as the linear combination of ten-angle data of a data-glove. It is calculated using the next equation.

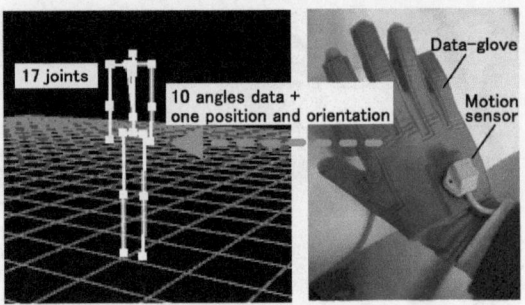

Fig. 3.1. Puppet/marionette model and its control interface.

$$p_i = a_{i,0}h_0 + a_{i,1}h_1 + \cdots + a_{i,9}h_9 + b_i \tag{3.1}$$

where, p_i is the angle of i-th joint of a puppet, $h_0, h_1, \cdots, h_9$ are ten-angle data of a data-glove and b_i is the initial angle of i-th joint of a puppet. $a_{i,0}, a_{i,1}, \cdots, a_{i,9}$ are coefficients arbitrarily specified by the user.

As for all joints of a puppet, equation (3.1) is transformed into the matrix expression.

$$P = \Pi \times H \tag{3.2}$$

where, P is a vector $[p0, p1, p2, \cdots p16]^T$, whose element p_i is also a vector of the x-, y-, and z-angle values of each puppet joint. H is a vector $[h0, h1, \cdots, h9,1]^T$, whose element is the angle value of each hand joint. Finally, Π is a matrix that means a mapping table and initial pose information as the following matrix.

$$\Pi = \begin{bmatrix} a_{0,0} & a_{0,1} & \cdots & a_{0,9} & b_0 \\ a_{1,0} & a_{1,1} & \cdots & a_{1,9} & b_1 \\ \vdots & \vdots & \ddots & \vdots & \vdots \\ a_{16,0} & a_{16,1} & \cdots & a_{16,9} & b_{16} \end{bmatrix} \tag{3.3}$$

A vector $[b_0, b_1, \cdots, b_{16}]^T$ specifies an initial pose. Its element means a vector of the initial x-, y- and z-angle values of each puppet joint.

Fig. 3.2 shows four poses of the hand and their four corresponding poses of a puppet. We define Pose 1 is an initial pose since the paper shape of a hand seems more natural rather than the stone shape. Using only one mapping table, by the one-hand poses in Pose2, 3 and 4, the poses of a puppet shown in the right group of Fig 3.2 are obtained for instance. This mapping is adequately specified by the user to make it easier for his/her hand to control the puppet.

3.2 Motion Generation Using Marionette Metaphor

As mentioned in Section 1, one mapping table allows us to make very few kinds of motions and it is insufficient in the practical use. So the system requests the user to

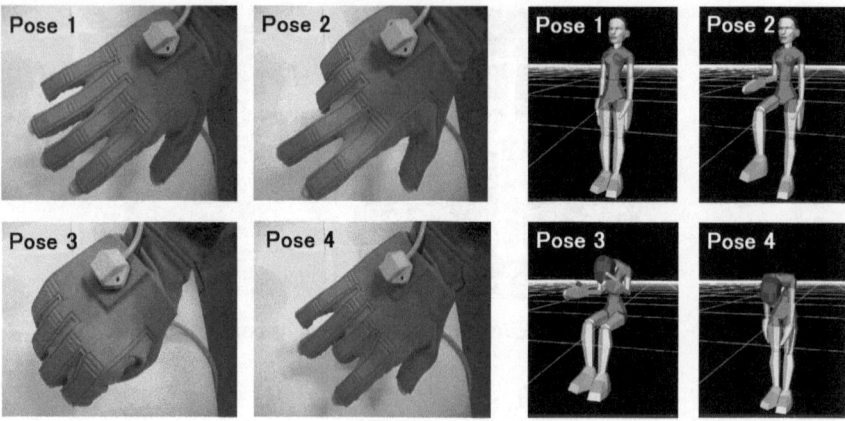

Fig. 3.2. Four one-hand poses and their corresponding puppet poses.

prepare multiple mapping tables and to choose one of them by the keyboard input properly. However, it was thought that this is inconvenient and more intuitive interface is needed. We introduced another real-time motion generation method using a marionette metaphor. This subsection treats motion effects of marionette metaphor, i.e., gravity field and ground contact constraints.

3.2.1 Motion Effect of Gravity Field

Similarly to a real marionette, the body of our marionette consisting of a waist, left and right hips, a chest, and left and right collars is treated as one rigid part. Fig. 3.3 shows five kinds of hand positions and poses in the upper group, and their corresponding marionette positions and poses in the lower group. First one (Pose 1) is a normal position and pose. Other four have a different orientation but their positions are almost the same. Second figure (Pose 2) and third figure (Pose 3) show that the hand fall down forward and that the hand go up backward respectively. These rotations of the marionette body correspond to pitch of the Euler Transformation. Fourth figure (Pose 4) and fifth figure (Pose 5) show the rotations of the marionette body correspond to roll of the Euler Transformation. Although there are no figures, the

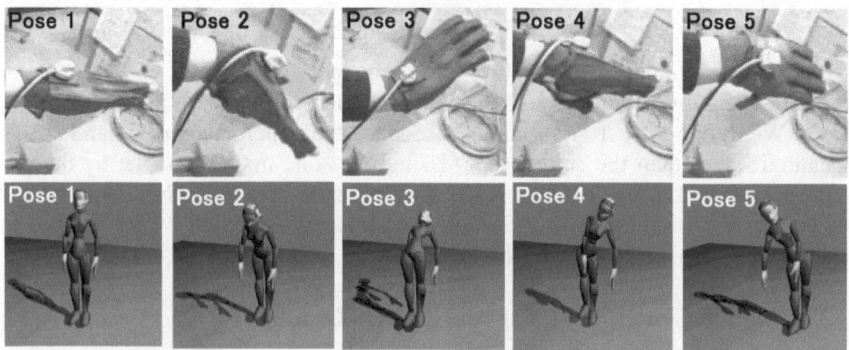

Fig. 3.3. Normal and four one-hand orientations and their corresponding marionette poses with gravity effect.

rotations of the marionette body correspond to head of the Euler Transformation is also possible. The marionette exists in the gravity field so its two arms and two legs always hang down. In this case, the positions of the hand is enough high so the ground contact constraint does not exist. Only gravity effect exists.

3.2.2 Motion Effect Based on Marionette Metaphor

Actually the arms of a real marionette are controlled by the strings connected to each of their hand, and the legs of the marionette are controlled by the strings connected to each of their knee. Fig. 3.4 shows another set of example poses those describe this effect. We used a mapping table similar to the one used to generate the poses of Fig. 3.2, that is, the thumb and little finger of the user hand control the marionette's legs and the index finger and third finger control the marionette's arms. Pose 1 means that the marionette right hand is pulled up by a virtual, invisible string. This virtual string is controlled by the hand action of the user, strictly speaking, by the action of the user's third finger. Pose 2 is almost the same as Pose 1. In this case, the marionette left hand is pulled up by the action of the user's index finger. In the case of Pose 3, the marionette both left and right hands are pulled up.

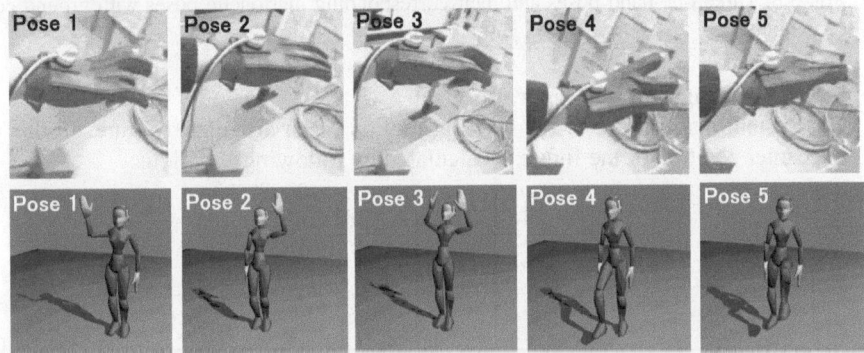

Fig. 3.4. Five one-hand poses and their corresponding strung marionette poses.

As for these poses, the inverse kinematics is partially used to determine the position of the intermediate joint, i.e., the elbows because the user's hand actions only control the position of each of the marionette's two hands. To carry out this, we introduced 2-links Inverse Kinematics. For its more detail, see the paper [10]. As for the remainder of Fig. 3.4, Pose 4 means that the marionette right knee is pulled up by a virtual, invisible string. This virtual string is controlled by the action of the user's little finger. Pose 5 is almost the same as Pose 4. In this case, the marionette left knee is pulled up by the action of the user's thumb. In the both cases, lower legs fall down due to the gravity effect.

3.2.3 Motion Effect of Ground Contact Constraint

As for a real marionette, ground contact constraint plays a significant role to effectively generate various motions. Fig. 3.5 shows another set of example poses concerning ground contact constraint. Left figure (Pose 1) is an initial pose. In this case, neither two feet nor two hands touch the ground. Center figure (Pose 2) means that two feet touch the ground due to the lower position of the waist since the user's hand position becomes lower. In this case, positions of both left and right knee are automatically calculated using 2-links Inverse Kinematics. Furthermore, right figure (Pose 3) of Fig. 3.5 shows a pose with both feet and hands contacting the ground.

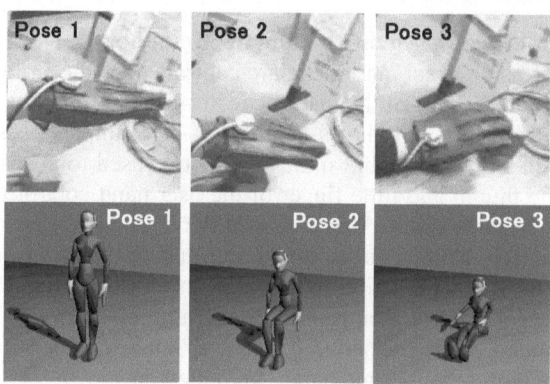

Fig. 3.5. Three one-hand poses and their corresponding marionette poses with ground contact constraints.

3.2.4 Walking Motion Generation

Our system also generates the walking motion of an articulated figure. In this case, the center position of the figure is calculated by following equations:

$$Z_{i+1}^{C} = \frac{Z_i^{RF} + Z_i^{LF}}{2} + Z^{MS} \times \cos \theta_i^{Y},$$

$$Y_{i+1}^{C} = Y^{MS},$$

$$X_{i+1}^{C} = \frac{X_i^{RF} + X_i^{LF}}{2} + Z^{MS} \times \sin \theta_i^{Y}, \qquad (3.4)$$

$$\theta_{i+1}^{Z} = \theta_{MS}^{Z}$$

$$\theta_{i+1}^{Y} = \theta_i^{Y} + \theta_{MS}^{Y},$$

$$\theta_{i+1}^{X} = \theta_{MS}^{X}.$$

Here, $X_{i+1}^{C}, Y_{i+1}^{C}, Z_{i+1}^{C}$ are the x, y, z component of the center position at $i+1$-th frame. X_i^{RF}, Z_i^{RF} are the x, z component of the right foot position at i-th frame, as well, X_i^{LF}, Z_i^{LF} are the x, z component of the left foot position. Y^{MS}, Z^{MS} are the y, z component of the position data sent by a motion sensor device. Its x component is not used in this case. $\theta_{i+1}^{X}, \theta_{i+1}^{Y}, \theta_{i+1}^{Z}$ are the rotation angles of the center along x-axis, y-axis, and z-axis respectively at $i+1$-th frame. θ_i^{Y} is the rotation angle along y-axis at i-th frame. $\theta_{MS}^{X}, \theta_{MS}^{Y}, \theta_{MS}^{Z}$ are the rotation angles data along x-axis, y-axis, and z-axis respectively, sent from a motion sensor device. It is possible to make a turn by changing θ_{MS}^{Y} and also control its speed by the change of Z^{MS}.

3.3 Discussion

Even if using conventional computer animation software, creation of the motions shown in Fig. 3.3, 3.4 and 3.5 is not easy, especially the motion of Fig. 3.5 is very difficult. However, using our system, the user can create those motions by his/her one-hand actions interactively in real time.

The main mathematical factor of our system is only 2-links Inverse Kinematics. This is very simple so its calculation cost is very low. Therefore, our system generates the motions demonstrated in this subsection in real time. As for the performance of the system, frame rate is around 18 fps using a standard PC, 850MHz Pentium III CPU, 640MB memory, and GeForce3 graphics. This value is satisfactory for interactive animation systems.

4 Motion Database System Using Symbolic Representation of Motion Data for Motion Searches

This section treats a motion database system using symbolic representation of motion data for motion searches. Especially we describe a system overview, our similarity measure of motion data and its evaluation results.

4.1 System Overview

Fig. 4.1 shows the system configuration of our motion database system. The system has original motion data as primary information and their symbolic representation data as secondary information in its motion database. When the user enters a query motion for similarity motion searches, the system generates the symbolic representation data from the query motion in order to compare it to each data in the secondary information and to output similar motions as the comparison result.

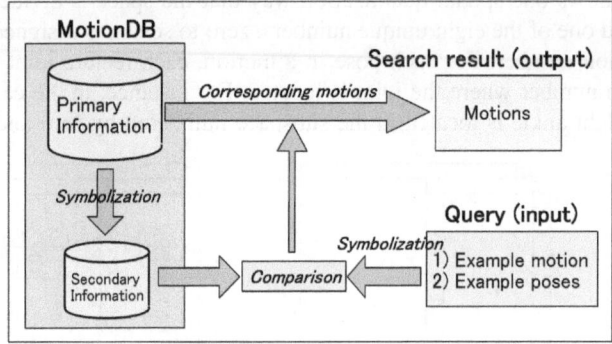

Fig. 4.1. System configuration.

4.2 Similarity Search of Motion Data

This subsection describes how to generate secondary information, i.e., symbolic representation data extracted from motion data by spatial quantization. This spatial quantization is applied to a few joints of an articulated figure model, which are semantically important joints called feature joints. First of all, we define feature joints in next sub-subsection. After that, we explain two spatial quantization ways, and introduce our similarity measure for similarity motion searches based on the spatial occurrence probability.

4.2.1 Feature Joints

If the quantization process to obtain secondary information is applied to all the joints of an articulated figure model, its calculation cost and the secondary information size become large. Then, if it is possible to determine small number of joints, those are semantically important or enough to characterize the corresponding motion, the quantization process should be applied to such a small number of joints. We decided four joints, i.e., a left wrist, right wrist, left ankle and right ankle, as feature joints because we assume that the positions of those joints are calculated using their parent joints information and then these joints have much significant information rather than the other joints. In the following sub- and sub-subsections, feature joints mean four joints, i.e., a left wrist, right wrist, left ankle and right ankle.

4.2.2 Spatial Quantization for Symbolic Representation of Motion Data

Each motion data consists of multiple sequential pose data. Our spatial quantization process is applied to each pose data and consequently multiple sequential symbolic representation data will be obtained after that. Strictly speaking, the symbolic representation data of each pose contains four symbol values, each of which means the location information of the corresponding feature joint. We treat two spatial quantization ways as shown in Fig. 4.2.

The space division is performed based on the relative position of each joint to the center of mass of an articulated figure model. That is, the center of mass of the model becomes the origin of a local coordinate system around the model. This spatial quantization is not influenced by the direction of the model in a motion. The left figure of Fig. 4.2 shows one spatial quantization way that the space is divided into eight subspaces and one of the eight unique numbers, zero to seven, is assigned to each of them as its region number. For each pose in a motion, each feature joint is represented as the region number where the joint is located. For instance, in the case of the left figure, the right ankle is located in the subspace numbered by zero and then it is repre-

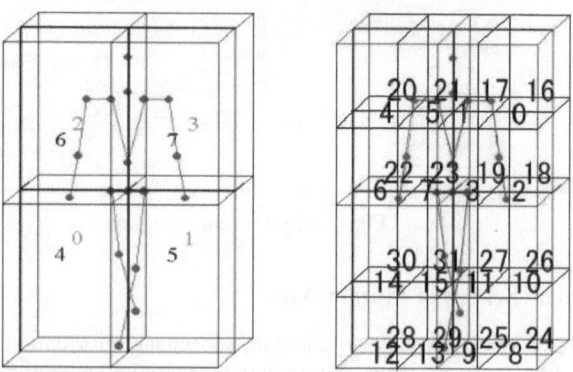

Fig. 4.2. Two different space division ways.

sented as the number 0, and the left ankle is located in the subspace numbered by 5 and then it is represented as the number 5. This is our symbolization process by the spatial quantization. Symbol values assigned to feature joints do not represent their strict positions, that is, there is ambiguity so that the secondary information consisting of such symbolic representation data seems available as the feature information of motions for similarity searches.

The papers [21, 22] proposed the same space division as the right figure of Fig. 4.2. In this paper, we propose another space division way shown in the right figure of Fig. 4.2 because this could obtain better results than the other several space division ways actually we tried. In the first trial, we decided to divide the space into 27 subspaces equally. In this case, we had to calculate the maximum space reachable for feature joints from the center of mass of a model. Then, we divided the space into 27 subspaces by dividing each X-, Y- and Z-direction into equally three segments. However, this division way is not good because in many motions, feature joints exist close to the center of mass so that outer regions of them are almost useless. As the second trial, we divided the same maximum space into 64 subspaces by dividing each direction equally into four segments. However, in this case, the number of regions is too many and most regions are useless. Especially outer regions are useless due to the same reason of the 27 division case. Finally we found that the space division shown in the right figure of Fig. 4.2 is the most efficient way in our trials. The space is divided into four segments in the both X- and Y-direction, and divided into two segments in the Z-direction. Totally the space is divided into 32 subspaces. Symbol values assigned to the subspaces are determined to satisfy that the difference of two symbol values of two adjoining subspaces is only one bit. Actual division points are decided as follows:

1) Three division points in X-direction: the origin, the midpoint between a left wrist and a left ankle, the midpoint between a right wrist and a right ankle.
2) Three division points in Y-direction: the origin, the midpoint between a shoulder and an elbow, the midpoint between a knee and an ankle.
3) One division point in Z-direction: the origin.

In the case of the right figure of Fig. 4.2, the positions of a left ankle, right ankle, left wrist and right wrist are symbolized with 9, 29, 26 and 14 respectively. This is the symbolization for one pose, and one pose data is represented as one set of symbol values like {9, 29, 26, 14}. This symbolization is applied to all pose data, and the corresponding motion data is represented as the sequence of sets of such symbol values. This symbolized data of a motion is used to generate the spatial occurrence probability explained in next sub-subsection.

4.2.3 Spatial Occurrence Probability

As mentioned previously, each motion data is a set of continuous pose data. By the symbolization process, the pose data at each frame time is represented as a set of four symbol values of feature joints. Contrarily, the motion of each feature joint in a whole motion is represented as a set of continuous symbol values. From the set, it is possible to calculate the spatial occurrence probability of the corresponding feature joint. Strictly speaking, the spatial occurrence probability means a probability distribution of subspaces in which the corresponding feature joint exist over the whole motion.

From one symbolized motion data, one set of four spatial occurrence probability data, i.e., four histograms shown in Fig. 4.3,.will be obtained. We use it for our similarity search as the feature information. For i-th feature joint, its occurrence probability of j-th region is calculated by the next equation.

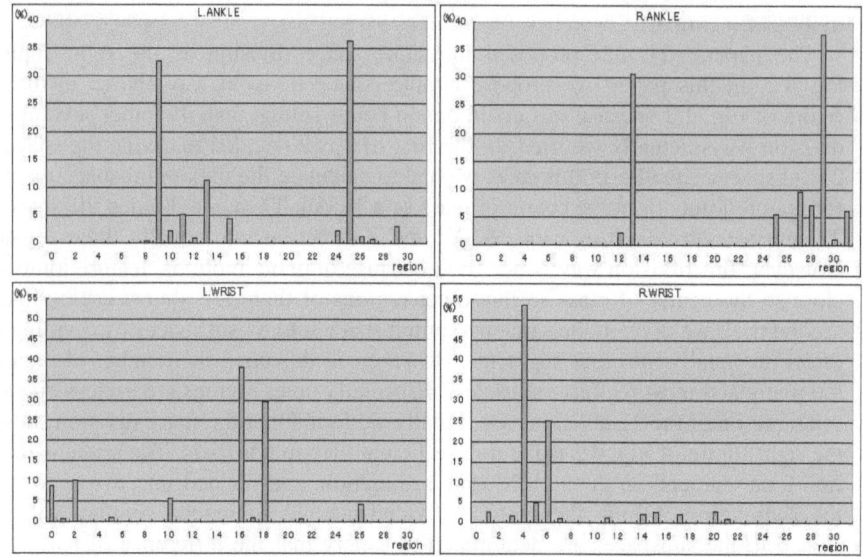

Fig. 4.3. Four histograms of a left wrist, right wrist, left ankle and right ankle.

$$p(i, j) = \frac{count(i, j)}{N} \quad (4.1)$$

Here, N is the number of frames in a symbolized motion data, $count(i,j)$ is the number of j-th region symbol values concerning i-th feature joint in a symbolized motion data.

4.2.4   Similarity Measure

In the case of the similarity search, our motion database system outputs motion data similar to the query motion entered by the user. Strictly speaking, the system calculates dissimilarity between a query motion and each motion of the motion database and then outputs motion data having the smaller dissimilarity value one by one. The dissimilarity value between two motions Q and T is calculated as Euclidean norm using the next equation.

$$E(Q,T) = \frac{1}{M} \sum_{i=0}^{M-1} \| Q(i) - T(i) \| = \frac{1}{M} \sum_{i=0}^{M-1} \sqrt{\sum_{j=0}^{N-1} (Q(i, j) - T(i, j))^2} \quad (4.2)$$

Here, $Q(i)$ and $T(i)$ are the histograms concerning feature joint i of two motions Q and T respectively. M is the number of feature joints. M is always 4. $Q(i, j)$ and $T(i, j)$ are the occurrence probabilities of region j concerning feature joint i of two motions Q and T respectively. N is the number of regions. In the case of the right figure of Fig. 4.2, N is 32.

4.3 Prototype Systems

Figure 4.4 shows the snapshot of our motion database system developed using *IntelligentBox*. This system searches motions from motion database, similar to the example motion chosen by the user. The system also searches motions including sequential key poses specified by the user as the query. This means exact match search. There are five same articulated figure models in the figure. The most left one is prepared for the preview of searched motions. One of the searched motions is also used as the query motion of the next similarity motion search. The other four models are prepared to specify query poses for the exact match motion search.

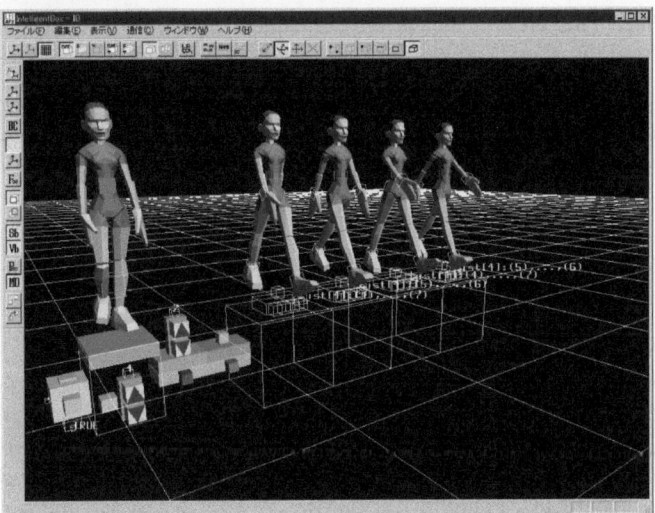

Fig. 4.4. Motion database system developed using *IntelligentBox*.

The system calculates the positions of feature joints to obtain the corresponding symbol values per each of the four poses and it obtains their symbolic representation data. Hence, the system retrieves motions whose symbolic representation data includes the symbolic representation data calculated from the four query poses. Although there are four models to specify query poses in the figure, it is possible to change the number of models by means of making their copies or deleting some of them interactively.

4.4 Experiments

This subsection presents experimental results of similarity searches for the evaluation of our proposed method. Before showing experimental results, we describe our motion database and evaluation measures.

4.4.1 Motion Database

For the evaluation of our motion search method, we had to prepare a motion database. We used a commercial product called "RIKIYA" [23]. It contains 300 motion data created by recording real human motions using a motion capture system. Unfortunately these 300 motions are composite motions like the sequence of primitive motions, e.g., the sequence of "walk", "tumble", "rise", and "walk" again. In the practical use, the user usually enters a primitive motion, e.g., "walk", "jump" etc., to search its similar motions. Therefore, we made seven classes of primitive motions, totally 61 primitive motions, from the 300 composite motions of "RIKIYA". Its details will be indicated in Table 4.1 and Table 4.2.

4.4.2 Evaluation Measures

We use the same three evaluation measures described in [24]. They are *First tier*, *Second tier* and *Nearest neighbor* as follows.

First Tier: This criteria means the percentage of top $(k–1)$ matches (excluding the query) from the query's class, where k is the number of motions in the class.

Second Tier: This criteria is the same type of result, but for the top $2(k–1)$ matches.

Nearest Neighbor: This criteria means the percentage of test in which the top match was from the query's class.

4.4.3 Experimental Results

As described above, we prepared 61 primitive motions by manually cutting out from original motion data. There are seven classes, i.e., "walk", "jump", "tumble", "rise", "sit down a chair", "kick by right leg", and "throw by right hand". We calculated the above evaluation measures for the similarity searches on these seven classes of primitive motions. Table 4.1 and 4.2 show evaluation results of the 8 division case and those of the 32 division case. These values are averages of the same class motions and all motion classes. The total search times to generate the results on 61 motions for the 8 division case and the 32 division case are around 4 seconds and around 5 seconds using a standard PC, Pentium III 500MHz CPU and 256 MB memory. Search times for one query motion in the 8 division case and in the 32 division case become 0.065 second and 0.082 second respectively. Most results of the 32 division case are equivalent or better than those of the 8 division case. For the accuracy, the motion classes "kick by right leg" and "throw by right hand" indicate not good value. One reason for this seems that these motions have high locality so that we should use only right leg or right hand as feature joints. Another reason may be that the number of motions in each of these classes is too small.

4.5 Discussion

Our motion database does not have a large number and many kinds of motions because we had to prepare it by manually cutting out primitive motions from composite motions of a commercial product database. For precise evaluations of the availability of our motion database system, we will have to prepare a motion database consisting of a large number and many kinds of motions. Currently we have been studying algorithms that help us to extract primitive motions from composite motions, and we have already proposed new method based on hierarchical curve simplification [25]. We will make a satisfactory motion database by the help of that method.

Table 4.1. Evaluation results on 32 division

Motion class	1st measure	2nd measure	3rd measure	# of motions
walk	0.905229	0.996732	1.000000	18
jump	0.393939	0.621212	0.666667	12
tumble	0.400000	0.555556	0.800000	10
rise	0.523810	0.666667	1.000000	7
sit down a chair	0.533333	0.633333	0.833333	6
kick by right leg	0.416667	0.666667	0.250000	4
throw by right hand	0.250000	0.333333	0.250000	4
All motion classes	0.566471	0.711770	0.786885	61

Table 4.2. Evaluation results on 8 division

Motion class	1st measure	2nd measure	3rd measure	# of motions
walk	0.937908	1.000000	1.000000	18
jump	0.295455	0.575758	0.500000	12
tumble	0.377778	0.688889	0.700000	10
rise	0.380952	0.547619	0.428571	7
sit down a chair	0.666667	0.666667	0.833333	6
kick by right leg	0.250000	0.333333	0.250000	4
throw by right hand	0.166667	0.250000	0.000000	4
All motion classes	0.533425	0.687945	0.655738	61

Moreover, as described in Section 3, we have proposed a real-time motion generation system using puppet/marionette metaphors. Using this system, the user can generate coarse motions of an articulated figure model by his/her hand actions in real time. Those motions are possible to be used as query motions for similarity motion searches. We are supposed to integrate the two systems to develop an intelligent motion management system.

5 Concluding Remarks

In this paper, we described intuitive interfaces for motion generation and motion search. These are research results on the interactive animation system achieved by our research group as the part of a research project "Intuitive Human Interface for Organizing and Accessing Intellectual Assets". We did these researches toward the development of a narrative database system in which narrative data would be represented as CG animations. As a result, we studied on intuitive interfaces for CG animation creation. For the motion design, we have proposed a component based motion editing environment, a real-time motion generation system using puppet/marionette metaphors and a motion database system by symbolic representation of motion data. In this paper, we mainly treated these topics. On the other hand, for the shape design, we have also proposed a polygonal model database management system that accepts hand sketch images as the query and outputs corresponding polygonal models by the silhouette image matching [26-28]. As well, we have other research results [29, 30]. Due to the page number limitation, we did not describe them in this paper. See each paper for its detail.

As future works, we will integrate all the research results mentioned in this paper in order to develop an interactive animation system using *IntelligentBox* towards the development of a narrative database system.

References

1. Okada, Y.: Intuitive Motion Editing Environment for Interactive Animation Systems, Proc. of Symposium on Visual Computing/Graphics and CAD, pp. 109-114, June 2001, (in Japanese).
2. Okada, Y., Component Based Motion Editing Environment for Game Character Design, Proc. of Second International Conference on Intelligent Games and Simulation, SCS Publication, pp. 22-26, 2001.
3. Witkin, A. and Kass, K.: Spacetime constraints, Proc. of SIGGRAPH'88, pp. 159-168, 1988.
4. Gleicher, M.: Motion editing with spacetime constraints, Proc. of SIGGRAPH'97, pp. 139-148, 1997.
5. Lee, J. and Shin, S.-Y.: A hierarchical approach to interactive motion editing for human-like figures, Proc. of SIGGRAPH'99, pp. 39-48, 1999.
6. Life Forms^{TM}, http://www.credo-interactive.com/products/lifeforms/lf_4-0_studio.html
7. Okada, Y. and Tanaka, Y., 1995: IntelligentBox: A Constructive Visual Software Development System for Interactive 3D Graphic Applications, Proc. of Computer Animation '95, IEEE Computer Society Press, pp. 114-125.
8. Okada, Y. and Tanaka, Y., 1998: Collaborative Environments in IntelligentBox for Distributed 3D Graphic Applications, The Visual Computer (CGS special issue), Vol. 14, No. 4, pp. 140-152.
9. Okada, Y., Real-time character animation using puppet metaphor, Workshop Note of the First International Workshop on Entertainment Computing (IWEC2002), pp. 86-93, 2002.
10. Okada, Y.: Real-time Motion Generation of Articulated Figures Using Puppet/Marionette Metaphor for Interactive Animation Systems, Proc. of the 3rd IASTED International Conference on Visualization, Imaging, and Image Processing (VIIP03), ACTA Press, pp. 13-18, Benalmadena, SPAIN, September 2003.
11. David J. Sturman, Computer puppetry., IEEE Computer Graphics and Applications, 18(1):38-45, January/February 1998.
12. Noser, H. and Thalmann, D., Sensor Based Synthetic Actors in a Tennis Game Simulation, Proc. of Computer Graphics International '97, IEEE Computer Society Press, pp.189-198, 1997.
13. Laszlo, J., Panne, M.van de, and Fiume, E., Interactive Control For Physically-Based Animation, SIGGRAPH2000, pp.201-208, 2000.
14. Oore, S. Terzopoulos, D. and Hinton, G. ,A Desktop Input Device and Interface for Interactive 3D Character Animation, Proc. of Graphics Interface 2002, 2002.
15. Oore, S. Terzopoulos, D. and Hinton, G. ,Local Physical Models for Interactive Character Animation, Computer Graphics Forum, Volume 21, Number 3, Proceedings of Eurographics 2002.

16. Unuma, M., Anjyo, K. and Takeuchi, R.: Fourier Principles for Emotion-based Human Figure Animation, Proc. SIGGRAPH95, ACM SIGGRAPH, pp. 91-96, 1995.
17. Osaki, R., Shimada, M. and Uehara, K.: A Motion Recognition Method by Using Primitive Motions, Proc. of the Fifth Working Conference on Visual Database Systems (VDB5), pp. 117-128, 2000.
18. Lim, Ik. S. and Thalmann, D.: Key-posture Extraction out of Human Motion Data by Curve Simplification, Proc. of 23rd Annual International Conference of the IEEE Engineering in Medicine and Biology Society (EMBC2001), vol. 2, pp. 1167-1169, 2001.
19. http://www.nissho-ele.co.jp/3d/
20. http://www.polhemus.com/
21. Watanabe, R., Okada, Y. and Niijima, K.: A motion search technique based on symbolized expression of pose data, Proc. of IPSJ 63rd all Japanese domestic conference, pp. 225-226, September 2001, (in Japanese).
22. Watanabe, R. Okada, Y. and Niijima, K.: A motion search system based on symbolized expression of pose data, Proc. of IPSJ 64th all Japanese domestic conference, pp. 49-50, March 2002, (in Japanese).
23. Viewworks, http://www.viewworks.co.jp/
24. Osada, R, et al: Matching 3D Models with Shape Distributions, Shape Modeling International, May 2001.
25. Etou, H., Okada, Y. and Niijima, K.: Feature Preserving Motion Compression Based on Curve Simplification, CD-ROM Proc. of ICME2004, 2004.
26. Okada, Y.: 3D Model Matching Based On Silhouette Image Matching, Proc. of CSCC2002 (Recent Advances in Circuits, Systems and Signal Processing), WSEAS Press, pp. 380-385, Rethimno Greece, July 2002.
27. Okada, Y.: 3D MODEL DATABASE SYSTEM BY HAND SKETCH QUERY, Proc. of IEEE International Conference on Multimedia and Expo, Vol. I, pp. 889-892, Lausanne, Switzerland, August 2002.
28. Okada, Y.: 3D Model Database System by Hand Sketch Query and Its Intuitive Interface, to appear in 13th European-Japanese Conference on Information Modeling and Knowledge Bases (13EJC), Kitakyushu, Japan, June 2003.
29. Akazawa, Y., Okada, Y. and Niijima, K.: REAL-TIME VIDEO BASED MOTION CAPTURE SYSTEM AS INTUITIVE 3D GAME INTERFACE, Proc. of Third International Conference on Intelligent Games and Simulation (GAME-ON2002), SCS Publication, pp. 22-28, London UK, November 2002.
30. Tanaka, Y., Okada, Y. and Niijima, K.: Treecube: 3D Visualization Tool for Hierarchical Information, to appear in 13th European-Japanese Conference on Information Modeling and Knowledge Bases (13EJC), Kitakyushu, Japan, June 2003.

Human-Agent Co-operation in Accessing and Communicating Knowledge Media – A Case in Medical Therapy Planning

Volker Dötsch[1], Kimihito Ito[2], and Klaus P. Jantke[3]

[1] Hochschule für Technik, Wirtschaft und Kultur Leipzig (FH),
Fachbereich Informatik, Mathematik und Naturwissenschaften
Postfach 301166, 04251 Leipzig, Germany
doetsch@imn.htwk-leipzig.de
[2] Hokkaido University Sapporo,
Meme Media Laboratory,
Nishi 8, Kita 13, Kita-ku, Sapporo, 060-8628 Japan
itok@meme.hokudai.ac.jp
[3] Deutsches Forschungszentrum für Künstliche Intelligenz,
Stuhlsatzenhausweg 3, 66123 Saarbrücken, Germany
jantke@dfki.de

Abstract. The concepts of memetics and the development of meme media implementations have set the stage for a new generation of knowledge processing systems in which knowledge evolution may take place. When the evolution of knowledge goes beyond the imagination of humans, we will arrive at a new quality of human-computer co-operation.

The evolution of knowledge is of a particular interest in domains where the future is clearly unforeseeable, but where a rapid growth of knowledge is highly desirable. Medical therapy is such an area of a particularly great importance.

IntelligentPad technologies as a form of meme media implementation are used to formulate and represent medical therapy knowledge, to set up meme pools and to allow for the evolution of knowledge beyond human expectations.

This paper is reporting about the authors' first steps and is intended to lay the cornerstone of a related research and development program.

1 Introduction and Motivation

Memetics is seen as outlined in the truly exciting books by Richard Dawkins [4], Susan Blackmore [3] and Yuzuru Tanaka [9]. Richard Dawkins has attracted the world's attention to the phenomena of cultural inheritance and has introduced his seminal concept named *meme*. Susan Blackmore has taken the initiative to discuss the relevance of Dawkins' perspective from a psychological and from a somehow philosophical point of view telling all of us that we are affected by Dawkins' work. It is, naturally, up to you whether or not you feel personally affected by memetics, and this might easily become a slightly esoteric discussion.

G. Grieser and Y. Tanaka (Eds.): Intuitive Human Interface 2004, LNAI 3359, pp. 68–87, 2004.

But Yuzuru Tanaka, fortunately, has seized Dawkins' suggestion and developed it towards concepts, implementations and applications in computer science. He has coined the key term *meme media*.

The present approach relies on Tanaka's trend-setting work taking Dawkins' and Blackmore's contributions seriously.

We want to contribute to the endeavour of enabling computer systems to foster true knowledge evolution – the benefit for humans will be paramount. This may be understood as a contribution to new knowledge media in action as envisaged by Mark Stefik [8].

There are two more or less independent starting points from which to undertake such an endeavour. One is technology development as an inevitable basis; see [6] for a recent publication of the second author. Another one is identifying existing meme pools and working on evolution-driving forces. For the present investigation, the first author has brought in the domain and currently undertakes corresponding work on knowledge processing and, in particular, knowledge generation as previously done by the third author; see [2], e.g.

In particular, the application domain chosen is medical therapy planning; Based on former work in planning for complex dynamic domains (see [1], [2]).

2 Peculiarities of the Application Domain

We briefly describe characteristics of the application domain to reveal it's appropriateness for a meme media based approach to foster knowledge evolution.

Planning is a traditional research area of Artificial Intelligence. Traditional planning was dominated by logical approaches and by procedures more or less deductive in spirit. Conventional actions in deductive planning have so-called preconditions and postconditions. Their executability can be logically verified, and they change the world in a deterministic manner such that corresponding effects can be logically recorded.

In contrast, many practically relevant application domains are complex and dynamic such that deductive planning is inadequate by nature.

Oksana Arnold [1] (see also [2]) has investigated planning in complex and dynamic environments like industrial process control. Chemical installations are characteristic application cases.

In those domains, automated reasoning, in general, and computer-assisted planning, in particular, is invoked when the underlying process is in trouble. Then, there is typically some lack of data and complete knowledge for deductive reasoning is not available. The most exciting planning tasks are inductive in spirit – planning is learning [2].

Reasoning over those application domains, especially computer-assisted or fully automated reasoning like diagnosis and control, is complicated by a number of peculiarities classified into three groups as follows [1]:

[i] fundamental peculiariries characterizing dynamics and complexity,

[ii] domain-specific dynamics,

[iii] derived, but essential peculiarities.

For every class of peculiarities, we are giving a few instances to illustrate the type of difficulties we are facing and going to attack by means of meme media technologies.

[i] Fundamental Peculiarities
- Several target parameters can not be controlled directly. For instance, a human's blood pressure can only be controlled through a number of indirect medications.
- There are several process parameters of which one can not regularly access current values. Repeated tests, though possible in principle, may by physically exhausting and mentally unacceptable to human patients.
- The execution of some actions may depend on external resources the availability of which may be locally undecidable. This is particularly true for actions which depend on environmental details like communication channels, transportation facilities and administrational customs.

[ii] Domain-Specific Dynamics
- Certain constraints underlying the executability of actions need to be satisfied throughout the whole execution period of some action. For instance, some medication may necessarily require the absence of fever.
- The execution of actions is time-consuming. The amount of time necessary to complete some actions can not be estimated, in general. Usually, so-called time-outs serve as an upper time limit for executing actions.
- Usually, there are alternative actions. Those actions may have advantages and disadvantages; there might be no clearly preferred decision.

[iii] Derived Peculiarities
- So far, the human body is only insufficiently understood. There are far too many process parameters to be taken into account. Data has to be dropped and, thus, all information is incomplete by nature.
- The state of the human body changes even in case no actions at all are executed. There is no assumption of persistency.
- There are many interacting processes, and even if a current plan is perfect, it may fail by an unexpectable interaction with some other process. For instance, a schedule of surgery may be perfect, but break down if some doctor falls ill. It may also surprisingly turn out that some therapy treatment is more exhausting for a patient than initially expected.

The domain of planning in complex, dynamic environments, in general, resp. medical therapy planning, in particular, is deemed highly appropriate for meme media applications. First, the building blocks of knowledge available in the area can be reasonably mapped to meme media objects. Second, a central type of knowledge manipulation in practice truly consists in plugging those building blocks together. Third, due to the complexity of the domain, the evolution of knowledge through successful assembly of building blocks and application of composite meme media objects is essentially unforeseeable. Fourth, the domain – especially the restricted medical case – is of great practical importance and does attract sufficient public interest such that there is hope to bridge the gap from academic cutting-edge investigations to sufficiently large application cases.

3   Therapy Plan Generation and Execution Scenarios

Before going into the details of memetics for medical therapy planning, we need a vision of the future of memetic knowledge processing and evolution.

In the medical domain, the importance of decisions to human beings, to their health and life, and the derived liability of decision makers form particular obstacles to automated knowledge processing. This is beyond the present paper, but it has to be taken into account.

The current state of affair is characterized by therapy planning completely done by humans who, at most, use computers as tools for typewriting, printing and documentation purposes.

In contrast to the current state of affair, information and communication technologies offer the prerequisites for automated knowledge processing ([1], e.g.). We are on the cusp of bringing memetics to work in this area, driven by our own interest to see knowledge evolution taking place.

How to proceed gradually? How to introduce memetic knowledge processing? How to embed science and technology under development into a quite complex environment?

The *plan generation* may be seen as a separated task depicted as a box in an IT infrastructure visualization. Other components are *constraint evaluation* having, so to call, a particular dynamic logic as plug-in, *plan execution*, and *monitoring* (see Figure 1).

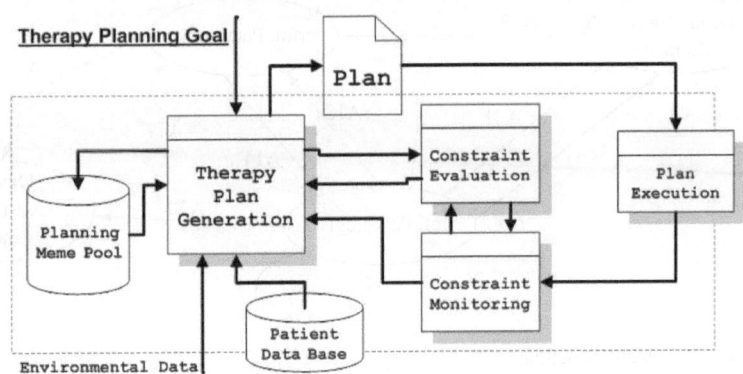

Fig. 1. Therapy Plan Generation in a Knowledge Processing Infrastructure

At a first stage, one may see `Therapy Plan Generation` as a task performed by hand. A meme media based planning tool may be invoked to support plan generation based on the `Planning Meme Pool`. If the employed logic is specified, `Constraint Evaluation` may be fully automated from the early beginning.

Re-planning is invoked when `Plan Monitoring` identifies invalid constraints.

On later stages of the implementation process, further components may be transformed into autonomous knowledge processing devices. But in contrast to process control [1], `Plan Execution` might never be completely automatic.

4   Medical Therapy Memes and Meme Pools

There is an enormous amount of knowledge in medical therapy which is currently more or less available. The authors are aware of the problem that making this knowledge available to computerized processing may take some time. Especially, a world-wide distribution of medical knowledge is not only facing technological obstacles, but also social, ethical, commercial, legal, and a large variety of other cultural difficulties. The authors refrain from going into these details and focus on scientific and technological investigations, exclusively.

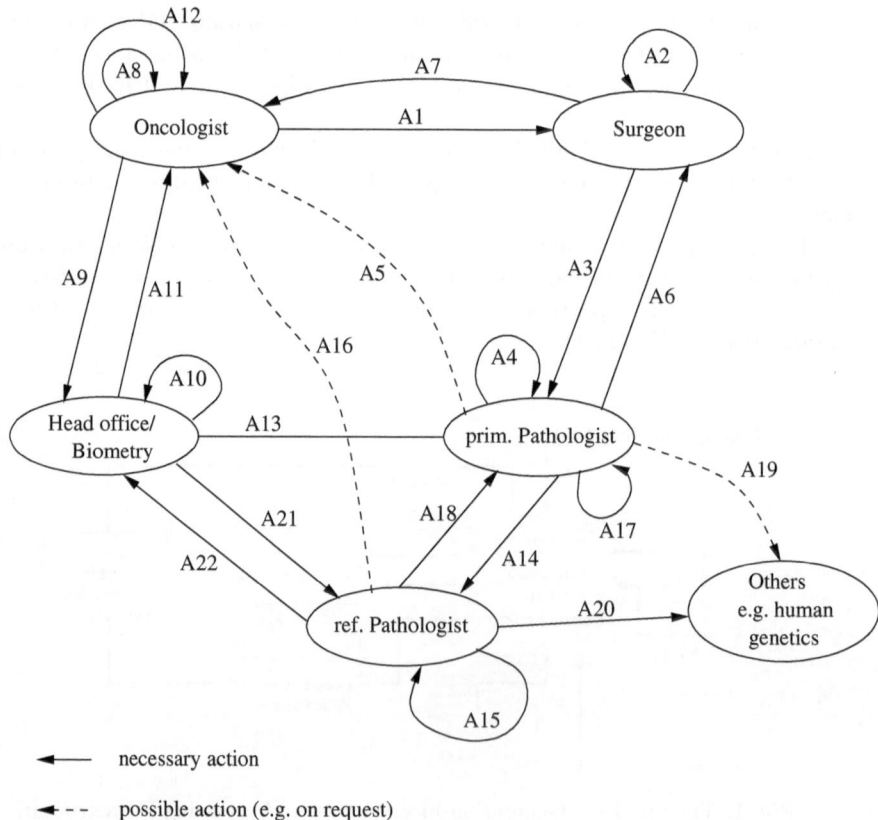

Fig. 2. Process of Patient Integration into a Randomized Clinical Trial in Germany

To avoid topical controversies on medical issues, for which the authors are not competent, the illustrations and examples stress more administrational activities in medical therapy than medication or direct physical treatment of patients. As a running example, we focus on the integration of patients into a randomized clinical trial as displayed in figure 2. Existing but finished protocols of German clinical trials on Non-Hodgkin-Lymphomas are taken as reference cases.

4.1   Basic Therapy Knowledge

There is a huge amount of elementary actions potentially taking place like the following which will be used subsequently:

[a 1] referral
[a 2] perform biopsy
[a 3] send data and tissue
[a 4] processing tissue, diagnostic findings
[a 5] send findings (if requested)
[a 6] send findings and data
[a 7] selection of an appropriate clinical trial
[a 8] patients registration (send data)
[a 9] randomization
[a 10] send data and the result of randomization
[a 11] plan treatment in detail and start treatment
[a 12] request to send data and tissue
[a 13] reference findings
[a 14] send reference findings (if requested)
[a 15] send reference findings
[a 16] compare findings and reference findings
[a 17] request data and reference findings of integrated patients

These actions as described in natural language are still incompletely specified and clearly generic in the sense that some of their corresponding parameters can vary. For instance, sending actions have parameters like sender, addressee and material to be sent.

Consequently, actions form a conventional class hierarchy where classes may have subclasses and instances which form the leaves when the hierarchy is seen as a tree.

In addition, actions usually have conditions (named constaints) under which they can be executed. Conditions are classified into start constraints and interval constraints. In medication and physical treatment, interval constraints are of crucial importance. Administrational processes are usually a little simpler and, therefore, interval constraints are less important. For simplicity, we confine ourselves to start constraints, first.

Here are two sample start constraint for actions with reference to the listing above.

[sc 7] The oncologist received diagnostic findings (and reference findings) and appropriate data.
[sc 11] The oncologist received the result of the randomization.

As briefly mentioned, the actions [a 1] to [a 17] listed above are classes which may have subclasses. They become instances by substituting parameters. For example, action class [a 3] has the instances [A 3], [A 14], [A 19], and [A 20] of sending tissue and data displayed in the process diagramm of figure 2.

Actions are represented as meme media objects which, in earlier days of AI, might have been called frames. They consist of a list of so-called slots containing all the relevant data ranging from an object's name over values for several parameters to constraints and certain flags like the one indicating whether execution has been started (cf. figure 3; for more details consult [9]).

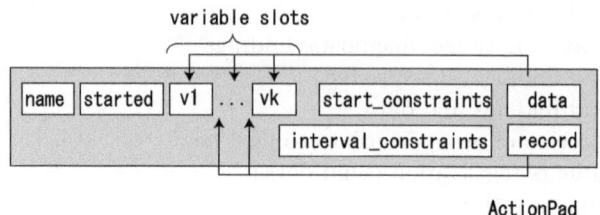

Fig. 3. A First Approach to Action Pads – The Slot Structure

Beyond former IntelligentPad applcations, the present one requires a specific type of relations between certain slots. There are some slots – those for start constraints and for interval constraints – that contain logical formulae. And these formulae contain variables which represent the content of some other slots.

4.2   Composite Plan Knowledge

Plan actions are building blocks which can be plugged together just like Lego toy blocks. A particular plan for the case under investigation is shown in figure 4. The naming of actions refers to the process model of figure 2.

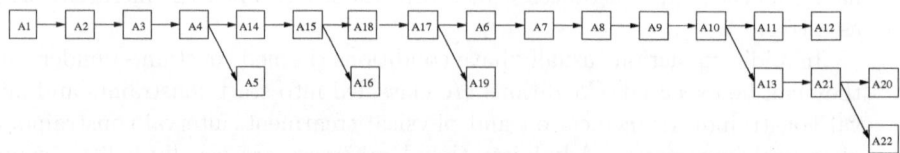

Fig. 4. A First Plan for Integration of a Patient into a Clinical Trial

Planning is plugging actions together in accordance with all the knowledge available. As explained in chapter 2, the ultimate goal is to come up with a plan consistent with everything known so far. Due to the vagueness and to the incompleteness of information, therapy planning is inductive in spirit and, thus, plan revision is frequently necessary (cf. [2]). Figure 4 displays an alternative.

The first plan is a more conservative one. Integrating a patient into a clinical trial is done only if reference findings are present. In contrast, the second alternative plan useful in seemingly urgent cases integrates a patient before reference findings did arrive. Especially in medication and physical treatment, there is usually a large number of alternatives.

Higher level actions usually consist of some structure according to subgoals to be reached either subsequently or potentially in parallel. They look like simple graphs. Planning is a stepwise refinement by substituting other actions for the nodes of those graphs. So, from a more structural perspective, planning is graph expansion. A planning step consists in plugging a graph into the node of a given graph under development.

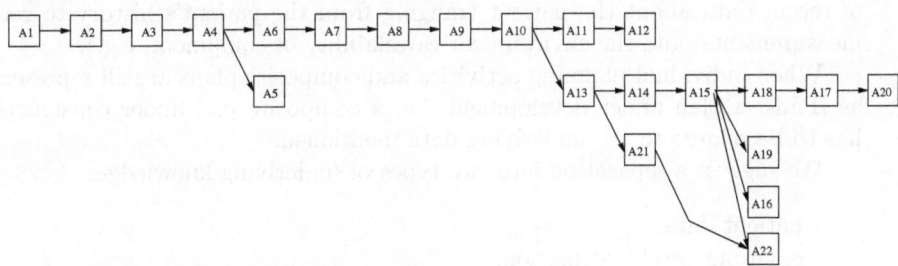

Fig. 5. An Alternative plan for Seemingly More Urgent Cases

Currently, all the work of planning and replanning is done by hand. Meme media technologies promise to gain efficieny by supporting the process of plugging actions together. The present paper aims at doing this automatically.

Plans as shown in figure 4 and 5 have to be represented as composite pads. Those pads result from elemtary pads or from other composite pads by plugging together, i.e. by establishing slot connections. The technicalities of this meme media manipulation process are subject of the following chapter.

Readers are advised to re-consult the communication architecture displayed in Figure 1. Therapy Plan Generation is the core activity yielding plans as output. Which plans are fit and suitable for execution depends on a rather dynamic environment including patients, doctors, medical stuff and environmental conditions like, for instance, available communication and transportation facilities. Even unforeseeable phenomena like weather conditions and, for instance, insect activities may interfere through impact on a patient's conditions.

Because of the complexity of the environment, we are far away from computer-controled plan execution, in general. The plans are executed by means of human activities. But constrained monitoring can be performed automatically to a large extent. To sum up, the evolutionary process through which plans are generated, are evaluated, may possibly succeed and may even survive for a longer period of time is only partially automated. Many agents – humans, computers, and others – work together.

The present approach focus the knowledge issues of this process with a certain emphasis on human-computer co-operation. The main agents are those that manipulate therapy planning knowledge. The authors' work aims at a shift in the division of labor such that a larger part of the knowledge processing is performed by computers.

Plan generation is meme media manipulation. Over time, it may result in a meme media evolution process.

5   Meme Media Manipulation and Development

When we think of meme media manipulation as taking meme media objects and plugging them together somehow like Lego toy building blocks – a methaphor frequently cited in [9] – we mostly focus on the manipulation of the core medical therapy knowledge.

But as pointed out above, we have to see the therapy knowledge in the light of recent data about the patient (ranging from the patient's history to recent measurements) and the environment (availability of equipment, e.g.).

When individual planning activities and composite plans are all represented as IPads, a plan under development, i.e. a composite pad under construction, has to be related to the underlying data mentioned.

We suggest a separation into two types of underlying knowledge:

- patient data,
- environmental information.

There are several arguments for such a distinction; a simple one is as follows. In different clinical environments there do exist conditions which are specific and not found in any other place. There are special communication connections to certain laboratories, there are special ways, distances, transportation facilities and the like to be respected, there are specific procedures of scheduling surgery and much more. All those peculiarities have to be taken into account. They can be bound directly to related action classes and will be inherited to individual actions upon instantiation time.

The separation of the underlying knowledge suggested above leads to different ways of accessing this knowledge during meme media manipulation.

In the present chapter, we go the step from *medical therapy memes* to *medical therapy meme media*. Knowledge will be encapsulated in meme media objects (knowledge media according to [8]) based on the IntelligentPad concept [9].

We have to discuss how patient data and environmental data can enter the meme media world and how knowledge about medical therapy, which is more procedural in spirit, can be formally represented to be put on top of the factual knowledge. These three aspects are shaping the present chapter.

5.1   IntelligentPad Technology for the Access to Patient Data

Increasingly, medical records of patients are being stored in databases. The main purpose of the computerization is to make treatment and accounting in hospitals efficient and, for legal reasons, comprehensible and undisputable.

To wrap such medical records into meme media objects, we follow the way that has been developed by Yuzuru Tanaka in his IntelligentPad research [9].

A MedicalRecordPad wraps any medical record stored in a medical database. It has slots for all medical data of a human according to a certain medical format. A MedicalRecordPad divides each medical record into a set of attribute-value pairs. Each attribute value is set to the slot with the same name as its attribute name. In its typical use on a MedicalRecordPad, it is pasted onto a

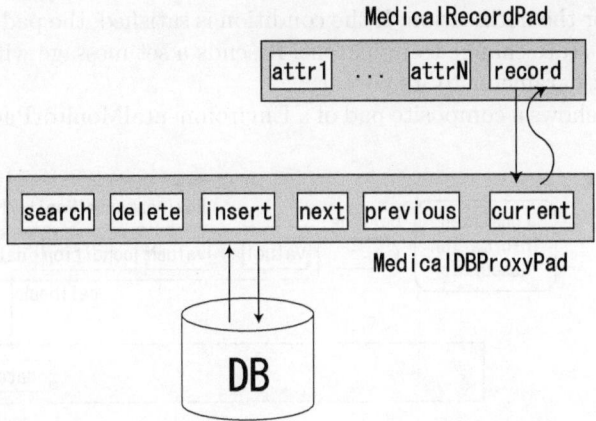

Fig. 6. Medical Record Access Architecture

MedicalDBProxyPad, which wraps basic database functions including search, insert, and delete.

Figure 6 displays a composite meme media object which is assembled of a MedicalRecordPad and a MedicalDBProxyPad.

Established meme media technology is invoked and adopted to the needs of the new domain.

5.2 IntelligentPad Technology for Environmental Embedding

Environmental data are very much like sensor information (see [1], e.g.) which is acquired somewhere outside.

Generally, there are two possible mechanisms of communication about environmental data – 'polling' and 'callbacks'. Polling is just periodical calling of a communication task for asking from time to time for the state of the environment by sending out requests for sensor data. On the other hand, callback is the way in which sensors notify the client that some event interesting to the client has been detected on the sensor. In response, the client invokes functions registered ahead of time. The use of callbacks provides event-driven planning. In this research, we adopt the mixed approach of polling and callbacks, according to the needs of clinical environments.

An EnvironmentalMonitorPad defines localized conditions and checks whether current and localized environmental information satisfies the conditions. In different clinical environments there do exist conditions which are specific and not found in any other place. Therefore, in different clinical environments different types of the EnvironmentalMonitorPad might be used.

An EnvironmentalMonitorPad has, at least, two slots named 'environmental data' and 'notification_constraints'. The slot 'environmental data' contains a set of attribute-value pairs of names of parameter and values of parameters. The slot 'notification_constraints' contains a formula that represents conditions to be satisfied for the notification. If the condition is satisfied, the pad notifies the environmental state change to its parent. It sends a set message with environmental data as its parameter to its parent.

Figure 7 shows a composite pad of a EnvironmentalMonitorPad and a BasePad.

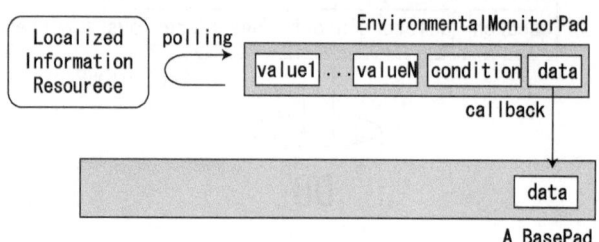

Fig. 7. Environmental Data Communication Architecture

Autonomous communication of a generated therapy plan, regardless whether the plan is handmade, automatically generated or resulting from an interactive session, is a highly interesting and novel issue. To the authors' very best knowledge, there is not much prior work (perhaps, nothing at all) on plans communicating autonomously with their environment. At least in the medical therapy planning domain, there are no related publications. A more detailed investigation will be postponed to a future publication.

5.3   IntelligentPad Technology to Represent Therapy Knowledge

In contrast to classical deductive planning, we never know about *executability* of a plan, because execution takes place in the future. All actions have constraints that must be satisfied at the beginning of an action or during the whole execution period. You never know whether or not all of the conditions will be true in the future. You can only check whether they are still possible from the perspective of the current knowledge. If there is nothing contradictory, the actions are considered *consistent*. If more information comes in, one may find out that consistency is lost.

Knowledge about medical therapy consists of an enormous amount of knowledge about elementary therapy actions and about ways to combine those actions into hopefully successful therapies. The latter is planning knowledge, from our present IT perspective. The core knowledge concerns individual actions and their related conditions of applicability. Knowledge of this type available in some location or, at least, in a human individual is forming a meme pool. Those meme pools are to be abstracted, formalized and represented as meme media pools.

The authors rely on the IntelligentPad concept by Yuzuru Tanaka [9], in general, and on the implementaional concepts of IntelligentPad, in particular. Therapy actions are mapped to so-called action pads.

An ActionPad (Figure 8) divides each medical record and environmental data into a set of attribute–value pairs in the same way as MedicalRecordPad descrived in the section 4.1.

Every ActionPad has the following four extra slots:

- action_name,
- action_started,
- start_constraint,
- interval_constraint.

The slot 'action_name' gives the name of this action, and the slot 'action_started' gives whether the action has already started or not. In the slots 'start_constraint' and 'interval_constraint', there are filled in logical formulae which may have variables. Those variables correspond to slot names of the action pad.

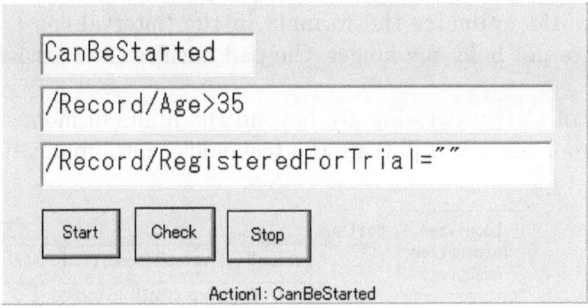

Fig. 8. Action Pads – Inhabitants of Medical Therapy Meme Media Pools

Every action pad has a method called 'Consistency Monitoring Method' (CMM, for short). Whenever an update of slot values takes place, this method is executed. It evaluates the formulae in the constraint slots. When the CMM computes for any constraint the value false, some activities are triggered. As a consequence, whenever data relevant to some action change, the action itself should check consistency.

Figure 9 shows the architecture of consistency checking with both patient data and environmental data. In its start_constraints slot, the ActionPad has the following constraint:

```
you_can_start(actionA) if constraints A, B, C hold.
```

And in its interval_constraints slot, the Pad has the following constraint:

```
you_can_continue(actionA) if constraints X,Y,Z hold.
```

ActionPad notifies that we can start actionA, if A, B, and C hold. This decision is made by replacing each variable v_i in A, B, C with the values of slot whose name is v_i. If actionA is started, the value of the slot 'action_started' will be turned into 'true'.

After the slightly simplified discussion of constraint monitoring above, the authors take the liberty of a short excursus on constraint monitoring in complex, dynamic, and non-persistent environments as laid out in [1] and [2].

Constraints are formulae that may express properties of process parameters to be satisfied in the future. Time plays an important role, and vagueness and incompleteness of knowledge about the future makes constraint evaluation somehow difficult. In fact, there is the need for a particular temporal logic.

Even more difficult, but also exciting, the choice of a suitable temporal logic has substantial impact on the whole knowledge processing under investigation.

To bring this to the point of memetics, the evolution of knowledge may deeply depend on the logics used in the planning process. To the authors' very best knowledge, there are no investigations at all about this problem area.

So, for the purpose of the present paper, we return to the simplified assumtion that there is any mechanism of reliable constraint evaluation.

During the actionA, whenever some value of slot in the ActionPad has been changed, CMM evaluates the formula in the 'interval_constraint' slots. If the formula does not hold any longer, the pad notifies the health care professionals involved.

Details of alert processing are beyond the limits of meme media technology and are important when putting the technology into application environments.

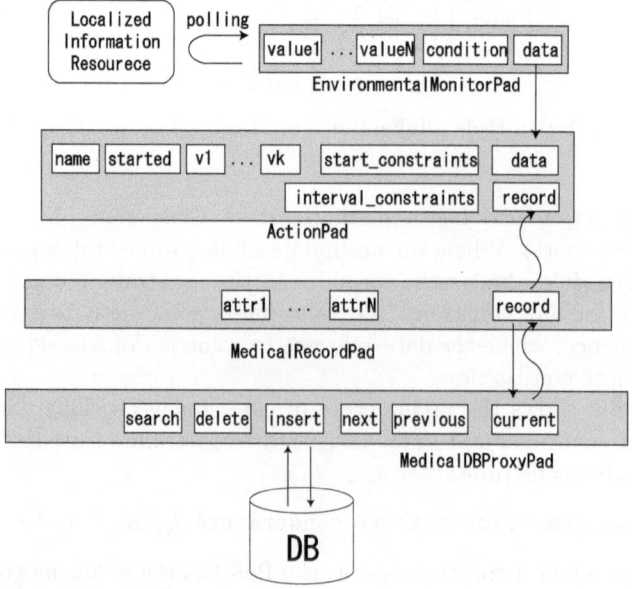

Fig. 9. Action Pad Communication Architecture

The present chapter's concepts are setting the stage for the representation of *medical therapy memes* truly as *medical therapy meme media.* On the basis of medical therapy meme media, computer-assisted or even automatic therapy plan generated can be introduced.

6 Automatic Planning and Knowledge Manipulation

This is a publication about memetics, about meme media technology and about knowledge evolution through meme media implementation and application. Planning in complex dynamic environments, especially medical therapy planning, serves as a testbed and demonstration case, only.

Therefore, the authors confine themselves to a treatment of the planning issue reduced to its essentials. More details can be found in [1], [2] and in some forthcoming publication about ongoing work of the first author.

Essentially, plan generation is seen as graph expansion. Medical therapy plans are hierarchically structured graphs.

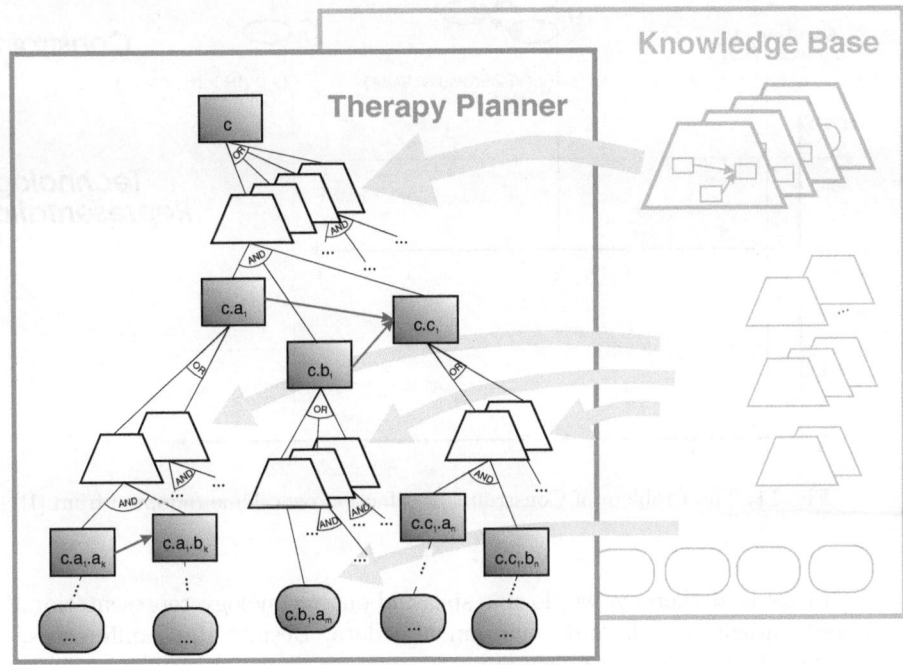

Fig. 10. Medical Therapy Planning as Hierarchical Graph Expansion

Planning starts with some highest level goal. For this goal, there are usually several alternative plan graphs which may be chosen and inserted. Alternatives can be ordered by preference values. As long as nodes of the stepwise extended graph are not yet atomic actions, they can be further expanded as illustrated in figure 10.

As discussed in chapter 2, complex dynamic environments do not provide sufficient information to decide plan executability. Planning is inductive by its very nature. But medical therapy actions depend on executability conditions expressed as constraints. Therefore, constraints need to be verified prior to execution.

Constraint supervision is necessary at planning time as well as during plan execution. Oksana Arnold has developed a sufficiently complete theoretical framework which can be carried over to medical therapy planning with a reasonably small amount of adaptation work.

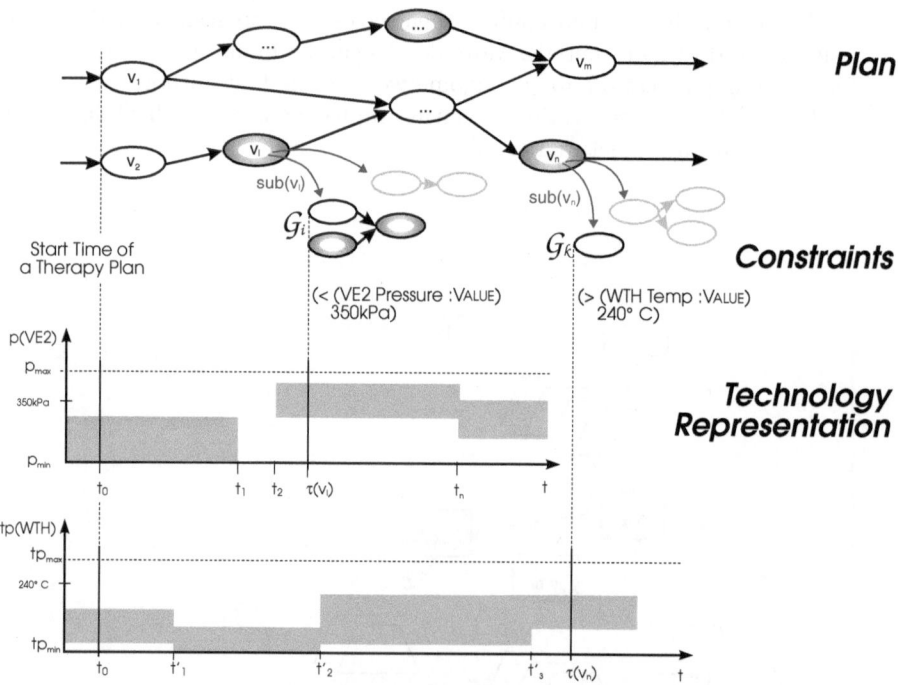

Fig. 11. The Problem of Constraint Satisfaction over Time (adopted from [1])

In medical therapy, we do not speak about technology representation, but about patient records and environmental data. Despite these differences, the constraint supervision problem appears as shown above. Actions inserted into a plan are consistent at planning time. Consistency has to be checked continuously. As soon as inconsistencies are detected, local plan revision is invoked. Action have to be replaced by other actions.

In our present approach, actions are pads and plans are more or less complex composite pads. Plan revision means a local reassembly of a composite pad.

The key message of the present chapter is that plan generation as sketched here can be performed automatically (cf. [1]). The first author is currently working on a variety of planning programs; details are to be published separately.

From the meme media point of view, planning programs do automatically assemble composite pads. According to the needs of a dynamic environment, plan revision my be frequently triggered. Ultimately, unforeseeable plans are generated and do succeed. Knowledge evolution takes place.

7   Meme Media Evolution Technologies

In the chapter 6 before, we have seen that planning can be done automatically as guarded graph expansion. But how does it work in detail that meme media evolution[1] is enabled?

Such as biological evolution has its internal mechanisms, so has meme media evolution. Though the present paper can not deal with all aspects of our quite complex research and development program, a brief look into the mechanisms of evolution seems desirable. A detailed discussion has to be postponed to a separate publication.

Automatic plan generation is a little like a robot playing with Lego building blocks. Under the peculiar conditions of a complex and dynamic domain and the absence of persistence, the outcome is usually unforeseeable, new and sometimes even innovative.

To stick with the metaphor of the playing robot for a moment, how does the robot find and choose its building blocks? How can the robot plug blocks together? In which way does the robot change a construction by unplugging blocks and inserting others instead?

Here, we do not ask for the strategy and for the supervision and control, but for the internal mechanisms of the present approach to meme media evolution.

Ultimately, a medical therapy plan is a tree-like graph outgrowing from a certain MedicalRecordPad as shown in figure 6. The leaves of the tree are actions to be executed at some future time point. From a conventional perspective, these leaves together with their partial ordering imposed by the underlying tree structure and with their immediate neighbouring relations inherited from the action hierarchy (cf. figure 10) form the plan.

Here, we are going to exemplify the meme media evolution technology by discussing three aspects in some more detail:

1. finding building blocks for planning,
2. finding consistent connections,
3. establishing new structures.

For finding suitable building blocks when generating a new plan, the planning algorithm needs to be able to search a meme pool for all available pads. In the authors' approach, pads have a lucid XML structure such that all relevant knowledge can be accessed.

The authors are aware of the requiorement for efficient implementations and for smooth embedding into given IT infrastructure. Nevertheless, the prefer a logical representation, in the sequel, for doubtless clarity.

---

[1] From the application perspective and at a first glance, this might seem to be a question of minor importance. Those interested in speeding up and advancing medical therapy planning might say that they don't care whether or not knowledge evolves, if only plan generation works well. But in the long run, if knowledge truly evolves, therapy planning will grow on an unforeseeably richer knowledge base. So, in its right perspective, the memetics' approach to knowledge evolution is substantial to medical therapy planning – and so is the present short chapter in this publication.

There is an implementation in Prolog which yields the desired behaviour with a predicate call as follows. For a given requirement `req`, we may search pad in a meme pool through the use of the following Prolog query:

```
?-pad_in_meme_pool(Pad),satisfy(Pad,req).
```

Let `p1` and `p2` be two pads. For a slot `s1` in `p1` and a slot `s2` in `p2`, the following Prolog query conncects `s1` to `s2`

```
?-connect(p1,s1,p2,s2).
```

where the predicate `connect` is defined accordingly. This is the point where automatic plan generation does really take place.

Connections established as above are not necessarily consistent. With an appropriate implementation of consistence checking – which is far beyond the present paper – one can step from just plugging pads together towards consistently establishing new structures.

```
?-satisfy(p1,s1,req1),satisfy(p2,s2,rec2),connect(p1,s1,p2,s2).
```

Whenever such a query succeeds the pad `p1` becomes a child of the pad `p2`, and `p2` becomes the parent of `p1`.

These steps of (automated) reasoning are some of the internal technicalities which take place when planning goes on and which, in the very end, are the establishing mechanisms of evolution.

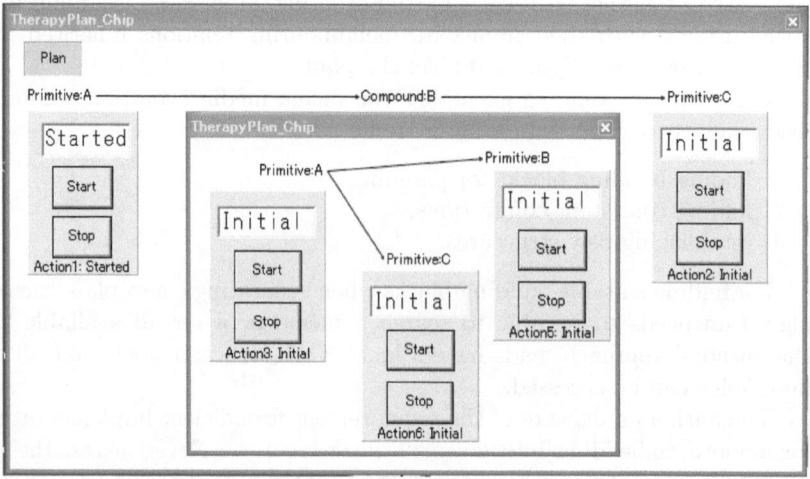

Fig. 12. Graph Expansion at Work Implemented in the CHIP Meme Media System

Last but not least, we should always be aware of the biotope issue [7] in meme media implementation and application:

We are the biotope or, at least, we belong to the biotope, together with all the regulations, formalisms and the like constraining social processes of health care.

8   Summary and Conclusions

Though our work is still in its earliest stage, it has brought up a number of insights and requirements which, in turn, lead to proper contributions to the current technology development. There are inventions in the large like, e.g., the introduction of sensor pads including the invention of corresponding architectural and communication concepts. And there are inventions in the small like, e.g., alternative approaches to communicate streams of patient data through pad hierarchies. One of them, the virtual slot approach resembles the view concept adopted from databases.

Another proposal recently brought up aims at the invention of agents that take care of constraint monitoring, for instance. A number of questions about agency do arise. Shall actions be seen as agents? If so, should these constraint monitoring agents sit inside of action agents? Or are they separately located and watching actions agents from a distance?

Talking about agency, we are obviously dealing with agents of a different time. As mentioned, there might be a hierarchical structure of nested agents. The modules of figure 1 may be seen as agents among which the planning agents plays a prominent role. The other distinguished agent is the one for plan execution. In the medical domain, this one may stay non-computerized for still some time. Thus, our general approach does inevitably rely on the communication between computer programs, between computerized agents and humans, and between humans, naturally.

Due to the lack of space and time, in particular, some quite exciting issues have not been discussed in sufficient detail. A crucial of them is the issue of communication among humans and therapy planning agents.

It is clear, especially in medical applications, that computer-generated results like medication, in detail, or like therapy, as a whole, do need to be given to humans for final confirmation. This, obviously, leads to the issue of communicating the computer's proposals to the human. Because mediacal therapy plans are generally hypothetic in nature, as discussed above in some detail, we are usually facing a lengthy sequence of communication acts. Understanding each other is a critical requirement which is, for the moment, postponed to a forthcoming investigation.

Acknowledgement

The authors are grateful to Yuzuru Tanaka for his influential work on meme media, in general, and for a manifold of activities supporting them in literally uncountably many ways. They also gratefully acknowledge the enormous help by Oksana Arnold beginning with her seminal work in planning and ranging to recent advice and kind permission to use material like some of the figures in the present publication. Oksana Arnold did a pioneering work on therapy planning in complex dynamic environments. Her achievements are still unsurpassed and have been serving as a rich source of inspiration.

References

1. Oksana Arnold. *Die Therapiesteuerungskomponente einer wissensbasierten System-architektur für Aufgaben der Prozeßführung.* infix, DISKI, Bd. 130, 1996.
2. Oksana Arnold and Klaus P. Jantke. Inductive Program Synthesis for Therapie Plan Generation. *New Generation Computing* 15 (1997) 1, pp. 27–58.
3. Susan Blackmore. *The Meme Machine.* Oxford University Press, 1999.
4. Richard Dawkins. *The Selfish Gene.* Oxford University Press, 1976.
5. Kimihito Ito. *CHIP(Collaborating Host-Independent Pads).* accessible under http://km.meme.hokudai.ac.jp/people/itok/CHIP/
6. Kimihito Ito and Yuzuru Tanaka. A Visual Environment for Web Application Composition. In *Proc of 14th ACM Conference on Hypertext and Hypermedia* 2003, pp. 184–193.
7. Klaus P. Jantke. *The Biotope Issue in Meme Media Implementation.* this volume, 2004.
8. Mark Stefik. The Next Knowledge Medium. *AI Magazine* 7 (1986) 1, 34–46.
9. Yuzuru Tanaka. *Meme Media and Meme Market Architectures.* IEEE Press and Wiley-Interscience, 2003.

Appendix: The Integration Process of a Patient into a Randomized Clinical Trial in Detail

First some general information about the application-example: the integration of a patient into a randomized clinical trial. Often a randomized clinical trial consists of several therapy protocols. For example, the protocols can differ in the age of the target group (e.g. one protocol for younger people and another protocol for elderly people). Each therapy protocol consists of several therapy-arms. The therapy-arms for one protocol can differ for example in duration, in dose or in accompanying supportive therapies. Normally patients will be distributed to the therapy-arms by randomization, in order to make the success of several therapy-arms comparable statistically.

The following example explains the connection between figure 2 and the plans in figures 4 and 5. This should give a slightly better understanding of the application domain.

Fig. 2 does not show a plan but a scheme of actions, which should be carried out in the normal case of the integration into a clinical trial. Because of different requirements in the application domain (state of health, certainty of the diagnosis) the integration can be based on different plans. We will not discuss the different requirements nor the variants of plans in this paper. The figures 4 and 5 are two examples for different plans.

The plan in Figure 4 starts with Action A1. Before A1 the patient is suspected of having malignant lymphoma. Action A1 is the referral of the patient to the biopsy. The biopsy will be performed by the surgeon (A2). The tissue (the result of the biopsy) and all necessary data will be sent to the primary pathologist because of the diagnosis (A3). The pathologist processes the tissue (e.g. by using paraffin) and creates a diagnosis (A4) – in our example: high malignant Non-Hodgkin-Lymphoma (NHL).

The primary pathologist sends the diagnosis and all accompanying data back to the surgeon (A6), who gives these data to the oncologist. If the oncologist asked the primary pathologist for data and diagnosis (A5), he gets that from the primary pathologist directly (A7).

Based on the diagnosis and the latest patient data the oncologist selects a suitable clinical trial and a therapy protocol (A8). In our example, this is the protocol NHL-B, which is a protocol of a German clinical trial on therapy of malignant Non-Hodgkin-Lymphomas.

The selection of a suitable protocol often is very complicated. There exist a lot of clinical trials, each has several protocols. The number of available protocols is very dynamic. The number of clinical trials increases and protocols are valid only for ca. 5 years. In general the description of clinical trials and protocols is not available in electronic form. They are books of 100 or more pages. As decision support for the selection process each therapy protocol has two lists of criteria; one list to qualify and another list to disqualify a patient for this protocol. Each list consists of 10 to 20 items. It is allowed to integrate a patient into a protocol only if all qualifying criteria are true and no condition in the second list holds. So the selection of a suitable clinical trial and a protocol is tedious handwork.

After the selection of a suitable therapy protocol (A8) the oncologist registers the patient for that protocol in the corresponding head office (A9). To do so, the patient's data and some signed forms have to be sent to the head office. The head office performs the randomization (A10). The oncologist gets the result of the randomization and all protocol-specific data (A11). Only than the treatment and the detailed therapy planning can start (A12).

To avoid diagnosis errors, the primary diagnosis must be confirmed by a reference diagnosis. The head office asks the primary pathologist to give the tissue and all necessary data to the reference pathologist (A13). At the same time the head office asks the reference pathologist for the reference diagnosis (A21). After the primary pathologist has sent data and tissue to the reference pathologist (A14), the reference pathologist produces the reference diagnosis (A15). This diagnosis is sent to the head office and to the primary pathologist (A22 and A18). The oncologist gets this diagnosis directly from the primary pathologist only if he requests it. If not, he gets the diagnosis via primary pathologist and surgeon some days later. Now the rest of the tissue can be used by other institutions (A20).

Finally the oncologist, primary pathologist, surgeon, and head office compare both diagnoses. If they match, all is fine. Otherwise one must stop the started treatment, make a new diagnosis, etc. But this case is neither shown nor discussed in the running case study of our present paper.

Accessing Related Web Resources
Through Annotated Documents

Jun Fujima and Yuzuru Tanaka

Meme Media Laboratory
Hokkaido University
N13 W8, Sapporo 0608628, Japan

Abstract. This paper proposes a new framework for organizing and accessing Web resources using loci defined on arbitrary Web documents. Our framework allows users to store Web resources in user-specified loci on a Web document to define a relation among them. This relation is retained as a set of tuples in a table called a Topica table. When users access such a locus, the resources associated with this locus are presented on the display screen. Each locus is associated with an attribute of the Topica table associated with this document. Our framework enables users to dynamically define such loci, called topoi, on arbitrary Web documents, and to input and/or output tuples of Web resources to and from a set of topoi defined on each of these Web documents. In addition, we propose a mechanism to access multiple related resources using a history of users' navigation through such documents.

1   Introduction

The resources on the World Wide Web [1] are now rapidly increasing their variety and accumulation. Such resources may be documents, data, application tools and services. To easily access desired resources on the Web, it is necessary to reorganize mutually related resources, and to store information about such relations somewhere on the Web.

Our question here is where to store such a relation so that the same user or even others can later easily access the same relation. No conventional information organization methods, such as table-based, hierarchical, or indexed one, are suitable for organizing and accessing a huge number of relations among Web resources.

Current Web tools do not support this task as well. For example, current Web browsers provide bookmark facilities. Although bookmark facilities allow users to organize Web resources using hierarchical structures, the increasing levels of hierarchy or its contents make it difficult for users to find desired resources.

The situation here is similar to the management and access of commodities in our societies. While commodities of the same type can be managed by a single database, there are so many different types that consumers cannot tell either which commodity belongs to which type, or which database manages which type. To solve this problem, we used to use documents or spaces to arrange

G. Grieser and Y. Tanaka (Eds.): Intuitive Human Interface 2004, LNAI 3359, pp. 88–98, 2004.

information about mutually related commodities. Examples include catalogs, stores, department stores, malls, and towns. In this paper, we use Web documents as such spaces.

From this point of view, we propose a framework that allows users to easily organize and access any Web resources using loci defined on arbitrary Web document. This framework allows users to dynamically specify any Web page portions to work as loci, and to store mutually related resources there. The resources and the relation among them are stored in an external server as relational annotations on this Web page. Users can find desired resources by accessing through such loci. In addition, we propose a method to access multiple mutually related resources by using a history of users' navigation through annotated Web documents as an access context.

2   Relational Annotation

2.1   Topica Framework

We proposed a framework, called a Topica framework, for organizing and accessing intellectual resources in 2000 [2]. Figure 1 shows the conceptual model of the Topica framework. A Topica document is used to select and arrange mutually related resources. The resources and mutual relations among them can be stored as a table in a Topica document. This table is called a Topica table. Each Topica document has some loci called topoi through which users can store and retrieve resources. Each topos is associated with an attribute of the corresponding Topica table. Each attribute of a Topica table may take as its value a character string, or a URI identifying another Topica document or resource.

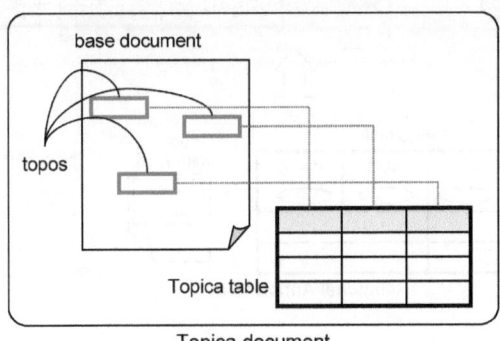

Fig. 1. The conceptual model of Topica framework.

A Topica document is implemented as an XML document including a reference to the Topica table. Topica table is implemented as an XML document or a table in RDBMS. Each topos has a name. A topos name works as an attribute name of the topica table. Different topoi may be associated with the same attribute of the same Topica table.

2.2   Requirements and Basic Concept of Relational Annotation

The Topica framework is not sufficient to support the organization and access of Web resources. Only the author who created a Topica document can define topoi. When users want to create a new Topica document, they must provide all the contents of this new document, its URI, and its Topica table.

Based on the above mentioned conceptual model, we have extended the Topica framework. There are many documents over the Web. In our new framework, users can make any Web page work as a Topica document. In addition, users can dynamically specify any set of arbitrarily chosen Web page portions to work as topoi, and store mutually related resources in these topoi.

The resources and the relation among them are stored as a Topica table in an HTTP server that is associated with the base Web page, and work as relational annotations on this Web page. Relational annotation means a set of annotations given at different locations with a relation defined among them. Web pages can be found by accessing search engines with appropriate search keys. Figure 2 shows an outline of our relational annotation framework. From users' point of view, it seems as if each Web document can directly store a Topica table. Each topos is associated with an attribute of the corresponding Topica table.

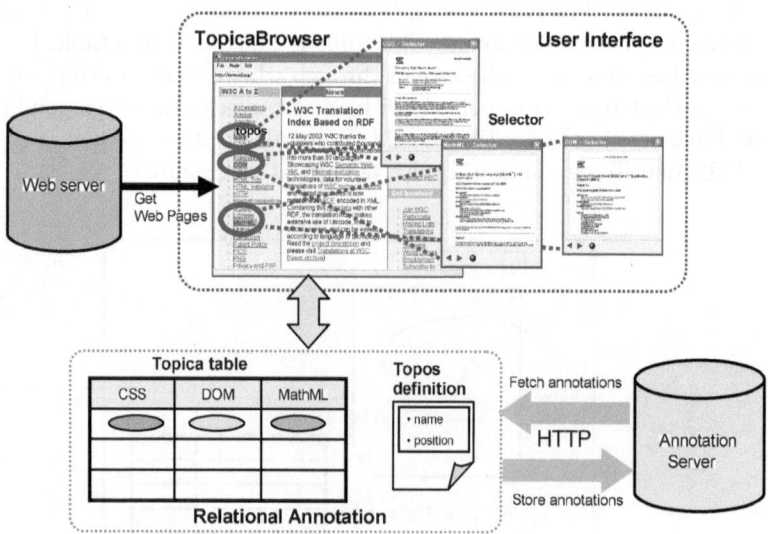

Fig. 2. The basic architecture of relational annotation framework.

2.3   Data Model in Relational Annotation Framework

Our system architecture uses annotation servers similar to the one developed for the Annotea architecture [3]. Information about topoi definition and resources stored in each topos are stored and managed independently from base Web documents. They are stored as RDF [4] documents in annotation servers. RDF is a standard description framework for representing information in the Web. Representing this annotation information as RDF descriptions enhances the interoperability between our framework and other Semantic Web applications.

A relation among stored resources is represented as an RDF description element which has elements, named by its topos names, as its children. Such elements are automatically created as RDF properties in the associated annotation server. For example, the tuple which has three topoi named 'css', 'dom', and 'mathml' has three string values, "Cascading Style Sheets", "Document Object Model" and "MathML". This tuple is represented as the following RDF description.

```
<r:Description r:about="http://www.w3.org">
  <css>Cascading Style Sheets</css>
  <dom>Document Object Model</dom>
  <mathml>MathML</mathml>
</r:Description>
```

Here, 'r' is the namespace prefix identifying an RDF syntax namespace.

The definition of a topos is represented as a 'topoi' element which is derived from an RDF description element. Each topoi element has 'topos' elements as its children. Each topos element has its name attribute and path attribute. Its name attribute specifies its name, while its path attribute indicates the position of the element specified as this topos.

We use an HTML-Path expression [5] in this paper to identify a portion in an HTML document. An HTML-Path expression is a specialization of an XPath [6] expression. In an HTML-Path expression, we can also use regular expressions that can be applied to text nodes. For example, the first h3 element in the body element's children is identified by

```
html[1]/body[1]/h3[1] .
```

In this expression, a regular expression can be used to specify a substring of this text node. This extension allows users to define a text substring, that is not a DOM tree node, to work as a topos. For example, if the above mentioned h3 element has a text node, 'Annotation System', as its child, this text substring 'Annotation' is identified by

```
html[1]/body[1]/h3[1]/text[([^\r\n]*)System] .
```

The following description shows the example of topoi definition on W3C top Web page shown in Figure 2.

```
<topoi r:about="http://www.w3.org">
  <topos name="css" path="/html[1]/body[1]/table[1]/.../a[3]" />
  <topos name="dom" path="/html[1]/body[1]/table[1]/.../a[6]" />
  <topos name="mathml" path="/html[1]/body[1]/.../a[12]" />
</topoi>
```

3   Resource Management Using Our Framework

3.1   Organizing Resources

To define a new topos on a Web document, users must first open this Web document using a special Web browser called TopicaBrowser. Through direct manipulations, users can specify any HTML/XML-node on this Web page to work as a topos. Users can name each topos, which is internally identified by its path expression of the node in the DOM tree of this Web page.

To store a new tuple in a Topica table through direct manipulation, users must input some resource to each of the all topoi using a TopicaBrowser. For the resource input to each topos, users can just drag out any resource from an arbitrary different Web page, and directly drop it into this topos. Such resources may be either text strings or URIs that point to other documents or files. The dropping of a resource into a topos does not immediately perform its registration to the topos. Users must specify an input resource or a null value for each of the all topoi on the same document by repeating these drag-and-drop operations. After finishing with this repetition, users can click the registration button on the TopicaBrowser to register the set of these simultaneously specified resources as a new tuple of the corresponding Topica table. User can store multiple tuples on the same document. They are stored in the same Topica table. The addition of a new topos or a new tuple to a document expands the Topica table horizontally or vertically.

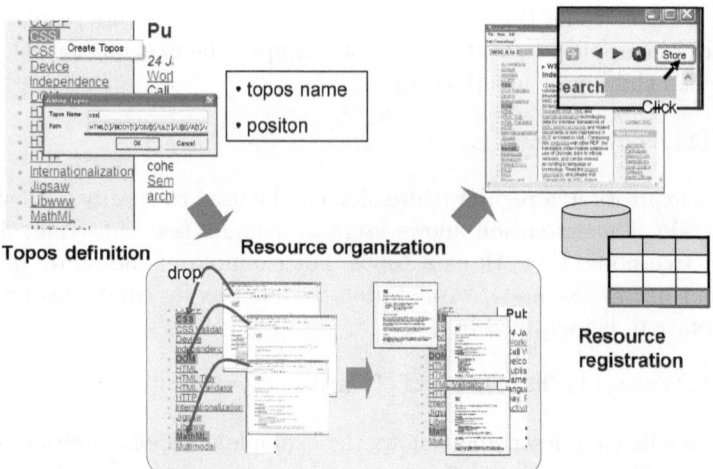

Fig. 3. Definition of topoi and resource registration in topoi.

Figure 3 shows the process of defining topoi and storing resources. Three anchor elements, 'CSS', 'DOM' and 'MathML', on the same W3C top Web page are defined to work as topoi. Each topos is specified to store the URI of the specification Web page for the corresponding technology. The Topica table in this example stores a single tuple.

3.2   Accessing Stored Resources Through Topoi

Multiple resources can be associated with each topos. They constitute the projection of the corresponding Topica table to the associated attribute. Users can access all of them through this topos. Users may click each topos to pop up its selector window. Such a selector window shows all the resources relevant to the clicked topos. Each selector window allows users to select some resources stored in the corresponding topos. Such a selection works as a relational selection operation on the corresponding attribute, and restricts the Topica table. This makes every other selector window show the projection of the restricted Topica table (figure 4). We call this operation a 'fix' operation, and its inverse a 'free' operation. Users may interactively use fix operations to gradually filter out unnecessary resources and/or those related to unnecessary resources.

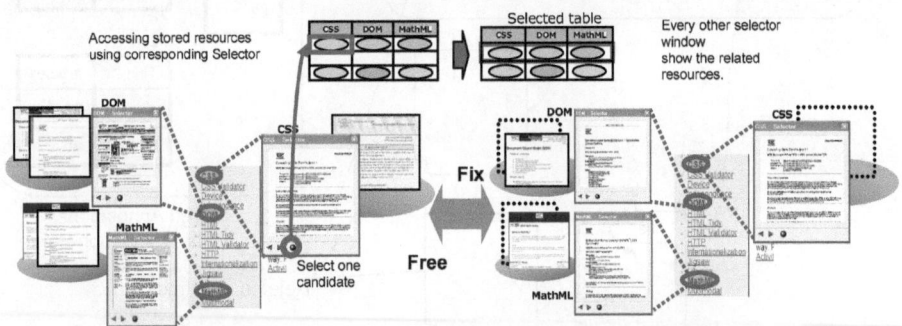

Fig. 4. Fix and Free operations in selector windows.

3.3   Communication with Annotation Servers

Users can query a server either to retrieve existing annotations, to post a new annotation, to modify an annotation, or to delete an annotation. Each communication between a client browser and an annotation server uses the standard HTTP protocol.

When a user opens a Web document on a TopicaBrowser, the browser asks the associated annotation servers whether they store annotations to this Web document. If some of them have any annotations, the TopicaBrowser gets all annotations from each annotation servers, and allows users to retrieve and display these annotations on this base Web document. When a user annotates this Web page using operations mentioned in section 3.2, the added annotations are stored in a currently accessed annotation server. Dropping another annotation server URI into the TopicaBrowser allows users to access a different user's or different community's annotation on the same base Web page.

4   Accessing Web Resources Using Navigation Paths

4.1   Navigation Among Annotated Documents

For the access of organized resources stored as relational annotations on Web documents, users may repetitively apply fix and free operations to gradually focus on desired resources. Users can reach desired Web pages using our relational annotation framework.

Let us consider the following user's navigation trough annotated Web documents (figure 5).

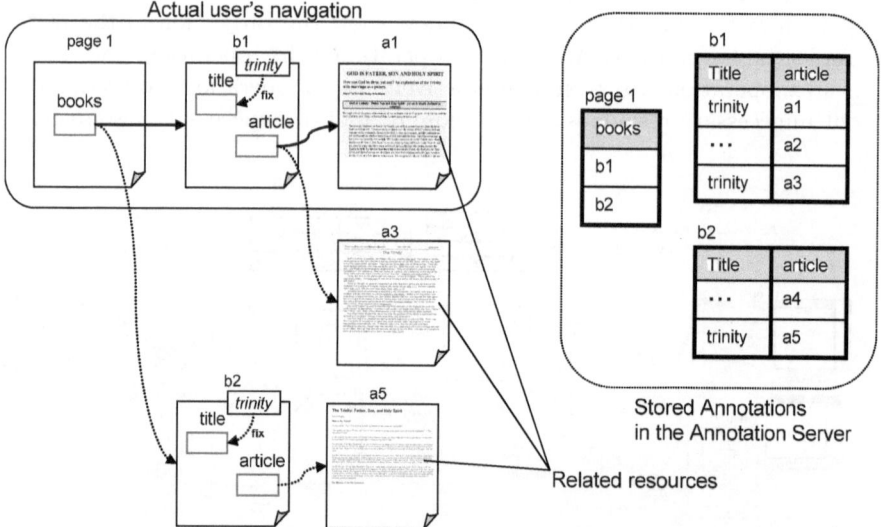

Fig. 5. The navigation example and related resources.

A user accesses an annotated Web page that has a topos for 'books'. The user may open a selector window and select one Web page from that topos. The selected page may also be annotated and have two topoi, 'title' and 'article'. The user may open the selector corresponding to the 'title' topos and select one string value "trinity". Then, the user can go to a Web document about the trinity.

In such a way, users can access a desired resource through several navigation steps. Here, if the user selects another Web page in the 'books' topos, or if the user selects another article in the 'article' topos, the document that the user finally obtain might be a different one. To get other candidates in this navigation, the user need to repeat such a navigation many times. In this section, we will propose our solution to this problem.

We consider such a single navigation path as a user's access context. Users should be able to automatically obtain a set of Web resources that belong to the same access context specified by the navigation path.

4.2   Navigation Path

When a user navigates through annotated Web documents using a Topica Browser, the browser records the user's navigation path. This recording task starts when a TopicaBrowser opens the first document.

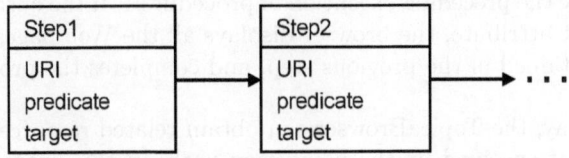

Fig. 6. The structure of navigation path.

We define the structure of a 'navigation path' as shown in figure 6. A navigation path is a sequence of steps visited encountered base documents. A step consists of a URI of the document, a 'predicate' specifying a condition applied to each of the topoi on the document by a user, and the 'target' specifying the topos name that was used to jump to the next document or resource. The 'predicate' attribute is given its condition when the user selects values of some topoi using the 'fix' operation.

For example, when a user performs the example navigation of section 4.1, the navigation path is recorded as shown in figure 7.

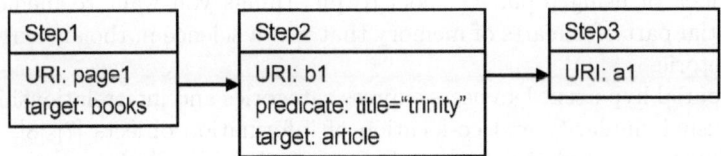

Fig. 7. The example structure of single navigation path.

The primary purpose of using a navigation path is to address a set of resources in relationally annotated Web documents. This paper uses this path structure to access all the Web resources obtained by choosing different target pages at each step of this given navigation path.

4.3   Accessing Related Web Resources

To obtain related resources, users may click 'get related resource' menu on a TopicaBrowser. Then, the TopicaBrowser automatically traces recorded navigation path to retrieve the set of related resources through the following method. Firstly, the TopicaBrowser accesses the Web page specified by the URI stored in the URI attribute of the first step of the given navigation path.

1. The TopicaBrowser asks the associated annotation servers whether they store tuples associated with the current URI and satisfying the condition specified by the 'predicate' attribute in this step. If the servers store such tuples, the browser gets the set of values of the topos specified by the 'target' attribute.
2. The TopicaBrowser recursively applies the procedure 1 to all the URIs obtained by the preceding execution of procedure 1. If the current step contains no target attribute, the browser displays all the Web pages specified by the URIs obtained in the previous step, and completes the processing.

In this way, the TopicaBrowser can obtain related resources using the same access context specified by the navigation path. In this process, the tracing of the path depends only on topoi conditions that are set by the user. The 'URI' attribute value is not used after the second step.

Applying this process to the example navigation path in figure 7, the TopicaBrowser firstly holds a URI 'page1'. Then the browser gets the set of URIs, 'b1' and 'b2' in figure 5, from associated annotation servers. Next, the browser moves to the second step of the navigation path, and asks annotation servers whether they store tuples that are associated with 'b1' or 'b2' and satisfying the condition *'title = "trinity"'*. As the result, the user can obtain documents 'a1', 'a3', and 'a5'.

5   Related Works

The idea of using topoi, i.e., loci to put things you want to memorize is the essential part of the arts of memory that was a science in the ancient Greek arts of rhetoric.

Spatial hypertext lets users express categories and interrelationships through the visual similarity and co-location of information objects [7] [8]. While spatial hypertext studies focus on the use of visual similarity and co-location of information objects to express relationships among objects, Topica framework focuses on how we can associate an n-ary relation among n topoi defined on a Web document.

Although there are many other Web annotation systems, many of them can not store relations among resources working as annotations. OHSs (Open Hypermedia Systems) allow links and annotations to be added to documents outside the author's control. Recently, OHS community has been developing various systems for augmenting the Web resources [9] [10].

The Semantic Web [11] is an extension of WWW and describes relationships among Web documents in RDF for the better manipulation and understanding of such relationships by computers and people. It is an important milestone for building a Semantic Web that users become able to associate RDF metadata with Web resources using Web annotation tools. Annotea [3] is a shared annotation framework based on an open RDF infrastructure. Annotations are represented by using W3C's standards such as RDF, XPointer [12], and XLink

[13]. Our system architecture also uses external RDF annotation servers similar to the Annotea architecture. Xspect [14] is a system to handle transformation between an open hypermedia format and XLink. CREAM [15] is an annotation framework that allows users to create relational metadata. It uses metadata that instantiate interrelated definitions of classes in a domain ontology using RDF based descriptions. S. Alexaki et al. [16] [17] proposed a formal model capturing RDF schema constructs and a declarative query language called RQL using generalized path expressions for taxonomies of labels.

Relational annotation is different from other annotation systems based on RDF, because topoi on the same Web document are related with each other by a Topica table stored in annotation servers. In addition, our framework does not assume any taxonomical structures among topos names. Users don't need to design the schema for new topos definition. All that the user has to do is to create new topoi on a Web document. Semantic Web aims to provide facilities for information resource providers and brokers to describe semantic relationships among resources. Relational annotation framework focuses on collaborative organization of resources.

6   Conclusions

This paper has proposed a framework for organizing and accessing Web resources. Our framework allows users to store mutually related resources as relational annotations on a Web document that is specified to work as a base of resource organization. For the access of these resources, users may simultaneously open selector windows of more than one topos to repetitively apply fix and free operations, and to gradually focus on desired resources. Our framework does not require any rewriting of Web pages working either as base documents of relational annotations or as resources stored on base documents. Moreover, our framework allows users to access related resources by tracing all the navigation paths similar to the specified one.

References

1. Berners-Lee, T., Cailliau, R., Luotonen, A., Nielsen, H.F., Secret, A.: The World-Wide Web. Commun. ACM **37** (1994) 76–82
2. Tanaka, Y., Fujima, J.: Meme Media and Topica Architectures for Editing, Distributing, and Managing Intellectual Assets. Kyoto International Conference on Digital Libraries 2000 (2001) 208–216
3. Kahan, J., Koivunen, M.R.: Annotea: an open RDF infrastructure for shared Web annotations. In: Proceedings of the tenth international conference on World Wide Web, ACM Press (2001) 623–632
4. Lassila, O., Swick, R.: Resource Description Framework (RDF) Model and Syntax Specification. W3C Recommendation (1999) http://www.w3.org/TR/1999/REC-rdf-syntax-19990222.
5. Ito, K., Tanaka, Y.: A Visual Environment for Dynamic Web Application Composition. In: Proceedings of the fourteenth ACM conference on Hypertext and hypermedia, ACM Press (2003) 184–193

6. Clark, J., DeRose, S.J.: XML Path Language (XPath) Version 1.0. W3C Recommendation (1999) http://www.w3.org/TR/xpath.
7. Shipman, F., Moore, J.M., Maloor, P., Hsieh, H., Akkapeddi, R.: Semantics happen: knowledge building in spatial hypertext. In: Proceedings of the Thirteenth ACM Conference on Hypertext. Spatial Hypertext (2002) 25–34
8. Marshall, C.C., Shipman, III, F.M.: Spatial hypertext and the practice of information triage. In: Proceedings of the Eighth ACM Conference on Hypertext. Structure and Spatiality (1997) 124–133
9. Anderson, K.M.: Integrating open hypermedia systems with the world wide web. In: Proceedings of the eighth ACM conference on Hypertext, ACM Press (1997) 157–166
10. Gronbaek, K., Bouvin, N.O., Sloth, L.: Designing Dexter-Based Hypermedia Services for the World Wide Web. In: Proceedings of the Eighth ACM Conference on Hypertext. WEB Integration and Application (1997) 146–156
11. Berners-Lee, T., Hendler, J., Lassila, O.: The semantic Web. Scientific American **284** (2001) 34–43
12. Daniel, R., DeRose, S., Maler, E.: XML Pointer Language (xpointer). W3C Recommendation candidate recommendation (2001) http://www.w3.org/TR/xptr.
13. DeRose, S., Maler, E., Orchard, D., Trafford, B.: XML Linking Language (XLink). W3C Recommendation 27 June 2001 (2001) http://www.w3.org/TR/xlink.
14. Christensen, B.G., Hansen, F.A., Bouvin, N.O.: Xspect: bridging open hypermedia and xlink. In: Proceedings of the twelfth international conference on World Wide Web, ACM Press (2003) 490–499
15. Handschuh, S., Staab, S.: Authoring and annotation of web pages in cream. In: Proceedings of the eleventh international conference on World Wide Web, ACM Press (2002) 462–473
16. Alexaki, S., Christophides, V., Karvounarakis, G., Plexousakis, D., Tolle, K., Amann, B., Fundulaki, I., Scholl, M., Vercoustre, A.: Managing RDF Metadata for Community Webs. In: Proceedings of the Workshop on The World Wide Web and Conceptual Modeling (ER2000). (2000) 140–151
17. Alexaki, S., Christophides, V., Karvounarakis, G., Plexousakis, D., Tolle, K.: On Storing Voluminous RDF Descriptions: The case of Web Portal Catalogs. In: Proceedings of the 4th International Workshop on the Web and Databases (WebDB'01). (2001)

The Biotope Issue
in Meme Media Implementations

Klaus P. Jantke

Deutsches Forschungszentrum für Künstliche Intelligenz,
Stuhlsatzenhausweg 3, 66123 Saarbrücken, Germany
jantke@dfki.de

Abstract. The concepts of memetics and the development of meme media implementations have set the stage for knowledge media evolution by which externalized human knowledge is becoming subject to a process of growth which can be boosted by technological means.

Computers acting in computer networks in co-operation with humans will constitute interactive knowledge media – another goal of Artificial Intelligence.

The key question is whether or not we will be able to establish proper meme pools in which memetic evolution finds an opportunity to take place. And if so, it is the question what conditions we have to provide for a dynamic evolution of meme media based knowledge. This is the biotope issue.

Properly dealing with the biotope issue is essential for a future development of meme media going beyond the limits of conventional software technologies. Thus, the biotope issue is not only just a philosophical or methodological foundation of meme media development, but a core problem which is frequently underestimated.

The aim of the present publication is to make the biotope issue seen in its right perspective – for the benefit of memetics and meme media development as a whole.

1 Motivation of a Seemingly Esoteric Discussion

Memetics is seen as outlined in the truly exciting books by Richard Dawkins [3], Susan Blackmore [1] and Yuzuru Tanaka [16]. Richard Dawkins has attracted the world's attention to the phenomena of cultural inheritance and has introduced his seminal concept named *meme*. Susan Blackmore has taken the initiative to discuss the relevance of Dawkins' perspective from a psychological and from a somehow philosophical point of view telling all of us that we are affected by Dawkins' work. It is, naturally, up to you whether or not you feel personally affected by memetics, and this might easily become a slightly esoteric discussion.

But Yuzuru Tanaka, fortunately, has seized Dawkins' suggestion and developed it toward concepts, implementations and applications in computer science. He has coined the key term *meme media*.

The present approach relies on Tanaka's trend-setting work taking Dawkins' and Blackmore's contributions seriously.

G. Grieser and Y. Tanaka (Eds.): Intuitive Human Interface 2004, LNAI 3359, pp. 99–107, 2004.

We want to contribute to the endeavour of enabling computer systems to foster true knowledge evolution – the benefit for humans will be paramount.

As Mark Stefik [15] has foreseen, there is a tendency towards externalization of knowledge into interactive electronic media, a trend which is considerably boosted by the spread of the Internet. Meme media pools are mushrooming.

Meme media objects or meme media, for short, are the inhabitants of these pools. How are they? Are they doing well?

Taking Dawkins' and Blackmore's contributions [3] and [1] seriously means to ask for the living conditions of meme media in their respective meme media pools. In the spirit of Tanaka [16], every pool of meme media is bringing with it the potential of knowledge evolution. The work is properly done, only if there is some progress recognizable and knowledge does evolve.

Otherwise, we have set up just another heap of data, like the Internet which is currently more a data cemetory than a knowledge source. Similar problems are known in every larger enterprise. They all have huge databases, but suffer from a lack of knowledge.

The biotope issue in meme media implementations is about making data more beneficial for humans, in general. Moreover, it stresses the issue of knowledge evolution which can potentially go beyond the limits of human expectations and imaginations, in particular. More technically speaking, this is the question of what to do to enable knowledge evolution.

When Tanaka's book [16] did appear, it seemed that the time has come for our data – or, at least, for some of them – to wake up and begin to evolve. But does this really happen? Where are the pools of evolving knowledge media?

It seems that we have some severe deficiencies. The life in our meme pools, not to mention our databases, is far behind its potentials. The biotope issue has been widely underestimated.

To say it very explicitly: We have to take care of the living conditions of our meme media. We have to think and work about technological measures which foster knowledge evolution.

A first step is to establish awareness of the biotope issue. This is a minimal aim of the present publication. One of the reviewers of the present paper's submitted version has seen the paper as an outline of a future research project. This, for sure, was *not* the author's intention. Instead of any separate project dealing with the biotope issue, everyone dealing with meme media theory, engineering and application should become aware of this issue and act appropriately. So, the biotope issue may disappear through the infusion into the meme media community's daily research and development practice. The present paper will have been successful as soon as there is no further need to refer to it. In other words, considering the biotope issue should become folklore in the meme media community.

Last but not least, there is another motivation for the author to raise a discussion about the biotope issue in meme media implementations – the quite serious difficulties in communicating the essentials of meme media concepts and meme media implementations.

The author has had numerous talks with representatives from industries about the essentials and the potentials of meme media, system demonstrations included. In general, meme media and IntelligentPad implementations have been seen as just another middleware approach.

There is some quite obvious reluctance to getting engaged in meme media applications. Just another middleware does not seem exciting enough to invest time or money. From this perspective, the biotope issues does possess a commercially relevant dimension.

2 Perspectives at the Biotope Issue

Recall Richard Dawkins' impressive report about a colony of birds, so-called saddlebacks, living quite isolated on islands near New Zealand [3]. There is a rather detailed documentation of the evolution of songs these birds are singing. To say it as explicit as possible: The songs are forming a meme pool in which evolution takes place, provably. These birds on the island are only the *habitat* in which the *songs are living*. The birds are forming the biotope for the songs. Having a little closer look, it may be reasonable to include the island, the wheather and the like into the biotope considerations.

Those birds are somehow building a biotope to their songs. We humans are similarly being biotopes to our thoughts. This is, at least, a possible perspective at the memes we are breeding in our brains. For humans, it is not easy to step back and agree with something else being more central than the self.

Chris Fileds is surveying and summarizing current work in cognitive science, the neurosciences and evolutionary psychology to come up with an answer to the question "Why do we talk to ourselves?" [8].

The summary is consistent with other work about evolutionary side effects of the humans' cognitive architecture. Fields concludes with the insight that we humans "talk to ourselves because we have to". There is a space in the human brain which works somehow like a buffer. Components of the brain write into this space and others read from it. Fields summarizes: "If our cognitive apparatus allowed different functional modules to easily access each other's representations in their native form, ... we might not need an inner voice at all." So, there are biological reasons for breeding memes.

In the present chapter of the paper, so far, we dealt only with memes, not yet with meme media.

Whenever and whereever we externalize knowledge into modular objects, especially on computers and computer networks, we are getting close to meme media. However, in many cases, the underlying implementation principles are not appropriate to stimulate evolution of the knowledge externalized. It turns out to be literally dead.

For already a dozen of years or so, Yuzuru Tanaka is striving hard to establish meme media implementations which allow for memetic evolution [16], at least in principle.

All these implementations have their respective conditions under which the meme media objects can be subject to evolution – the biotope issue.

To sum up briefly, is this again getting an esoteric discussion, to some extent? Not in the author's opinion! The brief discussion of the phenomenon of memes in biological reality has revealed that there are reasons for the existence of memes, and there is a variety of preconditions fostering the evolution of those memes. Analogously, we have to think about the conditions of meme media evolution, if we are interested in exploiting the potentials of knowledge evolution in computers and computer networks which goes beyond human expectations and estimations.

3   The Biotope Issue in Application Attempts

For the sake of a focussed discussion, we confine ourselves to IntelligentPad implementations, exclusively. The biotope issue discussion can not serve as an overview on meme media and memetics. Readers not satisfied with such a narrow view are directed to the underlying literature already cited, especially to [16]. The implementations envisaged here are of the type reported in [11], e.g. The present volume in which this paper appears will contain further examples galore.

3.1   Fundamental IT Constituents of IntelligentPad Biotopes

When knowledge is mapped onto computer systems and computer networks, minimal requirements concerning the hardware and the software are inevitable. Though this is absolutely trivial, is has to be seen as part of the biotope issue: One needs something before pads can begin to duplicate, to combine, to mutate, to cross-over and the like, i.e. before knowledge evolution can take place.

We all know the old and ever returning lie about platform-independend code. In contrast, we need to make explicit which assumptions are taken for granted that a certain meme media implementation can be launched.

In addition to a certain operating system, there may be the need for some environment like Microsoft's .NET framework. All this is agreeable, but is has to be made explicit.

3.2   Software Paradigms and Implementation Principles

IntelligentPad systems are complex IT systems that are never implemented from scratch. Every individual system approach takes advantage of some programming paradigm and exploits work done earlier. It usually takes some developing environment as a basis and adds some of its own basics. For instance, libraries are taken and extended according to the particular needs of the approach.

For illustration, in object oriented programming, classes are defined and particular pads are introduced as instances of those classes inheriting information such that the programming effort for individual pads is minimized.

Whatever approach is used, for many good reasons and in accordance with overwhelming experience, there is a need to make the assumptions explicit.

In most cases, there will be a tradeoff between independence of meme media objects and efficiency in their development process. Predefining functionalities upwards in a hierarchies and using functionalities located in libraries makes pads more lightweight, but makes them dependent on the presence of related files.

In general, there seems to be a deficiency in clarity about those implementation decisions together with a lack of discussion among developers and scientists. Most decisions seem to be ad hoc, instead of driven by a certain methodology.

3.3   IntelligentPad Application Development

When IntelligentPad technology is spread all over the world, there will be an increasing request for development support.

At a first glance, features of any meme media development environment do not really interfere with the biotope issue, as making the pads can be clearly separated from using the pads, i.e. from the pads' life.

But a closer look reveals that this is simply not true – it can not be true by the very nature of memetics. Birth and death can not be separated from life.

More technically speaking, when pads are generated dynamically according to unforeseeable needs of a dynamic domain – when evolution beyond human administration is going to take place – the way in which pads can be generated or not is an essential aspect of the biotope issue.

This can be seen in even more detail when currently widely independent approaches meet each other. Take, for instance, the dynamic plan generation approach from [7] and combine it with the application development approach of [6], where a so-called cockpit is proposed to support control of pad generation and maintenance. At the moment, the cockpit is really a tool supporting pad generation, but separated from the generated pads' lifecycle. In the future, more advanced cockpit functionality will be desirable. The medical therapy planning approach of [7] will lead to dynamic pad generation where details of monitoring and control of the generation process have impact on the direction of the ongoing meme media evolution.

3.4   Embedding IntelligentPad into Application Environments

It is with IntelligentPad application as it is with all other IT applications; they have to be embedded into some usually a priori given environment. Embedding requires interfaces.

From a strictly memetic point of view, the problem might be paraphrased as follows. On the one hand, meme media objects need to be able to meet each other, to communicate with each other and to do all those things that are necessary to enable evolution. Beyond this, on the other hand, they have to live in an environment and, therefore, need to sense the environment somehow.

Whenever we maroon our pads, we should carefully equip them with some ability of perception or, more generally, of communication.

There are, at least, to different approaches to embedding of pads into given IT infrastructures which do not mutually exclude each other. First, one may develop particular pads serving the whole community of inhabitants of some meme pool by arranging the communication with the surrounding world. Ito's so-called service wrapper pad [11] is a good representative of this approach. There are other solutions like, e.g., proxy pads to relational databases. Second, one may equip every pad with the ability to understand and speak some language. Still, we are far from releasing pads with natural language skills. For the moment, languages like HTTP may do (cf. [10]). In another environment, another language may be more appropriate. Are pads going to learn XML?

3.5   Domains of Evolving Externalized Knowledge

Clearly, in areas where no considerable evolution of knowledge takes place, there is no need for an in-depth discussion of the biotope issue.

Those areas are, perhaps, inappropriate for meme media technologies, as there is no remarkable advantage over other middleware approaches.

In contrast, domains where a considerable part of the knowledge is subject to a dynamic evolution are potentially attractive to attempts of invoking meme media technologies. Naturally, one still needs to find out whether knowledge is sufficiently modular and whether there are natural ways to map knowledge units to IntelligentPad objects.

Assume such an application domain has been identified, like medical therapy planning, see [7], e.g. What are particular aspects of the biotope issue to be taken into account, especially those beyond the aspects mentioned above?

In those domains, the evolution of knowledge takes place in accordance with disciplinary regulations and customs. Even local peculiarities come into play. For illustration, hospitals have usually their own procedures how decision makers are contacted and how plans are made.

When IntelligentPad technologies are in use, the evolution of pads does reflect those peculiarities. In other words, the culture of the environment including the non-IT environment has impact on the pads' culture. At least, there will be an interference.

It might be highly interesting to see whether or not certain human cultural environments can be distinguished by a different impact on knowledge evolution in meme media pools. Most probably, there will be more influential and less influential domains. One may expect that research and development will, as a side effect, reveal unwelcome insights.

Phenomena of the latter type, however, are beyond the scope of the present investigation and also far beyond the investigations planned for the future.

Instead, we go into a little more detail to illustrate what it means in practice to take the biotope issue into account. Pads of the CHIP system [10] are adapted to become classes and instances of medical therapy actions [7]. Plugging pads together results in therapy plans.

But what does it mean to plug pads together? Therapy knowledge may be located in distributed meme pools. Plugging pads together means to establish a certain inter-pad communication. The communication with some underlying patient data record pad is of a particular importance, because executability constraints have to be checked with respect to current patient data. According to the CHIP architecture, every pad has its own Web server. Pads are 'talking to each other' by means of http-get and http-post. Whenever changes occur in a pad somewhere down in the hierarchy of a composite pad, these changes are propagated upwards through the whole hierarchy.

The communication abilities of the CHIP pads are centrally located in some dynamic link library, thus being part of the biotope of these pads.

It turns out that peculiarities of the application domain of medical therapy planning result in special communication requirements. To mention just one, changes in the patient data record pad usually affect only a few pads within a large therapy plan. Instead of propagating changes through the whole hierarchically structured plan according to the `chip.dll`, it is more efficient and secure if one establishes a direct data exchange between therapy actions pads and the underlying patient data record pad.

In other words, certain peculiarities of the medical therapy planning domain lead the authors to changes in the biotope – the biotope issue has been recognized a central one.

4   Perspectives at Knowledge and Human Learning

There is recent interest in bridging the gap between meme media technologies and technology enhanced learning (e-learning, for short) like in [13] and [17], e.g. Work about so-called subjunctive interfaces [14] seems to be relevant as well. Meme media meet e-learning.

In the author's opinion, this is an enormously promising domain of research, development and applications, because human memes meet meme media and compliment each other. The key question for the conditions of both meme types' co-existence and, in particular, co-evolution has never before been made explicit.

In e-learning, human knowledge is not simply encoded in media objects, distributed over digital networks, and decoded at the other end. Knowledge is the result of construction processes when humans deal with content and actively engage in exploration, communication, experiment, and the like [2, 5]. It requires in-depth studies of different types (consult [4], e.g.) to reveal the mechanisms of learning.

On a more technological level, one may work about meme media technologies and tools for technology enhanced learning [13, 17]. Another approach may be to sort out didact principles to which meme media technologies seem to be especially suitable. Explorative learning, e.g., may be substantially supported by subjunctive interfaces as proposed and developed by Aran Lunzer [14].

As we know it from the arts (see [18] for an invaluable source of case studies), affecting the human means to find some way to get the human's memes engaged. The approach of e-learning concentrates on the art of connecting meme media to the human memes. From this perspective, storyboarding [12] comes into play. In the future, we will ponder, perhaps, about the biotope issue of human and meme media.

5   Summary and Conclusions

Instead of repeating the arguments from before, four theses are intended to summarize the author's viewpoint and – hopefully – to provoke some discussion among interested scientists, developers and users.

– The biotope issue is essential for memes in the biological reality. It is usually taken for granted. To meme media implementations, the biotope issue is of similar importance, but it is widely underestimated.
   A primary goal of the present paper is to attract attention to the biotope issue and to establish an awareness of the biotope issue in the scientific and engineering community.

– The most difficult point in the biotope issue discussion is that humans have to step back, have to give priority to the memes and have to consider themselves as part of the memes' and the meme media objects' biotope, only.
   Success of meme media implementations and applications requires some fundamental rethinking.

– There is a large variety of technical and technological details in meme media implementations which turn out to be substantial aspects of the biotope issue.
   Seeing the biotope issue in its right perspective is the only way to find a guideline for dealing with those seemingly minor implementational questions.

– The question for the biotope issue may be considered as a crucial criterion to distinguish those application domains that are appropriate to meme media approaches from those that are not.
   Simpler software technological problems that ask for a certain middleware solution do not require meme media, if there does not appear any biotope problem.

– Certain meme media implementations are best distinguished from concurring developments of information technologies by their evolutionary potentials. Only emphasis on the evolutionary potentials can make the meme media implementations successful.
   Thus, respecting the biotope issue is of strategic importance and has certain commercial relevance.

For a greater impact on meme media implementations and their usage, the present paper should result in some guideline or, at least, in some checklist to take the biotope issue appropriately into account.

The reader should be aware of a rather delicate aspect of memetics which complicates not only writing about the biotope issue, but also finding agreements about the essentials of memetics. Thinking about memetics thoroughly leads to the question about the human self. From a very strict memetic point of view (cf. [1] and [8]), there is no other human self than a story told us by our brain.

Last but not least, it is worth to point to the fact that a deeper discussion of the aspects systematized in chapter 3 of this paper does need more IntelligentPad development competence. The author depends very much on other colleagues and on ongoing experience with application attempts.

References

1. Susan Blackmore. *The Meme Machine*. Oxford University Press, 1999.
2. John D. Bransford, Ann L. Brown and Rodney R. Cocking. *How People Learn. Brain, Mind, Experience, and School*. National Academy Press, 2003.
3. Richard Dawkins. *The Selfish Gene*. Oxford University Press, 1976.
4. Antonio Damasio. *The Feeling of What Happens. Body and Emotion in the Making of Consciousness*. Hartcourt, Inc., 1999.
5. Brent Davis, Dennis Sumara and Rebecca Luce-Kapler. *Engaging Minds. Learning and Teaching in a Complex World*. Lawrence Erlbaum Associates, 2000.
6. Gerhard Degel. *Meme Media Development Control – The Cockpit Concept*. presentation on the Dagstuhl Workshop on Intutive Human Interfaces, March 1-5, 2004 (unpublished so far).
7. Volker Dötsch, Kimihito Ito and Klaus P. Jantke. *Human-Agent Co-operation in Accessing and Communicating Knowledge Media – A Case in Medical Therapy Planning*. this volume, 2004.
8. Chris Fiels. Why do we talk to ourselves?. *JETAI* 14 (2002) 4, 255–272.
9. Malcolm Gladwell. *The Tipping Point*. Little, Brown and Company, 2000.
10. Kimihito Ito. CHIP Users' Manual, http://ca.meme.hokudai.ac.jp/people/itok/CHIP/index.html. accessed on August 1, 2004.
11. Kimihito Ito and Yuzuru Tanaka. A Visual Environment for Web Application Composition. In *Proc of 14th ACM Conference on Hypertext and Hypermedia* 2003, pp. 184–193.
12. Klaus P. Jantke and Rainer Knauf. *Didactic Design through Storyboarding: Standard Concepts for Standard Tools*. First International Workshop on Dissemination of E-Learning Technologies and Applications, January 3-6, 2005, Cape Town, South Africa, (to appear).
13. Kimio Kashiwazaki, Yukiaki Kikuta, Makoto Ohigashi and Yuzuru Tanaka. *Interactive 3D Learning Contents Based on a 3D Meme Media Architecture*. First International Workshop on Dissemination of E-Learning Technologies and Applications, January 3-6, 2005, Cape Town, South Africa, (to appear).
14. Aran Lunzer. *Benefits of Subjunctive Interface Support for Exploratory Access to Online Resources*. this volume, 2004.
15. Mark Stefik. The Next Knowledge Medium. *AI Magazine* 7 (1986) 1, 34–46.
16. Yuzuru Tanaka. *Meme Media and Meme Market Architectures*. IEEE Press and Wiley-Interscience, 2003.
17. Yuzuru Tanaka. *Memetics Approach to the Dissemination of e-Learning Objects*. First International Workshop on Dissemination of E-Learning Technologies and Applications, January 3-6, 2005, Cape Town, South Africa, (to appear).
18. Andrej Tarkowskij. *Die versiegelte Zeit. Gedanken zur Kunst, zur Ästhetik und Poetik des Films*. Ullsten, 1984.

Meme Media Architecture
for Intuitively Accessing
and Organizing Intellectual Resources

Yuzuru Tanaka

Meme Media Laboratory, Hokkaido University
Sapporo, 060-8628 Japan

Abstract. With the growing need for interdisciplinary and international availability, distribution and exchange of intellectual resources including information, knowledge, ideas, pieces of work, and tools in reeditable and redistributable organic forms, we need new media technologies that externalize scientific, technological, and/or cultural knowledge fragments in an organic way, and promote their advanced use, international distribution, reuse, and reediting. These media may be called meme media since they carry what R. Dawkins called "memes". An accumulation of memes in a society forms a meme pool that functions like a gene pool. Meme pools will bring about rapid accumulations of memes, and require new technologies for the management and retrieval of memes. This paper first reviews our R&D on meme media, and then proposes their application to the Web to make it work as a meme pool for collaboratively reediting intellectual resources, as well as for intuitively accessing and organizing the huge accumulation of intellectual resources in our societies.

1 Introduction

Nowadays the research topics of science and technology are diversified and segmented into more and more categories. The number of interdisciplinary research topics has also increased. With increasingly sophisticated research on science and technology, there is a growing need for interdisciplinary and international availability, distribution and exchange of the latest research results, in reeditable and redistributable organic forms, including not only research papers and multimedia documents, but also various tools developed for measurement, analysis, inference, design, planning, simulation, and production. Similar needs are also growing for the interdisciplinary and international availability, distribution and exchange of ideas and works among artists, musicians, designers, architects, directors, and producers. We need new media technologies that externalize scientific, technological, and/or cultural knowledge fragments as intellectual resources in an organic way, and promote their advanced use, international distribution, reuse, and reediting.

Intellectual resources denote not only multimedia documents, but also application tools and services provided by local or remote servers. They cannot

G. Grieser and Y. Tanaka (Eds.): Intuitive Human Interface 2004, LNAI 3359, pp. 108–126, 2004.

be simply classified as information contents since they also include tools and services. Media to externalize some of our knowledge as intellectual resources and to distribute them among people are generally defined as knowledge media. Some knowledge media that provide direct manipulation operations for people to reedit and to redistribute their contents are called meme media.

Although WWW and browsers enabled us to publish and to browse intellectual resources, they do not enable people to reedit and redistribute memes published in meme media. When memes are liberated from their servers and distributed among people for their reediting and redistribution, they are accumulated in a society to form a meme pool, which will bring a rapid evolution of intellectual resources shared by this society. This will cause an explosive increase of intellectual resources similar to the flood of consumer products in our present consumer societies.

This paper first reviews meme media architectures, and then proposes the application of the meme media architecture to the Web to make it work as meme pools. This extension makes the Web work as a shared repository not only for publishing intellectual resources, but also for their collaborative reediting, as well as for their intuitive access and reorganization.

2   The Web and Meme Media

2.1   Why Meme Media?

The publication and reuse of intellectual resources using the Web technologies can be characterized by the schematic model in Figure 1. In the model, we do not have any support for extracting any portion of published Web pages, combining them together for their local reuse, or publishing the newly defined composite object as a new Web page. The composition here means not only textual combination but also functional composition of embedded tools and services. We need some support to reedit and redistribute Web contents for their further reuse.

It is widely recognized that a large portion of our paperwork consists of taking some portions of already existing documents, and rearranging their copies in

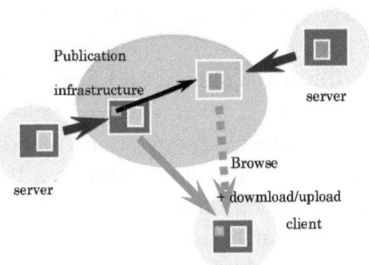

Fig. 1. The publication and reuse of intellectual assets using the Web technologies.

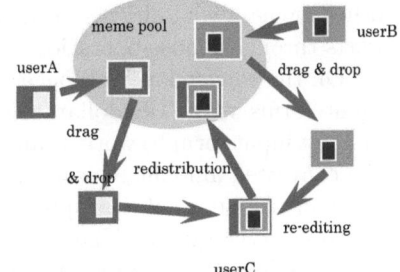

Fig. 2. Meme media technologies for the worldwide publication, reediting and redistribution of intellectual assets.

different formats on different forms. This tendency has been significantly growing since we began to perform our paperwork on personal computers. Since the reediting is so fundamental in our daily information processing, personal computers introduced the copy and paste operations as fundamental operations. Now, these operations are undoubtedly the most frequently used operations on digital contents. We need to make these operations applicable not only to multimedia documents but to documents with embedded tools and services.

Figure 2 shows a new model for the worldwide publication, reediting and redistribution of intellectual resources. As in the case of the Web, you can publish a set of your intellectual resources as a compound document into a worldwide publication repository. You can use a browser to view such documents. In addition to these operations, you can extract any portions of viewed documents as reusable components, combine them together to define a new compound document for your own use, and publish this new compound document into the repository for its reuse by other people. This new model of publishing, reediting and redistributing intellectual resources assumes that all these operations can be performed only through direct manipulation. Meme media technologies realize this new model. They provide the direct manipulation operations necessary for reediting and redistributing intellectual resources.

2.2   How Meme Media Change the Reuse of Web Contents?

Figures from 3 to 4 show an example process of reediting and redistributing intellectual resources over the Web. The meme media technologies provide these operations as generic operations on intellectual resources represented as meme media objects. This example accesses two Web pages, i.e., Lycos Finance Stock Quotes and Charts, and Yahoo Finance Currency Conversion (Figure 3). The former allows you to specify an arbitrary company, and then shows its current stock quote together with its stock quote chart. The latter allows you to specify two currencies and the amount in one of them, and then outputs its conversion to the other currency. Browsers showing the two Web pages are wrapped by meme media wrappers, and work as meme media objects. These wrapped browsers allow us to specify any input forms and/or any displayed objects such as character strings and images to work as I/O ports for the interoperation with other meme media objects. You can directly specify which portions to work as ports through mouse operations.

On the conversion Web page, you may fill in the source and target currency input forms with 'US dollar' and 'Japanese Yen'. Then you may specify the amount input form to work as an I/O port, and the character string representing the converted amount to work as an output port. You may connect a text I/O component to each of these ports, make the wrapped browser to hide its display, and resize it (Figure 3). The result is a currency conversion tool from US dollar to Japanese Yen. This tool wraps the Yahoo Finance Currency Conversion service, and works as an interoperable meme media object. Through mouse operations, you can also specify that the dollar input port will work as the primary port of this media object.

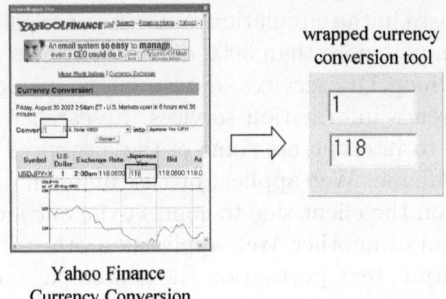

Yahoo Finance
Currency Conversion

wrapped currency
conversion tool

Fig. 3. The wrapping of the Yahoo Finance Currency Conversion page to create a new interoperable tool, simply by specifying the amount input form and the converted amount to work respectively as an I/O port and as an output port.

On the 'Stock Quote and Chart' Web page, you may input some company in the input form, and specify the output portion representing the current stock quote to work as an output port. Now, you can paste the wrapped currency conversion tool on this Stock Quote and Chart Web page, and connect the primary port of the conversion tool to the current stock quote port of the Stock Quote and Chart page (Figure 4). This defines a composite tool that combines two services provided by the two different servers. Now you may input a different company in the input form of the base Web page. Then the composite tool will return its current stock quote both in US dollar and in Japanese yen.

wrapped currency
conversion tool

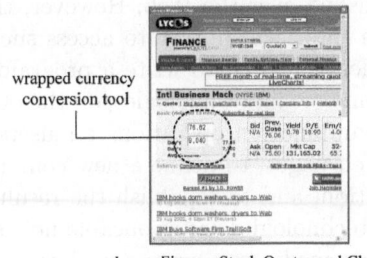

Lycos Finance Stock Quotes and Charts

Fig. 4. The pasting of the wrapped currency conversion tool on the Stock Quote and Chart Web page with the connection of the primary port of the conversion tool to the current stock quote port of the Stock Quote and Chart page.

Meme media technologies also allow us to republish this composite tool as a new Web page. Other people can access this Web page and reuse its composite function using a legacy Web browser.

The example above tells us how fundamental the reediting and redistribution operations are to the creative reuse of a large accumulation of available contents, application tools, and services. Such a memetic composition of a new meme media object from more than one available meme media object uses only direct manipulations, namely edit operations, on their view representations, or their phenotypes in biological terminology. The programs that define their contents including their embedded tools and services can be considered as their genotypes. Meme media objects allow us to edit their genotype through the direct editing of their phenotypes, which is fundamental in intuitively defining new intellectual resources from existing ones.

Our framework also opens a new vista in the circulation and reuse of scientific knowledge. In bioinformatics, for example, more than 3000 different services are now available on the Web. They include DB services, data analysis services, simulation services, and related reference information services. Researchers in this field, however, have no tools yet to interoperate some of these services for their own use. This has two reasons. Different Web applications use different data formats. In addition, there is no way on the client side to connect the output of one Web application to the input form of another Web application other than making a copy of the appropriate output text portion on the source page and pasting it in the input form of the target page. While SOAP allows you to write a program to functionally integrate more than one Web services, it is a server side programming tool, and hard to use for non-programmers. Our framework to extract and wrap Web applications uses HTML format for the data exchange. It allows us to visually specify what to extract and wrap, and which portions to export as slots. It allows us to use paste and peel pad operations to combine extracted Web contents together with other pads for the composition of a new functionally integrated tool.

2.3   Frequently Asked Questions on Meme Media Technologies

Some readers may think that Web Service technologies can provide us with similar functions for the interoperation among Web contents. Web Service technologies enable us to interoperate services published over the Web. However, they assume that the API (Application Program Interface) library to access such a service is a priori provided by its server side. You need to write a program to interoperate more than one Web service. Meme media technologies, on the other hand, provide only the client-side direct manipulation operations for users to reedit intellectual resources embedded in Web pages, to define a new combination of them together with their interoperation, and to republish the result as a new Web page. In addition, meme media technologies are applicable not only to the Web, but also to local objects. Meme media can wrap any documents and tools, and make each of them work as interoperable meme media object. Their wrapping, however, cannot use the same generic wrapper as in the case of wrapping Web contents. Different types of tools may require different wrappers.

Some other readers may become worried about the copyright problem. Copyright policies, however, have been reconsidered and modified every time when people introduced new media technologies. Whenever a new media technology is introduced, the consensus on new copyright policies gradually coevolves with new copyright protection and/or license management technologies. We have been, and are observing such coevolution of new policies with the Web technologies. Some have established closed services on the Web that are exclusive to their members, while others have established a closed network, such as the I-mode cellular phone network in Japan by NTT DoCoMo, to implement a micropayment scheme for charging each access to the registered information services. Many other types of license and account management are currently tried on the Web. The same situation will occur for meme media technologies.

2.4   Related Research

Some user-customizable portal sites such as MyYahoo provide another way to personalize Web pages. If a user has a priori registered his interests, the system will customize the Web page only to show what he is interested in.

HTML4.01 provides a special HTML tag `<iframe>`, or inline frame, for a Web page author to embed an arbitrary Web document in a newly defined Web page. However, it does not allow users browsing Web pages to directly specify either a Web document portion to extract or a location in the target document to insert the extracted document. They need to access and to edit HTML definitions of these Web pages.

Turquoise [1] and Internet Scrapbook [2] both adopt programming-by-demonstration technologies to support the reediting of Web documents. Users may demonstrate, on the screen, how to change the layout of a Web page to define a customized one, and apply the same editing rule whenever the Web page is accessed for refreshing. They enable users to change layouts, but not to extract any components, nor to functionally connect them together. Transpublishing [3] allows users to embed some portions of Web documents in a newly defined Web page. It also proposes license management and charge accounting technologies. The embedding requires the rewriting of the HTML definition using a special HTML tag to import a document.

Example tools for extracting a document component from a Web document include W4F [4], DEByE [5], and WbyE [6]. W4F provides a GUI support tool to define an extraction. Users, however, still need to write some script programs. The system creates a wrapper class written in Java from user's demonstrations. To use this wrapper class, users need to write program codes. DEByE provides a more powerful GUI support tool. However, it outputs the extracted document components in XML format. Its reuse requires some knowledge on XML. WbyE is an extension of DEByE. These systems, however, do not provide any tools for users to visually combine two wrapped Web applications, and to compose a single tool with an integrated function. There are also several research studies about recording and playing a macro operation on a Web browser. Such approach also requires users to have expertise to customize recorded operation sequences described in some language.

Up to now, hypermedia research groups have mainly focused their efforts on the linking services among intellectual assets for the navigation and the interoperability among them. They basically assumed that hypermedia contents were just viewed without making their copies, reediting, nor redistributing them among people. Over the last decade, the Open Hypermedia Working Group (OHSWG) has been working on a standard protocol to allow interoperability across a range of application software components. The group first focused on the separation of link services from document structures, which enables different hypermedia systems to interoperate with each other, and client applications to create, edit, and activate links which are managed in separate link databases [7]. Microcosm [8] and Multicard [9] are examples that worked as reference systems of link servers. The hypertext community also focused on the interoperability with database systems, which introduced higher level functionality: for example HyperBase [10] on a relational foundation, and HBI [11] on a semantic platform. The interoperability with databases also leads to the idea of separating component storage, run time and document content issues. The Dexter Hypertext Reference Model [12] proposed a layered architecture to separate them. As an alternative to such a layered architecture, the open hypertext community collaboratively developed a standard protocol OHP [13] for interdependent different services to interoperate with each other. These architectures worked as a basis to apply link services to the Web [14]. HyperDisco [15] and Chimera [16] proposed such interoperable service models, which were later applied to the Web [17] [18].

The OHSWG approach was basically based on the following principles: the separation of link services, and the standardization of a navigational and/or functional linking protocol among different applications and services. The standard protocol may rely on either API (Application Program Interface) libraries or an on-the-wire communication model using such a standard transport medium as socket. The group is further expanding the linking service functionality by introducing collaborative spatial structures [19], computational aspects, or dynamically defined abstract communication channels [20].

Meme media research that has been conducted independently from the open hypertext community has been focused on the replication, reediting, and redistribution of intellectual resources. To achieve this goal, our group adopted a visual wrapper architecture. Any component, whether it is an application or a service, small or large, is wrapped by a visual wrapper with direct manipulability and standard interface mechanism. These wrappers work as media to carry different types of intellectual resources. Our wrapper architecture allows users to define a composite media object by combining primitive media objects. Composite media objects allow further recombination. Users can exchange those composite media objects through the Internet.

Application of meme media technologies to OHS technologies simply means that objects in the latter framework are wrapped by meme media wrappers to become meme media objects. Such wrapping introduces meme media features to those objects without loosing any of their OHS features.

3   Basic Meme Media Architectures

3.1   IntelligentPad and IntelligentBox as Basic Meme Media Systems

We have been conducting research and development on meme media and meme pool architectures since 1987. We developed 2D and 3D meme media architectures 'IntelligentPad' and 'IntelligentBox' respectively in 1989 and in 1995 [21] [22] [23] [24] [25] [26], and have been working on their meme-pool and meme-market architectures [27] [28], as well as on their applications. These are summarized in [29].

In object-oriented component architectures, all types of knowledge fragments are defined as objects. IntelligentPad exploits both an object-oriented component architecture and a wrapper architecture. Instead of directly dealing with component objects, IntelligentPad wraps each object with a standard pad wrapper and treats it as a pad (Figure 5). Each pad has a card like view on the screen and a standard set of operations like 'move', 'resize', 'copy', 'paste', and 'peel'. Users can easily replicate any pad, paste a pad onto another, and peel a pad off a composite pad. A pad can be pasted on another pad to define both a physical containment relationship and a functional linkage between them. When a pad P2 is pasted on another pad P1, the pad P2 becomes a child of P1, and P1 becomes the parent of P2. No pad may have more than one parent pad. Each pad provides a list of slots that work as connection jacks of an AV-system component, and a single connection to a slot of another pad (Figure 5). You can functionally connect each child pad to one of the slots of its parent pad. Each pad uses a standard set of messages 'set' and 'gimme' to access a single slot of its parent pad, and another standard message 'update' to propagate changes of state to its child pads. In their default definitions, a 'set' message sends its parameter value to its recipient slot, while a 'gimme' message requests a value from its recipient slot.

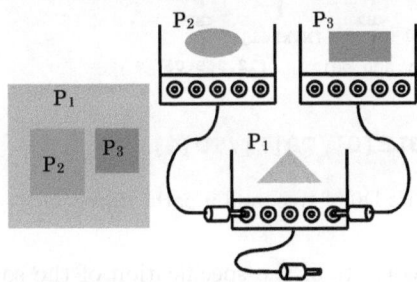

Fig. 5. A composite pad and its slot connection structure.

Pads can be pasted together to define various multimedia documents and application tools. Unless otherwise specified, composite pads are always decomposable and reeditable.

4   Wrapping Web Contents as Meme Media Objects

4.1   Extraction and Reediting of Web Contents

Web documents are defined in HTML format. An HTML view denotes an arbitrary HTML document portion represented in the HTML document format. The pad wrapper to wrap an arbitrary portion of a Web document needs to be capable of both specifying an arbitrary HTML view and rendering any HTML document. We call this pad wrapper an HTMLviewPad. Its rendering function is implemented by wrapping a legacy Web browser such as Netscape Navigator or Internet Explorer. In our implementation, we wrapped Internet Explorer.

The specification of an arbitrary HTML view over a given HTML document requires the capability of editing the internal representation of HTML documents, namely, DOM trees. The DOM tree representation allows you to identify any HTML-document portion, which corresponds to a DOM tree node, with its path expression. Figure 6 shows an HTML document with its DOM tree representation. The highlighted portion in the document corresponds to the highlighted node whose path expression is /HTML[0]/BODY[0]/TABLE[0]/TR[1]/TD[1]. A path expression is a concatenation of node identifiers along a path from the root to the specified node. Each node identifier consists of a node name, i.e., the tag given to this node element, and the number of its sibling nodes located to the left of this node.

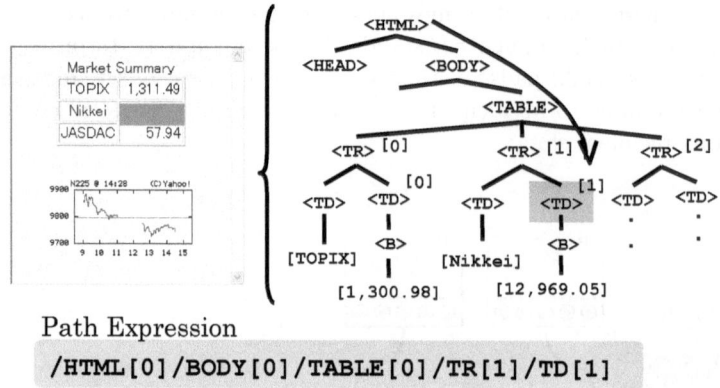

Path Expression
/HTML[0]/BODY[0]/TABLE[0]/TR[1]/TD[1]

Fig. 6. An HTML document with its DOM tree, and a path expression.

The definition of an HTML view consists of the specification of the source document, and a sequence of view editing operations. The specification of a source document uses its URL. Its retrieval is performed by the function 'getHTML' in such a way as

```
doc = getHTML("http://www.abc.com/index.html", null).
```

The second parameter will be used to specify a request to the Web server at the retrieval time. Such requests include POST and GET. The retrieved document is kept in DOM format. The editing of an HTML view is a sequence of DOM tree manipulation operations selected out of the followings:

1. EXTRACT : Delete all the nodes other than the sub tree with the specified node as its root.
2. REMOVE : Delete the sub tree with the specified node as its root.
3. INSERT : Insert a given DOM tree at the specified relative location of the specified node. You may select the relative location as CHILD, PARENT, BEFORE, or AFTER to insert the given DOM tree respectively as the last child, the parent, the last left sibling, or the first right sibling of the specified node.

An HTML view is specified as follows:

```
defined-view = source-view.DOM-tree-operation(node),
```

where source-view may be a Web document or another HTML document, and node is specified by its extended path expression.

You may specify two sub trees extracted either from the same Web document or from the different Web documents, and combine them to define a view.

```
doc = getHTML("http://www.abc.com/index.html", null);
view2 = doc
        .EXTRACT("/HTML/BODY/TABLE[0]/")
        .EXTRACT("/TABLE[0]/TR[0]/");
view1 = doc
        .EXTRACT("/HTML/BODY/TABLE[0]/")
        .INSERT("/TABLE[0]/TR[0]/", view2, BEFORE);
```

4.2   Direct Editing of HTML Views

Instead of specifying a path expression to identify a DOM tree node, we will make the HTMLviewPad to dynamically frame different extractable document portions for different mouse locations so that its user may move the mouse cursor around to see every extractable document portion. When the HTMLviewPad frames what you want to extract, you can drag the mouse to create another HTMLviewPad with this extracted document portion. The new HTMLviewPad renders the extracted DOM tree on itself. Figure 7 shows an example extraction using such a mouse-drag operation, which internally generates the following edit code.

```
doc = getHTML("http://www.abc.com/index.html", null);
view = doc
       .EXTRACT("/HTML/BODY/TABLE[0]/");
```

The HTMLviewPad provides a pop-up menu of view-edit operations including EXTRACT, REMOVE and INSERT. After you select an arbitrary portion, you may select either EXTRACT or REMOVE.

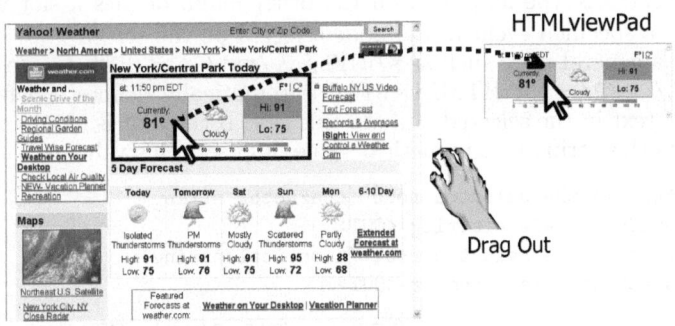

Fig. 7. Live extraction of an element using a mouse-drag operation.

The INSERT operation uses two HTMLviewPads showing a source HTML document and a target one. You may first specify INSERT operation from the menu, and specify the insertion location on the target document by directly specifying a document portion and then specifying relative location from a menu including CHILD, PARENT, BEFORE, and AFTER. Then, you may directly select a document portion on the source document, and drag and drop this portion on the target document. The dropped HTMLviewPad is deleted after the insertion.

4.3   Automatic Generation of Default Slots

The HTMLviewPad allows you to map any node values of its view and any events on its view to its newly defined slots. The definition of such a node-slot mapping takes the following form:

```
MAP(<node>, NameSpace),
```

where <node> is specified by its path expression and NameSpace defines a slot name. An example of such a mapping is as follows:

```
MAP("/HTML/BODY/P/txt( )", "#value")
```

Depending on the node type, the HTMLviewPad changes the node value evaluation to map the most appropriate value of a selected node to a newly defined slot. We call these evaluation rules node-mapping rules. Each node-mapping rule has the following syntax:

```
target-object => naming-rule(data-type)<MappingType>
```

```
naming-rule :      naming rule for the new slot
data-type   :      data type of the slot
MappingType :      <IN | OUT | EventListener | EventFire>
```

Slots defined with the OUT type are read-only ones. The IN-type mapping defines a rewritable slot. The rewriting of such a slot may change the display of the HTML view document. The EventListener-type mapping defines a slot that changes its value whenever an event occurs in the node selected on the screen. The EventFire-type mapping, on the other hand, defines a slot whose update triggers a specified event in the node selected on the screen.

For a general node such as </HTML/.../txt()>, </HTML/.../attr()>, or </HTML/.../P/>, the HTMLviewPad automatically defines a default slot, and sets the text in the selected node to this slot. If the text is a numerical string, it converts this string to a numerical value, and sets this value to the slot.

```
  a text in the selected node (character string)
=> NameSpace::#Text(string)<OUT>
  a text in the selected node (numerical string)
=> NameSpace::#Text(number)<OUT>
```

For a table node such as </HTML/.../TABLE/>, the HTMLviewPad converts the table value to its CSV (Comma-Separated Value) representation, and automatically maps it to a newly defined default slot of text type.

For an anchor node such as `</HTML/.../A/>`, the HTMLviewPad automatically performs the following three mappings to define three default slots:

```
  a text in the selected node
=> NameSpace::#Text(string, number)<OUT>
  href attribute of the selected node
=> NameSpace::#refURL(string)<OUT>
  URL of the target object
=> NameSpace::#jumpURL(string)<EventListener>
```

For example, let us consider a case in which we extract an anchor defined as follows:

```
<A href="./next.html">
Next Page
</A>
```

The first mapping sets the text "Next Page" to a string (or number) type default slot NameSpace::#Text. The second mapping sets the href "./next.html" to a string type default slot NameSpace::#refURL. The third mapping has the EventListener type. Whenever the anchor is clicked, the target URL is set to a string-type default slot NameSpace::#jumpURL.

For a form node such as `</HTML/.../FORM/>`, the HTMLviewPad automatically performs the following three mappings to define three default slots:

```
  the value attribute of the INPUT node with the name attribute
  in the selected node
=> NameSpace::#Input_type_name(string, number)<IN, OUT>
  Submit action
=> NameSpace::#FORM_Submit(boolean)<EventFire>
  the value obtained from the server
=> NameSpace::#FORM_Request(string)<EventListener>

  type = <text | password | file | checkbox | radio | hidden |
             submit | reset | button | image>
  name = <name> attribute in the INPUT node
```

For example, let us consider a case in which we extract a form defined as follows:

```
<FORM action="./search">
<INPUT Type=txt name=keyword >
<INPUT Type=submit value="search">
</FORM>
```

The first mapping rule for a form sets the input keyword to a string (or number) type default slot NameSpace::#Input_text_keyword. The second mapping rule is an EventFire-type mapping. Whenever a TRUE is set to a Boolean type default slot #FORM_Submit, the HTMLviewPad triggers a form-request event. The third mapping has the EventListener type. Whenever an event to send a form request occurs, the HTMLviewPad sets the corresponding query to a string type default slot NameSpace::#FORM_Request.

Each HTMLviewPad has the additional following four default slots. The #UpdateInterval slot specifies the time interval for the periodical polling of referenced HTTP servers. A view defined over a Web document refresh its contents by periodically retrieving this Web document in an HTTP server. The #Retrieval-Code slot stores the code to retrieve the source document. The #ViewEditing-Code slot stores the view definition code. The #MappingCode slot stores the mapping definition code. The HTMLviewPad updates itself by accessing the source document, whenever either the #RetrievalCode slot or the #ViewEdit-ingCod slot is accessed with a set message, the interval timer invokes the polling, a user specifies its update, or it becomes active after its loading from a file. In addition to these four slots, the HTMLviewPad automatically creates slots defined by the mapping code that is set to the #MappingCode slot.

4.4   Visual Definition of Slots for Extracted Web Contents

Our HTMLviewPad also allows users to visually specify any HTML-node to work as a slot. In its node specification mode, an HTMLviewPad frames different extractable document portions of its content document for different mouse locations so that its user may change the mouse location to see every selectable document portion. When the HTMLviewPad frames what you want to work as a slot, you can click the mouse to pop up a dialog box to name this slot. Since each extracted Web component uses an HTMLviewPad to render its contents, it also allows users to specify any of its portions to work as its slot. We call such a slot thus defined an HTML-node slot. The value of an HTML-node slot is the HTML view of the selected portion. The HTMLviewPad converts ill-formed HTML into well-formed HTML to construct its DOM-tree. Therefore, you may connect an HTMLviewPad to an HTML-node slot to view the corresponding HTML view. If the HTML-node slot holds an anchor node, the HTMLviewPad connected to this slot shows the target Web page.

Figure 3 shows an HTMLviewPad showing a Yahoo Web page with an embedded Web application to convert US dollar to Japanese yen based on the current exchange rate. On this pad, you can visually specify the input form for inputting dollar amount and the output text portion showing the equivalent yen amount to work as slots. The HTML-path of the input-form is represented as

```
HTML[0]/BODY[0]/DIV[0]/FORM[0]/INPUT[0]/text[(.*)],
```

while the HTML-path of the selected output text portion is represented as

```
HTML[0]/BODY[0]/TABLE[0]/TR[0]/TD[1]/A[0]/attr[href].
```

You may name the corresponding HTML-node slots as #dollarAmount and #yenAmount respectively. The HTMLviewPad allows you to suspend the rendering of its contents. In this mode, you may use an HTMLviewPad with an HTML view as a blank pad with an arbitrary size. Figure 3 shows, on its right hand side, a currency rate converter pad. We have defined this pad from the above mentioned Web page just by defining two slots, resizing the HTMLview-Pad, and pasting two text IO pads with their connections to #dollarAmount and #yenAmount slots.

Such a pad wraps a Web application, providing slots for the original's input forms and output text strings. We call such a pad a wrapped Web application. Since a wrapped Web application is such a pad that allows you to change its primary slot assignment, you may specify any one of its slots to work as a primary slot.

You can also wrap a Lycos' Web page for a realtime stock-price browsing service, defining a slot for the current stock price. Then you may paste the wrapped currency conversion Web application with its #dollarAmount specified as its primary slot on this wrapped Lycos stock-price page. We connect the conversion pad to the newly defined current stock price slot. For the input of different company names, you can use the input form of the original Web page. Since this Web application uses the same page layout for different companies, the same path expression correctly identifies the current stock-price information part for every different company.

5 Example Applications

5.1 Example Application of Live Documents

The HTMLviewPad allows us to extract an arbitrary HTML element from the Web document it displays. The direct dragging-out of this portion creates another HTMLviewPad showing the extracted portion. The periodic polling capability of the latter HTMLviewPad keeps the extracted document portion alive. You may paste such a live copy in a pad form on another pad with a slot connection for functional composition. You may also paste a pad on such a live copy in a pad form, and connect the former pad to one of the slots of the latter. Using such operations, you may compose an application pad integrated with live copies of document portions extracted from different Web pages.

Figure 8 shows the plotting of the NASA Space Station's orbit and Yohkoh Satellite's orbit. We used a world map with a plotting function. This map has a pair of #longitude[1] slot and #latitude[1] slot, and creates, on user's demand, more pairs of the same type slots with different indices. First, you need to access the home pages of the space station and the satellite. These pages show the longitude and the latitude of the current locations of these space vehicles. Then, you may make live copies of the longitude and the latitude in each Web page, and paste them on the world map with their connection respectively to #longitude[i] and #latitude[i] slots. The live copies from the space station Web page uses the first slot pair, while those from the satellite Web page uses the second slot pair. These live copies update their values every 10 seconds by polling the source Web pages. The independent two sequences of plotted locations show the orbits of the two space vehicles.

5.2 Composition with More Than One Wrapped Web Application

When applied to the over-the-counter services in e-banking, our framework enables financial planners to dynamically collect appropriate live information and

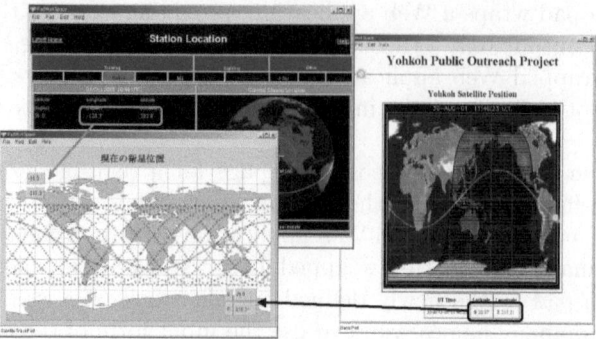

Fig. 8. The plotting of the NASA Space Station's orbit and Yohkoh Satellite's orbit.

Web applications from the Web as well as local Web pages that access internal databases, to dynamically combine them together for composing customized portfolios of live stock-market information, and to send it to their clients by e-mail. Financial planners can reedit the live portfolios according to their clients' demands. Clients can also reedit the proposed live portfolios to define summaries or focused information. They can also combine more than one live portfolio obtained from different financial planners to define a cross-comparison view.

Figure 9 shows a composite tool that integrates several public Web applications in bioinformatics including DDBJ's Blast homology search service, GenBank Report service, and PubMed's paper reference service. Blast service allows us to input a sample DNA sequence, and outputs genes with similar DNA sequences. We have specified the input form and the accession number of the first candidate sequence to work as slots. The accession number works as an anchor linking to a GenBank Report Web page containing the detail information about this gene. Its corresponding slot contains the URL to the target GenBank Report page. We have pasted an HTMLviewPad with its connection to this second slot. As a result, this child HTMLviewPad shows the corresponding GenBank Report page. This page contains bibliographic information about the related research papers. We have visually specified the title portion of the first research paper to work as a slot of this pad. We have also wrapped the PubMed service with its input form work as a slot. PubMed service returns a list of full documents that contains given keywords. We have made this slot to work as the primary slot. By pasting this wrapped PubMed service on the HTMLviewPad showing a GenBank Report page with its connection to the title slot, you will obtain a composite tool that functionally integrates these three services.

6   Redistribution and Publication of Meme Media Objects as Web Contents

Whenever you save a wrapped Web-document portion extracted from a Web page, the system saves only the pad type, namely 'HTMLviewPad', the values

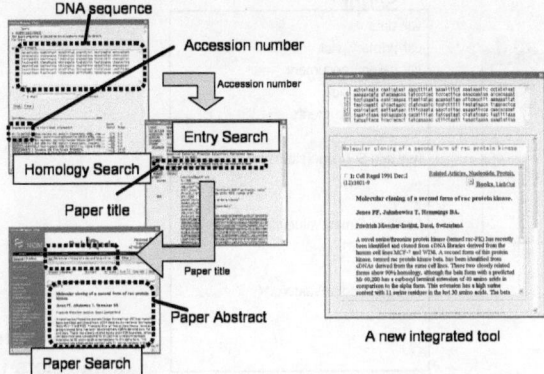

Fig. 9. Visual composition of a new tool that integrates DDBJ's Blast homology search service, GenBank Report service, and PubMed's paper reference service.

of the two slots, #RetrievalCode slot and #ViewEditingCode slot, and the path expression and name of each user-defined slot. Copies of such a live copy share only such meta information with the original. They access the source Web page whenever they need to update themselves. This is an important feature from a copyright point of view, since every update of such a copy requires a server access. The redistribution of a live copy across the Internet needs to send only its save format representation. When a live copy is activated on the destination platform, it invokes the retrieval code stored in #RetrievalCode slot, executes the view editing code in #ViewEditingCode slot to display only the defined portion of the retrieved Web document, and defines every user-defined slot. You can further extract any of its portions as a live copy.

For the reediting of extracted Web contents, our framework provides two methods. One of them allows you to insert an HTML view into another HTML view without any functional linkage. The other allows us to paste an HTML view as a pad on another HTML view as a pad with a slot connection between them. The former composition results in a new HTML view, while the latter composition is no longer an HTML view. In order to publish composed documents and/or tools as HTML documents in the Web, we need to convert non HTML view compositions to HTML views. We call such a conversion a flattening operation.

For the HTML representation of an HTML view working as a pad, we use script variables to represent its slots, its primary slot, its parent pad, the parent's slot it is connected, and the list of child pads. As shown in Figure 10, we use JavaScript to define SetValue function to set a new value to a specified slot, GimmeValue function to read out the value of a specified slot, and UpdateValue function to update the primary slot value and to invoke every child pad's UpdateValue function. To update the primary slot value, we define a script program to invoke the parent's GimmeValue function with the connection slot as its parameter, and to set the return value to the own primary slot. Figure 10 shows an HTML view defined with two slots #increment and #number and the

124   Yuzuru Tanaka

Script
```
var slots
var primary_slot
var parent_document
var parent_slot
var child_documents

function SetValue(slotname,value){
...
}
function GimmeValue(slotname){
...
}
function UpdateValue(...){
...
}
```

Fig. 10. A JavaScript program to define slots in an HTML view.

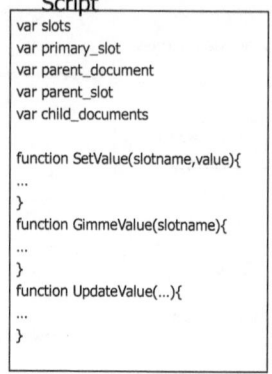

```
<HTML>
<BODY>
<INPUT type=text>
</BODY>
</HTML>
```
text.html

```
<HTML>
<BODY>
Button
</BODY>
</HTML>
```
button.html

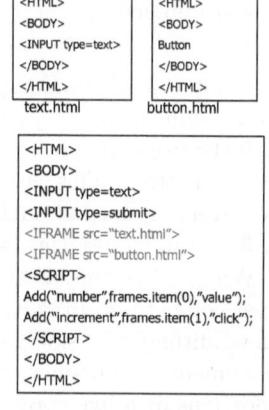

```
<HTML>
<BODY>
<INPUT type=text>
<INPUT type=submit>
<IFRAME src="text.html">
<IFRAME src="button.html">
<SCRIPT>
Add("number",frames.item(0),"value");
Add("increment",frames.item(1),"click");
</SCRIPT>
</BODY>
</HTML>
```
composite.html

Fig. 11. Use of a JavaScript program for an HTML-view composition with three HTML views.

three standard functions. This HTML view works as a counter with a number display and a button to increment the number. The HTML view defines these components in HTML.

Figure 11 shows an HTML view composition with three HTML views; two works as child pads of the other. The parent HTML view is the counter with two slots, #increment and #number. One child HTML view works as a button with its primary slot #click, while the other child HTML view works as a number display with its primary slot #value. The composition rewrites the HTML definition of the base pad to embed the HTML definitions of the other two using <IFRAME> tags, and adds a script code using <SCRIPT> tags to define slot connection linkages among them. The composed HTML view works exactly the same as a composite pad combining the pad representations of these three HTML views. Users may use a legacy Web browser to show this composite view and to play with it.

We may use this mechanism to flatten a composite pad that uses only those pads extracted from some Web pages.

7   Concluding Remarks

Meme media architectures work as the enabling technologies for interdisciplinary and international availability, distribution and exchange of intellectual assets including information, knowledge, ideas, pieces of work, and tools in reeditable and redistributable organic forms. When applied to the Web, they make the Web work as a meme pool with a huge accumulation of ready-to-use intellectual resources. Meme media over the Web will significantly accelerate the evolution of memes in our societies, which will lead to a need for new ways of organizing and accessing their huge accumulation.

This paper has first reviewed meme media architectures, and then proposed the application of the meme media architecture to the Web to make it work as meme pools. This extension makes the Web work as a shared repository not only for publishing intellectual resources, but also for their collaborative reediting and reorganization.

References

1. Miller, R., Myers, B.: Creating Dynamic World Wide Web Pages By Demonstration. Technical report, Carnegie Mellon University School of Computer Science (1997)
2. Sugiura, A., Koseki, Y.: Internet scrapbook: automating web browsing tasks by demonstration. In: Proceedings of the 11th annual ACM symposium on User interface software and technology, ACM Press (1998) 9–18
3. Nelson, T.: Transpublishing for Today's web: Our Overall Design and Why It is Simple (1999) http://www.sfc.keio.ac.jp/ted/TPUB/Tqdesign99.html.
4. Sahuguet, A., Azavant, F.: Building intelligent web applications using lightweight wrappers. Data Knowl. Eng. 36 (2001) 283–316
5. Ribeiro-Neto, B.A., Laender, A., da Silva, A.S.: Extracting semistructured data through examples. In: Proceedings of the 8th ACM International Conference On Informtion and Knowledge Management (CIKM'99). (1999) 91–101
6. Golgher, P.B., Laender, A.H.F., da Silva, A.S., Ribeiro-Neto, B.A.: An Example-Based Environment for Wrapper Generation. In: Proceedings of the Workshops on Conceptual Modeling Approaches for E-Business and The World Wide Web and Conceptual Modeling, Springer-Verlag (2000) 152–164
7. Carr, L., Hall, W., De Roure, D.: The evolution of hypertext link services. ACM Comput. Surv. 31 (1999) 9
8. Fountain, A.M., Hall, W., Heath, I., Davis, H.C.: Microcosm: An Open Model With Dynamic Linking. In: Proceedings of the ACM European Conference on Hypertext '90 (ECHT '90). (1990) 298–311
9. Rizk, A., Sauter, L.: Multicard: an open hypermedia system. In: Proceedings of the ACM conference on Hypertext, ACM Press (1992) 4–10
10. Schütt, H.A., Streitz, N.A.: HyperBase: a hypermedia engine based on a relational database management system. (1992) 95–108
11. Schase, J., Legget, J., et al.: Design and implementation of the hbi hyperbase management system. Electronic Publishing: Origination, Dissemination and Design 6 (1993) 35–63

12. Halasz, F., Schwartz, M.: The Dexter hypertext reference model. Commun. ACM **37** (1994) 30–39
13. Davis, H., Lewis, A., Rizk, A.: OHP: A Draft Proposal for an Open Hypermedia Protocol. In: Proceedings of ACM Hypertext '96, ACM Press (1996) 9
14. Grønbæk, K., Bouvin, N.O., Sloth, L.: Designing dexter-based hypermedia services for the world wide web. In: Proceedings of the eighth ACM conference on Hypertext, ACM Press (1997) 146–156
15. Wiil, U.K., Leggett, J.J.: The HyperDisco approach to open hypermedia systems. In: Proceedings of the the seventh ACM conference on Hypertext, ACM Press (1996) 140–148
16. Anderson, K., Taylor, R., Whitehead, E.: Chimera: Hypertext for heterogeneous software environments (1994)
17. Wiil, U.K., Leggett, J.J.: Workspaces: the HyperDisco approach to Internet distribution. In: Proceedings of the eighth ACM conference on Hypertext, ACM Press (1997) 13–23
18. Anderson, K.M.: Integrating open hypermedia systems with the World Wide Web. In: Proceedings of the eighth ACM conference on Hypertext, ACM Press (1997) 157–166
19. Reinert, O., Bucka-Lassen, D., Pedersen, C.A., Nürnberg, P.J.: Caos: a collaborative and open spatial structure service component with incremental spatial parsing. In: Proceedings of the tenth ACM Conference on Hypertext and hypermedia : returning to our diverse roots, ACM Press (1999) 49–50
20. Moreau, L., Gibbens, N., et. al.: SoFAR with DIM Agents. (In: Proceedings of the 5th International Conference on the Practical Application of Intelligent Agents and Multi-Agent Technology (PAAM 2000))
21. Tanaka, Y., Imataki, T.: A Hypermedia System allowing Functional Composition of Active Media Objects through Direct Manipulations. In: Proceedings of the IFIP '89, San Francisco, CA (1989) 541–546
22. Tanaka, Y., Nagasaki, A., Akaishi, M., Noguchi, T.: A synthetic media architecture for an object-oriented open platform. In: Proceedings of the IFIP 12th World Computer Congress on Personal Computers and Intelligent Systems - Information Processing '92 - Volume 3, North-Holland (1992) 104–110
23. Tanaka, Y.: From augmentation media to meme media: IntelligentPad and the world-wide repository of pads. In Kangassalo, H., et. al., eds.: Information Modelling and Knowledge Bases, VI, IOS Press (1995) 91–107
24. Tanaka, Y.: A Meme Media Architecture for Fine-Grain Component Software. In: Proceedings of the Second JSSST International Symposium on Object Technologies for Advanced Software, Springer-Verlag (1996) 190–214
25. Johnstone, B.: DIY Software. New Scientist **147** (1995) 26–31
26. Okada, Y., Tanaka, Y.: IntelligentBox: a constructive visual software development system for interactive 3D graphic applications. In: Proceedings of the Computer Animation, IEEE Computer Society (1995) 114
27. Tanaka, Y.: Meme media and a world-wide meme pool. In: Proceedings of the fourth ACM international conference on Multimedia, ACM Press (1996) 175–186
28. Tanaka, Y.: Memes: New Knowledge Media for Intellectual resources. Modern Simulation and Training **1** (2000) 22–25
29. Tanaka, Y.: Meme Media and Meme Market Architectures: Knowledge Media for Editing, Distributing, and Managing Intellectual Resources. IEEE Press & Wiley-Interscience (2003)

Enhancing Visual Perception
Using Dynamic Updating of Display

Toshio Kawashima[1], Takanori Terashima[2],
Takeshi Nagasaki[1], and Masashi Toda[1]

[1] Future University, Hakodate
116-2 Kamedanakano-cho, Hakodate
041-8655 Hokkaido, Japan
{kawasima,nagasaki,toda}@fun.ac.jp
[2] Miyagi University, School of Project Design
1 Gakuen, Taiwa-cho, 981-3298 Miyagi, Japan
terashima@myu.ac.jp

Abstract. In this report we propose two types of methods that enhance the visual perception of human. The first idea uses a type of change blindness, a short-term information suppression of visual information processing. This makes possible to provide visual stimulation to peripheral area of visual field without being noticed by the user. It can be used to separate "what you see" and "where you will see the next" when you design the screen of computer display. The second idea is to control the speed of reading text using visual stimulation to peripheral. We tested several types of leader for guiding eye-gaze. Experimental result shows that the leaders increase reading speed without loss of comprehensiveness.

1 Introduction

The most important sensation is often said to be vision because 40% of human brain is used for processing visual information. This fact indicates that information received via visual channels is the largest in the modality of sensation.

History. First visual display methods would be gesture to attract someone's attention. Our vision system is intrinsically inhomogeneous. The center of retina, fovea, has more receptors than the peripheral part of retina. Visual acuity is very high around retina from this reason, while very low in peripheral area. This inhomogeneity requires activeness of human vision system. Gesture would first be invented to attract attention by giving dynamic visual stimulus to peripheral area on retina. The second invention is characters that express meaning by a series of these primitive shapes. First characters were written on a flat surface such as board or paper. Characters had long been static expression, until movie technology was developed.

These two fundamental ideas are still a basic function of computer display. The first one is the blinking cursor. The second is text display.

G. Grieser and Y. Tanaka (Eds.): Intuitive Human Interface 2004, LNAI 3359, pp. 127–141, 2004.
© Springer-Verlag Berlin Heidelberg 2004

The third visual technology is movie and television. Early nineteenth century flipbook was invented. This idea that a sequence of discontinuous images causes motion perception was grown up to movie in the end of the nineteenth century. Thirty years later television was invented as the extension of this idea and raster scan display was developed for the display. At this stage dynamic visual stimulation and complex image pattern like characters were integrated in visual display.

After the last decade of the twentieth century, high resolution displays are commonly used in computer system but the principle of the display has not changed. The relation between display and human, however, has changed. The image rendered on a display is redrawn when an input device generates an event. This interactivity is essence of the current display system.

In addition, high spec graphic cards provide higher rendering speed and higher refresh rate up to 200Hz. In spite of the fact that the performance of a computer display already exceeds our perceptual limitation, the principle of visual display is intrinsically the same as movie.

Position of the Research in the Project Group. In the project of "Intuitive Human Interface for Organizing and Accessing Intellectual Assets" the role of our subgroup is to find a breakthrough of human interface from the viewpoints of engineering and psychology.

Previous researches of human interface have been focused on "real-world oriented" interaction systems that use special input devices to collect the information from human or on "virtual reality" that uses a special small head-mounted display or wall-type screens.

Many researches of information visualization have been also done but they use no feedback from observer's response at perception level.

Prof. Morita of Yamaguchi University, a group member of the subgroup, is interested in the computational model of vision. He proposes an eye-gaze control algorithm of foveal vision that uses a short-term memory to select the next fixation position. He applied his model to reading. In his research the model well simulates the saccades and fixations of human eye during reading textbook. He also applied the model to design a dynamic visual marker to guide eye-gaze. His researches will be reported in the workshop.

The authors of the paper are interested in the mechanism of visual cognition. Vision mechanism, especially saccadic suppression impresses us because it hides the change (or update) of image when the change occurs during the period of saccadic motion. We applied the phenomenon to design a computer display that updates the contents during use's eye movement without being noticed. Another research subject is eye leading for speed-reading. We designed an eye leading method to control eye-gaze.

Through the subproject we tried to increase the amount of information by assistant of computer based on the characteristic of human.

Organization of the Paper. The remainder of the paper is organized as follows. Section 2 briefly reviews mechanism of vision and the limitation of reception via visual display. In section 3 we propose two ideas of dynamic display of visual information. One is display-updating mechanism during saccade. The other is eye-gaze guidance for speed-reading. Section 4 discusses the possibility of new approaches of dynamic display based on psychology of vision. Finally, section 5 concludes our work.

2   Vision Mechanism and Visual Display

Human vision is an inhomogeneous sensory system. In the center of vision visual acuity is the greatest and drops off toward peripheral area [1]. The center is called fovea where the most of receptors are *cones* that are specialized for processing detail of the image. In the peripheral area the retina consists of *rods* that are sensitive to motion and are important for night vision. Because of the complementary system the human vision must be *active*.

Our vision system obtains only a part of scene during a fixation. By moving eyes repeatedly to the place where important information will be found, we are able to recognize the scene. This activeness is the essence of human vision.

The nature of foveal vision system is considered in typography. Bold-faced fonts and italic fonts are used to emphasize important words so that the words are easily found in peripheral vision. The action of shaking hand in the crowd attracts the attention because of the peripheral vision's sensitivity to moving object. These examples explain that visual display methods have been empirically designed to reflect the static characteristics of human vision system.

With the power of advanced computer, and with a sensing system that monitors the human activity, we are able to design more sophisticated display methods strongly based on vision psychology. For example, current computer display does not fully consider the two types of vision systems, foveal and peripheral. If a system observes eye-gaze as a measure of attention in real-time, the system updates the screen reflecting the status of the observer.

In this paper, we propose two types of ideas.

1. Updating screen during saccadic motion of eyes using the feedback from eye-tracking system
2. Text reader for speed-reading using the motion of text to lead the eye gaze

In the both ideas visual stimulation to peripheral vision guides the gaze direction to the stimulated point so that the point can be imaged in the fovea.

3   Designing Display Methods
Based on Vision Psychology

In this section we propose two approaches that control the eye movement for the design of visual display. Eye movement is necessary behavior for recognizing scene, and is also a very important index of human behavior that reflects *what he/she pays attention to now*.

3.1   Updating Screen During Saccadic Motion of Eyes

Typographical designs such as boldface font and spaces between words are said to be guides while reading text [2]. They work as static markers placed in the peripheral vision. Our idea is to place such markers at arbitrary positions of the display without being noticed. This idea seems paradoxical because a marker must be recognized as a marker by the user.

A solution of the paradox is to use *saccade* as a trigger of updating screen. Saccade is a rapid movement of eye between *fixations*. Fixation is a state that the eye gaze is moveing within a small area. The change of image during a saccade cannot be noticed because of saccadic suppression of visual sensitivity. This type of psychological phenomenon is called *change blindness* [3][4].

In the next section we examined screen updating during saccade. The experimental setup is composed of an eye-tracking system and a graphic display. We investigated a set of parameters that must be considered to design an experimental system.

3.2   Inducing Saccade Using Dynamic Typographic Motion

In the second idea we tried to induce eye-movement while reading text using typographic motion. Moving fonts on the screen is a common idea to attract the attention of the viewer. We used the idea to lead the eye gaze while reading text.

We investigated preferable type of guide for rapid reading, preferable length of text, and the limitation of reading speed.

4   Screen Update During Saccade

We have already mentioned about the idea that facilitate the reading. This section discusses the saccade detection by eye-tracking system, and the feasibility of the idea, that is, whether the screen modification without being noticed by reader is really possible, and how much saccadic suppression works effectively for it.

The eye movement while reading is discontinuous. It has two states that are called *fixations* and *saccades*. Fixations are the periods that the eyes are almost stationary; these periods are usually between 150 and 500ms. Between two successive fixations there are a period, called saccade, where the eyes are moving rapidly. People stare at a place and capture a certain length of text string; normally it is 5 to 8 characters in Japanese reading. Eye-gaze jumps onto the next place and captures the string again and again [1]. Fixated points depend on reader's knowledge, experience and difficulty of text document.

It is well known that a stimulus such as a blinking object can catch reader's attention. As the same reason we expect that gaze control is possible with the use of such stimuli. However, such stimulus may disturb reader's primary activity of understanding when it is too strong. Readers are likely only to follow the stimuli without understanding the sentence.

We are, thus, intrigued by peripheral vision and saccadic suppression. Visual acuity in peripheral vision is drastically worse than in fovea, and the image during saccade is not seen clearly. If the system stimulates in peripheral vision and erase it during saccade, eye gaze will be guided to the position of the stimulation while reader does not perceive its existence.

4.1 Computer Display and Saccadic Suppression

We conducted the following experiment to investigate saccadic suppression for computer display. Similar experiments were conducted by Triesch et. al. [5][7]. They developed a saccade contingent updating system using head mounted-display (HMD). But they did not measure the amount of saccadic suppression around saccadic eye-movement.

Method of Experiment. The percentages of perception to the change on the screen, under two situations, are compared to examine our idea.

The first test examines how much a subject is sensitive to the change on the screen (Fig.1-(a)). Subjects are asked to keep on looking at the center of screen. Two text strings are placed on both sides of the screen. These strings are 5-character nonsense Japanese words. One of those characters is replaced with other character at a random timing. The length of a nonsense word is chosen so as to be viewed with a single fixation.

The other test is to examine whether the same change is noticed if the change occurs during saccade (Fig.1-(b)). A subjects is asked to stare at a text string at one side. Then, the subject is asked to cause a saccade by moving the eyes rapidly to the text string at the other side of the screen. One of five characters at the destination which is randomly selected changes with a certain probability during the period.

We expect that the change in Fig.1-(a) is highly sensitive even though the change is shown in the peripheral vision, while percentage in Fig.1-(b) will decrease because of saccadic suppression. In addition, we tested various delay time between saccade detection and character update. It demonstrates the amount of the saccadic suppression with respect to the stage of eye movement.

Experimental Setup and Evaluation of Timing of the System. The system used in the experiment is shown in Fig.2. The system redraws the computer display when a signal is sent from a process that detects saccade of the subject. The left PC (PC1) observes the eye movements with a pair of CCD cameras. The images are sampled at 60Hz and are sent to ISCAN RK-464 and RK726PCI/RK620PC. Image processing of eye gaze detection is done within a single frame period. PC1 sends the parameters of eye gaze and other auxiliary information to another PC (PC2) via RS232C. PC2 calculates the distance of eye gaze between successive frames, and reports the saccade detection when the distance exceeds a threshold. When a saccade is detected display screen is updated. The display is a 1280-pixel 21 inch CRT (EIZO FlexScan T960) whose

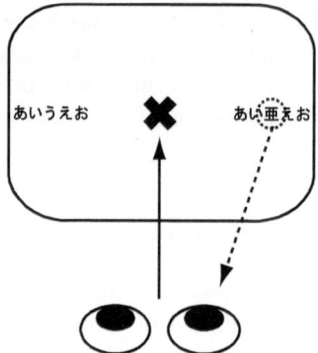 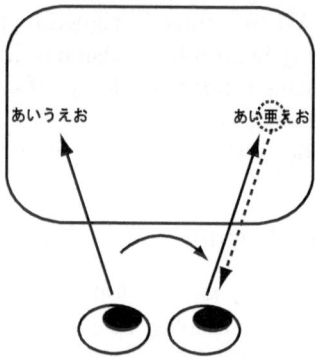

(a) Fix the eyes at the center of screen. Text strings are at both sides. One of characters randomly changes sometimes.

(b) Move the eyes intentinally from side to side. One of charecters at the destination changes during saccade.

Fig. 1. Two Experimental Conditions to Investigate Saccadic Suppression

refresh rate is 120Hz. This is the maximal resolution of the CRT at this frequency. The dot pitch of the CRT is 0.25mm. The graphic card used in the system is RADEON 8500.

We need to estimate the timing that the apparatus operates since the character update must be done within limited timing. In the system PC1 and PC2 operate asynchronously. Outline of the system operation is as follows.

1. PC1 captures the images of eyes and calculates the position of the eyes every t_s(ms). This is the sampling time of the eye-tracking system.
2. When the eyes start moving, PC1 captures the image t_s(ms) after t_0. The image processing of eye requires another t_s.
3. PC2 receives its coordinate after t_d(ms) because of the transmission latency of RS232C (≈ 1.8(ms)).
4. PC1 keeps capturing and sends the next position to PC2. It takes $t_s + t_d$.
5. PC2 calculates the difference between the positions of successive two frames. This calculation takes t_p(ms).
6. After the calculation, PC2 waits for v-sync signal and then redraws the screen. The maximal wait time is t_r(ms). Another t_r is required for redrawing.

We have confirmed the difference calculation is done within a refresh cycle of the video card. Therefore t_p is t_r for the worst case. Overall, the total time T needed to redraw after saccade is estimated by the following equation.

$$T = 3t_c + t_d + \Delta\tau + t_p + 2t_r$$
$$\approx 77 + \Delta\tau[\text{ms}]$$

where $\Delta\tau$ is the delay inserted to control the timing of redraw. The time schedule is illustrated in Fig.3.

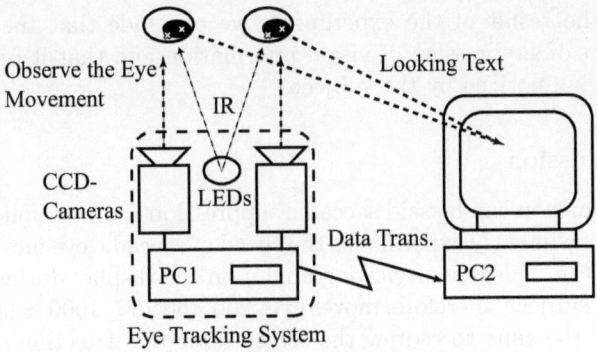

Fig. 2. System Overview

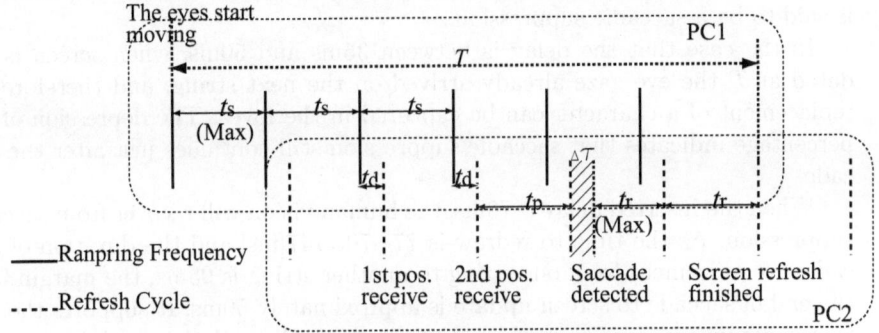

Fig. 3. Time Schedule

In the experiment, the width of the font is 28 pixels. Each nonsense text string consists of 5 characters, totally 140-pixel width. Thus 140 pixels are occupied at both sides of the screen. After all 1000-pixel width is the gap. Since saccade time for the gap is generally longer than T, display redrawing can be completed during saccadic movement.

4.2 Results

Subjects are two male and four female, age of 20 to 33. Table1 shows the percentage that the subject noticed the change in case of subjects looking at the center of the screen. Three subjects are sensitive to the change (marked in Table1-(a)). These three subjects are asked to detect the change during saccades. The delay $\Delta\tau$ is randomly chosen from 0, 35, 50, 70, and 105[ms]. The result is Table1-(b).

The percentage of (a) for subjects A, B and E is between 70 and 80. Since it is comparable to the percentage of (b) when the range of delay is from 70 to 105 ms, we can conclude that no suppression can be found in this range of delay. The percentage decreases when the delay is 35 to 50ms. Information is almost completely suppressed when the delay is zero.

From the result of the experiment, we conclude that the system controls the amount of suppression of visual information and that it updates the screen without being noticed by the subject.

4.3   Discussion

The phenomenon can be said saccadic suppression from the following discussion.

In the preliminary experiment, the speed of saccadic eye movement was about 200 pixels (i.e. 5 degree of viewing angle) on the display during 1/60 second on average. A subject, therefore, moves eyes $200 \times 60 \times 77/1000 \approx 900$(pixels) during T which is the time to redraw the screen after the detection of saccade. Thus, the estimated position of eye-gaze at T is just before the next string at the other side of the screen, and is close enough to detect the replacement of a character of the word according to the result of (a). Consequently, the decrease of percentage is said to be a saccadic suppression.

In the case that the delay is between 35ms and 50ms, when screen is updated at T the eye gaze already arrived on the next string, and therefore the replacement of a character can be captured in the fovea. The depression of the percentage indicates that saccadic suppression still continues just after the saccade.

When the inserted delay is 70ms, the human vision will recover from saccadic suppression. As the time to redraw is 77+70=147[ms] and the duration of saccadic eye movement from one string to another string is 95ms, the margin from the end of saccade to screen update is approximately 50ms. It supports the fact that saccadic suppression lasts about 50ms after the end of saccade [6].

When the delay is 105ms, the percentage is as high as (a). This is because the eyes have competely recovered from saccadic suppression.

The results are perfectly explained by the fact that stimulation to peripheral vision is suppressed during saccadic eye movement. The experiment also proves that text modification during saccade can be done without being noticed if saccade detection and image refresh are performed with appropriate timing.

Currently, the system works only if the eye movement is long enough on the screen because of the time for saccade detection and display redraw. For reading of a Japanese text, the average distance of saccade is only 2 to 5 characters (mostly 3 or 4)[1]. Suppose eye-gaze jumps 3.5 characters during a saccade, it is equivalent to 98 pixels of the screen in our system, or 2.8° of viewing direction. The duration of saccade is only 8.2ms! Video-based eye tracking systems is inadequate for this purpose. A solution is non-NTSC eye gaze measurement system whose sample rate is several times higher than video-based system.

5   Rapid Reading Guided by Eye Leading

5.1   General Aspect of Speed Reading

Paper is the most widely used media to carry information such as texts. Texts are often provided as electronic document today. The most characteristic difference

Table 1. Percentage that the change was noticed. (Noticed/Changed)

(a) The percentage that the subject noticed the change in the peripheral area when the eye gaze is fixed on the center of the screen. Three subjects are sensitive to the change.

	Age	Sex	Percentage(%)	
A:	32	F	30/ 34=88.2	√
B:	33	F	91/128=71.1	√
C:	20	M	35/118=29.7	
D:	20	F	56/108=51.9	
E:	28	M	73/ 99=73.7	√
F:	20	F	46/126=36.5	

(b) The percentage that the subject noticed the change when image is changed during saccade. The subjects are A, B, and E.

Delay	Percentage(%)
0	12/259= 4.6
35	60/224=26.8
50	84/210=40.0
70	172/228=75.4
105	204/235=86.8

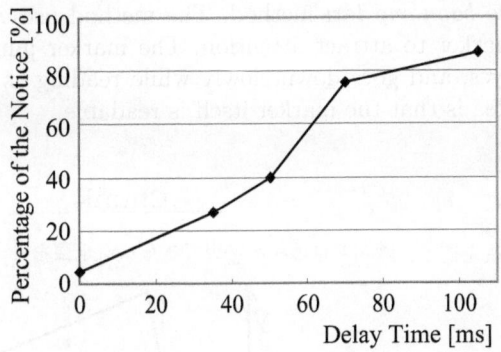

Fig. 4. Percentage of the Noticed to the Change in the Screen

is that electronic text can have many typographical variations in font style or in color. In addition electronic text can dynamically change the style of display according to user's reaction. Paper documents, on the other hand, are very static. We studied a preferable use of this characteristic to achieve effective reading on a computer screen.

A native Japanese typically reads 500 to 700 characters in a minute. The speed becomes more than 2,500 after a special training of rapid reading. The purpose of the research described in the section is to design such a speed-reading aided by computer system without any special training. We investigated the feasibility of the speed-reading with computer aid.

First we summarize known reasons that decrease the speed of reading text.

- Reading word by word
- Oral reading
- Reading with lip movement
- Talking in mind (Silent Reading)
- Regression of eye gaze
- Difficulty of line feed
- Irregular eye movement

If these problems are solved it can be possible to increase the speed of reading. In particular, we are interested in eye movement. Reading speed will increase when the eye movement becomes refined, e.g. less fixation, less regression, smooth line feed and shorter duration of fixation.

In previous researches various approach for speed reading have proposed such as Vertical Scrolling, Times Square Scrolling, Rapid Serial Visual Presentation (RSVP), Segmented Text, and Controlled-Rate Text [8]. None of them provide a satisfactory result, some of them are even worse. These approaches adopt different style of display from the usual text display, and this type of form show less information at once. We like to provide text document with usual form; our approach is not to move the text but to move the eyes on appropriate position and timing by giving a marker to catch reader's attention. If the marker is too salient, reader may only follow after the marker without reading. The marker must be selected so that it never disturb reading while it controls the eye's speed.

We propose *bouncing text* method. The method uses vertical movement of strings as a marker to attract attention. The marker jumps up to attract the attention of eyes, and goes down slowly while reading as shown in Fig.5. The point of the idea is that the marker itself is readable.

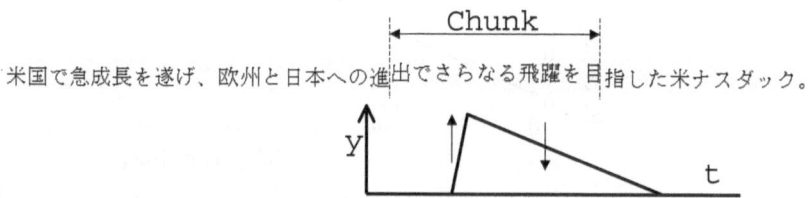

Fig. 5. Bouncing Text. Selected chunk moves up rapidly and then moves down slowly

5.2   Experiments

We examined how much effectively the bouncing text works for speed-reading. Texts used for the experiments are columns of a Japanese newspaper. Each column have 1100 characters on the average, roughly 60 characters×25 lines. Subjects read 30days of columns on the experiment. After reading each column they are asked to answer a questionaire which has three questions with three alternatives to check if the subject understand the topic. First, a subject reads a set of columns to derive ordinary reading speed. Then, a subject reads another set with eye leading, with bouncing text.

Each text is divided into chunks of characters on the experiment and bouncing text leads eyes chunk by chunk. The number of the chunk is seven or ten.

Experiment 1: Fixed Speed. Leading speed is 20% faster than the fastest pace on the first examination (ordinary reading). We checked whether if the lowering of understanding is found or not in the experiment with the questionnaire. No degradedness is found from the result.

Experiment 2: Variable Speed. Subject read a set of column as same as the previous experiment except that the speed of eye leading becomes 20% faster (slower) if three questions are all correct (not all correct). The final speed is expected to converge to the fastest speed of reading without lowing of understanding.

Experiment 3: Comparing Preference. We examined the preference of eye leading method. In the experiment another type of eye leading method that uses a simple red frame to enclose a chunk is tested to compare the performance and preference.

Totally, a subject is asked to answer the seven types of experiment summarized in Table 2.

Table 2. Types of Eye Leading Method

1 Ordinary reading
To check ordinary reading speed and personal difference
2 Bouncing text with 7-chracter chunk
To show the effect of eye leading
3 Bouncing text with 10-chracter chunk
To derive effective length of chunking
4 Bouncing text with 7-chracters chunk and variable speed
To estimate the limitation of reading speed
5 Eye leading with 7-chunk enclosed by a red frame
To see reader's preference of marker
6 Ordinary reading
To check learning effect

5.3   Results

Experiments were done about ten subjects. In the first experiment of ordinary reading, they read at 450-940 characters per minute and the average is about 660 char/min. The result is consistent with the previous reports (500-700 char/min). The score of the questionnaire is 1.9-2.6 on the average.

Fig.6, reading speed of each subject for 30 days of column, shows that reading speed depends on individual difference rather than difficulty of topic. The graph shows that the reading speed is almost stable except small fluctuation during 30 trials. No learning effect is found from the result of ordinary reading. Comparison of the score for each examination is shown in Fig.8. No significant difference of score was found among six types of leading method described in Table 2. The score for the second examination is slightly low, but it is not because of the reading speed since the others show higher score despite the similar pace of reading. From the result, we conclude that the eye leading does not lower the understanding during reading.

Then, how much faster can a subject read text? We define the limit reading speed as the state that the average of the three most recent score converges to

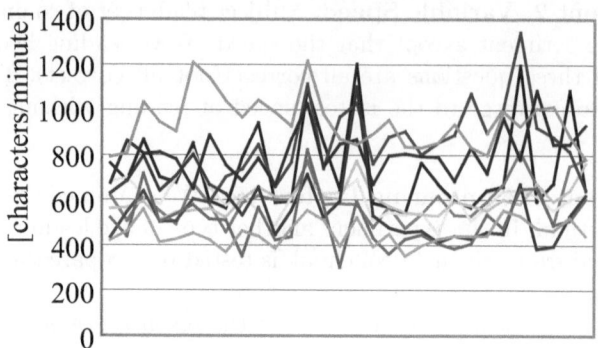

Fig. 6. Ordinary Reading Speed of Ten Subjects. Texts are columns of a newspaper for 30 days. (Experiment 1)

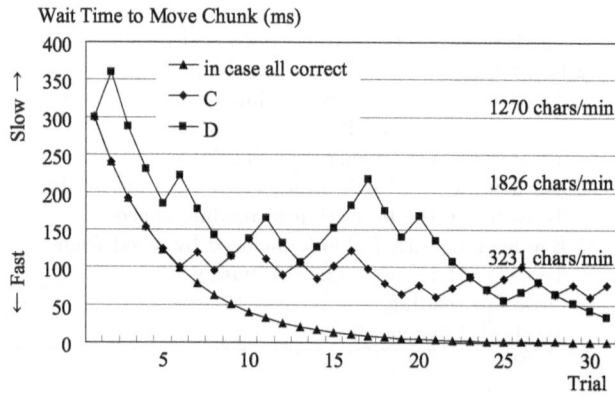

Fig. 7. The result of variable speed. (Experiment 2) of trial increases

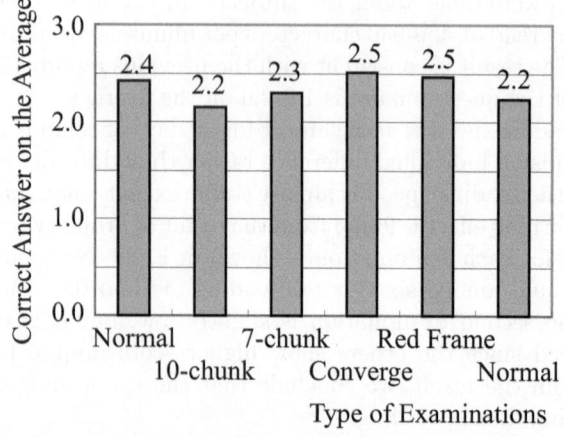

Fig. 8. Correct Answer for the Questionnaire (Experiment 3)

a certain value. In our experiment, the pace of reading is 300-700ms initially, converges to 60-160ms finally as shown in Fig.7. This number is 3.5-12 times faster than the ordinary reading, equivalent to 2500-7300 characters a minute while it is 450-940 initially. The average score when the speed converged was 2.5.

At the last of the series of experiment, subjects are asked to read ordinarily without eye leading again. Reading speed for the last test was 580-1100 char/min. The result is shown in Fig.9. This graph indicates that small learning effect between the 1st and the 6th experiments exists. However, the final speed of the 5th experiment is several times faster than the speed of the 6th experiment. This is a proof that eye leading accelerates reading speed.

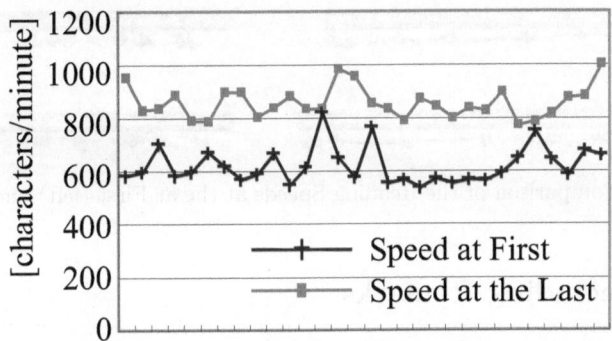

Fig. 9. Comparison of reading speeds for type 1 and for type 6 in Table 2

5.4   Discussion

Does Bouncing Text Leads Eye Gaze? – Yes and No. We can conclude from the experiments that the speed-reading *with computer assistant* is possible. But it does not mean that *speed-reading with fixation control* is possible because the method only control the pace of eye-movement. As we discussed about speed-reading with eye leading in this section, optimal control of fixation position is desirable.

The result of this section showed a hint of eye-gaze control for speed-reading. Subjects says that they could intuitively accustom to the speed-reading with bouncing text. This type of visual stimulation is essentially a calm technology of display. It is less disruptive than other visual cues, such as color, slant, and thickness.

The Size of Chunk and the Position of Fixation. The location of the fixation in the case of 7-character chunk are similar to ordinary reading rather than that of 10-charater chunk as shown in Fig.10. It is generally said that eyes see 5-8 characters at a fixation; 10 characters may be too long. This might be a reason why the score for 10-character chunk is lower than others.

We only tested columns of a newspaper constantly divided by equal length in the text. The preference expected to be improved if chunking is done syntactically, and if leading is done considering the semantics of text.

It is, however, not so simple because the reading speed and the length of saccade depends on the difficulty of the text. When the text is a light fiction the speed is high and the saccade length is long, on the other hand, low speed and short saccade with frequent regressions when a text of philosophy.

Fig. 10. Comparison of the Reading Speeds at the at First (left) and the Last (right)

6   Concluding Remarks

In the project we demonstrated a possibility of new display methods. They use dynamic image updating methods that take into account psychological effects. In the research we experimented two types of display based on eye-gaze control.

The first method uses a psychological phenomenon called saccadic suppression, in which information transmission is suppressed during rapid eye movement. Using saccadic suppression mechanism, a kind of change blindness, the image on the display can be changed gradually without being perceived by the subject. Such information control mechanisms can cause un-natural psychological experiences to the user. A few reseachers already started to use the change blind effect. Intille proposes *Change Blind Information Display*. His idea is to design an intelligent interface system between ubiquitous displays and computer to reduce disruption caused by display updating [9].

The second method accelerates the speed of eye movement while reading. In human vision, the destination of eye movement is computed based on peripheral vision. Eye movement, therefore, can be controlled by some sophisticated displaying method to the periphery. Our system presents moving cues to attract attention in peripheral vision using computer graphics to guide eye movement.

As stated in Prof. Morita's report in this proceedings, human model of vision is, actually, more sophisticated than we expected. The human vision is non-uniform, dynamic and task-oriented system. We have used only a little part of knowledge of human to design a display. So, there may be further possibility in displaying method.

We indicated ideas of dynamic visual display in the future. We, of course, need further work to realize a practical system. As movie was invented one hundred yeas ago, novel display method will be invented. There is no doubt that collaboration of engineers and psychologists is necessary to promote these ideas.

References

1. R. Osaka, "Experimental Psychology of Eye Movements", The University of Nagoya Press, Japan, 1993.
2. K. Rayner and A. Pollatsek, "The Psychology of Reading", Lawrence Erlbaum Associates, UK, 1989
3. R. A. Rensink, "Seeing, sensing, and scrutinizing", Vision Research, 40, pp. 1469–1487, 2000
4. D. J. Simons, "Curent Approaches to Change Blindness", Visual Cognition, 7, (1/2/3), pp. 1–15, 2000
5. J. Triesch, B. T. Sullivan, M. M. Hayhoe and D. H. Ballard, "Saccade Contingent Updating in Virtual Reality", Proceedings of the symposium on ETRA 2002: eye tracking research and applications symposium, pp. 95–102, 2002
6. "Dependence of Visual Suppression on the Amplitude of Saccade and Blinks" Vision Research, (26), 11, pp. 1815–1824, 1986
7. J. Truesch, D. H. Ballard, M. M. Hayhoe, "What you see is what you need", Journal of Vision, (3), pp. 86–94, 2003
8. M. S. Castelhano, P. Muter, "Optimizing the reading of electronic text using rapid serial visual presentation" Behaviour & Information Technology, (20), 4, pp. 237–247, 2001
9. S. S. Intille, "Change Blind Information Display for Ubiqutous Computing Environments", UbiComp 2002, LNCS2498, pp. 91–106, 2002

3D Space Framework
for the Multi-facet Accessing
of Database Records

Makoto Ohigashi and Yuzuru Tanaka

Meme Media Laboratory, Hokkaido University,
N.13 W.8, Kita-ku Sapporo 060-8628, Japan
{ohigashi,tanaka}@meme.hokudai.ac.jp

Abstract. This paper proposes a framework for the construction of a 3D information access space that supports users to intuitively access large amounts of information. To cope with a large set of database records, we need a dynamic method for organizing and accessing records through multiple different views, such as topological, temporal, categorical, hierarchical and alphabetical views. In the proposed information space architecture, each record is visualized together with its related views, called facets. Each facet is provided as a 3D window-like component that displays a relevant information space on its surface and works as an entrance gate to the space. Through facet components, we can catch a glimpse of more detailed or related information spaces. We can also access relevant records by diving into arbitrarily chosen one of these spaces. Users can dynamically edit these multiple views in order to change the navigation and visualization functions by directly selecting and manipulating facet components.

1 Introduction

Recently, interactive information visualization of a large set of data or records is one of the most perspective applications of interactive 3D graphics. Simultaneously, the growth of the storage technologies derives a large set of data or records in databases. To cope with such volumes of information, users need efficient methods for organizing and accessing database records through various types of views. Conventional 3D visualization systems provide efficient methods for accessing a large amount of information[1, 2]. However, these systems provide *static* information spaces tightly coupled with the data structure, such as hierarchical data on the file systems[3–5] or nested-relations in an OODB[6, 7]. To support efficient access to large amounts of information, it is necessary to change the navigating functions dynamically such a way R.S.Wurman described[8].

CastingNet[9] is a hypermedia system for organizing and accessing semi-structured data such as those over the WWW. This system represents each data item as a frame with a list of attributes, and a relationship among frames as an axis associated with one attribute of frames. Users can combine some axes

G. Grieser and Y. Tanaka (Eds.): Intuitive Human Interface 2004, LNAI 3359, pp. 142–158, 2004.

to organize a large set of frames. This approach allows users to define an axis using only one attribute. However, in order to obtain the required information from a large information repository, it is necessary to narrow down a large set of information by restricting the multiple attributes of data or records.

This paper proposes a framework for generating a 3D information space that supports users to organize and access information through multiple views. Our approach enables users to change their navigation and visualization functions dynamically in order to obtain their required information. In the proposed information space architecture, each database record is visualized together with multiple different views of the record, called facets. A facet works as a basis for organizing and accessing database records related to an arbitrary number of attributes. It allows users to organize and access database records through various views, including topological, temporal, categorical, hierarchical and alphabetical views, as R.S. Wurman said[8].

This paper also proposes a component-based framework for automatic creation of a proposed information access space. We construct a multi-facet information access space as a composition with 3D interactive components. It allows users to access relevant information by diving into another space repeatedly through arbitrarily chosen one of the facets. Furthermore, users can dynamically change their navigation and visualization functions by directly selecting and manipulating facet components.

The remainder of the paper is organized as follows. In chapter 2, we describe the concept of our proposed information access space, called MFIS. Chapter 3 gives the details of the implementation architecture and the automatic creation mechanism of an MFIS. Chapter 4 illustrates an example spatial navigation in an MFIS and an experimental evaluation. Finally, we make some concluding remarks.

2   The Concept

In order to obtain the required information from a large information repository, we need to explore information through multiple different views, including categorical, topological and temporal views. This paper proposes a 3D information access space that supports such explorations by associating multiple views with each database record. These views are called *facets* of each record. The information space, in which each record is visualized together with multiple facets, is called a Multi-Facet Information access Space, or an MFIS for short.

In this chapter, we illustrate the concept of a multi-facet of a record and a new information access method through such multiple facets. Next, we suggest the mappings of such an information access process to the users' navigation process in virtual spaces.

2.1   Multi-facet Information Access

Fig. 1 shows the concept of a multi-facet information access. In order to simplify the following explanations, let us use a historical database relation R, which

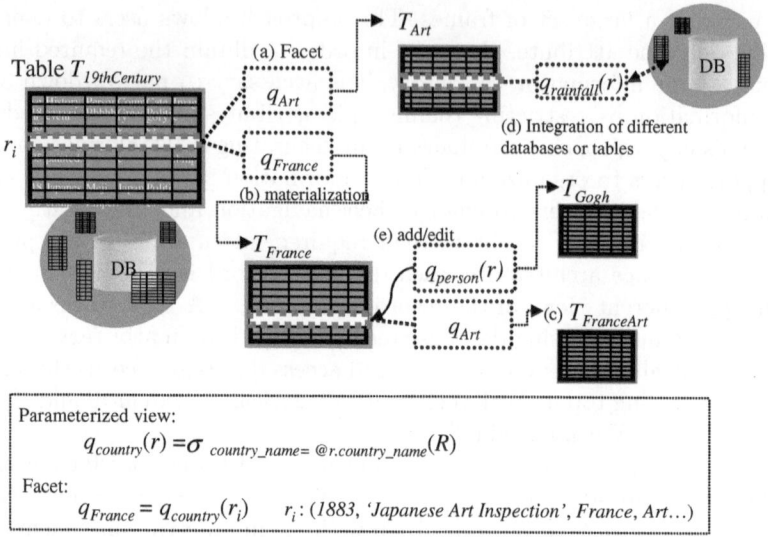

Fig. 1. The Multi-Facet Information Access.

contains attributes (*year, title, country_name, category, person_name, ...*). A relational table $T_{19thCentury}$ in Fig. 1 is the result of a query $q_{19thCentury}(= \sigma_{1800<year\leq1900}(R))$. The following discussion, which used the specific relation R, is easily applicable to general relations. Furthermore, our architecture can be easily extended to cope with more than one relation as described in later subsection.

Multi-facet of a Record. In relational data model, we can consider an arbitrary query as a virtual relation, or a virtual table, called a database view[10]. It means that users can define an arbitrary new viewpoint as a database view. Suppose that users may browse the relation R through different views, including temporal(such as "19th century", "1870's" or "1998"), topological("Europe", "Germany" or "Berlin"), alphabetical(e.g. concerned with "Vincent van Gogh") and categorical(scientific, political, economical or artistic, etc.) views. We can define these views as parameterized queries, i.e. parameterized views. For instance, a topological view is defined as a following record-parameterized view,

$$q_{country}(r) = \sigma_{Country(r)}(R)$$
$$Country(r) : country\_name = @r.\mathbf{country\_name}$$

where @r.**country_name** part is the value of *country_name* attribute of a record r. When this view is instantiated by a record value, it becomes a **facet** of this record, e.g. the $q_{country}(r)$ is instantiated by the record r_i(*1883, 'Japanese Art Inspection', France, Art, ...*) to become a France facet q_{France}(see Fig. 1(a)). Other records similarly instantiate this view to work as a Japan facet or Germany facet etc.

We can define more complicated facet using two or more attributes. The following parameterized view q_{decade} gives a temporal and categorical view of focusing on, for example, the economical events in the decade around "the Great Depression(1837)".

$$q_{decade}(r) = \sigma_{Decade(r)}(R)$$
$$Decade(r) : category = @r.\text{category}$$
$$\wedge @r.\text{year} - 5 \leq year \leq @r.\text{year} + 5$$

Associating various types of parameterized views with a record, users can browse multiple different facets of the database record.

Facets Using Different Databases or Relations. A data model that gives multiple viewpoints to a single table is commonly referred to as a star schema model[11]. A star schema model contains a centralized table known as a fact table and its highly normalized tables known as dimension tables. However, this model has some operational limitations due to the distinction of these two tables. Our approach allows users to use different tables in the same or different databases for the definition of a facet because it is given as an arbitrary database view(see Fig. 1(d)). Suppose that a relational table S is a weather database relation, we can define the following facet combining a historical table R and a weather table S,

$$q_{rainfall}(r) = \Pi_{S.month, S.rainfall}(\sigma_{Rainfall(r)}(R \bowtie S))$$
$$Rainfall(r) : S.country = @r.\text{country} \wedge S.year = @r.\text{year}.$$

This facet defines a view that represents local monthly precipitation related to a historical event r. Furthermore, we can define another facet using these or other relation tables, and associate it with one of the record in the table T_{Art}.

Information Access Through Facets. In general information retrieval systems, users can obtain the required information through the recursive querying process, i.e. modifying existing queries and retrieving their results repeatedly. Turning now to the facets, an existing query is modified by the instantiation of a parameterized view, and its result is retrieved by the materialization of the instantiated view(see Fig. 1(b)). In such a process, we consider two different retrieving methods according to the users' intentions. (i) One is a method to retrieve the relevant information by specifying a new condition or integrating different relations as described in the above subsection. (ii) The other is a method to narrow down the current view by restricting the condition of the current focusing view. Consider now the case of the facet q_{France} in Fig. 1, we can define the following two types of facets,

(i) $q_{France} = \sigma_{Country(r_i)}(R)$

(ii) $q_{France} = \sigma_{Country(r_i)}(q_{19thCentury}) = \sigma_{Country(r_i) \wedge 1800 < year \leq 1900}(R)$

The facet (i) q_{France} selects historical events in France *of all date* from the relational table R. The other facet (ii) q_{France} selects historical events in France *in the 19th century*. The former facet is called an *extensional* facet and the latter is called a *restrictive* facet. Using the restrictive facets recursively, users can narrow down large tables. Through the two *restrictive* facets q_{France} and q_{Art} as shown in Fig. 1(c), we can obtain the relational table $T_{FranceArt}$ that contains the Artistic events in France in the 19th century.

Customization of the Facets. Associating an arbitrary parameterized view with a record, user can browse database through a new viewpoint. For example, let us consider the case that a user needs to associate a new alphabetical view 'person' with one record in the table T_{France} as shown in Fig. 1(e). First, users define a parameterized view $q_{person}(r)(= \sigma_{person\_name=@r.person\_name}(R))$. When the user associates it with the record $(\ldots, Gogh, \ldots)$, it makes a new facet q_{Gogh} of the record. Then, the facet retrieves a table T_{Gogh} containing records concerned with the whole Gogh's life in a database R.

2.2 Mapping of Database Elements to 3D Objects

The purpose of our work is to associate the database exploration process with a spatial navigation process in virtual spaces. In order to create such an information access space, we need a method to map database elements, such as relational tables, records and facets, to component objects in virtual spaces. Table 1 shows our mapping framework between database elements and component objects in virtual spaces. Fig. 2 shows the virtual space generated from the result of the mapping of the database elements in Fig. 1.

A database table is mapped into an individual virtual space, e.g. the relational table $T_{19thCentury}$ in Fig. 1 is mapped to the 19thCentury-Space in Fig. 2. Each record in a relational table is mapped into a record object in a virtual space, e.g. records in the relational table T_{France} are mapped to record objects in *France*-Space. A record object is a 3D visual object that holds the value of a corresponding record as a list of attribute values. A facet of a record is mapped to a facet object of a record object, e.g. the facets q_{France} and q_{Art} of the record r_i are mapped to the facet objects f_{France} and f_{Art} of the record object r_i. The result table of the materialized facet is also mapped to a virtual space. A facet object displays the mapped space on its surface like a 3D window and works as an entrance gate to it, e.g. the facet object f_{France} displays the *France*-Space and enables us to enter this space.

Table 1. Primitive database constructs and their corresponding contents in a virtual space.

database constructs	virtual space elements
relational table/view	virtual space
record in a table	record object in a virtual space
facet of a record	facet object of a record object

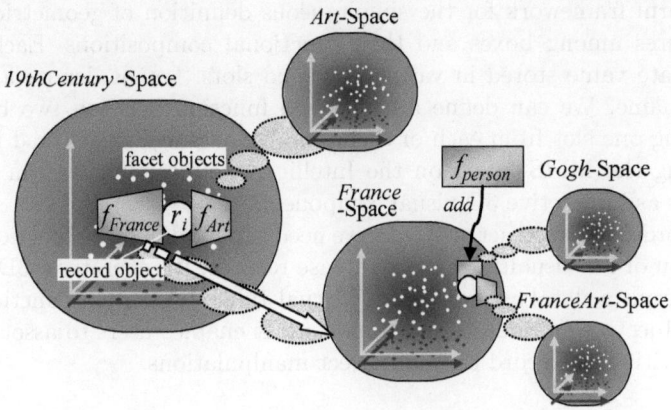

Fig. 2. The Multi-Facet Information Access Space.

These mappings result in the information access space as shown in Fig. 2, where users can explore database records through virtual space navigations. In this space, users can first browse the relational table $T_{19thCentury}$ by traveling around in the $19thCentury$-Space. Selecting one of the facet objects surrounding a focused record object, we can browse the relevant records of the focused record by diving into another information space. In Fig. 2, the user selects the facet object f_{France} surrounding the record object r_i and dives into the $France$-Space through this facet object. Let us denote this navigating function as follows,

$$19thCentury \xrightarrow{f_{country}} France.$$

The Addition of an *extensional* facet object f_{person} to one of the records in the $France$-Space enables users to access a new information space $Gogh$-Space. Let us also denote this navigating function as follows,

$$France \xrightarrow{\downarrow \tilde{f}_{person}} Gogh.$$

The proposed Information Space Architecture allows users to access a large information repository through the recursive spatial navigation. Furthermore, such navigation may retrieve the related information from different tables int the same or different databases in such a way as described in section 2.1.

3   Component-Based Framework

This chapter describes the details of our component-based framework for automatic creation of an MFIS. We use the IntelligentBox system[12] as the basis of construction of an MFIS. IntelligentBox system is a component-based visual software development system for interactive 3D graphic applications. This system represents objects as interactive 3D visual components, called boxes. It provides a uniform framework for the simultaneous definition of geometrical compound structures among boxes and their functional compositions. Each box has its own state value stored in variables, called slots. Let us denote a slot name as #slot_name. We can define a compound function between two boxes through selecting one slot from each of them and connecting the selected two slots. Developing the MFIS based on the IntelligentBox system, we can provide facet objects as interactive 3D visual components.

In order to construct an MFIS, we need two fundamental functions. One is the function of 3D visualization of database records. It generates a 3D visualization space from a database table or a virtual table. The other function provides a facet object as an interactive component. It enables users to associate arbitrary views with each record through direct manipulations.

3.1   3D Visualization of Database Records

A 3D visualization function of the retrieval records is realized by a Database Record Reification Box (DRRB)[13]. A DRRB is a composite box which visualizes database records as interactive components using user-defined visualization scheme. A DRRB consists of three basic components, including (i) a query evaluation, (ii) the visual representation of each record and (iii) the arrangement of a set of records, as shown in the Fig. 3(a).

A DBProxyBox works as an interface between a database management system(DBMS) and the IntelligentBox system. Users can use a set of database functions through a DBProxyBox. A DataSetManagementBox(DSMBox) virtually reifies each database record as an interactive component. A DSMBox stores a template box for visualizing the retrieved records. A GeometricalManagementBox (GMBox) geometrically arranges a set of records in a 3D virtual space. A GMBox holds a set of GM function boxes which specify a rule of records arrangement by composing a set of primitive geometrical functions, such as a coordinate origin box and coordinate axis boxes.

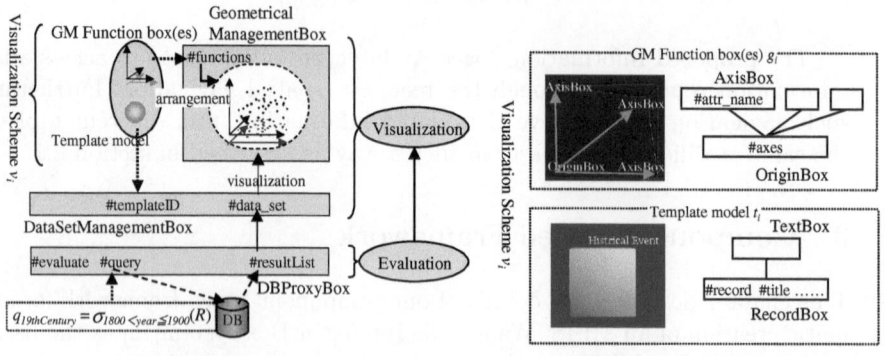

(a) The component-based architecture   (b) An example visualization scheme

Fig. 3. A Database Record Reification Box(DRRB).

Fig. 3(b) shows an example visualization scheme. A visualization scheme needs two types of visual mappings, an intrinsic mapping and an extrinsic mapping[14]. A visualization scheme consists of a template model and GM function boxes. A template model defines an intrinsic mapping which specifies how to represent each record. A template model consists of a RecordBox and a set of attribute representation boxes. We can use an arbitrary box provided by the IntelligentBox system as an attribute representation box. In Fig. 3(b), the template model t_i includes a TextBox that represents the value of the attribute slot #title of the RecordBox. GM function boxes define an extrinsic mapping which specifies how to arrange a set of records geometrically. Each of the GM function boxes is a primitive geometrical function box such as an OriginBox and an AxisBox. In Fig. 3(b), the GM function box g_i consists of an OriginBox and three Axis boxes. The #attr_name slot of each AxisBox specifies the corresponding name of attribute.

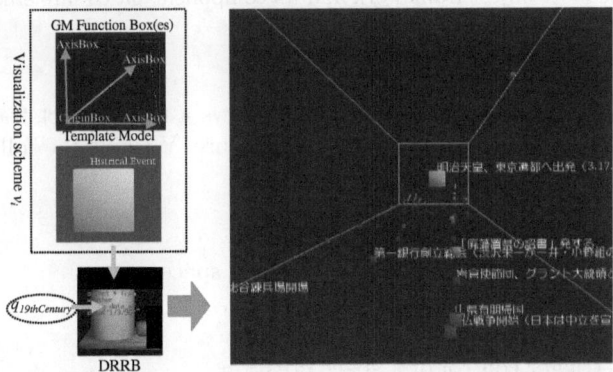

Fig. 4. An example visualization space of the table $T_{19thCentury}$.

Fig. 4 shows an example visualization space automatically generated by the DRRB which uses the visualization scheme v_i in Fig 3(b). In this example, a query $q_{19thCentury}$ is set in the #query slot of the DBProxyBox. The DBProxyBox retrieves the result table $T_{19thCentury}$ from a DBMS. The DSMBox and the GMBox generate the $19thCentury$-Space from the table $T_{19thCentury}$. Each record object represents the value of the attribute #title, because it is generated according to the template model t_i. The GM function box g_i arranges a set of record objects in the 3D space. In this case, the *category* attribute is mapped to the x-axis box, the *importance* attribute to the y-axis box, and the *year* attribute to the z-axis box. This space allows users to explore the history events in the 19th century.

3.2   Facet Object

In order to associate multiple different viewpoints with each of the record objects in the above space, a facet object needs a mechanism to be combined

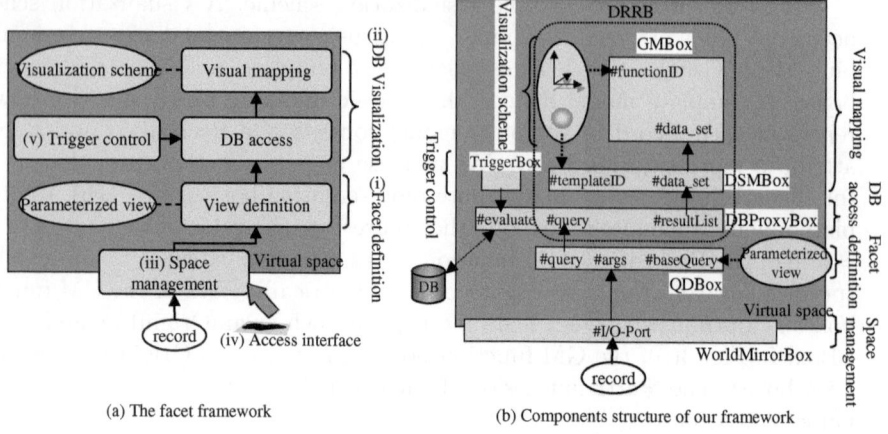

(a) The facet framework

(b) Components structure of our framework

Fig. 5. The facet-object framework and its component-based implementation architecture.

with an arbitrary record object. Fig. 5 shows a facet-object framework and its component-based implementation architecture. We give the following five functions to a facet component.

(i) a definition of a facet,
(ii) the mapping of a facet to a virtual space,
(iii) a representation of a virtual space,
(iv) an access interface to a virtual space,
(v) a trigger control of a space creation.

The function (i) enables users to associate different views with each of the database records. Each view is defined as a parameterized view. When a facet object is connected to a record object, a facet object specifies a facet from a given parameterized view. For example, when a parameterized view $q_{country}(r)$ is connected with a record (1878, 'The Treaty of Berlin', Germany, Politics, ...), it becomes a facet $q_{Germany}$. This function is provided by a QueryDefinitionBox(QDBox). A QDBox holds a parameterized view in the #baseQuery slot. When it receives a record value in its #args slot, it defines a facet from the parameterized view, and it stores the facet in the #query slot.

The function (ii) generates a visualization space from a facet. This function consists of two primitive functions, a query evaluation and a visualization of the retrieved records using a pre-registered visualization scheme. These functions are implemented as the functions of DRRB described in the previous section.

The function (iii) displays an arbitrary virtual space like a 3D window, in order to represent multiple facet objects together with a record object. Many preceding researches proposed such a function[15–17]. However, these systems provide no mechanism to define a functional linkage between a virtual space object and another objects. This means that it is impossible to combine a facet object with a record object. Therefore, we need a WorldMirrorBox[18] as the basis of a facet object. A WorldMirrorBox allows us to embed a 3D space in another 3D space environment. Users can see the contents of the embedded space through this 3D window-like WorldMirrorBox. Furthermore, we need another function that sends a record value to the #args slot of the QDBox in its embedded space. So, we extend the function of WorldMirrorBox to be able to send a record value to the inside objects through its #I/O-Port slot.

The function (iv) is provided by the World Mirror. The WorldMirrorBox allows users to dive into the embedded space. When a user has a collision with a WorldMirrorBox, the user can dive into the embedded space. It allows uses to navigate through the different spaces.

The function (v) is implemented as a TriggerBox. Since the MFIS structure is hierarchically nested, we need to control the timing of each space creation. A TriggerBox is connected with the #evaluate slot of the DBProxyBox. The DRRB generates a visualization space only when a TriggerBox issues a signal. A TriggerBox issues a signal only when a user enters to the space that includes a facet component. Each space is generated dynamically according to the user's database explorations process.

We realize the facet function by constructing these components as the structure as illustrated in Fig. 5(b).

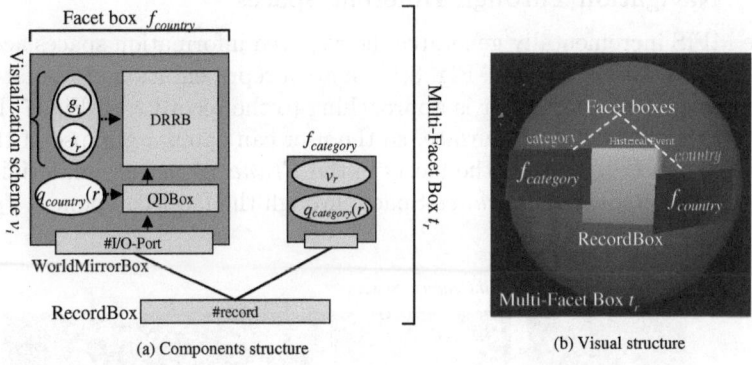

Fig. 6. A multi-facet box structure used as a template model for generating an MFIS and an example visual design.

3.3 Multi-facet Component

A multi-facet component consists of a record object and an arbitrary number of facet objects. The structure of a multi-facet component is shown in Fig. 6. Visualizing all the retrieval records as multi-facet components, we can construct an MFIS. The base component of a multi-facet component is a RecordBox. All the facet objects are connected to the #record slot of the RecordBox. When a facet object receives a record value, it assigns the value to a parameterized view stored in the #baseQuery slot of the QDBox. In Fig. 6, the facet object

$f_{country}$ holds a parameterized view $q_{country}(r)$, and the facet object $f_{category}$ holds another parameterized view $q_{category}(r)$. Using this multi-facet component t_r as the template model in each facet object recursively, we can incrementally create an infinitely nested MFIS.

3.4   Automatic Creation Process

Fig. 7 shows an example MFIS automatically generated by the DRRB in Fig. 3 which uses the multi-facet component in Fig. 6 as its template model. The DBProxyBox holds the query $q_{19thCentury}$. When a trigger signal is sent to the #evaluate slot of the DBProxyBox, the DRRB makes a copy of the multi-facet component for each of the retrieval records, and geometrically distributes a set of visualized records. The RecordBox of each multi-facet component receives the corresponding record value. When the record value is sent to all the connected facet components, each facet component defines an appropriate facet and materializes it, and it generates the result visualization space. As shown in Fig. 7, the facet component $f_{country}$ connected with the record object r_i (*1883, 'The 1st Japanese Art Inspection', France, Art, ...*) specifies a facet q_{France} from the parameterized view $q_{country}(r)$. Then, it generates a *France*-Space.

4   Spatial Navigation

4.1   Navigation Through Different Spaces

The MFIS incrementally generates the required information spaces according to the users' access behaviors. Fig. 8(a) shows a representation of the facet component f_{France} when the user is approaching to the record r_i in Fig. 7. It displays the *France*-Space on its surface, so the user can catch a glimpse of that space. As shown in Fig. 8(b), all the facets in the *France*-Space are materialized when the user enters into the *France*-Space through the facet component f_{France}. By

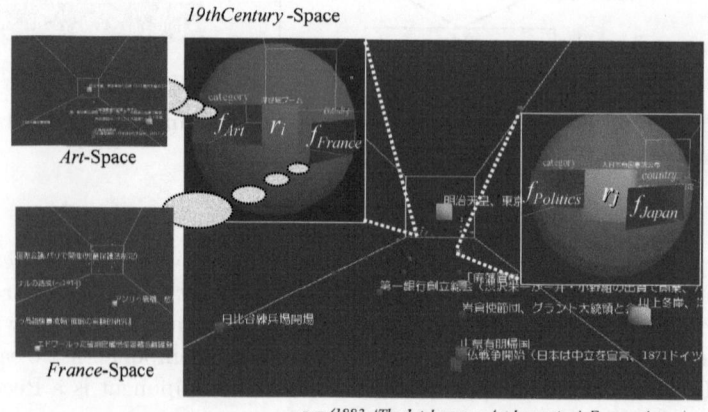

r_i = (1883, 'The 1st Japanese Art Inspection', France, Art, ...)
r_j = (1889, 'The Constitution of the Empire', Japan, Politics, ...)

Fig. 7. An example MFIS automatically generated by our framework.

traversing over the different spaces, users can narrow down a large set of records or retrieve the relevant records from different tables in the same or different databases.

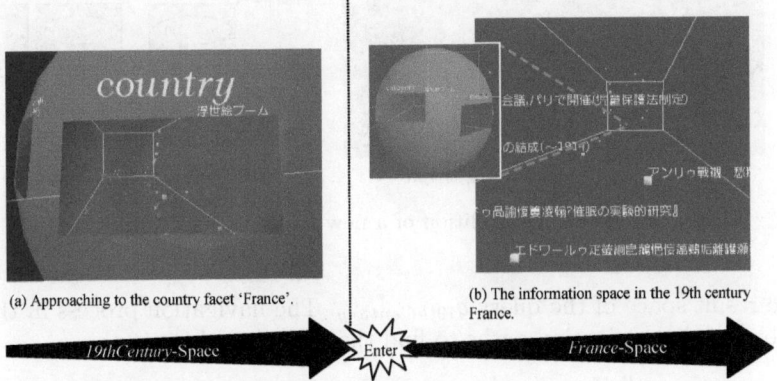

(a) Approaching to the country facet 'France'.

(b) The information space in the 19th century France.

19thCentury-Space   Enter   *France*-Space

Fig. 8. The process of entering into the *France*-Space.

4.2   Modification of Navigation Functions

As shown in the preceding, we can explore database records by traversing access different spaces using the pre-registered multiple facets. However, in order to obtain the required information, it is also necessary for users to modify the views dynamically on their navigation process. Our approach provides each facet component as an interactive component. It means that users can dynamically edit navigation functions through direct manipulations of facet components.

Fig. 9 shows an example modification of a facet component. The left panel in Fig. 9(a) shows a list of the pre-registered facet objects. Fig. 9(b) shows a change of the components structure of a multi-facet component when a facet is added. Suppose that a user needs to add a new viewpoint 'person' to one of the records. When the user selects a facet component f_{person} from the list panel and connects it to the RecordBox by drag-and-drop, the facet component instantiates the parameterized view $q_{person}(r)$ by the record value. If the *person_name* attribute value is '*Gogh*', it defines a facet q_{Gogh}. The TriggerBox of the facet component f_{Gogh} issues a trigger signal. Then, the facet component generates a *Gogh*-Space and displays that space on its surface. It means that it becomes to be possible for the user to access a new visualization space *Gogh*-Space.

In this way, our approach enables users to change their viewpoints dynamically in order to access different information spaces.

4.3   Example Navigation

Fig. 10 illustrates an example navigation in an MFIS generated from the historical table R described in Section 2.1. The *19thCentury*-Space in Fig.10(a) is

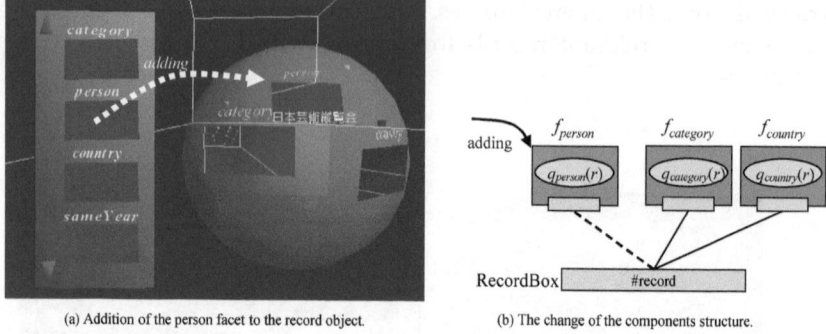

(a) Addition of the person facet to the record object.   (b) The change of the components structure.

Fig. 9. The addition of a new facet to a record object.

the result space of the query $q_{19thCentury}$. The navigation process in this figure is one of the navigation paths to find the following objective α,

α : *all the records concerned with a painter*
who has made a copy of the UKIYOE in France.

We assume that we start our navigation from the $19thCentury$-Space. As described in Section 2.2, we can denote a candidate navigation path as follows,

$$19thCentury \xrightarrow[0.161]{f_{country}} France \xrightarrow[0.341]{f_{category}} Art \xrightarrow[0.107]{\downarrow \tilde{f}_{person}} Gogh,$$

where the number under the first arrow shows the ratio of the entrances to $France$-Space in the total records in the $19thCentury$-Space. Such a ratio indicates how easy to enter the next space. The notation $\downarrow \tilde{f}_{person}$ means the addition of an extensional facet object f_{person} to a record.

In the $19thCentury$-Space shown in Fig. 10(a), each record object has two types of facets, $q_{country}(r)$ and $q_{category}(r)$. Through the restrictive facet object f_{France} of the record "The Napoleonic Code", we can enter the $France$-Space as shown in Fig. 10(b). Note that the 16.1% records in the $19thCentury$-Space have facet object f_{France}, which means that we can enter the $France$-Space through any of them. This navigation leads to the narrow down of the historical events to those *in France* in the 19th century.

In a similar way, entering the $FranceArt$-Space through one of the restrictive facet objects f_{Art} covering the 34.1% records in the $France$-Space, we can narrow down the historical events to the 399 historical events concerned with *France Art* in the 19th century(see Fig. 10(c)). In this space, we can see the records "The 1st Japanese Art Inspection" or "The Exhibition of UKIYOE", which suggest that the Japanese arts were in fashion around that time in France. The record "The copy of Japanese UKIYOE" is found in the neighborhood of them. As shown in Fig. 10(c), adding an *extensional* facet object f_{person} to the record, the facet generates the $Gogh$-Space as shown in Fig. 10(d). In the $Gogh$-Space, we can see Gogh's life. We may see that he was born in the Netherlands and immigrated to France where the Japanese arts are in fashion at that time.

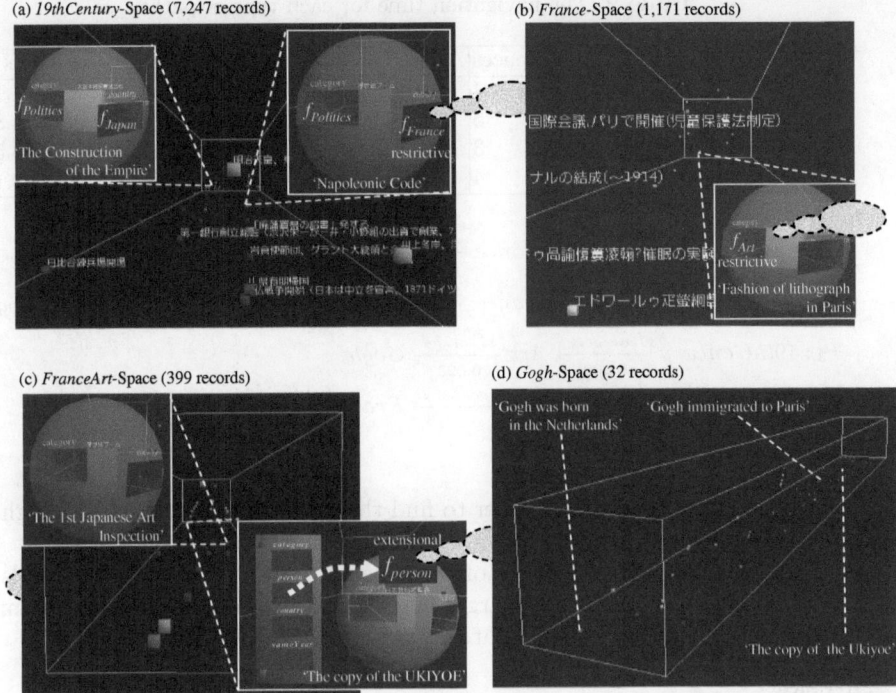

Fig. 10. An example navigation of a historical database in the MFIS.

4.4   Experiments

This section describes the experiment to show the effectiveness of the information access in which the user who is not familiar with databases issues the complicated queries described in chapter 2 using the interfaces realized in chapter 3. In order to address the advantage of the MFIS approach over the conventional query specifications, it may be appropriate to report how long time users spent to reach to the destination space. First, we gave the objective α, *"Find all the records concerned with a painter who has made a copy of the UKIYOE in France."*, to 10 users, and recorded their access behaviors starting from the 19thCentury-Space to the destination Gogh-Space. Before the experiments, they learned the way to move freely in a virtual space. And the 4 facets, $f_{country}$, $f_{category}$, f_{person} and f_{decade}, are given to them.

Table 2 shows times they spent to reach the Gogh-Space using the four different navigation paths, P_1, P_2, P_3 and P_4. These paths are given below the table. The average time denotes how much time they spent in one space. The path P_1 introduced in Fig. 10 needs the average time of almost 61 seconds. The P_4 takes almost 62 seconds in similar process to the P_1. The P_2 takes the longest total time of about 75 seconds, because it required 5 steps to reach the destination. However, it takes the least time of about 15 seconds per one space. On the other hand, the P_3 needs only 3 steps, but it takes the longest average time of almost 23 seconds. The reason why P_3 takes so much time per

Table 2. The navigation time for each type of paths.

Navigation Path	Number of Spaces	Average Time(s/space)	Total Time(s)
P_1	4	15.27	61.10
P_2	5	14.97	74.85
P_3	3	22.85	68.56
P_4	4	15.53	62.11

$$P_1 : 19thCentury \xrightarrow[0.161]{f_{country}} France \xrightarrow[0.341]{f_{category}} Art \xrightarrow[0.107]{\downarrow \tilde{f}_{person}} Gogh$$

$$P_2 : 19thCentury \xrightarrow[0.161]{f_{country}} France \xrightarrow[0.341]{f_{category}} Art \xrightarrow[0.190]{\downarrow f_{decade}} Decade \xrightarrow[0.160]{\downarrow \tilde{f}_{person}} Gogh$$

$$P_3 : 19thCentury \xrightarrow[0.200]{f_{category}} Art \xrightarrow[0.022]{\downarrow \tilde{f}_{person}} Gogh$$

$$P_4 : 19thCentury \xrightarrow[0.200]{f_{category}} Art \xrightarrow[0.274]{f_{country}} France \xrightarrow[0.107]{\downarrow \tilde{f}_{person}} Gogh$$

one space is that it forces the user to find the 2.2% records related to 'Gogh' in the *Art*-Space.

Even if a user may take any of these paths, it takes only 66.65 seconds on the average to navigate to the target in an MFIS. However, the SQL statement for the same navigation as the path P_2 has the following complexity,

q_{France} :

> Select *attr_list*
> From $q_{19thCentury}$
> Where *country_name = subquery$_{country}$*

subquery$_{country}$:

> Select *country_name*
> From $q_{19thCentury}$
> Where *title = 'Napoleonic Code'*

q_{Art} :

> Select *attr_list*
> From q_{France}
> Where *category = subquery$_{category}$*

subquery$_{category}$:

> Select *category*
> From q_{France}
> Where *title = 'The fashion of Lithograph in Paris'*

q_{Decade} :

> Select *attr_list*
> From q_{Art}
> Where *year $\geq$ subquery$_{year}$ − 5 And year $\leq$ subquery$_{year}$ + 5*

$subquery_{year}$:

> Select $year$
> From q_{Art}
> Where $title$ = 'The 1st Japanese Art Inspection'

q_{Gogh} :

> Select $attr\_list$
> From R
> Where $person\_name$ = $subquery_{person}$

$subquery_{person}$:

> Select $person\_name$
> From R
> Where $title$ = 'The copy of the UKIYOE'.

This query needs to specify conditions such as

$$title = \text{'The 1st Japanese Art Inspection'}$$

and

$$title = \text{'The copy of the UKIYOE'.}$$

However, it is difficult to specify these conditions correctly in advance without reading any attribute values of relevant records. Our approach allows users to specify these predicates by focusing on one of the records or selecting one of the facets in a virtual space repeatedly. It means that users can issue the above complicated queries only by traversing over the virtual spaces.

In this experiment, the user issues a set of queries to narrow down large tables. However, users can also issue more complicated queries, such as a query which joins different tables in the same or different databases, using the same interface in our proposal space.

The result of our experiment shows that our approach provides much more rapid and intuitive access to such target records than conventional query specifications.

5   Conclusion

In this paper, we have proposed an MFIS and its component-based implementation framework. In oder to support efficient explorations of a large amount of information, it is required to define and dynamically change the viewpoints for organizing and accessing them as R.S.Wurman said. First, we have proposed a framework for generating a 3D information space that enables users to organize and access database records through various different views. In this space, users can dynamically change their navigation functions to obtain the required information from a large information repository. This paper has also proposed a component-based framework for the automatic creation of a proposed information access space. The proposed framework allows users to explore a large amount of information by diving from a record in one information space to another space related to the record repeatedly. Moreover, it enables users to manipulate and select one of the facet components to change the navigation and the visualization functions dynamically. The result of our experiment shows the advantage of our approach over the conventional query specifications.

References

1. Card, S.K., Robertson, G.G., Mackinlay, J.D.: The information visualizer, an information workspace. In: Proc. ACM Conf. on Human Factors in Computing Systems(CHI'91). (1991) 181–188
2. Card, S.K., Mackinlay, J.D., Shneiderman, B.: Reading in Information Visualization Using Vision to Think. Morgan Kaufmann (1999)
3. Rekimoto, J., Green, M.: The Information Cube: Using Transparency in 3D Information Visualization. In: Proc. Third Annual Workshop on Information Technologies & Systems (WITS'93). (1993) 125–132
4. Robertson, G.G., Mackinlay, J.D., Card, S.K.: Cone trees: Animated 3D visualizations of hierarchical information. In: Proc. ACM Conf. on Human Factors in Computing Systems(CHI'91). (1991) 189–194
5. Silicon Graphics, Inc.: FSN: File System Navigator. online manual edn. (1992)
6. Boyle, J., Leishman, S., Fothergill, J., Gray, P.: WIMPS to 3D: design of a visual language for a database. Technical report, Aberdeen University (1994)
7. Massari, A., Saladini, L., Hemmja, M., Sisinni, F.: Virgilio : A non-immersive VR system to browse multimedia databases. In: Proc. of IEEE Intel. Conf. on Multimedia Computing and Systems. (1997)
8. Wurman, R.S.: Information Anxiety. Doubleday (1989)
9. Masuda, Y., Ishitobi, Y., Ueda, M.: Frame-axis model for automatic information organizing and spatial navigation. In: Proc. ACM European Conf. on Hypermedia technology. (1994) 146–157
10. C.J.Date: An Introduction to Database Systems. Addison-Wesley (1990) Fifth Edition.
11. Kimball, R.: The Data Warehouse Toolkit: Practical Techniques for Building Dimensional Data Warehouses. John Wiley & Sons (1996)
12. Okada, Y., Tanaka, Y.: IntelligentBox: A constructive visual software developement system for interactive 3D graphic apprications. In: Proc. of Computer Animation'95. (1995) 114–125
13. Ohigashi, M., Tanaka, Y.: A framework for the virtual reification of database records. IPSJ **42** (2001) 80–91
14. Benedikt, M.: Cyberspace: Some Proposals in Cyberspace: First Steps. MIT Press (1991)
15. Elvins, T.T., Nadeau, D.R., Kirsh, D.: Worldlets - 3D thumbnails for wayfinding in virtual environments. In: Proc. ACM User Interface Software and Technology Symposium-CUIST'97. (1997)
16. Stoakley, R., Conway, M.J., Pausch, R.: Virtual reality on a WIM: Interactive worlds in miniature. In: Proc. Conf. ACM SIGCHI. (1995)
17. Viega, J., Conway, M.J., Williams, G., Pausch, R.: 3D Magic Lenses. In: Proc. ACM UIST'96. (1996) 51–58
18. Itoh, M., Tanaka, Y.: WorldMirror and WorldBottle: Components for embedding multiple spaces in a 3D virtual environment. Jounal of IPSJ **42** (2001) 2403–2414

Integrated Visualization Framework for Relational Databases and Web Resources

Tsuyoshi Sugibuchi and Yuzuru Tanaka

Meme Media Laboratory, Hokkaido University 060-8628 Sapporo, Japan
{buchi,tanaka}@meme.hokudai.ac.jp

Abstract. In this paper we propose an integrated visualization framework for relational databases and Web resources. Using our *VERD framework*, users can dynamically integrate local databases and Web resources and interactively construct various visualizations. Users can define data integration and visualization by constructing a flow diagram consisting of various *operators* through direct manipulation. The principal idea of this framework is to manipulate Web resources, visualizations, and database relations through visual components based on relational schemata and integrate them based on the relational database model. In VERD framework, two types of special view relations are used for representing visualizations and for treating Web resources as database relations. Hence, in VERD framework, a Web resource can be combined with database relations as if it is also a local relation. Similarly, VERD framework specifies visual mapping between source data relations and visualization representations by means of relational operations. VERD framework supports various interactive visualization operations including 'details-on-demand', 'drill-down', and 'brushing-and-linking' These operations are performed by modifying view relations associated with visualizations.

1 Introduction

Good information visualizations can reveal significant abstraction of data when the scale and the complexity exceeds the human capability to interpret data records from reading only them, and help users to find hidden trends or structures from a data set. In addition, adding interactivity to information visualizations is useful for exploring a large set of multivariate data. The interactive manipulation of visualization allows users to dynamically change visualization parameters, so that user can scan a large data set, focus on a meaningful portion of data, and find trends or patterns. Many interactive techniques including brushing-and-linking, *dynamic queries* [14], multiscale visualization, and multiple visualization coordination have been studied. Moreover, the interactive definition or construction of visualization is another useful technique for data exploration tasks and has been applied in many scientific visualization systems and database visualization systems. In these systems, users can construct a visualization system, suitable both for the source data and for the user's mental model, quickly to test user's hypotheses.

G. Grieser and Y. Tanaka (Eds.): Intuitive Human Interface 2004, LNAI 3359, pp. 159–174, 2004.

Dynamic information integration is also a useful technique to find rules from a complicated data set. By combining other related data with data of our current concern, we can introduce another viewpoint on current data. For instance, we may find an unforeseen trend from a market data by comparing it with a weather data. The World-Wide-Web is a universal data repository providing a huge amount of data for various application domains. Contents distributed over the WWW include more dynamic or graphical contents than records stored in DBMSs. Moreover, many Web application pages provide various services like Web searching, online dictionaries, shopping, and engineering calculations. If we can extract such contents and services from arbitrary Web pages and dynamically integrate them together with the target data of our current concern, we can extensively extend our data analysis capabilities.

In this paper we propose a new visualization framework we call VERD (Visualization Environment based on the Relational Database model). VERD framework allows users to integrate local database relations with related Web contents, and provides an interactive environment to visualize integrated data resources in various ways.

The following is an outline of VERD framework.

The relational database model has been adopted as a theoretical basis of VERD framework to integrate heterogeneous data resources and visualizations. In VERD framework, each data resource and each visualization display are manipulated through operations on relational schemata. In particular, we define special view relations to uniformly treat both visualizations and Web resources as relational schemata. A *visualization view relation* is a view relation to represent a visualization. A *Web view relation* is also a view relation to represent a set of related Web resources. Hence, data integration and visualization are both performed by uniformly applying relational operations to local database relations, Web view relations, and visualization view relations.

VERD framework introduces interactivity into data integration and visualization tasks by using the following mechanism. VERD framework provides a set of interactive components called *operators*. Each operator corresponds to a user's primitive operation for specifying data integration and visualization. Each visualization is defined as a flow diagram consisting of operators and connections among them. To integrate arbitrary Web resources with our visualization, we use Web wrappers to define a view relation among mutually related contents over the Web. We have developed a lightweight Web wrapper algorithm and a graphical interface for users to specify Web wrappers through direct manipulations. By using this interface, users can interactively and quickly specify Web wrappers on demand in their data exploration task.

This paper is organized as follows. In Section 2, we describe our basic framework for interactive database visualization. In particular in Section 2, we focus on how VERD framework works with visualization view relations. In Section 3, we show how Web resources can be integrated with database visualizations. We describe the details of Web view relations and an outline of our Web wrapper. Then in Section 4, we describe how VERD framework is implemented. In Section 5, we discuss the related research works. Finally, we conclude our paper with some remarks.

2   VERD Framework

2.1   Visualization View

A visualization view is a relational representation of a visualization. In the relational database model, a virtual relation which provides a schema for some application is called a view relation. Our visualization view relation is an extension of this view relation to deel with graphical representation and location of each records. Visualization of source data is equivalent to defining a visualization view relation on a source relation. In VERD framework, a source data can be associated with a visualization scheme by using relational operations. Visualization view relations are dynamically constructed and modified in a visualization task.

A schema of a visualization view has *visualization attributes*. Each visualization attribute corresponds to a visualization property such as location, color, size, and angle. A type of each visualization attribute is identified by its name. In other words, the name of each attribute is used by our visualization system to associate its value with an appropriate visual property.

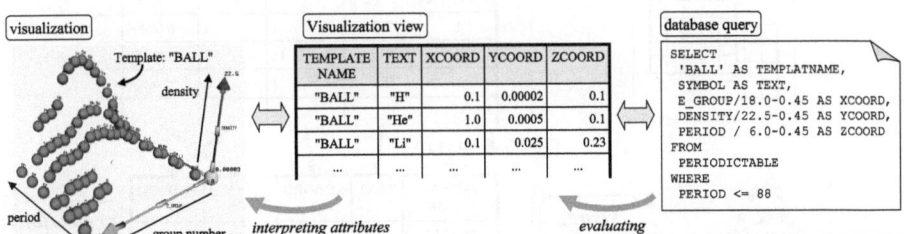

Fig. 1. Visualization view example

Figure 1 shows an example visualization and a visualization view relation corresponding to this visualization. This 3D scatter plot visualization represents a periodic table of elements. In this visualization, each element is represented as a ball. The three coordinate values of each ball are associated with the group, the period, and the density of each element. A textual label attached to each ball shows the name of each element. The schema of a visualization view relation illustrated in Figure 1 has visualization attributes corresponding to the four visual properties, X, Y, Z coordinates and the text label. A TEMPLATENAME attribute is included in this schema to specify a template. A template is a visual component to represent each database record. Some template has both a visual shape and a data representation function for displaying the text, changing the color, and morphing the shape. Users can compose a new template by combining visual primitive components. The template used in this example visualization consists of a simple ball primitive and a component displaying a text string. The virtual dimension of visualization can be expanded by combining additional visual primitives with the template. This operation is equivalent to adding new visualization attributes to a visualization view.

A visual mapping for associating source data with a visualization is equivalent to a relational operation which projects a source relation onto a visualization view schema. Figure 2 illustrates an example of a visual mapping. In this example, the SYMBOL attribute is directly projected onto the TEXT attribute. On the other hand, the computed attributes derived from the attributes E_GROUP, PERIOD, and DENSITY are associated with the three coordinate attributes. These computations normalize the locations of visible data elements to arrange all of them in the visualization area. This projection operation can be described as a database query given in Figure 1. In this query description, the name of the source data relation appears in the FROM clause, and the visual mapping is specified in the SELECT clause. This query also specifies conditions to visualize only those elements with their atomic numbers less than 88. When our visualization system performs this visualization, this query is evaluated by the DBMS. Then, our system creates this visualization from the query evaluation result.

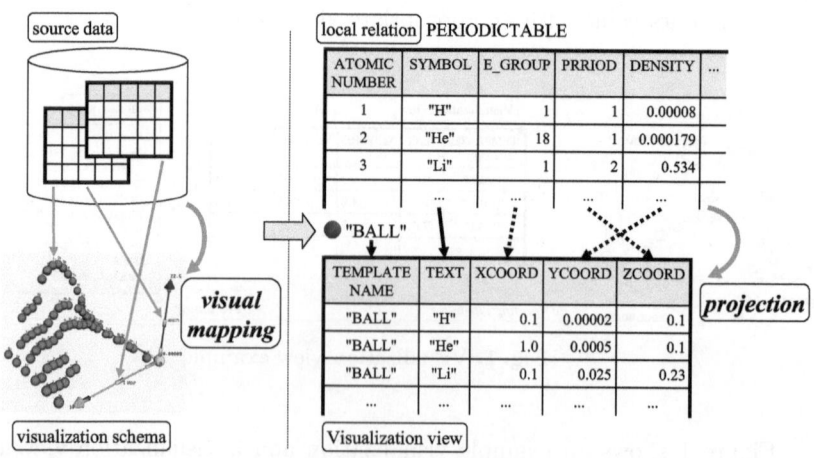

Fig. 2. Visual mapping

Each visualization operation is performed by deriving a new visualization view relation from another visualization view relation. VERD framework allows users to magnify a portion of visualization, to combine other data with the current visualization, and to coordinate more than one visualization. Figure 3 shows that each visualization operation is performed as a view modification operation. This figure shows that not only a visualization but also its portion can be represented as a visualization view relation. This feature is useful for performing interactive data exploration tasks by directly combining visual components.

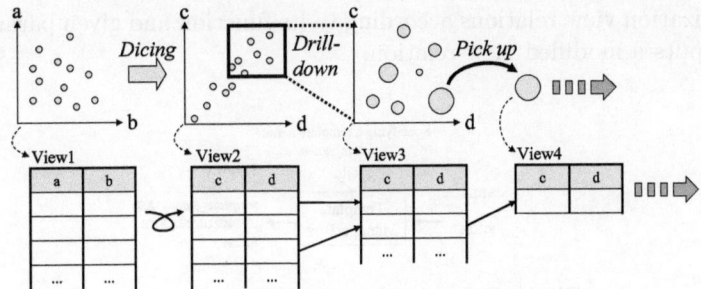

Fig. 3. View modification

2.2 Operators

VERD framework allows users to interactively specify visualizations. For this purpose, VERD framework provides a set of *operators*. Users can define a visualization by constructing a flow diagram consisting of operators.

Table 1. Operators for specifying representations

Name	in / out	parameter	function
TemplateManagerBox	$V \rightarrow V'$	*template name*	applying a template
AxisBox, OriginBox	$V \rightarrow V'$	*attribute name*	specifying a coordinate system
ContainerBox	$V \rightarrow V$		displaying visualization results
OverlayBox	$V^1 + V^2 \rightarrow V'$		overlaying several visualizations

Table 2. Operators for specifying queries

Name	in / out	parameter	function
TableBox	$\phi \rightarrow V$	*table name*	selecting a database relation
SelectBox	$\sigma(V) \rightarrow V'$	(*spacial position*)	selecting records it encloses
RecordFilterBox	$\sigma(V) \rightarrow V'$	*condition*	adding a new condition
JoinBox	$V^1 \bowtie V^2 \rightarrow V'$	*join condition*	joining two relations

Table 1 and 2 show operators provided by VERD framework. These operators can be classified into two categories, visual specifiers and query specifiers. Note that each operator does not correspond to either a relational operation or a clause of a database query. Each operator is designed to correspond to a user's primitive operation for specifying visualizations and database queries.

Operators perform their functions by executing composite operations consisting of several relational operations. Each operator takes single or multiple visualization view relations as its input. Some types of operators take parameters specified by users. Most parameters (e.g. the name of the table to visualize) are directly specified. Parameters of some types of operators (e.g. SelectBox) are specified by spatially arranging these operators. Each operator modifies input visualization view relations according to its function and given parameters, then it outputs a modified view relation.

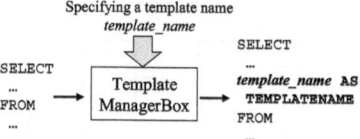

Fig. 4. Example of query rewriting by an operator

Each operator modifies visualization views relation by rewriting database queries that specify that views. Figure 4 shows that a TemplateManagerBox performs its function by rewriting an input query to specify the value of TEMPLATE-NAME attribute. *A query flow diagram* is a flow diagram consisting of such operators and connections among them, and it works as an SQL query generator for specifying visualization view relations. Figure 5 shows a query flow flow diagram that specifies the visualization in Figure 1. Database queries flow through this diagram, and are modified by each operator.

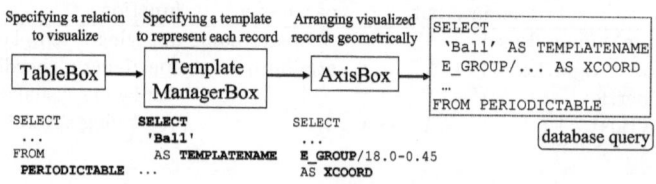

Fig. 5. Example of a query flow diagram

Operators are also interactive components. Users can combine operators by connecting their jacks and plugs as if they connect AV components. Figure 6 shows a screenshot of a query flow diagram specifying the visualization illustrated in Figure 1.

2.3   Visualization Examples

Magic Lens. Figure 7 illustrates an example query flow diagram that defines a magic lens [1]. It displays detailed information about records included in the selected region. In this example, a base of a magic lens, which is represented as a rectangular frame, consists of a SelectBox and an OverlayBox. The Select-Box specifies a region to apply additional representations, and the OverlayBox overlays new representations over the original visualization. By just dropping operator components into this frame, users can specify representations that the magic lens applies to each target record. Users can apply additional representations by dropping such a magic lens into some visualization result.

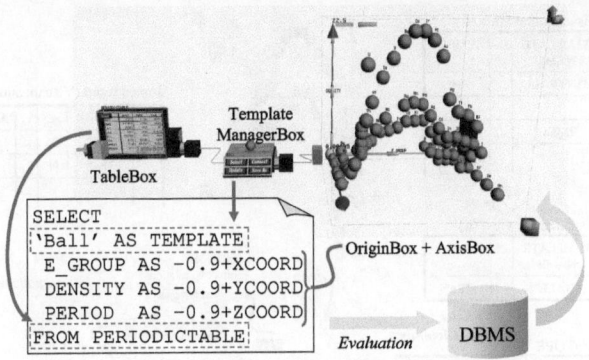

Fig. 6. Screenshot of a query flow diagram

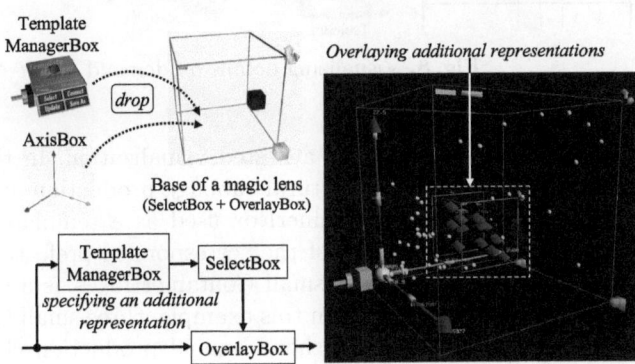

Fig. 7. Magic lens

Visualizing Details on Demand. In VERD framework, any portion of visualization corresponds to some view relation. Therefore, each component contained in a visualization result can also work as a view relation. Figure 8 illustrates a visualization process starting with the visualization result obtained in Figure 6. In this example, visualization (A) corresponds to a visualization view relation (i), and each ball representing an atom corresponds to a small visualization view relation with a single tuple represented by this ball.

Such a portion working as a visualization view relation can be joined with another relation. In this example, the isotopes of ruthenium are retrieved by joining a relation storing major isotope data with a relation (ii) corresponding to ruthenium, and visualized as the visualization (B). A user can visualize isotopes of various elements by only dropping balls into a SelectBox.

Nested Visualization. Figure 9 shows an example of nested queries and nested visualizations. This example visualizes the prefectural cabbage production in Japan. In this example, a ContainerBox is used as a template to visualize each prefecture. This template has two tiny AxisBoxes. This template is designed to visualize an annual cabbage production change of each prefecture. A Container-

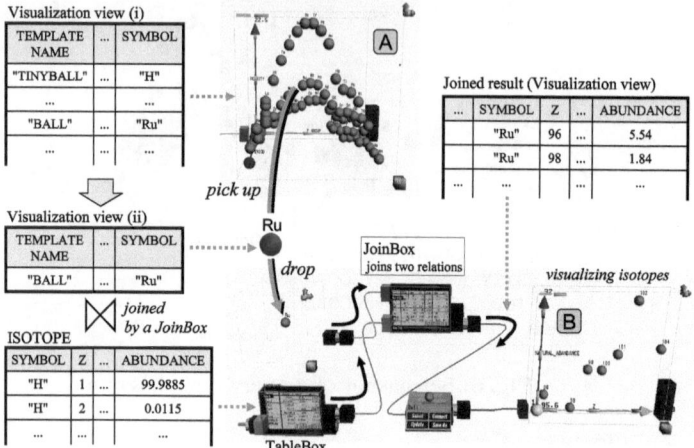

Fig. 8. Visualizing details on demand

Box used as a template gives users a nested visualization. In this example, a large ContainerBox visualizes prefectural cabbage production amounts in 1991 as shown in (A). Each small ContainerBox used as a template visualizes the annual cabbage production change of the corresponded prefecture as shown in (B). Users can select each of these small ContainerBoxes as a source data set to visualize its related information. In this example, three small ContainerBoxes are selected. The visualization (C) shows annual production changes of three similar vegetables, cabbage, Chinese cabbage, and lettuce, in the selected different prefectures. In this example, users can see the general trend of lettuce production which have increased instead of Chinese cabbage.

3   Integration with Related Web Resources

In this section, we extend our VDRD framework to integrate database contents with related Web contents.

3.1   Web View Relations

In VERD framework, Web resources are integrated with local databases based on the relational database model. In our approach, we extract data from a target Web document into a tabular form, and access it through a relational view called *a Web view relation*. A Web view relation associates a relational schema to relevant Web resources. Therefore, data integration between local relations and related Web resources is performed by specifying relational operations between local relations and Web view relations.

To perform data integration among heterogeneous Web resources, we have to associate the set of these Web resources to a general data structure like a relational table. This is a difficult task because each Web document has a complicate

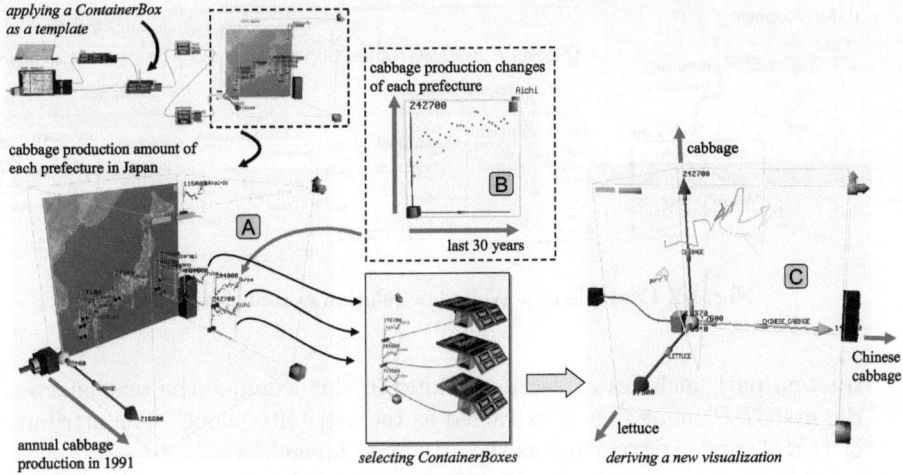

Fig. 9. Example of a nested visualization

and different structure. However, we can make this task easier by focusing only on required portions of documents and by associating them to a relational table. To perform this operation, we need *a Web wrapper* for extracting mutually related resources from Web documents. Moreover, we need an interactive way of quickly developing a Web wrapper.

Generally speaking, a wrapper means a software tool for extracting structured information from unstructured data or semi-structured data. A Web wrappers extracts a relation from a set of HTML documents distributed over the WWW. There are many studies on information extraction from Web documents. Various ways of implementing Web wrappers have been already proposed. In this work, we adopted a DOM (document object model) -pattern-based wrapper. An HTML document is a semi-structured document whose structure can be represented as a DOM tree. Our wrapper scans a DOM tree of a source HTML document, and finds a sub tree that matches with a given template pattern. Then the wrapper extracts data values from the found sub tree, and imports them as attribute values of the Web view relation.

A specification of a Web wrapper is described using the extraction path notation. The extraction path notation is an extension of the XPATH [2] notation. Extended features include the notation for specifying branched patterns of DOM fragments. Data mapping between HTML nodes and the attributes of a Web view relation can be specified using the extraction path notation.

Figure 10 shows an example of a Web wrapper and its specification described using the extraction path notation. Our notation uses a comma and braces to specify branched patterns for matching. In this example, the first and the second $\langle TD \rangle$ nodes appearing in each row of a table are selected. Attribute values or texts of HTML nodes of the matching sub tree are associated with the attributes of the Web view relation schema. For this purpose, the description of each ex-

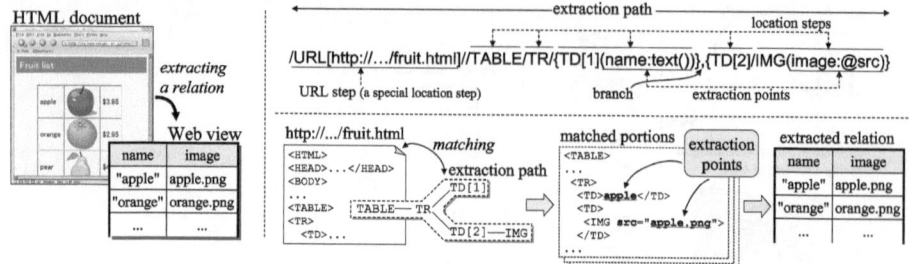

Fig. 10. Example of a Web view relation and an extraction path

traction path includes extraction points. In this example the text enclosed by the first $\langle TD \rangle$ node tags is extracted as the attribute 'name'. The attribute src of $\langle IMG \rangle$ node is extracted as the attribute 'image'.

Our notation uses backward references to define more complicated extractions. Moreover, source information may be often distributed in a set of HTML documents related to each other by hyperlinks. A Web view must be defined by visiting all the related HTML documents. Our notation for describing extraction paths is designed to satisfy these requirements.

3.2   User Interface for Specifying Web Wrappers

Our visualization system provides a graphical user interface to specify Web wrappers. Our interface has the dynamic previewing mechanism for supporting users to quickly and interactively specify an arbitrary Web wrapper. Usually, the wrapper specifying process has many repetitions of try-and-error tasks. To specify a wrapper that correctly works, a user tries to extract data using a provisional wrapper specification, and repeat the refinement of the current wrapper specification. The purpose of our dynamic previewing interface is to improve the wrapper specification task by shortening the time required for each try-and-error step.

Figure 11 shows on outline of this interface. To quickly specify a wrapper specification, our system uses a wrapper induction algorithm that generates a wrapper specification from given examples of extracted data. We developed a lightweight algorithm for the wrapper induction. With this algorithm, our system generates a wrapper from example HTML nodes selected from the source Web page within 100 miliseconds.

Our system provides a Web browser interface for users to directly specify extraction examples on a Web page. Users can select an HTML node as an example through mouse operations. Moreover, when the mouse cursor is moved, our browser immediately selects an HTML node under the mouse cursor as a candidate example, and generates a Web wrapper from a set of example nodes. The generated wrapper is executed immediately, then extracted HTML nodes by this wrapper are highlighted in the browser interface as an extraction preview. The latency time required for completing a preview update after a mouse cursor movement is less than 100 milliseconds.

Selecting an HTML node as an extraction example

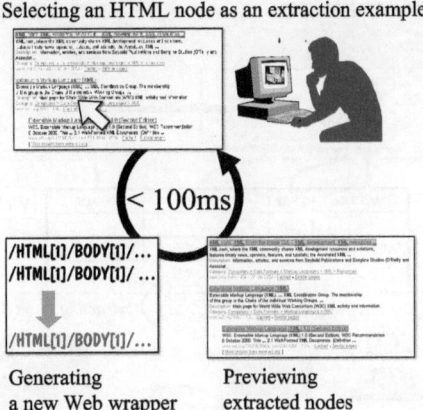

Generating
a new Web wrapper

Previewing
extracted nodes

Fig. 11. The architecture of dynamic previewing

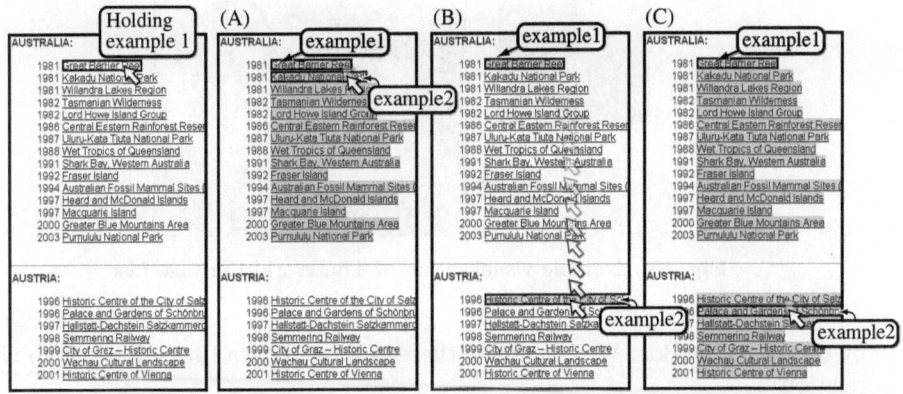

Fig. 12. Example of dynamic previewing for specifying wrapper

Figure 12 shows that our interface smoothly highlights items to be extracted in response to the mouse movement. In this example, a user is specifying a Web wrapper on 'The World Heritage List' page presented by UNESCO [3]. The dynamically updated preview suggests various patterns of extraction results such as (A) all heritages of one nation, (B) the heritage that appears first in each nation's heritage list, and (C) all the heritages of all the nations. User can quickly find good extractions by only moving the mouse cursor over the target Web page.

3.3   Visualization Example Integrated with Web Resources

VERD framework provides a special operator called a *WebViewBox* to execute a Web wrapper defined using an extraction path expression. Figure 13 shows an example of visualizing information of the world heritages by using this operator. In this example, the nation's name, the registration year, the name and photograph of each heritage are extracted from 'The World Heritage List' Web site

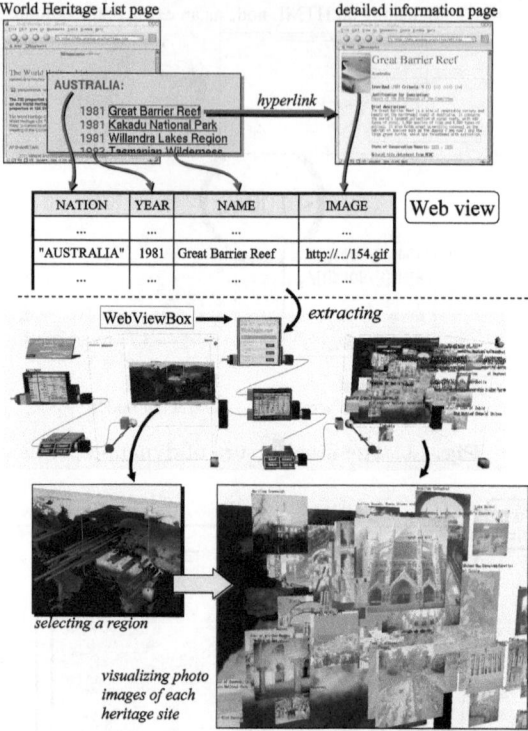

Fig. 13. Example visualization of The World Heritage List

by the WebViewBox. We can access these extracted data through the Web view relation.

In this example, we created a visualization from data stored in a local database. The GDP, longitude and latitude of each nation are obtained from a local database, and are visualized as the left visualization in Figure 13. Then, we select nations in Europe by using a SelectBox, and join the selected portion with the Web view relation. As a result, each heritage's photograph obtained from UNESCO's page is visualized in the right visualization, and is spatially arranged according to the longitude and the latitude obtained from a local database.

3.4   Wrapping Web Applications

In VERD framework, a function of each Web application is also abstracted as a relational view. A function of a Web application is treated as a relation between user's requests and system's answers. This relation is considered as a Web view relation. Each Web application's transaction that consists of a user's request and an application's answer is treated as an instance tuple of the Web view relation. Because each transaction corresponds to each tuple, this abstract method works well for stateless services that process each transaction independently of other transactions. Typical Web applications like search services and online dictionaries are of this type.

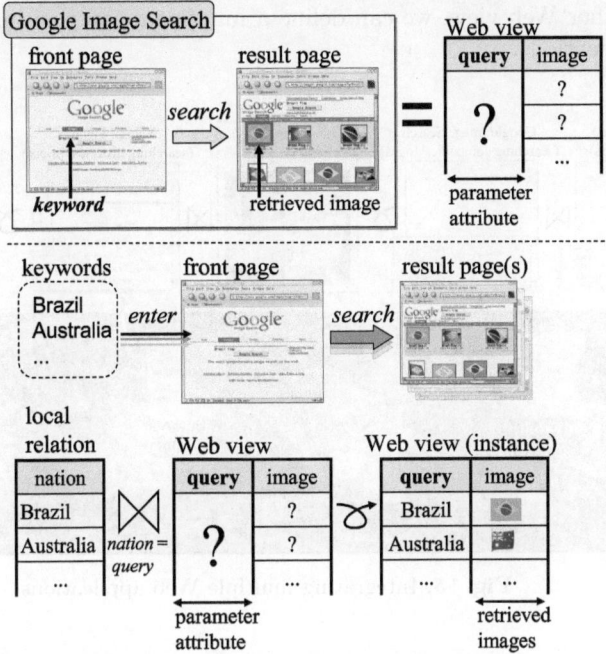

Fig. 14. Wrapping a Web application

To use a Web application, users have to fill in a form of an HTML page with parameter values, and to send a request as well as these parameter values to the corresponding Web server by using HTTP. We associate parameters of a Web application with the special attributes of the Web view relation. These Web view attributes are called *parameter attributes*. Usually a Web application returns an HTML document as a reply to the user's request. Therefore, we can extract return values from a Web application by specifying a Web view on the returned page.

A Web view relation with parameter attributes is also a view relation. However, when we try to obtain instance values of such a Web view relation, we need to specify a set of candidate values of its parameter attributes. These candidate values of parameter attributes are sent to the Web application page one by one, and, for each of them, a relation is extracted from the reply pages to fill in other attribute values of the Web view relation. In most cases, such candidate values of parameter attributes are specified by a relational join with another relation.

In Figure 14, we define a Web view relation by wrapping the Google Image Search service. This Web view relation extracts a set of URLs that point to images with the highest rank in the Google image search for each given keyword. This Web view relation has a parameter attribute to specify a keyword. This parameter attribute can be associated with nation names through a relational join with a local relation about nations in the world. As a result, for each nation, the image with the highest rank is extracted. By joining a Web view relation with another Web view, we can define a functional composition combining two Web applications.

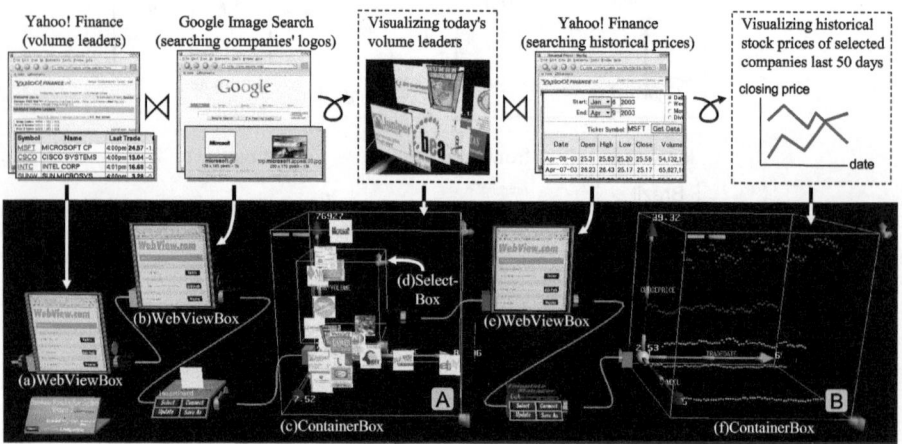

Fig. 15. Integrating multiple Web applications

Figure 15 shows an example functional composition of Web applications. In this example, the Web view relation specified by the WebViewBox (a) extracts today's volume leaders of NASDAQ market, and follows hyperlinks to the profile pages to extract the full names of the companies. The WebViewBox (b) defines a Web view relation by wrapping the Google Image Search service. This Web view is joined with the Web view specified by (a) to search for the logo images of the retrieved companies. The ContainerBox (c) visualizes extracted data by representing each company with its logo image and by arranging such logos geometrically in a 3D space according to the last trade price, the price change, and the trading volume of company stocks. The SelectBox (d) is used to select companies it encloses. A view relation corresponding to the selected companies is further joined with another Web view relation that is specified by the WebViewBox (e) to retrieve stock prices in the last 50 days. As a result, the stock prices of the selected companies during the last 50 days are visualized by the ContainerBox (f).

4   Implementation

We have implemented our system using a 3D visual component-ware system IntelligentBox [4]. The IntelligentBox system architecture provides 3D visual components called boxes. Each box is an interactive and functional component, and has slots as a logical interface for accessing its internal state. Users can specify slot connections between two boxes to define operation inter between them. We have implemented operator components as boxes. This allows us to connect operators using slot connections.

5   Related Work

There are many studies on interactive information visualization. DEVise [5] and Tioga-2 [6] are similar systems to the system proposed in this paper. These systems are based on the relational database model. In contrast to these systems that can represent an individual visualization display as a relation, VERD framework can further represent each constituent element of visualizations as a relation. This feature of VERD framework allows us to flexibly construct exploratory data visualization environment. For instance, the details-on-demand interface we showed in 2.3 can be easily constructed by naturally applying VERD framework because each visual component is also associated with a visualization view relation.

The flow diagram is a popular model for defining visual programming environments, and has been adopted by many interactive visualization systems such as AVS [8], DataExplorer [9], and Tioga-2 [6]. However, these systems distinguish components constituting flow diagrams from components constituting visualizations. On the other hand, in VERD framework, both types of components are equivalent in outputting some visualization view relations. Therefore, our system allows mixed use of operators and visualizations, and allows us to construct complicated visualizations such as the nested visualization example in Section 2.3.

Supporting OLAP (online analytic processing) operations is a future topic of our study. Polaris [10] is a visualization system for OLAP and it allows us to explore in a large dataset by using several OLAP operations such as drilling-down and pivoting. This system works well with one multidimensional dataset. Extended VERD framework will support dynamic data combination between multidimensional datasets and other datasets.

Data extraction from Web documents is one of the active research areas in the last decade. Many studies for the Web wrapping have been reported. In particular, several studies [11] [12] proposed graphical interfaces for specifying wrappers, but these studies have not focused their attention on repetitive try-and-error refinement of wrappers. LEXiKON [13] allows us to incrementally refine a wrapper through try-and-error repetitions. However, each trial step takes long because it has only a conventional Web form interface. Our wrapper definition interface for repetitive refinement is closely related to *dynamic query interfaces* [14]. Both a dynamic querying interface and our interface tightly associate a visualization with user's manipulations and allow users to quickly scan in a large exploration space of parameter values or extraction examples.

6   Concluding Remarks

In this paper we have proposed a new framework which provides an integrated environment for visualizing both database records and Web content objects. In our VERD framework, each visualization corresponds to a view relation, and is specified by a database query. Users can create such queries by interactively combining operator components. In addition, we have extended this framework to support the relational data extraction from HTML documents over the Web. Users can extract relations from the Web by specifying Web view relations, and combine them with local database relations to visualize database records together with their related Web contents. VERD framework can also define functional compositions of Web applications by using relational operations.

References

1. Benjamin B. Bederson and James D. Hollan and Ken Perlin and Jonathan Meyer and David Bacon and George W. Furnas. Pad++: A Zoomable Graphical Sketchpad For Exploring Alternate Interface Physics. *Journal of Visual Languages and Computing*, 7(1), pp. 3-32, 1996.
2. XML Path Language (XPath). http://www.w3c.org/TR/xpath/
3. The World Heritage List. http://whc.unesco.org/heritage.htm
4. Y. Okada and Y. Tanaka. IntelligentBox:a constructive visual software development system for interactive 3D graphic applications. *Proc. of the Computer Animation 1995 Conference*, pp. 114-125, 1995.
5. Miron Livny, Raghu Ramakrishnan, Kevin Beyer, Guangshun Chen, Donko Donjerkovic, Shilpa Lawande, Jussi Myllymaki, and Kent Wenger. DEVise: Integrated Querying and Visual Exploration of Large Datasets. *Proc. of ACM SIGMOD '97*, pp. 301-312, May, 1997.
6. Alexander Aiken, Jolly Chen, Michael Stonebraker, and Allison Woodruff. Tioga-2: A Direct Manipulation Database Visualization Environment. *Proc. of the 12th International Conference on Data Engineering*, pp. 208-217, February, 1996.
7. Chris North, Ben Shneiderman. Snap-Together Visualization: A User Interface for Coordinating Visualizations via Relational Schemata. *Proc. of ACM AVI 2000*, May, 2000.
8. Craig Upson, Jr. Thomas Faulhaber, David Kamins, David Laidlaw, David Schlegel, Jeffery Vroom, Robert Gurwitz, and Andries van Dam. The Application Visualization System: A computational environment for scientific visualization. *IEEE Computer Graphics and Applications*, 9(4), pp. 30-42, 2000.
9. Bruce Lucas, Gregory D. Abram, Nancy S. Collins, David A. Epstein, Donna L. Greesh, and Kevin P. McAul. An architecture for a scientific visualization system. *Proc. of IEEE Visualization '92*, pp. 107-114, October, 1992.
10. Chris Stolte, Diane Tang and Pat Hanrahan. Polaris: A System for Query, Analysis, and Visualization of Multidimensional Relational Databases. *IEEE Visualization and Computer Graphics*, 8(1), pp. 52065, Jan/Mar 2002
11. Ling Liu, Calton Pu, Wei Han. XWRAP: An XML-enabled wrapper construction system for Web information sources. *Proc. of the 16th International Conference on Data Engineering*, pp. 611-621, March, 2000.
12. lberto H. F. Laender, Berthier Ribeiro-Neto, and Altigran S. da Silva. DEByE - Data Extraction By Example. *Data and Knowledge Engineering* 40(2), pp. 121-154, 2002.
13. Gunter Grieser, Klaus P. Jantke, Steffen Lange. Gunter Grieser, Klaus P. Jantke, Steffen Lange *Proc. of 13th Int. Conference on Algorithmic Learning Theory*, pp. 173-187, 2002.
14. Ben Shneiderman. Dynamic queries for visual information seeking. *IEEE Software*, 11(6), pp. 70-77, 1994.

Discovering Implicit Relationships
in a Web of Contexts

Mina Akaishi[1] and Nicolas Spyratos[2],[*]

[1] RCAST, University of Tokyo,
4-6-1 Komaba Meguro-ku Tokyo 153-8904, Japan
mina@ai.rcast.u-tokyo.ac.jp
[2] Université de Paris-Sud, Laboratoire de Recherche en Informatique,
LRI-Bât 490, 91405 Orsay Cedex, France
spyratos@lri.fr

Abstract. We propose a framework for discovering implicit relationships between descriptors and objects in large information bases. Typical examples of such information bases are large collections of Web pages, where the anchors play the role of descriptors for distant web pages, and the web pages themselves play the role of the described objects. Our approach assumes that the contents of the information base are organized into manageable subsets called *contexts*, each user setting up his(her) own web of contexts. While setting up a web of contexts, a user may create implicit relationships between descriptors and objects (relationships of which the user may not even be aware). We provide a framework for discovering such implicit relationships in a web of user-defined contexts; this is done based on extended notions of synonymy/homonymy using descriptor and object paths.

1 Introduction

The rapid proliferation of information sources in recent years and the advent of the Internet have created a world wide web of interconnected information resources. Today, the Web represents the largest collection of information resources that an individual has ever been able to access – and it is continuously growing at accelerating paces.

Several kinds of tools have been developed to help individual users to access Web resources. The so-called search engines are the most popular among these tools, as they allow users to access the resources they index using a very simple search mechanism, namely keywords or combinations of keywords.

There is however a price to pay by users for the simplicity of the search mechanism: the answers obtained from search engines usually contain large amounts of information that is not related to what the user had in mind when asking the question. This problem comes from the fact that any given search engine indexes

[*] Work by this author was partially supported by the DELOS EU Network of Excellence in Digital Libraries, Contract No G038-507618.

G. Grieser and Y. Tanaka (Eds.): Intuitive Human Interface 2004, LNAI 3359, pp. 175–188, 2004.
© Springer-Verlag Berlin Heidelberg 2004

resources that cater to the interests of very large and highly heterogeneous populations of users. So, on the one hand we have a large collection of information resources (hereafter referred to as the *information base*), and on the other hand a very large and highly heterogeneous population of users.

To cope with this situation, in previous work [4, 1, 3], we introduced a personalization mechanism that allows each user to define his (her) own sub-collections of resources of interest and interconnect them for later (and more convenient) use. Such "customized" sub-collections is what we called in [6] user contexts, or simply *contexts*. Intuitively, a context is a set of resources (hereafter referred to as *objects*) within which each resource is associated with two items: a set of *descriptors* and a set of *references* to other contexts. More formally, a context is a set of triples of the form: ⟨*descriptors, object, references*⟩.

Perhaps the simplest example of context is the directory of a department store. In most department stores, this directory is usually located on the ground floor (facing the entering customers) and looks like the table of Figure 1(a). A directory, consists of a number of lines and each line contains one or more keywords describing items for sale in the store plus the floor on which the items can be found. For example, in the directory of table 1(a), the first line contains the keywords "Perfumes" and "Cosmetics" plus the indication "ground floor" meaning that such items are found on the ground floor. Similarly, the second line indicates that women's clothing can be found on the first floor, and so on.

We can view the department store directory as a context whose contents are triples of the form: ⟨*keywords, line-number, floor-number*⟩, as shown in Figure 1(b). Under this view, the keywords are the descriptors, the line-number is the object and the floor-number is just another context, i.e., of a floor context. Each floor context, in turn, is again a set of triples, where each triple consists of a set of keywords, a floor sector number and a subsector number (assuming the sector is divided into sub-sectors, otherwise the sub-sector number is set to Nil, indicating that the floor sector is not divided into sub-sectors).

A customer entering the department store looks at (or "accesses") the directory, and then examines one by one the triples of the directory. Aided by the descriptors the customer selects a floor number, i.e., a new context. Once on the selected floor, the customer repeats the same steps (but this time looking at the floor directory) in order to find the exact sector on the floor where the items of interest are located. Note however that the items themselves are *not* part of the sector context. In other words, the context mechanism just helps you find *where* the items of interest are located, based on their descriptors – disregarding *what* these items are. Incidentally, when the items of interest are information items, such as electronic documents, then their descriptors are usually referred to as *metadata* – as opposed to the actual data contained in the information item.

It is important to note that a context is a "light-weight" abstraction mechanism, different from the usual abstraction mechanisms (such as classification, attribution and inheritance). However, it can be used orthogonally together with those mechanisms.

In the context mechanism introduced in [6–8], there are only three types of entities, namely object identifiers, context identifiers and descriptors; for sim-

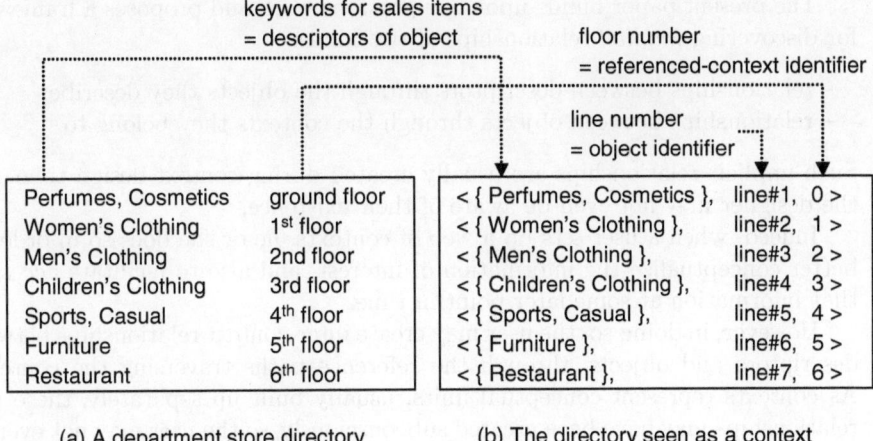

keywords for sales items
= descriptors of object

floor number
= referenced-context identifier

line number
= object identifier

Perfumes, Cosmetics	ground floor
Women's Clothing	1st floor
Men's Clothing	2nd floor
Children's Clothing	3rd floor
Sports, Casual	4th floor
Furniture	5th floor
Restaurant	6th floor

< { Perfumes, Cosmetics }, line#1, 0 >
< { Women's Clothing }, line#2, 1 >
< { Men's Clothing }, line#3 2 >
< { Children's Clothing }, line#4 3 >
< { Sports, Casual }, line#5, 4 >
< { Furniture }, line#6, 5 >
< { Restaurant }, line#7, 6 >

(a) A department store directory   (b) The directory seen as a context

Fig. 1. An example of contexts.

plicity, we call object identifiers simply *objects* and context identifiers simply *contexts*. We assume that the set of objects, the set of contexts and the set of descriptors are mutually disjoint sets. As a consequence, a context cannot belong to the contents of any other context. However, a context can be referred to from within another context.

It is important to note that our context mechanism is not concerned with the content or internal structure of the objects: as long as the objects are identifiable, they can belong to the contents of any context. Actually, the information base itself is considered as a context – the context containing all the objects of the information base.

It is also important to note that our context mechanism has a minimal interference with the normal operation of the information base: it can be implemented on top of the system managing the information base, at a minimal cost. Our previous example of the department store directory illustrates this point quite clearly.

There are two main reasons for using a web of contexts on top of an existing information base:

(a) to allow users to define their own, personalized sub-collections, and to describe objects using familiar names (local to the sub-collection);

(b) to speed-up searching for desired objects, by traversing appropriate contexts.

Once again, we stress the fact that searching for desired objects is based solely on object descriptors, i.e., without consideration of content or internal object structure. This is precisely the reason why, earlier on, we called our context mechanism a "light-weight" abstraction mechanism.

In previous work [2, 5, 4, 1, 3], we have presented a mechanism for context management, in a web of inter-related contexts, i.e., a set of tools for creation or deletion of a context, insertion/deletion/modification of a triple in a context, search for objects of interest in a context, and traversal of contexts in search of a context of interest.

The present paper builds upon our previous work and proposes a framework for discovering *implicit* relationships of two kinds:

- relationships between descriptors through the objects they describe;
- relationships between objects through the contexts they belong to.

Such implicit relationships are usually created during context design time, and the designer may not even be aware of their existence.

Indeed, when a user sets up a web of contexts, he or she does so in order to better conceptualize the information of interest, and also to facilitate access to that information at some later point in time.

However, in doing so, the user may create inter-context relationships between descriptors and objects, through the reference paths traversing the contexts. As contexts represent conceptual units, usually built up separately, these new relationships may have been created subconsciously, so the user may not even be aware of their existence. As a consequence, showing to the user such unexpected (and sometimes surprising) relationships, may prove useful to the user in several ways, including re-thinking the web of contexts already created.

The main contribution of this paper is to provide a framework for the discovery of implicit relationships between descriptors and between objects in a web of user-defined contexts.

The remainder of this paper is organized as follows. In section 2 we recall the definition of context that we use, as well as some auxiliary concepts. In section 3, we define implicit relationships formally, and we present examples of tracing such relationships. Finally, in section 4 we offer some concluding remarks.

2   Context

In this section, we define the notion of context that we use, as well as a notion of path for context traversal. Our definitions are inspired from the notion of context presented in [6–8], with some extensions.

2.1   The Notion of Context

A context consists of an identifier c plus a *content*. The content of c is a set of triples of the form, $\langle object\text{-}descriptors, object, object\text{-}references \rangle$, where *object-descriptors* is a set of descriptions of the object content and *object-references* is a possibly empty set of other contexts.

We note that, contrary to [6–8], we allow our contexts to have multiple references. This feature allows greater flexibility and provides for higher expressive power. We also note that an object descriptor can be a piece of text, an image, a sound score, or anything that helps describe the content of the object; it can even be an "object viewer"[4, 1, 3], i.e., a tool allowing the user to just have a look at the contents of the object.

In some application environments the object descriptors are just keywords, and such keywords may come from a controlled vocabulary. Furthermore, such a vocabulary may be structured by a subsumption relation. For example, if the objects are the books of a computer science library then their descriptors most likely will be keywords from the ACM Computing Classification System (ACM, 1999, http://www.acm.org/class/). However, for the purposes of this paper, it is immaterial whether descriptor definitions follow given rules or not.

What is important to keep in mind is that descriptors and references are context dependent: an object can belong to different contexts and may have different names and/or different references in each context. This feature is useful when we want to view an object from several different perspectives.

2.2   Accessing Information Through Paths

Accessing information in a web of contexts often involves navigating from one context to another by following references, i.e., by traversing contexts. From an object within a given context, we can reach any object that belongs to one of its references and, recursively, any object that lies on a path. A path is a sequence of pairs of the form (c_i, t_i), $i = 1, ..., n$, where

(i) c_i is a context and $t_i = \langle d_i, o_i, r_i \rangle$ is a triple in the content of c_i, and

(ii) c_{i+1} is in r_i, for $i = 1, ..., n\text{-}1$.

Paths form the basis for reaching objects in a context navigating through the references of objects. Actually, the query language presented in [8] is a path-language.

3   Implicit Relationships

As we mentioned earlier, each context is a conceptual unit, probably set up separately by its designer then connected through references to other contexts, in a web of contexts. In this section, we describe the framework for discovering *implicit* relationships in a web of contexts.

3.1   Implicit Relationships Between Descriptors Through Objects

In any specific context, each descriptor describes one or more objects in that context, and each object has one or more descriptors describing it . For example, in a library context, the term **Programming** may describe one or more different books concerning programming, and a book concerning programming may also have the term **Theory** associated to it (e.g., if it's a book concerning the theory of programming).

We define the *extension* of a descriptor to be the set of all objects with which the descriptor is associated, and the *intension* of an object to be the set of all descriptors with which the object is associated. More formally we have:

Definition 1.

- Let c be a context, and let d be a descriptor in c.

  The *extension* of d in c, denoted by $E_c(d)$, is defined as follows:

$$E_c(d) = \{o | (d, o, r) \text{ is in } c\}$$

– Let c be a context, and let o be an object in c.
The *intension* of o in c, denoted by $I_c(o)$, is defined as follows:

$$I_c(o) = \{d | (d, o, r) \text{ is in } c\}$$

Clearly, E_c and I_c can be seen as set-valued functions, the former receiving a descriptor as input and returning a set of objects, while the latter receiving an object as input and returning a set of descriptors.

We note that all objects in $E_c(d)$ are related by the fact that they all share the descriptor d, i.e. they are *homonyms*, and all descriptors in $I_c(o)$ are related by the fact that they all describe the same object o, i.e. they are *synonyms*. However, these relationships are *explicit*, in the sense that it is the context designer that has explicitly defined them, at context design time. By "composing" these explicit relationships one can define *implicit* relationships as well, either between descriptors or between objects.

Indeed, the above definitions are given with respect to a single context c. However, we can extend them easily to a web of contexts, by replacing the set of descriptors appearing in c with the set of descriptors appearing in the whole web of contexts, and the set of objects appearing in c with the set of objects appearing in the whole web of contexts.

First, let us call *environment* of a descriptor d any context in which d appears, and let us denote by $Env(d)$ the set of all environments of d. Then, we can generalize the notion of extension over the whole web of contexts as follows:

$$E(d) = \bigcup_{c \in Env(d)} E_c(d).$$

Next, let us call *facet* of an object o, any context in which o appears, and let us denote by $Fac(o)$ the set of all facets of o. Then, we can generalize the notion of intension over the whole web of contexts as follows:

$$I(o) = \bigcup_{c \in Fac(o)} I_c(o).$$

E and I can be seen as set-valued functions extending the functions E_c and I_c (seen earlier) over the whole web of contexts. The implicit relationships between descriptors that we have in mind are obtained by composing the functions E and I to obtain a monotonic operator over sets of descriptors. This operator is denoted by IE and it is defined as follows: for every set of descriptors D, $IE(D) = I(E(D))$.

Clearly, the function IE is monotonic with respect to set inclusion, so its repeated application attains a fixpoint, say after n_0 steps (assuming the set of all descriptors is finite): $(IE)^{n_0+1}(D) = (IE)^{n_0}(D)$. We define two descriptors d and d' to be equivalent, denoted $d \approx d'$, if $(IE)^{n_0}(d) = (IE)^{n_0}(d')$.

Clearly, the relation $\approx$ is an equivalence relation over the set of all descriptors, and its equivalence classes describe all relationships (explicit and implicit) that exist among descriptors. The following algorithm computes the equivalence classes of descriptors under the relation $\approx$:

1. Pick a descriptor not yet "visited".
2. Apply E to find a set of objects, then apply I to the result to find a set of descriptors.
3. Repeat 2 until fixpoint.
4. Repeat 1-3 until all descriptors are visited.

In what follows, we present a number of examples showing the usefulness of the relation $\approx$ between descriptors.

c_{p1}: Profile

KITANO Takeshi	o_1	$\{c_{p1}\}$
Family	o_{10}	$\{c_{10}\}$
Movies	o_{11}	$\{c_{m1}\cdots\}$
-	-	-

c_{m1}: ZATOICHI

ZATOICHI	o_{m1}	-
Director	o_1	$\{c_{p1}\}$
Scriptwriter	o_1	$\{c_{p1}\}$
Actor, Zatoichi	o_1	$\{c_1, c_2\}$
-	-	-

c_{m2}: SEVEN SAMURAI

SEVEN SAMURAI	o_{m2}	-
Director	o_2	$\{c_{p2}\}$
Scriptwriter	o_2	$\{c_{p2}\}$
Actor, Kikuchiyo	o_3	$\{c_{p3}\}$
-	-	-

c_{p2}: Profile

KUROSAWA Akira	o_2	$\{c_{p2}\}$
Family	o_{20}	$\{c_{20}\}$
Movies	o_{21}	$\{c_{m2}\cdots\}$
-	-	-

Fig. 2. An example of a web of contexts.

Figure 2 shows a simple example of a web of contexts. The context c_{p1} is a context identifier, and *"profile"* is the name of the context. *"KITANO"* is a name of object o_1, and refers to the context c_{p1}. In the same context, the object o_{11} in named *"Movies"* and refers a set of contexts that includes the context c_{m1}. That context c_{m1} contains information about the movie *"ZATOICHI"*.

Let us see now if there is an implicit relation between *"KITANO"* and *"KUROSAWA"* through these contexts.

$E(\text{``KITANO"}) = \{o_1\}$
$IE(\text{``KITANO"}) = \{\text{``KITANO"}, \text{``Takeshi"}, \text{``Director"}, \text{``Scriptwriter"},$
$\text{``Actor"}, \text{``Zatoichi"}\}$
$E(IE(\text{``KITANO"})) = \{o_1, o_2\}$
$(IE)^2(\text{``KITANO"}) = \{\text{``KITANO"}, \text{``Takeshi"}, \text{``Director"}, \text{``Scriptwriter"},$
$\text{``Actor"}, \text{``Zatoichi"}, \text{``KUROSAWA"}, \text{``Akira"}\}$

$E(\text{``}KUROSAWA\text{''}) = \{o_2\}$
$IE(\text{``}KUROSAWA\text{''}) = \{\text{``}KUROSAWA\text{''}, \text{``}Akira\text{''}, \text{``}Director\text{''},$
$\text{``}Scriptwriter\text{''}\}$
$E(IE(\text{``}KUROSAWA\text{''})) = \{o_2, o_1\}$
$(IE)^2(\text{``}KUROSAWA\text{''}) = \{\text{``}KUROSAWA\text{''}, \text{``}Akira\text{''}, \text{``}Director\text{''},$
$\text{``}Scriptwriter\text{''}, \text{``}KITANO\text{''}, \text{``}Takeshi\text{''}, \text{``}Actor\text{''}, \text{``}Zatoichi\text{''}\}$

$(IE)^2(\text{``}KITANO\text{''}) = (IE)^2(\text{``}KUROSAWA\text{''})$, therefore, $\text{``}KITANO\text{''} \approx$ $\text{``}KUROSAWA\text{''}$. The descriptors $\text{``}KITANO\text{''}$ and $\text{``}KUROSAWA\text{''}$ are equivalent. This means that a set of implicit relation paths, or $IR\text{-}path$, exists between these two descriptors:

$IR - paths(\text{``}KITANO\text{''}, \text{``}KUROSAWA\text{''})$
$\quad = \{\text{``}KITANO\text{''}.o_1.\text{``}Director\text{''}.o_2.\text{``}KUROSAWA\text{''},$
$\qquad \text{``}KITANO\text{''}.o_1.\text{``}Scriptwriter\text{''}.o_2.\text{``}KUROSAWA\text{''}\}$

The first path means that object o_1 has $\text{``}KITANO\text{''}$ as a descriptor and $\text{``}Director\text{''}$ as another descriptor. Futhermore, $\text{``}Director\text{''}$ is also the descriptor of object $o_2$ whose $\text{``}KUROSAWA\text{''}$ is another descriptor. So this path suggests the relation that both $\text{``}KITANO\text{''}$ and $\text{``}KUROSAWA\text{''}$ are directors of movies. In the same way, the second path means that they are also scriptwriters of movies.

Figure 3 shows connections from each object to descriptors. Descriptors around an object are synonyms of the object, they are results of the function I for each object. In this figure, there is no relation (path) between $\text{``}KITANO\text{''}$ and $\text{``}KUROSAWA\text{''}$. Figure 4 shows a result of the function IE for each object. Then the relations between $\text{``}KITANO\text{''}$ and $\text{``}KUROSAWA\text{''}$ appeare on the graph. Those paths are given by $IR\text{-}paths(\text{``}KITANO\text{''}, \text{``}KUROSAWA\text{''})$.

3.2   Implicit Relationships Between Objects Through Facets

We now define implicit relationships between objects through facets. First, we recall that a facet of an object o is any context to which o belongs, and we denote by $Fac(o)$ the set of all facets of o. Moreover, given a context c, we denote by $El(c)$ the set of all objects appearing in c, that is,

$$El(c) = \{o | (d, o, r) \text{ is in } c\}$$

Clearly, Fac and El can be seen as functions, the former receiving an object as input and returning a set of contexts, while the latter receiving a context as input and returning a set of objects.

The implicit relationships between objects that we have in mind are obtained by composing the functions Fac and El to obtain a monotonic operator over sets of objects. This operator is denoted by $ElFac$ and it is defined as follows: for every set of objects O, $ElFac(O) = El(Fac(O))$.

Clearly, the function $ElFac$ is monotonic with respect to set inclusion, so its repeated application attains a fixpoint, say after n_0 steps (assuming the set of

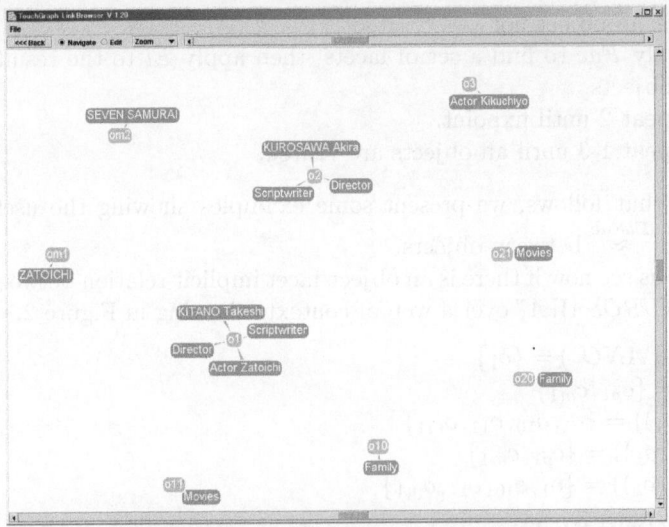

Fig. 3. Synonyms around each object.

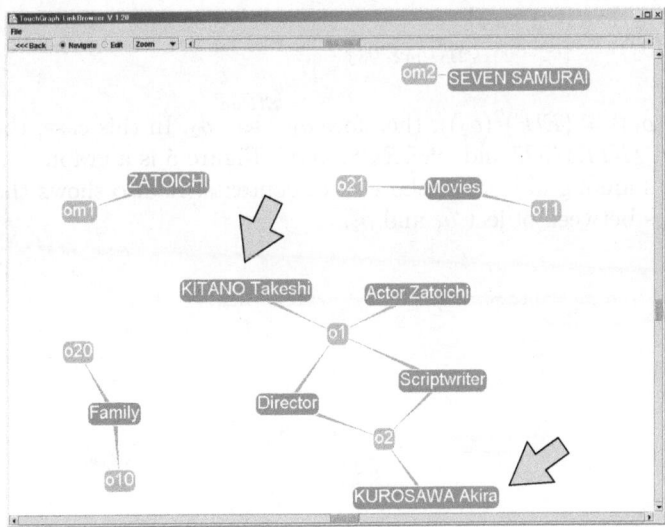

Fig. 4. Implicit relationships between objects and descriptors.

all objects is finite): $(ElFac)^{n_0+1}(O) = (ElFac)^{n_0}(O)$. We define two objects o and o' to be equivalent, denoted $o \stackrel{ElFac}{\approx} o'$, if $(ElFac)^{n_0}(o) = (ElFac)^{n_0}(o')$.

Clearly, the relation $\stackrel{ElFac}{\approx}$ is an equivalence relation over the set of all objects, and its equivalence classes describe all relationships (explicit and implicit) that exist among objects. The following algorithm computes the equivalence classes of objects under the relation $\stackrel{ElFac}{\approx}$:

1. Pick an object not yet "visited".
2. Apply *Fac* to find a set of facets, then apply *El* to the result to find a set of objects.
3. Repeat 2 until fixpoint.
4. Repeat 1-3 until all objects are visited.

In what follows, we present some examples showing the usefulness of the relation $\overset{ElFac}{\approx}$ between objects.

Let us see now if there is an object-facet implicit relation between *"KITANO"* and *"KUROSAWA"* over a web of contexts showing in Figure 2.

$E("KITANO") = \{o_1\}$
$F(o_1) = \{c_{p1}, c_{m1}\}$
$El(F(o_1)) = \{o_1, o_{10}, o_{11}, o_{m1}\}$
$F(ElF(o_1)) = \{c_{p1}, c_{m1}\}$
$(ElF)^2(o_1)) = \{o_1, o_{10}, o_{11}, o_{m1}\}$

$E("KUROSAWA") = \{o_2\}$
$F(o_2) = \{c_{p2}, c_{m2}\}$
$El(F(o_2)) = \{o_2, o_{20}, o_{21}, o_{m2}, o_3\}$
$F(ElF(o_2)) = \{c_{p2}, c_{m2}\}$
$(ElF)^2(o_2)) = \{o_2, o_{20}, o_{21}, o_{m2}, o_3\}$

$(ElF)^2(o_1)) \neq (ElF)^2(o_2))$, therefore $o_1 \overset{ElFac}{\not\approx} o_2$. In this case, there is no path between *"KITANO"* and *"KUROSAWA"*. Figure 5 is a graph to show the relationships among objects in the web of contexts. It also shows there is no relationships between object o_1 and o_2.

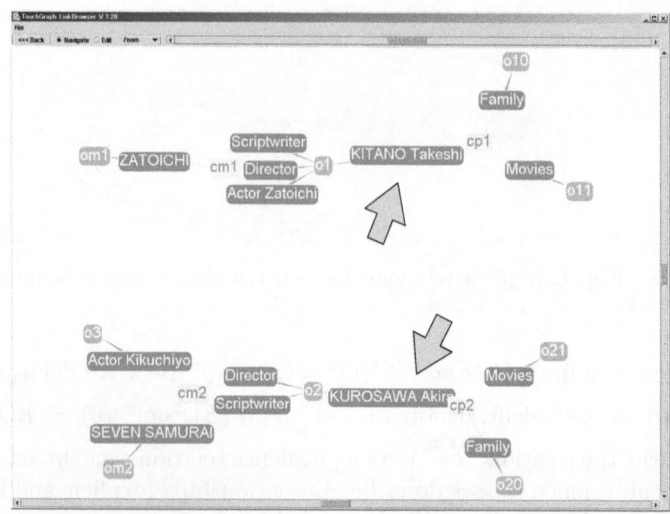

Fig. 5. Implicit Relationships between objects and facets.

c_{p1}: Profile of KITANO Takeshi

KITANO Takeshi	o_1	$\{c_{p1}\}$
Daughter	o_{10}	$\{c_{10}\}$
Movies	o_{11}	$\{c_{m1}\cdots\}$
-	-	-

c_{m1}: ZATOICHI

ZATOICHI	o_{m1}	-
Director	o_1	$\{c_{p1}\}$
Scriptwriter	o_1	$\{c_{p1}\}$
Costume Designer	o_5	$\{c_{p3}\}$
Actor, Zatoichi	o_1	$\{c_1, c_2\}$
-	-	-

c_{p2}: Profile of KUROSAWA Akira

KUROSAWA Akira	o_2	$\{c_{p2}\}$
Movies	o_{21}	$\{c_{m2}\cdots\}$
Son	o_4	$\{c_{p4}\}$
Daughter	o_5	$\{c_{p3}\}$
-	-	-

c_{m2}: SEVEN SAMURAI

SEVEN SAMURAI	o_{m2}	-
Director	o_2	$\{c_{p2}\}$
Scriptwriter	o_2	$\{c_{p2}\}$
Actor, Kikuchiyo	o_3	$\{c_{p3}\}$
-	-	-

c_{p3}: Profile of KUROSAWA Kazuko

KUROSAWA Kazuko	o_5	$\{c_{p3}\}$
Movies	o_{51}	$\{c_{m1}\cdots\}$
Brother	o_4	$\{c_{p4}\}$
Father	o_2	$\{c_{p2}\}$
-	-	-

Fig. 6. A example of a web of contexts.

Then, let us consider about object-facet implicit relations between *"KITANO"* and *"KUROSAWA"* in Figure 6.

$E(``KITANOTakeshi") = \{o_1\}$
$F(o_1) = \{c_{p1}, c_{m1}\}$
$El(F(o_1)) = \{o_1, o_{10}, o_{11}, o_{m1}, o_5\}$
$F(ElF(o_1)) = \{c_{p1}, c_{m1}, c_{p3}\}$
$(ElF)^2(o_1)) = \{o_1, o_{10}, o_{11}, o_{m1}, o_5, o_{51}, o_4, o_2\}$
$F(ElF^2(o_1)) = \{c_{p1}, c_{m1}, c_{p3}, c_{p2}, c_{m2}\}$
$(ElF)^3(o_1)) = \{o_1, o_{10}, o_{11}, o_{m1}, o_5, o_{51}, o_2, o_{21}, o_5, o_{m2}, o_3\}$

$E(``KUROSAWAAkira") = \{o_2\}$
$F(o_2) = \{c_{p2}, c_{p3}, c_{m2}\}$
$El(F(o_2)) = \{o_2, o_{21}, o_4, o_5, o_{51}, o_{m2}, o_3\}$
$F(ElF(o_2)) = \{c_{p2}, c_{p3}, c_{m2}, c_{m1}\}$
$(ElF)^2(o_2)) = \{o_2, o_{21}, o_4, o_5, o_{51}, o_{m2}, o_3, o_{m1}, o_1\}$
$F(ElF^2(o_2)) = \{c_{p2}, c_{p3}, c_{m2}, c_{m1}, c_{p1}\}$
$(ElF)^3(o_2)) = \{o_2, o_{21}, o_4, o_5, o_{51}, o_{m2}, o_3, o_{m1}, o_1, o_{10}, o_{11}\}$

In this case, $(ElF)^3(o_1)) = (ElF)^3(o_2))$. Therefore, $o_1 \overset{ElFac}{\approx} o_2$. There are several paths between the objects o_1 and o_2:

P_1: o_1. *"Director"- "Costume Designer".o_5. "KUROSAWA Kazuko"*
- *"Father".o_2*,
P_2: o_1. *"Director"- "Costume Designer".o_5. "KUROSAWA Kazuko"*
- *"Brother".o_4. "Son"- "KUROSAWA Akira".o_2*,

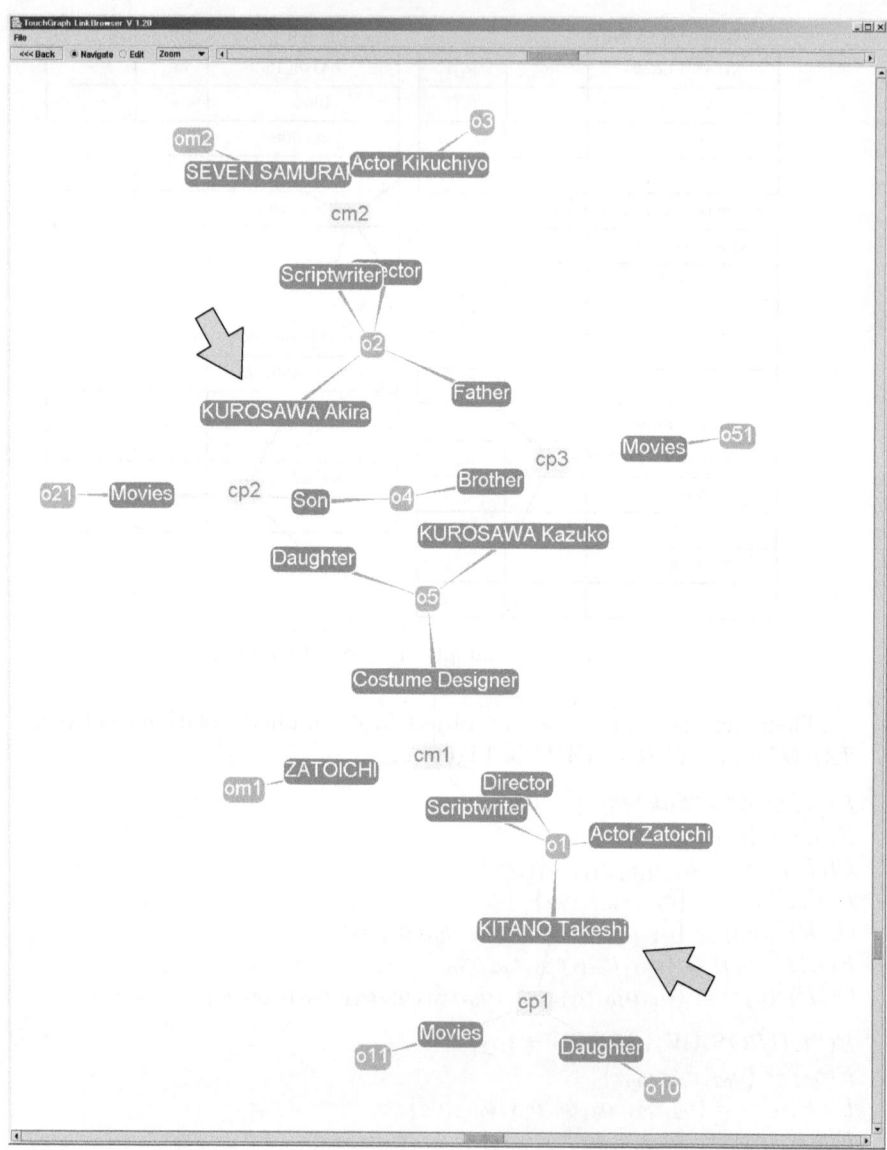

Fig. 7. Implicit Relationships between objects and facets.

P_3: o_1. *"Director"-"Costume Designer".o_5."Daughter"*
- *"KUROSAWA Akira".o_2,*
P_4: o_1. *"Director"-"Costume Designer".o_5."Daughter"*
- *"Son".o_4."Brother"-"Father".o_2,*

Therefore,
$IR\text{-}paths_{ElFac}(E(\text{"KITANO Takeshi"}), E(\text{"KUROSAWA Akira"}))$
$= \{P_1, P_2, P_3, P_4 ......\}.$

The first path is interpreted as follows. *"KITANO Takeshi"* is the *"Director"* of the movie *"ZATOICHI"*. In the same movie, *"KUROSAWA Kazuko"*, whose *"Father"* is *"KUROSAWA Akira"*, works as *"Costume Designer"*. Such an Implicit Relationship would be found as follows.

"KITANO Takeshi" is a descriptor of the object o_1 in the context c_{p1}. The object o_1 has *"Director"* as a descriptor in the context c_{m1}. In the context c_{m1}, there is an object o_5 named *"Costume Designer"*. The object o_5 has *"KURO-SAWA Kazuko"* as a descriptor in the context c_{p3}. In the context c_{p3}, there is an object o_2 named *"Father"*. The object o_2 has *"KUROSAWA Akira"* as a descriptor in the context c_{p2}.

Figure 7 is a graph to show the relationships among objects in the web of contexts. It also shows there are several paths between object o_1 and o_2. Figure 8 shows one of paths between object o_1 and o_2.

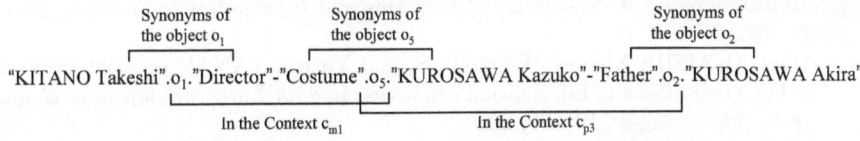

Fig. 8. A path between *"KITANO Takeshi"* and *"KUROSAWA Akira"*.

4 Concluding Remarks

We have defined two types of implicit relationships that may exist in a web of contexts in large information bases. We have also proposed a framework for discovering implicit relationships between descriptors through objects, and between objects through facets. This framework allows a user to discover relationships of which the user may not even be aware of when setting up the web of contexts. Apart from being of interest in their own right, such relationships could help in useful re-organizations of the web of contexts.

We have implemented these concepts in the form of what we call Information Access Space, based on the IntelligentBox System [4, 1, 3].

We believe that, in its present state, our framework can be useful only in "sparse" web of contexts, i.e. when each context references only a small number of other contexts. In each case, the equivalence classes of descriptors and/or objects are likely to be of relatively small size, hence to convey useful information. However, if the contexts are highly interconnected then these equivalence classes may be of very large size, hence difficult to exploit by users. We are currently investigating different types of "constraints", (i.e. additional properties) that the relationships between descriptors or between objects shold satisfy to make them intuitively appealing to (and manageable by) the users.

Acknowledgements

The authors would like to thank Yuzuru Tanaka (Hokkaido University), Takeshi Sunaga (Tama Art University), Kengo Dohtani (Tama Art University) and others for their constructive comments.

References

1. Mina AKAISHI, Makoto OHIGASHI, Nicolas SPYRATOS, and Yuzuru TANAKA. Information access space framework over contextualized information base. In *Seventh International Conference on Information Visualisation (IV 2003)*, pages 414–420, 2003.
2. Mina AKAISHI, Nicolas SPYRATOS, and Yuzuru TANAKA. A component-based application framework for context-driven information access. In *The 11th European-Japanese Conference on Information Modeling and Knowledge Bases*, pages 242–253, 2001.
3. Mina AKAISHI, Nicolas SPYRATOS, and Yuzuru TANAKA. Construction of information access space based on a contextualized information base. In *7th World Multiconference on Systemics, Cybernetics and Informatics (SCI 2003)*, pages 24–29, 2003.
4. Mina AKAISHI, Nicolas SPYRATOS, and Yuzuru TANAKA. Contextual search in large collections of information resources. In *13th European-Japanese Conference (EJC 2003)*, pages 313–320, 2003.
5. Mina AKAISHI, Hiroyuki YAMAMOTO, Makoto OHIGASHI, Nicolas SPYRATOS, and Yuzuru TANAKA. 3D visual construction of a context-based information access space. In *The 12th European-Japanese Conference on Information Modeling and Knowledge Bases*, pages 24–37, 2002.
6. M. Teodorakis, A. Analyti, P. Constantopoulos, and N Spyratos. Context in information bases. In *Proc, of the 3rd Int. Conference on Cooperative Information Systems (coopIS '98)*, pages 260–270, 1998.
7. M. Theodorakis, A. Analyti, P. Constantopoulos, and N. Spyratos. Contextualization as an abstraction mechanism for conceptual modelling. In *Proc. of the 18th Intern. Conference on Conceptual Modelling (ER '99)*, pages 475–489, 1999.
8. M. Theodorakis, A. Analyti, P. Constantopoulos, and N Spyratos. Querying contextualized information bases. In *Proc. of the 24th Intern. Conference on Information and Communication Technologies and Programming (ICT&P '99)*, pages 260–270, 1999.

On Information Organization in Annotation Systems

Panos Constantopoulos, Martin Doerr, Maria Theodoridou, and Manos Tzobanakis

Institute of Computer Science, FORTH
Heraklion, Crete, Greece
{panos,martin,maria,tzoban}@ics.forth.gr

Abstract. A rich semantic model of annotation is presented that distinguishes several annotation types, uses controlled vocabulary where appropriate, and supports multi-facetted characterization of documents, annotation of parts of documents as well as of entire documents, and annotation of document associations besides annotation of single documents. This model has served as the basis for implementing a powerful annotation system included in an advanced digital library system.

1 Introduction

According to the *New Oxford English Dictionary*, an annotation is "a note by way of explanation or comment added to a text or diagram". As such, annotations are primarily personal records of reading and interpretation, but they also often serve as shared records of work and opinion within specific scientific or professional communities. In the world of paper documents annotations are usually found either as arbitrary textual comments, or as characterizations according to specific aspects of interest. These can be unstructured and very personal, or they can be relatively structured, following certain rules with regard to aspects of annotation and format (usually established within a community). In what concerns the physical carrier of an annotation, this can be the annotated document itself or a separate document, usually a note card. In either case an annotation can be thought of as a distinct, yet 'secondary' document referring to a 'primary' one.

In the world of digital documents, annotations are mostly encountered in the context of digital libraries, scientific databases and document management systems, and they share the purpose and nature of traditional paper annotations. They can be incorporated in the documents, or they can be treated as (secondary) documents themselves, referring to other documents, which can be documents of independent origin ("primary" documents), or other annotations. When treated as documents, annotations may reside in an autonomous annotation base, to which all the usual document management services apply. Alternatively, they can be collocated with the documents they annotate.

Digital annotations present higher potential than paper annotations for supporting discourse within scientific or professional communities, especially by virtue of the possibility offered by the World Wide Web to uniformly access distinct annotation servers. The cost to be paid for realizing this potential is a compelling need to ensure common interpretations of the data elements contained in the annotations both by the programs accessing and manipulating them and by the people using them. This, in turn, implies a need for common information organization schemes.

G. Grieser and Y. Tanaka (Eds.): Intuitive Human Interface 2004, LNAI 3359, pp. 189–200, 2004.
© Springer-Verlag Berlin Heidelberg 2004

Furthermore it must be noted that the interfaces provided by annotation systems available to date compare rather unfavorably with the ease and freedom of writing on the margin or on note cards. As a partial compensation, some other productivity gain should be offered, such as the integration of annotation with other services.

Prominent issues in annotation system design include accommodating variety in user styles and needs, establishing community-agreed representations of annotations and transparently incorporating annotation in a wider set of electronic services, e.g. a digital library [1].

In the work reported here we address the above issues in the context of designing the annotation service for the SCHOLNET digital library system [2, 3], intended to support scholarly research. Thus the annotation service is expected (a) to offer a level of organization of information that matches the needs of a disciplined scholarly annotation practice, and (b) to be integrated with other services of the DL system. In this paper we focus on the definition of a semantic model of annotation, which provides the scheme for information organization supported by the annotation server. The resulting annotation record corresponds to a set of Dublin Core metadata elements.

In section 2 we review the types and content of annotations and the functionality of a number of annotation systems. In section 3 we introduce the semantic annotation model developed. Implementation considerations and the SCHOLNET project are briefly presented in section 4. Finally, section 5 contains concluding remarks.

2   Annotation and Annotation Systems

Annotations and annotation systems can be distinguished with respect to several criteria, such as formality, context-dependence, lexical and syntactic types, knowledge representation (language and annotation model), software architecture, data management, and access facilities.

Marshall [4] considers the distinction between *informal* annotations, such as personal notes on the margin, and *formal* ones, effectively metadata following standards, with values assigned according to conventional authorities. Semantic models, such as the one introduced here, are properly deemed as formal. Context dependence refers to whether an annotation carries enough information, in the form of appropriate markup, in order to be uniformly interpreted, by humans or by software agents. In Marshall's terms, *explicit* annotations admit uniform interpretation, while *tacit* ones, such as telegraphic personal annotations, rely on context for their interpretation, restricted only to some humans.

With regard to the lexical and syntactic constructs used to express annotations, several distinctions can be drawn.

By medium: Annotations can be lexical (text or hyperlink), visual (icon or highlighting), or acoustic (audio signal).

By locality of reference: Annotations may refer to entire texts (most common case), parts of texts or both (e.g., Amaya [5]). In some systems annotation links are provided at the end of a document (e.g., CritSuit [6]), while in other systems links are added at points in the document, either predefined by the author (e.g., CoNote [7]), or arbitrary (e.g., Amaya, Commentor [8]). In the latter case, of course, there is a validation issue in view of document updates.

By process: Three types of annotations can be defined: textual, link and semantic [1].

Textual annotation involves adding some form of free text commentary to a document (in general, resource), aimed primarily at human readers. Annotea [9] is an example of a system supporting this process. The SWISS-PROT database [10] is another example, in which the system contains protein sequence information together with descriptions of structure, functions, etc. An important point is that these descriptions (i.e., the annotations) are data of interest in themselves and they are treated as such, i.e. they can be accessed and processed independently of the primary data they annotate.

Link annotation provides information in the form of the contents of a link destination, rather than an explicit piece of text or other data. In a sense it can be considered as an extension of textual annotation. Examples of this kind, also primarily destined for human users, are the Distribution Links Service [11] and 3rd Voice [12].

Semantic annotation, finally, assigns markup elements according to a specified model, which take values from controlled vocabularies, and it aims at both human readers and software agents. This approach aims at explicitly associating fragments of resources with (representations of) concepts in the domain of discourse and should be contrasted with the previous two, in which such association is only effected ad hoc in the mind of the person reading the annotation. Some examples of systems adopting this approach (at varying degrees of formality) are SHOE [13], Ontobroker [14], COHSE [15] and SCHOLNET.

An important issue arising in semantic annotation systems is that of choosing an information representation model, i.e. a model of the annotation function expressed in some representation language and a controlled vocabulary from which data values are to be drawn. Annotation models usually include a set of annotation types and they vary in formality and detail, with implications both in terms of suitability for software agents and usability for humans. Almost every annotation system has its own model. For instance, the characterizations assigned to an annotation by the systems Amaya, HyperNews [16], Principia Cybernetica [17] and COHSE are listed in Table 1 below.

The first three systems provide characterizations that pertain to a position statement, yet at different levels of detail. Amaya and Principia Cybernetica provide relatively broad categories to which a position statement may be classified. They both include categories for comment (Amaya, PC: 'comment'), explanation (Amaya: 'example', 'explanation', PC: 'illustration') and suggested change (Amaya: change, PC: correction). PC also has categories relating to agreement/approval (refutation, confirmation), whereas Amaya has categories for advisory comments (advice), questions, as well as a general reference link with vague semantics (see also). HyperNews, on the other hand, offers a mixture of broad and narrow categories: comment ('note'), special categories of comment ('warning', 'feedback'), a bookmark category suggesting value ('idea'), an ephemeral bookmark ('news'), various degrees of agreement/approval ('ok', 'sad', 'angry', 'agree', 'disagree'), question, and a general reference link with vague semantics ('more'). All systems address only in part the aspects of scholarly criticism, and the vocabulary they offer does not display any structure that would convey some information about the function of annotation and the concepts involved.

Table 1. Examples of annotation characterizations

System	Annotation characterizations
Amaya	advice, change, comment, example, explanation, question, see also
HyperNews	question, note, warning, feedback, idea, more, news, ok, sad, angry, agree, disagree
Principia Cybernetica	comment, refutation, confirmation, correction, illustration
COHSE	decoration, linking, instance identification, instance reference, aboutness, pertinence

COHSE follows a different approach: it provides a set of constructs that enable associating arbitrary concepts with resource fragments. This association can take various forms essentially corresponding to the instantiation and attribution mechanisms of conceptual modelling. The high generality of this model, although seemingly a strength, is actually a weakness because it ignores the pragmatic aspects of annotation and consequently fails to provide guidance to the users as to which concepts to employ for characterizing resource fragments.

The annotation types offered by most systems are relatively few. Whether they are adequate or which set of types would better serve user requirements is an issue that calls for systematic empirical evaluation. In the absence of such results, we are inclined to make the working hypothesis that a rich model supporting accurate, fine grain characterizations would be more instrumental within a specialized scientific or professional community. The members of such communities usually share concepts, conventions and ways of working. Not only are they able to benefit from an adequately elaborated information model, but they also often require specificity and advanced functionality as productivity supports. In this paper we propose a model that represents the annotation function in higher precision and detail than previous ones, aimed specifically at supporting scholarly communities.

With regard to the referent of annotation, we note that what systems mostly support is annotation of primary documents and, sometimes, annotation of annotations. In both cases annotation refers to a single document, therefore it carries the interpretation of that document by a particular reader. A possible extension might be to have annotations that interpret the association between the contents of two primary documents.

Some systems employ expressive knowledge representation languages in order to support their information models and the formulation and evaluation of complex queries. This is the case, e.g., with Amaya, that employs RDF [18], and SCHOLNET, that employs SIS-Telos [19], which are equivalent with regard to expressive power.

Finally, some remarks about software architecture, data management, and access facilities of annotation systems. We restrict our interest to systems for the WWW, as this currently is the premium common platform for information access and collaboration. In general systems treat annotations as autonomous entities, managed separately from the primary documents, either locally or by some annotation server(s). Local management can be done either by the machine handling the annotated document (collocation) or by the machine supporting the annotation activity. In the case of multiple annotation servers, it is generally not possible for a client to know about all of them. So, each client communicates with a specific server which can subsequently negotiate information requests with other servers. Alternatively, the user may declare a set of servers to directly and exclusively communicate with (the policy of Amaya, rather restrictive). Most systems support only predetermined queries (CoNote also supports customized ones) and they employ no DBMS for storing annotations.

3   A Semantic Annotation Model

We now introduce a model for semantic annotation intended primarily to support scholarly communities. Following the analysis in the previous section, the model is designed to provide a structured and detailed representation of information, to serve as guide for formulating judgments and interpretations of documents, and to enable flexibility and elaboration. Specifically:

1. Annotations are treated as documents themselves. Being created by reference to other documents they are considered as *secondary documents*.
2. All kinds of documents (*primary* and *secondary*) can have annotations reflecting the interpretation of their contents by the annotator. This is termed *single annotation*.
3. A pair of primary documents can have annotations reflecting the interpretation of the association between their respective contents by the annotator. This is termed *associative annotation*.
4. Annotation on parts of documents is possible, as well as on entire documents.
5. Annotation is *multi-facetted*: annotation types are grouped into families representing distinct annotation aspects, or dimensions, called *facets*. Annotation types from different facets can be combined to produce a multi-dimensional characterization of the document. Here we define three facets, namely *PositionType, EvaluationType* and *RecordType* (see below).

Annotation types of the first two facets express intentional, rather than syntactic categories: we are primarily interested in capturing the intention of the annotator, rather than classifying the annotation by its syntactic form. The third facet includes both semantic and syntactic categories for descriptive purposes.

Each annotation type admits certain values. These may either belong to a controlled vocabulary [20], giving rise to an enumerated type, or be free text. Where appropriate, a controlled vocabulary provides a closed selection of terms, which facilitates the uniform and precise expression of meanings. Uniformity is thus promoted both across users and over time, which, in turn, supports communication and common practice. On the more technical side, the use of controlled vocabularies enhances retrieval performance. A controlled vocabulary may evolve in time following a predetermined process.

Our semantic model is developed on two abstraction levels: a level of categories and a more abstract level of meta-categories. In terms of the Telos knowledge representation language [21] actually used to implement the system, these correspond to the instantiation levels of simple classes and meta-classes respectively. Classes (or, categories) can be classified as instances of meta-classes (meta-categories), just like atomic objects and data values can be classified as instances of classes, on the basis of some common property. For clarity the meta-class and the simple class levels of the model are presented separately.

The meta-class level of the model organizes the kinds of documents and annotations from a number of aspects. Thus the following classes are introduced:

- *DocumentClass*: It contains all the different kinds (classes) of documents, i.e., PrimaryDocument, Annotation, SingleAnnotation, AssociativeAnnotation, and, by convention, Document.

- *AnnotationClass:* Annotations are distinguished into *classes* according to their functional relationship with the documents they refer to. So, AnnotationClass contains the classes: SingleAnnotation, AssociativeAnnotation and, by convention, Annotation. Since annotations are treated as documents, the various annotation classes are also included in DocumentClass.

- *AnnotationType*: Annotations are further distinguished into *types* according to the annotator's intention they serve. From the intentional point of view, we identify three main aspects of annotation: criticism, evaluation and description. Accordingly, AnnotationType is divided into three subclasses, called facets, which contain as elements the different annotation types. This organization makes explicit the intentional distinctions of annotation types. Consequently it allows performing annotation from multiple aspects by jointly employing annotation types from the different facets. Note that the elements of AnnotationType are entities at the simple class level, which are distributed as elements to the facets. Technically they can also be subclasses of the class Annotation. We define four subclasses of AnnotationType, the three facets and one auxiliary meta-class:

  o *PositionType*: Set of types characterizing position statements or leads for personal use of a document.
  o *EvaluationType*: Set of types representing evaluation criteria.
  o *RecordType*: Set of types containing descriptive information about the document.
  o *ControlledVoc*: This is an auxiliary meta-class used for identifying enumerated types (controlled vocabularies). Each of its elements also belongs to one of the intentional facets.

The meta-class level of the model is depicted in Figure 1. The annotation types, categorized by facet, are listed in Table 2. The semantics of the annotation types are given in Table 3 (a,b,c).

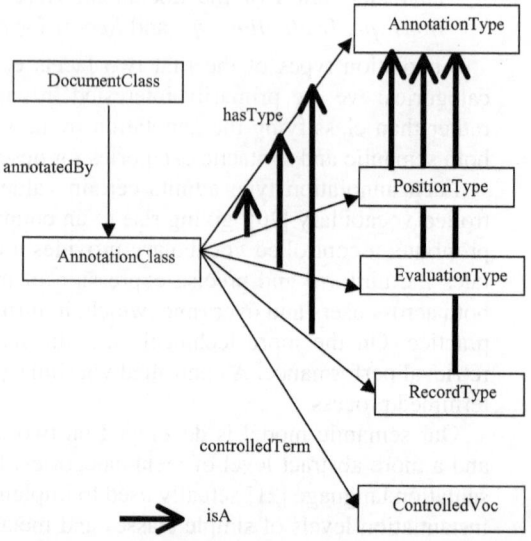

Fig. 1. Annotation model, meta-class level

Table 2. Annotation types by facet. Controlled value types are shown in italics

PositionType	EvaluationType	RecordType
Agreement	*Needs*	*DocumentNature*
Contribution	*Interest*	*Genre*
Explanation	*Writing*	Figure
Summary	*Clarity*	Table
Inspiration	*TargetReader*	Excerpt
Observation	*Value*	DocumentSubject
Question	*Originality*	
	OverallRating	
	Remark	

Table 3a. Semantics of the annotation types, PositionType facet

PositionType	
Agreement	Strong Agreement, Moderate Agreement, Weak Agreement, Disagreement
Contribution	An addendum to the document created by the reader
Explanation	An explanation volunteered by the reader. Free text.
Summary	A summary of (part of) the document produced by the reader. Free text.
Inspiration	An idea that came to the reader's mind after reading (part of) the document. Free text.
Observation	An observation made by the reader relative to (part of) the document. Free text.
Question	A question triggered in the mind of the reader by (some part of) the document. Free text.

Table 3b. Semantics of the annotation types, EvaluationType facet

EvaluationType	
Needs	Needs correction, Needs elaboration
Interest	Very interesting, Interesting, Moderately interesting, Uninteresting
Writing	Adequate analysis of the problem, Background information adequately presented, Enough evidence to support the conclusions, Provokes discussion, Logically arranged and organized
Clarity	Clearly written, Additional examples required to clarify the meaning
SuitableReader	Expert, Novice, Amateur
Value	Permanent value, Limited value
Originality	High, Medium, Low, None
OverallRating	Excellent, Very Good, Good, Acceptable, Unacceptable
Remark	Comment about the document. Free text.

Table 3c. Semantics of the annotation types, RecordType facet

RecordType	
DocumentNature	Theoretical, Design, Technical, Narrative, etc.
Genre	Book, Review, Original Paper, Survey, M.Sc. Thesis, Ph.D. Thesis, etc.
Figure	The presence of a figure at a specific point in the document is indicated.
Table	The presence of a table at a specific point in the document is indicated.
Excerpt	An excerpt from the document.
DocumentSubject	Characterization of the subject. Free text.

The PositionType facet includes annotation types that are intended to be a record of the thoughts generated to the reader by the document, appropriately categorized (Question, Explanation, Inspiration, Observation, Contribution), a personal summary (Summary), or an indication of the degree of agreement (Agreement) of the reader with statements or entire passages contained in the document. The latter can be effectively provided by choosing from a list of values, so Agreement takes values from a controlled vocabulary. The other position types are more appropriately expressed in the form of free text.

The EvaluationType facet includes annotation types intended to record the outcome of a structured evaluation of a document, like the one that takes place when evaluating an article submitted for publication. Such an evaluation may also be effected in the course of reading the document for other reasons, yet record can be taken of the evaluation in the same manner. Most of the annotation types in this facet have controlled vocabularies (Needs, Interest, Writing, Clarity, TargetReader, Value, Originality, OverallRating), so as to enable calibration of evaluations and to facilitate comparison of documents on the basis of those evaluations. On the other hand, Remark is expressed in free text.

The RecordType facet, finally, includes annotation types intended for document description. Of those, DocumentNature and Genre are enumerated types that serve for classifying a document, DocumentSubject allows a free text description of the subject, while Figure and Table indicate the presence of figures and tables, and Excerpt identifies a passage as excerpt from a document.

Note that the controlled values listed for enumerated types in Table 2 are indicative. In fact, the annotation model allows a significant degree of disciplined adaptation: terms in a controlled vocabulary may be altered, added or deleted, in order to better fit the needs and terminology of a user community. Similarly, annotation types in a facet may be renamed, added or deleted. Each such decision is confined within the scope of the relevant category, i.e. the annotation type of the vocabulary or the facet of the annotation type. It is reasonable to conjecture that types will exhibit less variability than vocabularies. One step further, we can expect the facets to be the part of the model with universal applicability, thus to remain invariable across applications, although renaming, adding or deleting facets is in principle possible.

The simple class level of the model, on the other hand, is presented in Figure 2. This part of the model mainly captures the operational relationships between annotations and documents already discussed above. Note that, by virtue of the hasType attribute assigned to AnnotationClass (see Figure 1), the class Annotation admits as attributes all the annotation types listed in Table 1. Specific values of these types are assigned to instances of Annotation, i.e. to specific annotations, observing restrictions that may apply (e.g., integrity constraints enforced by the UI in the SCHOLNET system). Finally, Annotation has the attribute AnnotationRecord (AR) which is a Dublin Core – conformant record (see section on implementation below).

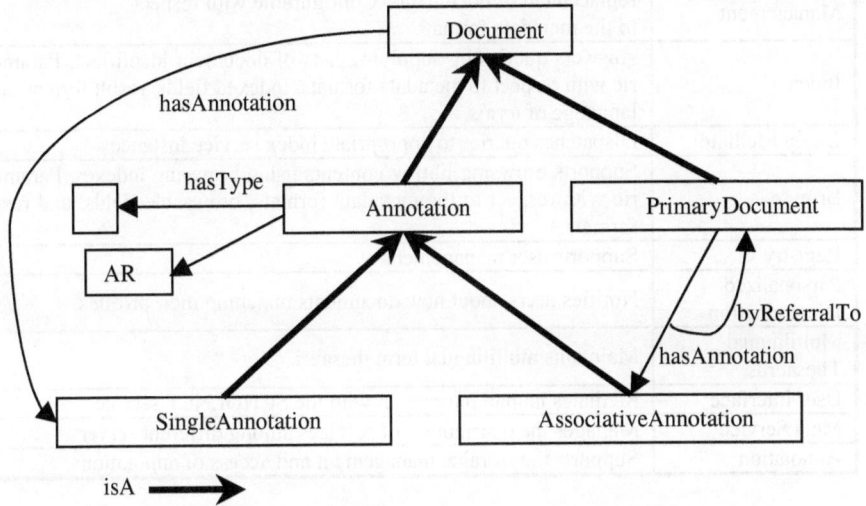

Fig. 2. Annotation model, simple class level

4 Implementation

An annotation service was designed and implemented as part of the SCHOLNET digital library system on the basis of the above model. Here we give a brief description of SCHOLNET and of the annotation service that we have implemented.

SCHOLNET [2, 3] is a EU IST 5th Framework project aimed at designing and building a second generation DL system supporting communication and collaboration within scholarly communities. The SCHOLNET system included support for non-textual data types, hypermedia annotation and personalized information, in addition to more "standard" DL services, such as information acquisition, description, archiving, access, cross-language search and retrieval, and dissemination.

The design of the SCHOLNET system follows the architectural principles developed for OpenDLib [22]. It consists of an open, networked federation of services that co-operate in a manner more complex than usual client-server. Specifically, a service can act as both "provider" and "consumer" and sharing relationships can be defined for any set of services. The services can be centralized, distributed or replicated on different servers. Thus, in an actual SCHOLNET-based DL system, multiple instances of the same service type may be hosted on different servers of different organizations, where a service may require functionality from other services in order to perform its task. Communication among services is based on the Open Library Protocol (OLP) [23]. OLP requests are expressed as URLs embedded in HTTP requests. Structured

Table 4. SCHOLNET digital library services

Service	Function
Repository	Stores and disseminates documents
Multimedia Storage	Stores and disseminates video
Library Management	Supports the submission, withdrawal, and replacement of documents. Configurable with respect to the metadata formats
Index	Answers queries by supplying lists of document identifiers. Parametric with respect to metadata formats, indexed fields, result formats and language of terms.
Query Mediator	Dispatches queries to appropriate index service instances.
Browse	Supports browsing library contents using browsing indexes. Parametric with respect to the metadata formats, browsable fields, and result formats.
Registry	Supports user management.
Personalized Dissemination	Notifies users about new documents matching their profiles.
Multilingual Thesaurus	Maintains multilingual term thesauri.
User Interface	Mediates human interaction with the SCHOLNET services.
Meta Service	Manages the distribution of services among different servers.
Annotation	Supports the storage, management and access of annotations.

requests and responses are formulated in XML. The services provided by SCHOLNET along with their function are listed in Table 4.

The Annotation service [24] provides functions of storage, retrieval and deletion of annotations. A client-server architecture is employed with data management undertaken by SIS [19], a high performance system based on the structural part of the Telos knowledge representation language [21], with expressive power equivalent to RDF/S. A rich set of predefined queries is coded in Java, through which routines of the SIS API are invoked. The annotations are written in XML according to specified DTDs. The choices concerning programming environment ensure maximum interoperability. In what concerns the annotation storage server, it was decided to use a separate server from the one serving the documents chiefly in the interest of autonomy.

To ensure semantic interoperability with other systems, a descriptive record of annotations has been devised that conforms to a subset of the Dublin Core [25] metadata. The fields of the annotation record along with their Dublin Core counterparts are listed in Table 5.

5 Conclusion

We have presented a semantic model of annotation in the context of scholarly work, on the basis of which we have implemented an annotation service as part of the SCHOLNET digital library system. Compared to other existing annotation systems, our model offers a richer information organization scheme in terms of structure and detail. It specifies several annotation types grouped in three facets according to re-

Table 5. Dublin Core – conformant annotation record

Dublin Core elements	SCHOLNET annotation record fields	
Identifier	annotation_id *mandatory*	Unique id of the annotation
Creator	author *mandatory*	Login name of author of the annotation
date.modified	date *mandatory*	Creation date
subject	type *mandatory*	Annotation Type
subject	Subject	List of keywords
description	Text	Free text
rights	Project	List of projects whose members are granted access
rights	Group	List of groups whose members are granted access
relation.reference	program	Program/project providing working context to the annotation
relation.reference	links.toValue	document or annotation handle, pointer inside a document, external URL
format	SCHOLNET annotation DTD	

spective aspects of annotation. By combining types from different facets, one can achieve high specificity in defining annotations. This can be a distinct advantage for a tool intended for use by specialized scientists and professionals. Consistency of annotation and retrieval are further supported by the use of controlled vocabularies where appropriate. The rigorously specified semantic model enables a shared understanding of annotations and therefore their use as a genuine part of a broader community knowledge repository or memory system, such as a digital library. In addition, a semantic model allows defining mappings between variations of annotation records therefore enhancing interoperability. Finally, the model supports annotation of parts of documents as well as of entire documents, and annotation of document associations besides annotation of single documents. Clearly, the information organization for annotation presented here is independent of its embodiment in the implemented annotation service.

Current shortcomings of the annotation service include the lack of non-textual annotations, and the lack of a general query facility. The former can be remedied and the latter is probably less vital than it seems at first sight, as indicated by experience with several SIS applications, in which parametric query classes can be identified.

Finally, it remains to carry out an evaluation of the annotation service in a realistic setting. This is planned to be a laboratory-wide application of the SCHOLNET digital library as a groupware.

References

1. Bechhofer, S. et al.: The Semantics of Semantic Annotation, ODBASE:1st Intl Conf. on Ontologies, Databases, and Applications of Semantics for Large Scale Information Systems. LNCS, Vol. 2519. Springer-Verlag, Irvine, California (2002) 1151—1167

2. SCHOLNET Project Homepage. http://www.ercim.org/SCHOLNET
3. SCHOLNET: A Digital Library Testbed to Support Networked Scholarly Communities. http://www.ics.forth.gr/isl/projects/projects_individual.jsp?ProjectID=4
4. Marshall, C.C.: Towards an ecology of hypertext annotation, Proc. HT98, ACM Conf. on Hypertext, pp. 40-49, Pittsburgh PA, USA, 1998.
5. AMAYA, W3C's Editor/Browser, http://www.w3.org/Amaya
6. Yee, K.-P.: CritLink Mediator, http://crit.org
7. Davis, J.: CoNote, 1994, http://www.cs.cornell.edu/home/dph/annotation/annotations.html
8. Roescheisen, M., Mogensen, C., and Winograd, T.: Shared Web Annotations As A Platform for Third-Party Value-Added Information Providers: Architecture, Protocols, and Usage Examples (1994)
   http://www-diglib.stanford.edu/diglib/pub/reports/commentor.html
9. Annotea, W3C, Annotea Project, http://www.w3.org/2001/Annotea
10. SWISS-PROT Annotated Protein Sequence database, http://www.expasy.org.
11. Carr, L., De Roure, D., Hall, W. and Hill, G.: The Distributed Link Service: A Tool for Publishers, Authors and Readers, WWW Journal, 1(1) (1995) 647-656
12. Margolis, M. and Resnick, D.: Third Voice: Vox Populi Vox Dei?, First Monday, 4(10) (1999) http://www.firstmonday.dk/issues/issue4_10/margolis
13. Heflin, J., Hendler, J. and Luke, S.: SHOE: A Knowledge Representation Language for Internet Applications, Technical Report CS-TR-4078 (UMIACS TR-99-71), Dept. of Computer Science, University of Maryland (1999)
14. Decker, S., Erdmann, M., Fensel, D. and Studer, R.: Ontobroker: Ontology Based Access to Distributed and Semi-Structured Information. In: Meersman, R., Tari, Z. and Stevens, S. (eds.): Semantic Issues in Multimedia Systems. Proc. DS-8, Kluwer (1999) 351-369
15. Carr, L., Bechhofer, S., Goble, C.A. and Hall, W.: Conceptual Linking: Ontology-based Open Hypermedia. Proc. WWW10, Hong Kong (May 2001)
16. Konstantas, D. and Morin, J. H.: HyperNews Hypermedia Newspaper. http://cui.unige.ch/OSG/projects/media/hypernews.html
17. Heylingen, F.: About the Principia Cybernetica Server, March 2002. http://pespmc1.vub.ac.be/SERVER.html
18. Lassila, O., Swick, R. R.: Resource Description Framework (RDF) Model and Syntax Specification. http://www.w3.org/TR/1999/REC-rdf-syntax-19990222
19. The Semantic Index System – SIS. http://www.ics.forth.gr/isl/r-d-activities/sis.html
20. Svenonius, E.: Design of controlled vocabularies, in Encyclopedia of Library and Information Science, Marcel Dekker (1989)
21. Mylopoulos, J.: Conceptual Modeling and Telos. In: Loucopoulos, P. and Zicari, R. (eds.): Conceptual Modeling, Databases and CASE: An Integrated View of Information System Development. Wiley (1992)
22. Castelli, D., Pagano, P.: A System for Building Expandable Digital Libraries, Proc. JCDL '03, Houston, Texas (May 2003) 335-345
23. Information Society RTD Standards Implementation Report, November 2001. http://www.diffuse.org/0111-rtd.html
24. Tzobanakis, M.: An Annotation System for digital documents, M.Sc. Thesis, Dept. of Computer Science, University of Crete (2003)
   http://www.ics.forth.gr/isl/publications/paperlink/Tzobanakis.pdf
25. Metadata Resources, Dublin Core-DC. http://www.ukoln.ac.uk/metadata/resources/dc/
26. Interactive Electronic Publishing, Web based tools for document annotation, http://www.elpub.org

Modelling Learning Subjects as Relationships

Martin Doerr

Institute of Computer Science,
Foundation for Research and Technology – Hellas,
Science and Technology Park of Crete,
Vassilika Vouton, P.O. Box 1385, GR 711 10, Heraklion, Crete, Greece
martin@ics.forth.gr

Abstract. This paper describes a novel intellectual structure for the subject space of material designed for selective autodidactic learning in a large knowledge base. This structure is based on a systematic theory-driven connection of categorical and factual knowledge. It is further based on the idea, that relevant subjects in such a system should be propositions, represented as categorical relationships. Informal inferences between concept hierarchies and categorical relationships are presented. The structure is implemented in a system for training of art conservators in diagnostic knowledge. Multiple systematic ways are implemented to give the user access and overview over large amounts of such subject propositions, that try to overcome the typical mismatch between a user-formulated request and the terms understood by the system, and the general disorientation of users in larger electronic media. The system is right now being presented to users with a first small population of cases.

1 Introduction

There is an increasing public interest to employ information systems for learning. Several factors give rise to high expectations in the potential of information systems as learning and training means for the near future:

1. the ability of database technology to provide effective access to information assets within large amounts of information;
2. the ease of updating database contents to the latest state of knowledge;
3. the possibility to guide the user on multiple paths through the training material - in contrast to the mostly sequential organization of contents in printed books;
4. the possibility to dynamically adapt content presentation to the specific interests and abilities of user groups;
5. the potential to replace human instructors by suitable interactions of the user with the system.

So far, didactics have been studied and applied since a long time. The principles to create a good didactic text, diagrams and other graphical representations for teaching purposes seem to be well understood. Presentations used in the traditional sequential teaching method are increasingly provided on the Web as so-called "course material". The vision is however, that the user himself has the possibility to explore the learning material following his/her interests, professional needs and pace of understanding. In

G. Grieser and Y. Tanaka (Eds.): Intuitive Human Interface 2004, LNAI 3359, pp. 201–214, 2004.

environments that offer by far more knowledge than any individual ever needs or is capable to memorize, the development of effective methods allowing the user to select specific contents seems to be critical.

To our understanding, it seems still to be poorly understood how to structure intellectually the subject space of a domain such that a user can clearly identify where his/her "original question" would be answered. Typically current systems organize the major individual concepts of the domain of discourse in a thesaurus and use them as a kind of subject headings for the learning assets (see e.g. [1]). We propose here the thesis that the true subject and the original user questions about scientific problems are propositions based on relationships rather than the array of individual concepts normally offered as index. Therefore we believe that there is a fundamental intellectual mismatch between the current way to organize the subject space of a scientific domain and the users questions. We further observe that frequently factual and categorical knowledge is neither well distinguished nor well related in subject spaces. A subject "rivers" might refer to a document about how riverbeds are formed and evolve, or about an actual river, or both. "Planets" may not include "Earth" etc.

In this paper, we make arguments that categorical and factual relationships should be central to the intellectual structure of a subject space for learning systems. Novel in this idea are not the general knowledge representation structures employed, but the ontological interpretation of the literature subject and its relationships to the information assets. This idea has been applied to create a prototype of an electronic training handbook for art conservators on the interpretation of multispectral images in the framework of the European funded project CRISATEL [2]. A museum can employ only few conservators, which are frequently confronted with an incredible amount of different materials, techniques, chemical agents and effects. The necessary knowledge for their daily work often exceeds the capacity of any individual. As in medicine, fast access to very detailed knowledge is often critical to preserve objects of immense value. Therefore art conservators already maintain several internationally operating information services about chemical agents and others.

Reliable access to highly specialized knowledge is required, and an organization of the resource that allows for quick understanding of what the resource contains and what it does **not** contain. Further, efficient and highly selective presentation of content is required, that answers comprehensively the problem.

The prototype is the result of an interdisciplinary collaboration of domain (art conservation) and IT experts. The specific conceptual model we have developed and the prototype itself can be easily generalized to training systems for diagnostic knowledge and experience in any other domain. A first experimentation with real end users will take place in the further course of the project.

The organization of this paper is as follows. In section 2 we make theoretical arguments for the role of categorical and factual relationships and their use to structure the index of a learning system. In section 3 we present the core conceptual model of the CRISATEL electronic handbook as a model to organize diagnostic knowledge and experience for autodidactic learning and the subsequent implementation. In section 4 we present related work. In section 5 we draw conclusions and refer to future work.

2 The Learning Subject Space

In this section we make theoretical arguments for the role of categorical and factual relationships and their use to structure the subject space of a learning system.

In an environment designed for autodidactic learning the user seeks knowledge. Let us take here a naïve position and say: Knowledge can be anything that reasonably complements the phrase "I know that...". By learning we mean here only acquisition of such knowledge by the human user (in contrast e.g. to learning skills by active training). In a typical subject catalogue, the user will be confronted with terms for individuals or individual concepts such as "dog", "meat", "Cathedral of Monreale", "gold". None of those expresses knowledge in that sense, however propositions such as "dogs eat meat", "the Cathedral of Monreale contains gold" do express knowledge. We take the position that individual concepts are constituents of knowledge, just as wheels are parts of cars but not cars themselves. Let us take the first phrase "dogs eat meat". Three elementary questions match directly with this proposition: "Do dogs eat meat", "what do dogs eat", "which animals eat meat", and the metaquestion "does this resource know what dogs eat?". A subject like "dogs" alone might be suitable as subject for students interested in acquiring spherical knowledge of everything about dogs. It is rather unspecific to seek answers to any real question.

2.1 About Concepts and Knowledge

Following the terminology of the TELOS knowledge representation language [3] we distinguish between Individuals and Attributes[1]. Universals are called classes, which can be either Individual Classes or Attributes Classes, whereas particulars are called Tokens, Individual Tokens or Attribute Tokens respectively. Individuals comprise equivalents of RDFS classes and their instances (URLs, URIs etc.) whereas attributes are similar to properties[2] and their instances in RDFS. Interpreting knowledge elements as TELOS propositions that imply individuals, we can distinguish between at least three kinds of knowledge elements:

1. Categorical[3] knowledge, such as: "Cats eat fish"
2. Factual knowledge, such as: "My cat ate my mullet"
3. Cross-categorical knowledge, such as "The Cathedral of Monreale contains gold"

Categorical knowledge elements are propositions consisting of two Individual Classes and a relationship between those that can either be an attribute class or an IsA relationship. Factual knowledge elements are propositions consisting of two Individual Tokens and an Attribute Token as relation between those. Categorical knowledge is characteristic for the learning contents in sciences like physics, biology etc., such as

---

[1] In the more recent theory of [4] Individuals are equivalent to "Nodes" and attributes to "Arrows".

[2] In contrast to formalizations of RDFS, a TELOS Attribute is an object in its own right. It can have more than one instance for the same combination of domain and range values and attributes of its own.

[3] The term "categorical knowledge" is used here in the sense of "relational universals, and "factual knowledge" in the same sense of "material facts" in [5].

"cats eat fish", whereas factual knowledge appears in these sciences as *examples* or *experience* from individual experiments or research expeditions and fieldwork. Historical studies on the other side focus on factual knowledge such as "Alexander the Great marched into Persia", whereas categorical knowledge appears in humanities as non-stringent *classification* of phenomena, such as "competition for limited resources can be a reason for war".

One can interpret n-ary relationships more generally as concepts that depend existentially on the attribution of two or more individual concepts. TELOS attributes are binary relationships, n-ary relationships can be simulated in TELOS using an Individual Class with n attributes as intermediate node.

Cross-categorical([5]) knowledge elements consist of an Individual Token, an Individual Class and a relation between those. The relation can be either an Attribute Token or an "instance of" relationship. Whereas the "instance of" relationship is part of all KR models, other cross-categorical knowledge elements have rarely been modelled or studied. However, cross-categorical knowledge elements are frequent in the knowledge acquisition process about real world phenomena in all kinds of scientific, historical or archaeological investigations, such as "this dress was made for wedding" or "this man was killed with a knife". A formal treatment of such propositions can be found in [6], and examples of application in [7]. We will not go into more detail here.

2.2   Problems of Matching User Questions at the Categorical Level

Matching a user question against a semantic network is relatively easy at the factual level. System and user *share* the same notion of *identity* of the Individual Tokens implied, be it people, objects, documents etc. The only technical difficulty for the user is to find out which identifiers the system uses for these Tokens. Several techniques such as exhaustive lists of alternative names, contextual data of the item etc. can significantly help users to find the Tokens they have in mind. For instance, data like "Spanish painter of Greek origin, 16th century" can help to find Domenikos Theotokopoulos, also known as "El Greco", in an information system. If the kinds of relationship maintained by the system are few and known to the user, even a question implying a relationship, such as "who were the teachers of El Greco" can easily be matched.

Matching a user question against a semantic network at the categorical level is more difficult. Generalizations and specializations of concepts are potentially unlimited. Even though natural languages comprise limited sets of terms, virtually any group of people elaborating a domain comes up with different variant concepts. Characteristically, George Lakoff [8] reports nine interpretations of the term "true mother", with no common set of instances for all of them. Therefore the chance is high, that an information system does not contain precisely a concept referred to in a user question. However, the user is frequently not interested in precisely this concept, but can solve his problem with a more specialized or more general answer. Therefore many systems present their concepts as IsA hierarchies or thesauri to the user, so that he/she can navigate through the available concepts until finding a suitable match. The same difficulty holds for geopolitical units and time intervals.

If the user actually is interested in an n-ary relation rather than the concept itself, the problem increases dramatically by the combination of the related concepts. There is a very low chance to hit the combination of concepts under which the system provides access to the knowledge the user is looking for. We suspect that this is the reason why users do not like the "advanced search" facilities regularly offered, and not the intellectual difficulty to use them - as normally argued. Most scientific databases return zero hits to many reasonable advanced questions. The major thesis we propose in this paper is that a subject indexed tailored to scientific questions must be based on suitable inference mechanisms guiding the user effectively to the relevant relations.

2.3 Inferences on Categorical Knowledge

Fig. 1 illustrates possible levels of knowledge in the system versus an original user question of the kind: "Would my Birma cat eat the fish on my table?". If we assume strict inheritance, an Attribute Class holds for all subclasses of its domain and range class. An information system can hence infer that the question "Do all Birma cats eat mullets?" is answered on the level "all cats eat any kind of fish". This is the first inference we implemented to assist search for relationships. It is completely transparent to the user. It could be supported by a Description Logic system such as FACT, CLASSIC and others.

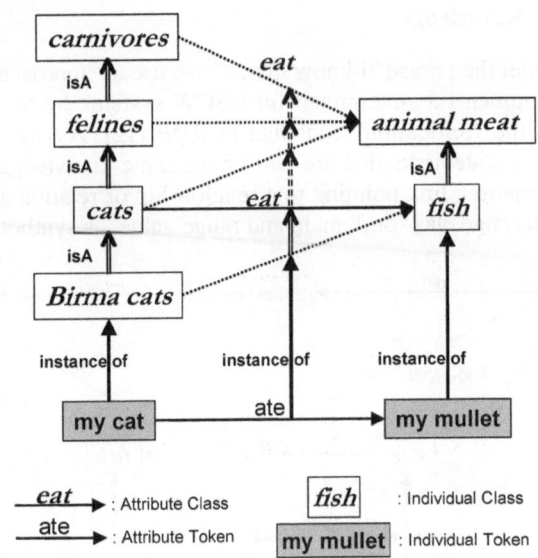

Fig. 1. Would my Birma cat eat my fish?

There is however another kind of "inheritance" towards generalization. The phrase "all cats eat any kind of fish" can be generalized upwards such as "There exist kinds of felines that eat fish", "There exist kinds of carnivores that eat kinds of animal meat" and "fish may be eaten by carnivores". Generalizations exist for all combinations of superclasses of the domain and range class. This second inference is also implemented in our prototype. More precisely, we point the user to the original rela-tionship. It is more important for searching, as it points the user from a general con-cept to specialized knowledge down to the factual level.

Together, these inferences are powerful means to give access to knowledge in the form of relationships.

However, we have not provided a formal theory about the possible quantifiers "all" "some" etc. appearing in such categorical statements and the effect on inheritance and generalization, nor have we come over such work for subject indexing. This is not trivial. See for example the variations: "garter snakes eat only fish" etc. This is a topic for future work.

In addition to providing a browser for navigation through the subject network and its inferences, we use two-dimensional tables that display the existence of relation-ships between combinations of key concepts (base level concepts, see below) as a kind of global view (see Fig. 6).

3 A Model for Learning Diagnostic Experience

In this chapter we present the conceptual model of the CRISATEL system and give some examples of the access modes it supports.

3.1 Scientific Knowledge

In order to model the phrase "I know that..." we use an approach [9] similar to Toul-min's microarguments as interpreted for CSCW systems by Streitz et al. [10], [11], and similar to the "reification" construct in RDF [12]. As argued in [12], we need statements about statements that are part of the same knowledge base. In contrast to the latter, we regard a link pointing to a relationship or relation as sufficient to imply the domain and range class or domain and range value, as symbolized in Fig. 2.

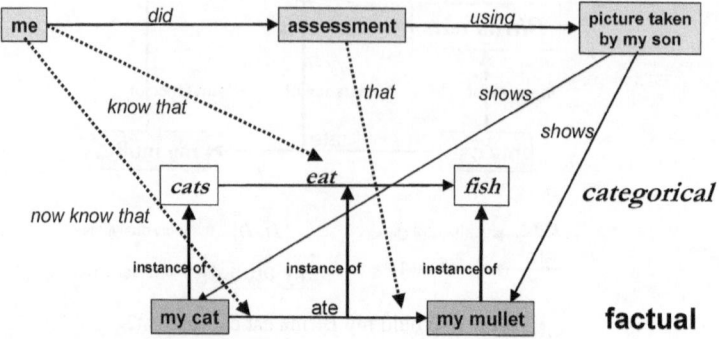

Fig. 2. Model for a Case of Knowledge Acquisition by Investigation.

Fig. 2 presents a model for the following example: Let us assume, I had a mullet in my kitchen, and the mullet disappeared. My son took a photo with my cat next to my mullet. Since I know, that cats eat fish (categorical), using the photo as indication I assess that my cat ate my mullet. Now I know that my cat ate my mullet (factual).

I also know now, that my cat in particular eats fish (cross-categorical). From enough similar observations, one can conclude that cats eat fish in general (categorical).

The interpretation of the picture in combination with background knowledge allows for creating knowledge. This example is quite characteristic for a wide class of scientific knowledge acquisition. Knowledge is produced in an assessment activity, using some investigation method that provides evidence. A categorical theory is used to interpret the actual process that caused the evidence. The reader should also note that the picture itself does not contain knowledge in this narrower sense. The difficulties of automatic image recognition demonstrate the complexity of the interpretation step. In the following sections of this paper, we shall develop in detail a model of a training system for the art object conservation domain where knowledge is produced by assessment or diagnosis. We expect however, that other kinds of scientific knowledge, such as application of certain methods to solve technological challenges etc. can be addressed with a quite similar methodology.

3.2   CRISATEL and Art Conservation

Let us give us here a short presentation of the CRISATEL Project such that the reader can understand the choices made for this learning system. CRISATEL is a three-years project funded by the European 5th Framework, IST Program, with full title: "Conservation Restoration Innovation Systems for Image Capture and digital Archiving to enhance Training Education and lifelong Learning", that started in September 2001. In this project, high definition digitization equipment for multispectral images and the software for evaluation of the images and the interpretation of these images by the art conservator is developed. The latter is the application described here.

The characteristic phenomena studied by art conservators on art objects are:

- Technique: The way the art object was produced.
- Material: Materials used for the production or modification of the object, some of which are incorporated in the object. Knowledge about technique and material allows for conclusions about the chronology, provenance and authenticity of the object and constrains the conservation and restoration methods to be applied.
- Alteration: Changes the object undergoes due to aging or environmental influences, even casual damages by museum visitors. This knowledge is the base for preventive conservation or restoration measures. Alterations are like diseases, there are infinite details of causes, reactions, possible treatments and their side effects.
- Interventions: The way the object has been modified by its keepers. This concept overlaps with the production Techniques. Some are the same, some are characteristic for later interventions only. This knowledge is useful to avoid misinterpretations about the chronology and provenance of the object and constrains the conservation and restoration methods to be applied. It allows for conclusion about the history and authenticity of the object.

The variety of the above phenomena, environmental factors, chemical agents for conservation and their side effects, and new investigation methods develop faster than education can follow. It exceeds the capacity of any specialist. Art conservators need effective access to learn the general knowledge needed to analyse phenomena specific to their working environment and to match observed phenomena with examples and general knowledge. The CRISATEL Electronic Handbook aims at becoming such a training site for art conservators in the interpretation of multispectral images, but it may in the future develop to render other kinds of knowledge as well.

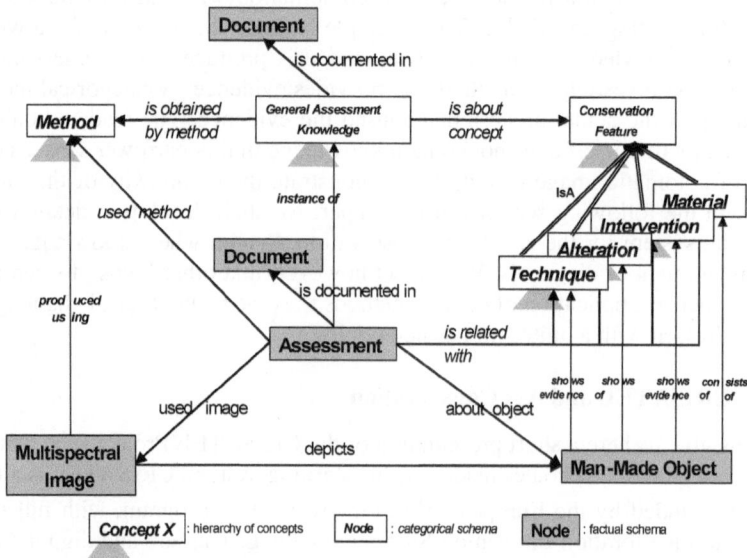

Fig. 3. Conceptual Model of the CRISATEL handbook.

3.3   The CRISATEL Handbook Model

The Conceptual Model of the CRISATEL handbook is based on the above considerations about scientific knowledge. It is presented in an abbreviated form in Fig. 3. The grey triangles symbolize standard thesaurus relationships following ISO2788, that allow for organizing individual concepts into hierarchies. We interpret the hierarchical relationship "BT/NT" as equivalent to "IsA"; "Method" and "Conservation Feature" as equivalent to individual concepts; and the node "General assessment Knowledge" as a relationship between those. On this basis we implemented the first two inferences described in section 2.3. The nodes "Multispectral Image" and "Man-Made Object" also have characteristic additional attributes (metadata) not shown here.

To the degree possible, concepts are taken from the CIDOC Conceptual Reference Model (ISO/CD21127) [13]. Those are: E22 Man-Made Object, E13 Attribute Assessment (here "Assessment"), E31Document, E29 Design or Procedure (here: Method), E57 Material. With respect to the general model in Fig. 2 we make significant simplifications and optimizations. These are based on observations about limitations in this specific application:

In the envisaged training environment, there is typically one source for each knowledge element: an empirical report about factual knowledge or a didactic text for categorical knowledge. Therefore we can contract the factual assessment itself with the observed relationship between the respective object (painting) and the observed feature. The feature itself is implicitly represented by the object itself, and described in the text of the assessment. The event of image taking is regarded as the instantiation of method used. It is captured by the metadata of the image (not shown in Fig. 3). As additional index, the assessment and the image is classified categorically by the kind of method applied, and the assessment is classified categorically by the kind of feature found.

A typical assessment could be: "Mr LeGrand found in the frame of the Mona Lisa wormholes by the X-Ray image X002456 taken on the 5th of September". The actual feature can be seen on the image, and is of kind "wormhole". The applied method is represented by the metadata of image X002456. In the sequence, the object is also classified by "shows wormholes". The assessment is classified in addition as "used method X-Ray" and "is related with "wormhole". This assessment is an instance of an application of the General Assessment Knowledge "wormholes can be found by low-energy X-Ray". Hence it will appear in the subject index under the latter, as well as under "X-Ray" and "wormhole" and all their generalizations.

As on the factual level, we simplify the categorical level: The categorical knowledge, that a specific investigation method can be applied to find certain kinds of phenomena, and the knowledge about how to apply the method on a painting, is interpreted as a relationship between Method and Conservation Feature, which we call "General Assessment Knowledge". All observations are about paintings only, so that a relationship, about on which kind of objects the diagnostic method is applied, needs not to appear in the categorical knowledge. Each instance of General Assessment Knowledge is documented by a didactic text (Document), and is regarded to represent the class of all factual assessments that apply the respective method and find the respective kind of feature.

The model for the categorical level must actually be seen as a metaschema, as its instances represent classes for the factual level (after expanding the simplifications described above). The CRISATEL Model for learning diagnostic knowledge in art conservation is an example of a coherent model for managing the categorical and factual knowledge of a domain.

3.4 User Interface Issues

The user interface and access modes are the result of a careful requirements analysis and design by art conservators and our laboratory, in particular in collaboration with Maria Chatzidaki, professor for art conservation in Athens. It is a direct application of the ideas described in section 2 and the adaptations to the specific application described in section 3.3. Basically it provides access through all nodes shown in Fig 3. It tries to capture all aspects relevant to art conservators, and to overcome the typical lack of overview users have in electronic media. It tries in particular to make the amount and distribution of content completely visible to the user. We regard this as very important in order to give the user an understanding of the coverage and completeness of the content provided, and the security that all relevant contents for his/her problem is at one comprehensible place and nowhere else. Fundamental to that are: the indexing of general knowledge as a specific relationship of individual concepts, the assumed instantiation relationship of actual assessments to the general knowledge implemented by the subject index, and the inferences described in section 2.3, together with a careful construction of the hierarchical relationships of the thesauri.

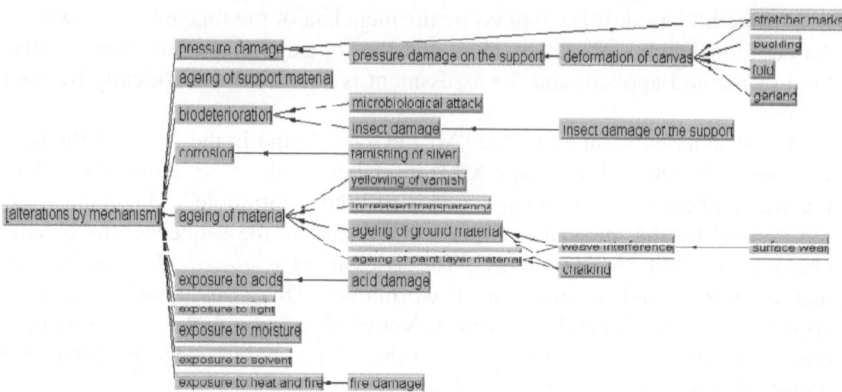

Fig. 4. Example of the graphical representation of a (poly)hierarchy of terms. All terms carry respective hyperlinks.

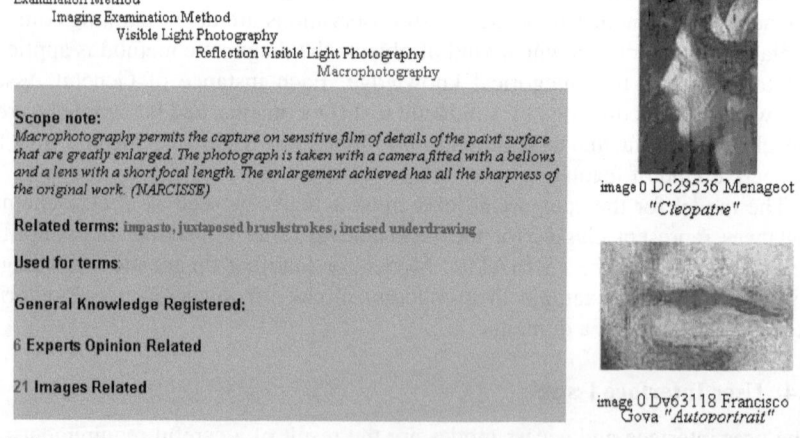

Fig. 5. Example of the template for the full description of a term. All terms, images and numbers carry respective hyperlinks.

The handbook starts with introductory texts explaining the functions of the handbook and basic art conservation concepts. The major intellectual structure is implemented by five complete thesauri compatible with ISO2788, which have been developed by Maria Chatzidaki and our lab, extending the flat vocabulary from the European projects NARCISSE and CRISTAL by semantic relationships, "node labels" and terms from major literature of the domain . They describe:

- Materials
- Evidence of Technique, Marks and Traces
- Alterations
- Interventions
- Investigation Methods

All thesauri are thematically constraint to the domain of conservation of paintings (a more detailed description will follow in a separate publication). Each thesaurus contains some hundred or more terms and is polyhierarchically structured, so that all possible direct subsumptions are modeled. The latter is necessary in order to create the complete instantiation of the implemented inferences described in section 2.3. Access is by graphical representations of the (poly)hierarchy (see Fig. 4) and by navigation through the full descriptions of the terms and their relationships (see Fig. 5). In particular, the terms are related to General Knowledge, objects, images and example assessments. We expect that a systematic compilation of all kinds of General Knowledge will needs several thousand nodes. The Louvre Conservation Laboratory (C2RMF) e.g. has tens of thousands of conservation reports with image material associated.

A complete graphical representation of the five thesauri and the General Knowledge relationships in between would exceed any comprehensible form. Therefore another systematic means to provide an overview was designed: For each thesaurus, a so-called "base level" of terms was selected. The term "base level" is taken from a series of cognitive studies in the late eighties as e.g. described by George Lakoff [8]. Here we create by "base level terms" a partition of the conceptual space concrete enough to render a notion of the application, and abstract enough to be understood on one glance, i.e. some ten or more terms per thesaurus. So the combinations of the 4 "basic" investigation methods with each base level of the other thesauri separately are displayed as 4 two-dimensional distribution maps (see Fig. 6). Each matrix element contains the frequency and an index to the General Knowledge nodes "under" this combination (see second inference in section 2.3). By that means, we can give an overview of about 400 cases on four pages. This should be sufficient to provide the user with a systematic overview about several thousand described cases.

ALTERATIONS	auto radiography	infrared photography	infrared reflectography	macro photography	optical microscopy	radio graphy	raking light photography	scanning electron microscopy	ultraviolet photography	visible light photography
alteration of paint layer							1			
alteration of the ground										
alteration of the support						1				
alteration of varnish										

Fig. 6. Example of the template for the distribution of General Knowledge nodes with respect to combinations of base level terms. The frequencies in the table link to the respective nodes.

Finally we provide direct search interfaces by all relations and metadata to paintings, assessments and images, as well as two-dimensional distribution maps of paintings by creation period and support, by creation period and technique, and by creation period and investigation method. The first inference in section 2.3 is transparently implemented in all queries.

4   Related Work

Even though Knowledge Representation languages like TELOS [3], KIF , RDF/S [14], OWL etc. and numerous expert systems are based on the analysis of knowledge into propositions since the conception of Semantic Networks, and at least some CSCW systems are based on such "microarguments" (e.g.: [10], [11]), subject catalogues and learning systems are slow to follow this paradigm. Most prominent example is "LOM" [1], the draft standard for learning object metadata by IEEE. LOM is integral part of [15], a conceptual model for the discorvery, creation, and management of learning resources and the aggregation of simple assets into more complex learning resources organized into predefined sequences of delivery. In LOM, the subject is defined by General Keyword (1.5), General Coverage (1.6) and Classification (9).

The latter way of subject indexing is the normal practice of general purpose libraries. The general subject can be modified by geographic or temporal restrictions, the "Coverage", e.g. in the Dublin Core Metadata Element Set (DCMES) [16] and the MARC formats. For the cases we discuss here, the notion of subject most accepted by bibliographers is the "aboutness", i.e. the document is "about" an individual concept, without further specification of what that might mean in the specific case. A more detailed analysis of the possible senses of a subject in library practice can be found in [17]. A very good ontological analysis of the notion of subject in the sense of "aboutness" can be found in [18].

A good example of an advanced, well-designed learning system in the sense we discuss here is the ADEPT [19]. It deals with teaching geology. Concepts are described with a frame-based knowledge representation formalism including relations between those concepts, which allows for navigation through "concept maps". The authors mention, that didactic texts are sometimes attached to relationships. Nevertheless, primary access is via individual concepts relevant for geology, like "landslides", "riverbeds" etc.

An indexing approach quite close to ours are the "enriched thesauri" of Hazewinkel [20]: It is based on "...key phrases...long enough to carry real information (single words in science only rarely do so)", so called Prepositional Noun Phrases (PNP) extracted from texts automatically. There is a partial order of genericity/specificity applied by a statistical algorithm and the phrases are related to individual concepts of a classification scheme. These PNPs are similar in their semantics to the propositions we use indexing. However, there is no clear ontological principle yet of how to structure the vast amount of propositions retrieved, which is of the order of a hundred thousand for a typical domain [20].

The major difference to our approach is that we construct the indexing propositions and their semantic relationships by a relatively compact intellectual analysis of the domain rather than automatically, and that we exploit inheritance along IsA relations to deduce the numerous relevant relationships that are implied by the resulting structure. The major advantage is that we have an explicit theory that allows us to guide the user more effectively, even in larger semantic structures.

On the other hand, the use of a semantic network or expert system as only resource for learning is neither very useful, since a learning system should not only consist of domain knowledge but also contain the didactic rendering and packaging of knowledge into didactic units and describe the didactic relationships. We have therefore chosen a hybrid approach of documents embedded in a semantic network that captures the core concepts and relationships. In particular, we model the relationships corresponding to the questions the user expects to be answered as n-ary relationships with associated didactic or scientific texts. One may regard this semantic network as a kind of metadata for those texts. The prototype system is implemented on top of the SIS semantic network database, which implements the static part of the TELOS knowledge representation model ([21], [4], [3]).

5 Conclusions and Future Work

We have implemented an intellectual structure novel to the subject space of material designed for selective autodidactic learning in a large knowledge base. This structure is based on a systematic theory-driven connection of categorical knowledge and factual knowledge. It is further based on the idea, that relevant subjects in such a system should be propositions, represented as categorical relationships. Navigation and querying of categorical relationships is assisted by two different kinds of inferences of generalization/specialization. The associated thesauri are systematically structured so that these inferences yield the expected result in all cases.

We have tried to find systematic ways to give the user access and overview about large amounts of such relationships. By that we have tried to overcome the typical mismatch between a user formulated request and the terms understood by the system. The user interface is richer in access modes than any system known to the author.

The system is right now being presented to users with a first small population of cases. The idea is to import half-automatically a larger amount of factual knowledge from existing description at the Louvre laboratory. The real value of the system cannot be tested before several hundreds of texts are loaded.

Even though the method has been applied to a very simple case, i.e. the application of investigation methods to detect features on an object, we believe that it can be generalized widely. Obviously it can at least be generalized to diagnostic knowledge in general.

The formalization of the semantics of the inferences described in section 2.3 deserve further investigation. Currently there is no ontological theory that would describe inferences of the "aboutness" relation from semantic relationships between subjects.

References

1. Draft Standard for Learning Object Metadata, Version 6.4, Institute of Electrical and Electronics Engineering, Inc. (IEEE), IEEE P1484.12.1/D6.4, New York, March 4, (2002).
2. http://www.crisatel.jussieu.fr
3. Mylopoylos, J., Borgida, A., Jarke, M., Koubarakis, M.: Telos: Representing Knowledge about Information Systems. ACM Transactions on Information Systems, Vol. 8, No. 4 (1990)
4. Analyti, A., Spyratos, N., Constantopoulos, P., Doerr, M.: Inheritance under Participation Constraints and Disjointness. Proceedings of the 8th European-Japanese Conference on Information Modelling and Knowledge Bases, Tampere (May 1998) 269-287
5. Guizzardi, G., Herre, H., Wagner, G.: On the General Ontological Foundations of Conceptual Modeling. In Proceedings of 21th International Conference on Conceptual Modeling (ER 2002). Springer-Verlag, Berlin, Lecture Notes in Computer Science
6. Analyti, A., Spyratos, N., Constantopoulos, P.: Deriving and Retrieving Contextual Categorical Information through Instance Inheritance. Fundamenta Informaticae 33. IOS Press (1998), 1-37

7. Doerr, M., Plexousakis, D., Bekiari, Ch.: A Metamodel for Part-Whole Relationships for Reasoning on Missing Parts and Reconstruction. In Hideko S.Kunii, Sushil Jajodia, Arne Solvberg, (eds.): Conceptual Modeling – ER 2001, 20th International Conference on Conceptual Modeling. Springer Verlag, Berlin, Yokohama, Japan (2001) 412-425, ISBN 3-540-42866-6

8. Lakoff, G.: Women, Fire, and Dangerous Things: What Categories Reveal about the Mind. University of Chicago Press, Chicago (1987)

9. Doerr, M.: Reference Information Acquisition and Coordination, in: "ASIS'97 -Digital Collections: Implications for Users, Funders, Developers and Maintainers. Proceedings of the 60th Annual Meeting of the American Society for Information Sciences", November 1-6 '97, Washington, Vol. 34, pp 295-312, Information Today Inc.: Medford, New Jersey, (1997). ISBN 1-57387-048-X

10. Streitz, N.A., Haake, J.M., Hannemann, J., Lemke, A.C., Schuler, W., Schütt, H.A., Thüring, M.: SEPIA: A Cooperative Hypermedia Authoring Environment. In: Proceedings of the 2nd ACM Conference on Hypertext (Hypertext'89) (1989) 343-364

11. Streitz, N.A., Haake, J.M., Hannemann, J., Lemke, A.C., Schuler, W., Schütt, H.A., Thüring, M.: SEPIA: A Cooperative Hypermedia Authoring Environment. In: Proceedings of the 4th ACM Conference on Hypertext (ECHT'89), Milan (1992) 11-2264

12. Hayes, P. (ed.): RDF Semantics - World Wide Web Consortium Proposed Recommendation 15 December 2003 http://www.w3.org/TR/2003/PR-rdf-mt-20031215

13. Crofts, N., Doerr, M., Gill, T., Stiff, M. (ed.): Definition of the CIDOC object-oriented Conceptual Reference Model. (version 3.2) (September 2001) http://cidoc.ics.forth.gr. This document is the source for ISO/CD 21127

14. Karvounarakis, G., Christophides, V., Plexousakis, D., Alexaki,S.: Querying RDF Descriptions for Community Web Portals. In Proc. of the 17 France National Conf. on Databases BDA. Agadir, Maroc., 29 October - 2 November 2001, http://139.91.183.30:9090/RDF/publications/sigmod2000.html

15. Advanced Distributed Learning (ADL). Sharable Content Object Reference Model (SCORM®), Version 1.3 Working Draft 1 (2003) (http://web.syr.edu/~jqin/LO/LOV/index.html)

16. Baker, Th.: A Grammar of Dublin Core. D-Lib Magazine, 6(10) (2000)

17. Le Boeuf, P.: FRBR and further. In: Cataloging & Classification Quarterly. Vol. 32, No.4 (2001) 15-52. ISSN 0163-9374

18. Welty, C., Jenkins, J.: Formal Ontology for Subject. Knowledge and Data Engineering. 31(2), Elsevier (1999) 155-182

19. Smith, T.R., Ancona, D., Buchel, O., Freeston, M., Heller, W., Nottrott, R., Tierney, T., Ushakou, A.: The ADEPT Concept-Based Digital Learning Environment. In Koch, T. Solvberg, I.T. (eds.): Research and Advanced Technology for Digital Libraries, 7th European Conference, ECDL 2003, Trohdheim, Norway, August 2003. Lecture Notes in Computer Science, Vol 2769. Springel-Verlag, Berlin Heidelberg New York (2003) 300-312

20. Hazewinkel, M.: Enriched Thesauri and their Uses in Information Retrieval and Storage, in: FIRST DELOS WORKSHOP, An Overview on Projects and Research Activities in Digital Library Related Fields, Sophia Antipolis, France 4-6 March 1996, ERCIM Workshop Proceedings – No. 97-W001

21. Constantopoulos, P., Doerr, M.: The semantic index system: A brief presentation. Heraklion - Crete, Greece: FORTH, Institute of Computer Science, Information Systems and Software Technology Group - Working Paper #6 (1993)

Formalizing Retrieval Goal Change by Prioritized Abduction

Ken Satoh

National Institute of Informatics
2-1-2 Hitotsubashi, Chiyoda-ku, Tokyo, 101-8430, Japan
ksatoh@nii.ac.jp

Abstract. When we traverse over the Internet to search information, we sometimes change an object which we are looking for, in other word, change a *retrieval goal* according to additional information obtained during search.

In this paper, we give a formalization of such a goal change by prioritized abduction and extend the method to a "retrieval command adviser". We assume a chain of logical rules to satisfy a purpose of the retrieval where bottom conditions are retrieval goals represented as abducible propositions. Abducing these retrieval goals leads to accomplishment of the retrieval purpose. Moreover, we introduce another kind of abducible propositions to represent applicability of logical rules. This applicability abducible is attached to a logical rule and used to detect which rules are used. Then, together with priority over these applicability abducibles to express strength of the associated rules, we determine which rules should preferably be applicable and hence we infer the most appropriate retrieval command which is derived from the most preferable rules. If the observed information is changed, then the applicability of rules is changed and according to the applicability abducibles, we change our retrieval goal. We believe that this mechanism explains a retrieval goal change.

Then, we extend the method to construct a "retrieval command adviser" which suggests better retrieval command than the initial command given by a user. We translate the above logical rules into another form which is used for predicting a purpose of give a command. When a user give a command then the system predict the purpose of a command using the newly introduced rules and then according to the initial logic rules and priorities, we infer the most appropriate retrieval command.

1 Introduction

Thanks to the advent of the Internet, we can get a large amount of information which we could not obtain without it. Then, we have, however, faced a new problem of information retrieval where we cannot easily get information which we want since there is much irrelevant information in the Internet and cannot filter them in an appropriate manner. In this case, he/she rambles around the Internet and only he/she hopes is just a luck to find his/her intended object

G. Grieser and Y. Tanaka (Eds.): Intuitive Human Interface 2004, LNAI 3359, pp. 215–232, 2004.

fortuitously. In such a situation, a user sometimes encounters a situation during a search over the Internet that he/she sometimes changes a retrieval goal when he/she finds a more interesting object than the one which he/she pursues. We believe that this kind of retrieval change is a kind of discovery when the user finds more appropriate object for his/her purpose.

Consider the following motivating example of a retrieval goal change[1].

- Prof. Tanaka would like to improve his English and he thinks that watching English movies helps his goal. So, he searches for a video recorder to watch movies.
- He firstly searches a video recorder with a noise reduction facility to watch English movie frequently with the video recorder.
- During the search, he happens to know the existence of a video recorder with English closed caption facility[2]. Then, he changes a retrieval goal to try to find such a video recorder with closed caption facility.

Although the ultimate purpose of the search is to improve English, his search has changed from a video recorder with a fine resolution to one with a closed caption facility. If we knew the ultimate purpose beforehand, we could advise the more sophisticated retrieval activity, but sometimes a user unconsciously retrieve relevant but not best information without knowing his/her ultimate purpose. To support for such a better search, we believe that a formalization of the phenomena should be done at the first place. By the formalization, we could develop a system with a more clear view to what we should do for an advice to the user. Refer to [7] for further motivation.

In this paper, we regard this kind of retrieval goal change as preference reasoning over rules with the assumption that we have the following rules and priority over the rules beforehand.

1. To improve English, watch English movies frequently.
2. To improve English, watch English captioned movies.
   This rule has a high priority over the previous rule.
3. To watch English movie frequently, search a video recorder with a fine resolution.
4. To watch English captioned movies, search a video recorder with a closed caption facility.
5. Only if we find a video recorder with a closed caption facility, we search other video recorders with a closed caption facility since we assume that the search for a video recorder with a closed caption facility will fail. In other words, if we search video recorders with a closed caption facility, we must have found at least one such video recorder beforehand.

The first and the second rules represent two possibilities to fulfill the ultimate purpose of this information retrieval activity which is "improving English". This

---

[1] This example was given by Prof. Yuzuru Tanaka from Hokkaido University.
[2] A closed caption facility is to show English sentences spoken in a movie at the bottom of screen.

ultimate purpose is replaced by another sub-purpose and there are two alternatives for this; one is to watch English movies frequently and the other is to watch captioned English movies. In order to watch English movies frequently, we search a video recorder with a fine resolution (the third rule) and in order to watch English captioned movies, we search a video recorder with a closed caption (the fourth rule). Although watching English captioned movies is more preferable to watching English movies frequently, we firstly search a video recorder with a fine resolution since we believe that finding a video recorder with a closed caption facility is very difficult according to the fifth rule.

In this initial situation, retrieving a video recorder with a fine resolution is the most preferable retrieval command since it satisfies all the rules and preferences. Note that we believe nonexistence of a video recorder with a closed caption facility and so, we cannot search a video recorder with a closed caption facility. Then, the fifth rule is also satisfied by not searching such a video recorder.

Suppose that we find a video recorder with a closed caption facility during the search. Then, implausibility of existence of a video recorder with a closed caption facility is rebutted. Then, to satisfy the fifth rule, we need to make the retrieval of other video recorder with a closed caption facility. Then, there arise two possibilities to satisfy the ultimate purpose of improving English. One is using a video with a fine resolution which leads to frequent watch of movies and the other is using a video with a closed caption facility which leads to watching captioned movies. Since we have a preference of watching captioned movies (the second rule) over frequent watch (the first rule), we choose the second one and as a result, we search other video recorder with a closed caption.

This kind of inference cannot be formalized in a deductive way. Since the deduction is "monotonic", that is, once we get an inferred result, we can no longer retract the result in a deduction. Therefore, to understand the phenomena, we need other reasoning formalism. Standard approach to this kind of problem is to use *nonmonotonic reasoning* and we actually gave a formal framework of retrieval goal change in [13] by using prioritized circumscription [10]. However, the previous formalization was just a specification of the most appropriate retrieval goal and did not concern computational issues very much.

In this paper, we give another but more computation-oriented formalism using *prioritized abduction*. Abduction [6] is used to complement unknown information by making hypothesis. In this paper, we use the abduction for two purposes; one is to represent retrieval commands and the other is to represent applicability of logical rules. We assume a chain of logical rules to satisfy a purpose of the retrieval where bottom conditions consists of retrieval goal abducibles. We also assume a prioritization over logical rules or success predictions of retrieval command which represents strength of satisfaction of rule of success of retrieval command. To make use of such prioritization we introduce the latter kind of abducibles in order to detect which rules are used. Then, together with priority over applicability abducibles, we determine which rules should preferably be applicable and hence we infer the most appropriate retrieval command.

If the ultimate purpose of the search is known beforehand, the above mechanism is enough. But for a practical system, it is desirable to give the appropriate retrieval command even if the ultimate purpose is not known. To solve this problem, we extend the method to construct a "retrieval command adviser" which suggests better retrieval command than the initial command given by a user. We translate the above logical rules into another form which is used for predicting a purpose of give a command. When a user give a command then the system predict the purpose of a command using the newly introduced rules and then according to the initial logic rules and priorities, we infer the most appropriate retrieval command.

There are research of applying nonmonotonic reasoning to information retrieval and/or adaptive information filtering[1–4, 8]. [1–3, 8] formalize relevance (or in other words, aboutness) between terms by using preference reasoning. They regard information conveyed in information carrier as logical relation between the carrier and the information. Then, the system becomes nonmonotonic since information carriers of term t is not necessary information carriers of two terms t and s, that is, the system violates monotonicity. They formalize this phenomena in terms of preference relation over information carriers that some carriers which are relevant with the term t is not less preferable if we consider carriers having both t and s. Another work related with aboutness is [4] which formalizes the concept of aboutness by default logic. These research are regarded as a formalization to explain the behavior of the current system while we give a new formalization of user behavior.

The structure of this paper is as follows. Firstly, we formalize two examples of retrieval goal change; One is the above video recorder example and the other is the goal change of a customer at a shop. Then, we generalize examples to show a formal framework for the goal change. Then, we extend this framework to a "retrieval command adviser".

2   Formalization of Retrieval Goal Change

In this section, we firstly discuss formalizations of two examples in a retrieval goal change by prioritized abduction and then generalize them into a formal framework to compute the most appropriate retrieval goal.

2.1   Video Recorder Example

We give a formalization of the video recorder example in the introduction using the prioritized abduction. We represent the rules of the video recorder example in an abductive logic program[3] as follows.

1. To improve English, watch English movies frequently.
   $I \leftarrow Appli_1^*, W$
   where I means "improving English" and $Appli_1^*$ is the abducible to express applicability of this rule, and W means "watching English movies frequently".

---

[3] For the precise definition of an abductive logic program, refer to the appendix.

2. To improve English, watch English captioned movies.
   $I \leftarrow Appli_2^*, S$
   where $Appli_2^*$ is the abducible for applicability of this rule, and S means "watching English movies which shows a caption".

3. To watch English movies frequently, search a video recorder with a fine resolution.
   $W \leftarrow F^*$
   where F^* means "searching a video recorder with a fine resolution".

4. To watch English movies which shows a caption, search a video recorder with a closed caption facility.
   $S \leftarrow C^*$
   where C^* means "searching a video recorder with a closed caption facility".

5. If we decide to search video recorders with a closed caption facility, there must be at least one video recorder found.
   $\perp \leftarrow C^*, \textbf{not } cond(C)$
   $cond(C) \leftarrow E$
   where $\perp$ means contradiction and E means "there exits a video recorder with a closed caption facility found".

6. We assume that there is very few video recorders with a closed caption facility.
   Thanks to "negation as failure", we do not need to represent this rule. E is true if and only if E is explicitly mentioned in the program.

7. We put priority over applicability abducibles as

$$\langle \{Appli_1^*\} < \{Appli_2^*\} \rangle$$

We use a top-down proof procedure proposed in [12] for a query processing to compute generalized stable models and then choose most preferable stable models w.r.t. a goal expressing the ultimate purpose[4]. The intuitive meaning of the most preferable models is that we consider only the necessary abducibles to derive a goal and these abducibles should be the most plausible ones. The below shows the actual log of our top-down proof procedure implemented in SICStus Prolog. Program denotes the rules defined as above. The symbol "-" means "negation as failure" and "0" means contradiction, and a proposition with "*" attached is an abducible. In the following execution, we firstly ask ?-start.

We ask ?-start. Then, we compute all the stable models denoted as Stable Models and then we choose the most preferable stable model denoted as Most Preferable Stable Models.

Program
```
start<- improve_english                          (0)
improve_english<- appli1*,frequentwatch          (1)
improve_english<- appli2*,shownEnglishsentence   (2)
frequentwatch<- find_noisereductionVCR*          (3)
```

---

[4] See the precise definition of generalized stable models and most preferable stable models w.r.t. a goal in the appendix.

```
shownEnglishsentence<- find_englishcaptionVCR*                        (4)
0<- find_englishcaptionVCR*,-cond(find_englishcaptionVCR)             (5)
cond(find_englishcaptionVCR)<- exists_englishcaptionVCR               (6)
```

```
Hierarchy for Abducibles
[[appli1*],[appli2*]]
```

```
Stable Models
```

```
Model 1
improve_english
frequentwatch
find_noisereductionVCR*
appli1*
start
```

```
Most Preferable Stable Models
improve_english
frequentwatch
find_noisereductionVCR*
appli1*
start
```

We intuitively explain how to compute the most appropriate command.

1. To derive the goal ?-start. We find the rule (0) and we then need to derive improve_english.
2. There are two rules to derive improve_english, (1) and (2).
3. To apply the rule (1), we need to abduce appli1* and show frequentwatch.
4. To show frequentwatch, we need to abduce find_noisereductionVCR* by the rule (3). Therefore, this derivation results in the model which includes abducibles of appli1* and find_noisereductionVCR*.
5. On the other hand, to apply the rule (2), we need to abduce appli2* and and show shownEnglishsentence. To show shownEnglishsentence, we need to abduce find_englishcaptionVCR* by the rule (4). Abducing find_englishcaptionVCR* leads to consistency check of the integrity constraint (5) where we need to show cond(find_englishcaptionVCR) is derived. However, to show cond(find_englishcaptionVCR), we need to show exists_englishcaptionVCR by the rule (6), but we cannot show this since there is no rule for exists_englishcaptionVCR. Therefore this inference results in a violation of the integrity constraint (5) and therefore no derivation cannot succeed.
6. Therefore, the most preferable stable model w.r.t. the goal expressing the ultimate purpose is the only one which includes find_noisereductionVCR* and appli1* only. Thus, the current performed retrieval command is the best command in this context.

During the search, suppose that we found a video recorder with a closed caption. we add `exists_englishcaptionVCR<-` to the program

```
Program
start<- improve_english                                              (0)
improve_english<- appli1*,frequentwatch                             (1)
improve_english<- appli2*,shownEnglishsentence                      (2)
frequentwatch<- find_noisereductionVCR*                             (3)
shownEnglishsentence<- find_englishcaptionVCR*                      (4)
0<- find_englishcaptionVCR*,-cond(find_englishcaptionVCR)           (5)
cond(find_englishcaptionVCR)<- exists_englishcaptionVCR             (6)
exists_englishcaptionVCR<-                                          (7)


Hierarchy for Abducibles
[[appli1*],[appli2*]]


Stable Models

Model 1
improve_english
frequentwatch
find_noisereductionVCR*
appli1*
start

Model 2
cond(find_englishcaptionVCR)
exists_englishcaptionVCR
improve_english
shownEnglishsentence
find_englishcaptionVCR*
appli2*
start

Most Preferable Stable Models
cond(find_englishcaptionVCR)
exists_englishcaptionVCR
improve_english
shownEnglishsentence
find_englishcaptionVCR*
appli2*
start
```

In this situation, not only the previous derivation is possible to result in "Model 1", but also the failed derivation of the latter rule (2) to show `improve_english` becomes now successful since `exists_englishcaptionVCR` can be inferred by the rule (7). This new derivation results in "Model 2".

Therefore, there are two models which has a different realization of `improve_english`. However, the latter model using `appli2*` is more preferable to the former model using `appli1*` thanks to the hierarchy of abducibles and therefore, the latter model is chosen. Then, in the new most preferable stable model, `find_englishcaption` becomes true. Therefore, for the new situation, the system now suggests a search for a video recorder with a closed caption. This reasoning explains the retrieval goal change.

2.2   Salesclerk Example

This is not an example for information retrieval, but the real conversation happening in the shop shown in [14]. We show this example in order to show not only generality of our analysis, but also possibility of giving new facility to the Internet shopping.

A Japanese female customer came to the shop to buy a jacket, but the jacket under her consideration was short and then, the conversation happened as follows (the conversation is translated into English).

Customer: This (jacket) is a little short, isn't it?

Salesclerk: Such a design is popular this year. Almost every shop deals with short ones. Do you prefer longer one?

Customer: Too short to cover my waist...

Salesclerk: It depends on the balance with your skirt or pants. 'cause you're now wearing shorter tight skirt, you think that way, but if wearing a long skirt, you will feel better.

This conversation successfully led to the purchase of a jacket and even a skirt(!). Shoji et al. analyze this case as follows:

> The customer's mental world was changed from one where the relevant attribute is length of jacket to another where different attribute called balance is relevant. Through the conversation, the capable salesclerk shown in the case could grasp the customer's wish that she make herself look as good-shaped as possible, and induce the appropriate goal (short but well-balanced jacket) in accordance with it.

This example is also a kind of retrieval goal change (from longer jacket to short jacket with well-balanced long skirt). If we assume the following logical rules, we can formalize this change as well.

1. A customer believes that the following hold:
   To have a good shape, hide a body.
   To have hide a body, find a long skirt.
2. A salesclerk has different rules to implement "good-shape" as follows:
   To have a good shape, have a good balance.
   To have a good balance, find a short jacket and a well-balanced long skirt.
3. We assume that the salesclerk knowledge is more preferable (or reliable).

In this case, not only the logical rule but also the priority between rules is dynamically added. The second set of rules is more preferable to the first set of rules (because of the current boom). Note that the second set of rules is not in the customer's knowledge at the initial situation and only after the salesclerk's statement, "It depends on the balance with your skirt or pants.", the customer came to know the rules and also priority of the rules by the statement "Such a design is popular this year. Almost every shop deals with short ones."

We represent the rules of salesclerk example in an abductive logic program as follows.

1. To have a good shape, hide a body.
   $G \leftarrow H$
   where G means "having a good shape and H means "hide one's body".
2. To have hide a body, find a long skirt. $H \leftarrow Appli_1^*, L^*$
   where L^* means "finding a long jacket".

The below shows the actual log of our proof procedure for this program.

```
Program
start<- good_shape                          (0)
good_shape<- hidebody                       (1)
hidebody<- appli1*,find_longjacket*         (2)

Hierarchy for Abducibles
[[abd(appli1)]]

Stable Models

Model 1
good_shape
balance
find_longskirt*
appli1*
start

Most Preferable Stable Models
good_shape
balance
find_longskirt*
appli1*
start
```

By starting with ?-start we try to satisfy good_shape. To satisfy good_shape there is only one rule (1) and therefore, find_longskirt* is the only possibility to satisfy good_shape.

Later, suppose that salesclerk says that the balanced combination of a short jacket and a long skirt also helps a good-shape. Then, we introduce the new rule according to the salesclerk.

3. To have a good shape, have a good balance.

   $G \leftarrow B$

   where B means "having a good balance".
4. To have a good balance, find a short jacket and a well-balanced long skirt.

   $B \leftarrow Appli_2^*, S^*, W^*$

   where S^* means "finding a short jacket" and W^* means "finding a well-balanced long skirt".

```
Program
start<- good_shape                                          (0)
good_shape<- hidebody                                       (1)
hidebody<- appli1*,find_longjacket*                         (2)
good_shape<- balance                                        (3)
balance<- appli2*,find_shortjacket*,find_longskirt*         (4)


Hierarchy for Abducibles
[[abd(appli1)],[abd(appli2)]]

Stable Models

Model 1
good_shape
hidebody
find_longjacket*
appli1*
start

Model 2
good_shape
balance
find_longskirt*
find_shortjacket*
appli2*
start

Most Preferable Stable Models
good_shape
balance
find_longskirt*
find_shortjacket*
appli2*
start
```

By starting with ?-start we try to satisfy good_shape. In this situation there are two rules (1) and (3) to satisfy good_shape. Using (1) and (2), we conclude find_longskirt* as a retrieval command and assume appli1* to satisfy the purpose. As an alternative derivation, using (3) and (4), we conclude `find_longskirt*` and `find_shortjacket*` as retrieval commands and assume `appli2*` to satisfy the purpose. However, thanks to the hierarchy of abducibles, The second model is chosen and `find_longskirt*` and `find_shortjacket*` become the most appropriate commands in the new situation.

2.3   Formal Framework for Goal Change

Now, we give a formal framework by generalizing the above example. We divide atomic propositions into four categories:

1. The first kind is called *purpose proposition* which expresses the ultimate purpose of the retrieval and a sub-purpose which leads to the ultimate purpose. In the video recorder example, the purpose propositions are I, W and S where W and S are sub-purposes of I.
2. The second kind is called *observation proposition* which expresses the current information context corresponding with the results obtained so far. In the video recorder example, the observation proposition is E.
3. The third kind is called *retrieval abducible* which expresses a retrieval command. In the video recorder example, the retrieval abducibles are F^* and C^*.
4. The fourth kind is called *applicability abducible* which expresses applicability of the rule. In the video recorder example, the applicability abducibles are $Appli_1^*$ and $Appli_2^*$.

In the prioritized abductive logic programming, we construct the following rules.

- $P \leftarrow Appli^*, L_1, ..., L_n$
  where P is a purpose proposition and $Appli^*$ is an applicability abducible meaning that this rule is applicable, and L_i is a sub-purpose proposition, P_i or a retrieval abducible which of the form R_i^*. Note that $Appli^*$ can be omitted.
- $\perp \leftarrow R^*, \text{not } cond(R)$
  $cond(R) \leftarrow C_1, ..., C_n$
  where R^* is a retrieval abducible and $C_1, ..., C_n$ are observation propositions. These rules means that if we assume R^*, all of C_i's should be satisfied.

- We give a priority over the above rules by putting abducibles for application in the higher hierarchy for more important rules.
- Most preferable solution: A solution which satisfies a goal with necessary and the most preferable rules defined by the most preferable stable models.

3   Retrieval Command Adviser

3.1   Abductive Framework to Guess the Purpose
and Infer the Most Appropriate Command for the Purpose

In the above examples, we firstly give the retrieval purpose as a top goal and then infer the most appropriate retrieval command. However, a user sometimes does not know his/her real purpose of information retrieval and may not be able to express the true purpose. In this section, in stead of user's providing the purpose, a system predict the purpose from user's initial retrieval command. An image of the system is depicted in Fig. 1. A user firstly gives an initial retrieval command then the prioritized abductive logic program guesses the ultimate purpose using a bottom-up execution of logical rules from the given command. Then, the program tries to figure out the most appropriate retrieval command which fulfils the purpose in a top-down manner.

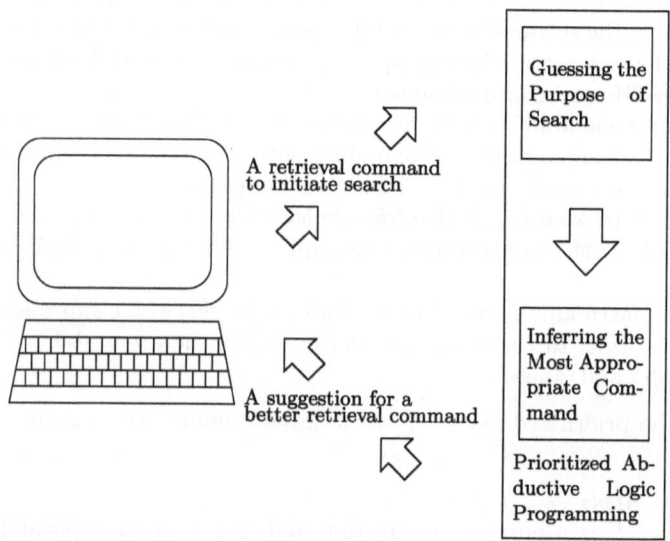

Fig. 1. Retrieval Goal Suggestion System

We add the following rules for prediction together with the previous rules.

- For the ultimate purpose, we introduce the following rule:
  $\bot \leftarrow pos(P), \text{not } P$
  where $\bot$ means contradiction and $pos(P)$ is a proposition meaning that a user invokes a retrieval action related with the ultimate purpose P. This rule is used to search other rules satisfying P when some retrieval action related with P is taken.
- $pos(P) \leftarrow L'_1$
  ...
  $pos(P) \leftarrow L'_n$
  where L'_i expresses that some action of information retrieval has been taken (denoted as $action(R_i)$), or some sub-purpose is fulfilled (denoted as $pos(P_i)$) and each "$pos(P) \leftarrow L'_i$" rule expresses that an action or a sub-purpose L'_i might lead to fulfilment of the purpose P.

The first integrity constraint means that if the prediction of an ultimate purpose is made, then we must try to satisfy the purpose. The latter rules are used to detect relevancy of actions or sub-purposes with an ultimate purpose. By these rules, we can find the hidden ultimate purpose for the initial retrieval command given by a user.

3.2 Video Recorder Example

Now, we apply the above framework to the video recorder example. We show additional rules below.

1. $\perp \leftarrow pos(I), \text{not } I$
   where I means "improving English".
2. To improve English, watch English movies frequently.
   $pos(I) \leftarrow pos(W)$
3. To watch English movies frequently, search a video recorder with a fine resolution.
   $pos(W) \leftarrow action(F)$
4. To improve English, watch English movies showing English caption.
   $pos(I) \leftarrow pos(S)$
5. To watch English movies showing English caption, search a video recorder with a closed caption facility.
   $pos(S) \leftarrow action(C)$

In the following execution, we start the situation when action, `action(find_noisereductionVCR)`, is taken by adding the rules of (0) and (1) and ask `?-start`.

Then, we try to guess the ultimate purpose of this retrieval and give the most appropriate retrieval command.

```
Program
start<- action(find_noisereductionVCR)                              (0)
action(find_noisereductionVCR)<-                                    (1)
0<- pos(improve_english),-improve_english                           (2)
improve_english<- appli1*,frequentwatch                             (3)
pos(improve_english)<- pos(frequentwatch)                           (4)
frequentwatch<- find_noisereductionVCR*                             (5)
pos(frequentwatch)<- action(find_noisereductionVCR)                 (6)
improve_english<- appli2*,shownEnglishsentence                      (7)
pos(improve_english)<- pos(shownEnglishsentence)                    (8)
shownEnglishsentence<- find_englishcaptionVCR*                      (9)
pos(shownEnglishsentence)<- action(find_englishcaptionVCR)         (10)
0<- find_englishcaptionVCR*,-cond(find_englishcaptionVCR)          (11)
cond(find_englishcaptionVCR)<- exists_englishcaptionVCR            (12)

Hierarchy for Abducibles
[[abd(appli1)],[abd(appli2)]]
```

```
Stable Models

Model 1
improve_english
frequentwatch
find_noisereductionVCR*
appli1*
pos(improve_english)
pos(frequentwatch)
start
action(find_noisereductionVCR)

Most Preferable Stable Models
improve_english
frequentwatch
find_noisereductionVCR*
appli1*
pos(improve_english)
pos(frequentwatch)
start
action(find_noisereductionVCR)
```

1. To derive the goal ?-start. We find the rule (0) and reduce the goal into ?-action(find_noisereductionVCR). Then, we find the rule (1) to derive the goal. However, in our procedure, we need to check the consistency of this derivation since some integrity constraint related with this derivation might be violated.
2. Therefore, from action(find_noisereductionVCR), we use a rule in a bottom-up manner to check consistency. Then by the rule (10) pos(shown Englishsentence) is inferred. And we continue to check the consistency of pos(shownEnglishsentence). Then, we find pos(improve_english) to be derived by the rule (8).
3. Then, we need to show that the integrity constraint (2), ''0<-pos(improve_ english),-improve_english'', is not violated. To show this, we need to derive improve_english. If we cannot show that improve_english is derived, then (2) is violated and there is no answer.
4. There are two rules to derive improve_english, (3) and (7).
5. To apply the rule (3), we need to abduce appli1* and show frequentwatch. To show frequentwatch, we need to abduce find_noisereductionVCR* by the rule (5). Therefore, this derivation results in the model which includes appli1* and find_noisereductionVCR*.
6. On the other hand, to apply the rule (7), we need to abduce appli2* and and show shownEnglishsentence. However, it fails as shown in the previous log.
7. Therefore, the most preferable stable model is the one which includes find_ noisereductionVCR* and appli1* only. Thus, the current performed retrieval command is the best command in this context.

During the search, suppose that we found a video recorder with a closed caption. we add `exists_englishcaptionVCR<-` to the program

```
Program
start<- action(find_noisereductionVCR)                              (0)
action(find_noisereductionVCR)<-                                    (1)
0<- pos(improve_english),-improve_english                           (2)
improve_english<- appli1*,frequentwatch                             (3)
pos(improve_english)<- pos(frequentwatch)                           (4)
frequentwatch<- find_noisereductionVCR*                             (5)
pos(frequentwatch)<- action(find_noisereductionVCR)                 (6)
improve_english<- appli2*,shownEnglishsentence                      (7)
pos(improve_english)<- pos(shownEnglishsentence)                    (8)
shownEnglishsentence<- find_englishcaptionVCR*                      (9)
pos(shownEnglishsentence)<- action(find_englishcaptionVCR)         (10)
0<- find_englishcaptionVCR*,-cond(find_englishcaptionVCR)          (11)
cond(find_englishcaptionVCR)<- exists_englishcaptionVCR            (12)
exists_englishcaptionVCR<-                                         (13)


Hierarchy for Abducibles
[[abd(appli1)],[abd(appli2)]]


Stable Models

Model 1
improve_english
frequentwatch
find_noisereductionVCR*
appli1*
pos(improve_english)
pos(frequentwatch)
start
action(find_noisereductionVCR)

Model 2
cond(find_englishcaptionVCR)
exists_englishcaptionVCR
improve_english
shownEnglishsentence
find_englishcaptionVCR*
appli2*
pos(improve_english)
pos(frequentwatch)
start
action(find_noisereductionVCR)
```

```
Most Preferable Stable Models
cond(find_englishcaptionVCR)
exists_englishcaptionVCR
improve_english
shownEnglishsentence
find_englishcaptionVCR*
appli2*
pos(improve_english)
pos(frequentwatch)
start
action(find_noisereductionVCR)
```

In this situation, there are two models which realize `improve_english` in a different way. However, thanks to hierarchy of abducibles the latter model is chosen. Then, in the new most preferable stable model, `find_englishcaption` becomes true. Therefore, for the new situation, the system now suggests a search for a video recorder with a closed caption in stead of the current retrieval command to search a video recorder with a fine resolution.

4   Conclusion

This paper presents a formal analysis of retrieval goal change in information retrieval task. We demonstrated the appropriateness of the formalization using examples. Moreover, using prioritized abductive logic programming, the system suggests the appropriate change of retrieval command based on the initial command given by a user. We believe that this analysis will be a basis of intelligent agents which make more creative suggestion for information retrieval.

However, this is just the first step and there are a lot of things to be done:

- How to obtain various purposes?
- How to obtain logical rules?
- How to obtain preference over rules?
- How to change preferences if new information is obtained?

We would like to investigate the above concern toward an implementation of more helpful cooperative agent for information retrieval.

Acknowledgements. This research is partly supported by JSPS Research for the Future Program. I thank for Yuzuru Tanaka from Hokkaido University for providing me an important motivating example for this research. I also thank Bob Kowalski from Imperial College for instructive comments on the research and Mina Akaishi from Hokkaido University for useful comments on the paper and anonymous referees for constructive comments to improve the paper.

Appendix: Definitions of Generalized Stable Models and Most Preferable Stable Models

Firstly, we give definitions related with abductive logic programming.

Definition 1. *[5]. Since we only consider propositions or grounded atoms, it is sufficient to consider a propositional version of abductive logic programming below.*

An abductive framework *is a pair* $\langle P, A \rangle$ *where A is a set of propositional symbols, called* abducible propositions *and P is a set of rules each of whose head is not in A. We call a proposition in A an* abducible.

The following is a definition of a generalized stable model which can manipulate abducibles in abductive logic programming.

Definition 2. *A rule R is of the form:*

$$H \leftarrow P_1, ..., P_j, \sim N_1, ..., \sim N_h$$

where H, $P_1, ..., P_j, N_1, ..., N_h$ *are propositions.*

We call H *the* head *of the rule* R *denoted as* $head(R)$ *and* $P_1, ..., P_j, \sim N_1, ..., \sim N_h$ *the* body *of the rule denoted as* $body(R)$. *If* $H = \bot$, *we sometimes call the rule an* integrity constraint.

Definition 3. *Let M be a set of propositions and* P^M *be the following program.*

$$P^M = \{H \leftarrow B_1, ..., B_l|$$
$$\text{``}H \leftarrow B_1, ..., B_l, \sim A_1, ..., \sim A_h.\text{''} \in P \text{ and } A_i \notin M \text{ for each } i = 1, ..., h.\}$$

Let $min(P^M)$ *be the least model of* P^M. *A* stable model *for a logic program* P *is* M *iff* $M = min(P^M)$ *and* $\bot \notin M$.

We say that P *is consistent if* P *has a stable model.*

Definition 4. *[5]. Let* $\langle P, A \rangle$ *be an abductive framework and* Θ *be a set of abducibles. A* generalized stable model $M(\Theta)$ *is a stable model of* $P \cup \{H \leftarrow |H \in \Theta\}$.

We say that a model $M(\Theta)$ *is a* generalized stable model with a minimal set of abducibles Θ *if there is no generalized stable model* $M(\Theta')$ *such that* Θ' *is a proper subset of* Θ.

Now, we extend the above framework with prioritization over abducibles. We firstly introduce a hierarchy over abducibles

$$\langle A_1 < A_2 ... < A_n \rangle$$

where A_i is a set of abducibles meaning that an abducible $a_i \in A_i$ should not be assumed more strongly than $a_j \in A_j$ if $i \leq j$, in other words, a hypothesis in A_j is more plausible than one in A_i.

According to the above hierarchy, we give a order over generalized stable models.

Definition 5. *Let* M_1, M_2 *be generalized stable models with a minimal set of abducibles of an abductive logic program. We say* $M_2 \preceq M_1$ *(M_1 is preferable to M_2.) if there is some $1 \leq j \leq n$ s.t. for every $1 \leq i \leq j - 1$, $A_i(M_2) = A_i(M_1)$*

and $A_j(M_2) \supseteq A_j(M_1)$ where $A_i(M)$ is a set of abducibles which are in A_i of $\langle A_1 < A_2... < A_i < ... < A_n \rangle$ and are true in M [5].

We write $M_2 \prec M_1$ as $M_2 \preceq M_1$ and not $M_1 \preceq M_2$.

The most preferable stable model w.r.t. a goal G of an abductive logic program P is a stable model with a minimal set of abducibles M of P s.t. it satisfies G and there is no stable model with a minimal set of abducibles M' of P s.t. it satisfies G and $M \prec M'$.

References

1. Amati,G., and Georgatos, Relevance as Deduction: A Logical View of Information Retrieval, *Proc. of the Second Workshop on Information Retrieval, Uncertainty and Logic (WIRUL'96)*, pp. 21 – 26 (1996).
2. Bruza, P., and Huibers, T.W.C., A Study of Aboutness in Information Retrieval, *Artificial Intelligence Review*, Vol. 10, No. 5-6, pp. 381 – 407 (1996).
3. P.D. Bruza and B. van Linder, Preferential Models of Query by Navigation, F. Crestani, M. Lalmas, and C.J. van Rijsbergen (eds), *Information Retrieval: Uncertainty and Logics*, Kluwer Academic Publishers, pp. 73 – 96 (1998)
4. Hunter, A., Intelligent Text Handling Using Default Logic, *Proc. of the Eighth IEEE International Conference on Tools with Artificial Intelligence (TAI'96)* pp. 34 – 40 (1996).
5. Kakas, A. C., and Mancarella, P., "Generalized Stable Models: A Semantics for Abduction", *Proc. of ECAI'90* pp. 385 – 391 (1990).
6. Kakas, A. C., Kowalski, R., and Toni, F., "The Role of Abduction in Logic Programming", Handbook of Logic in Artificial Intelligence and Logic Programming 5, pp. 235 – 324, D.M. Gabbay, C.J. Hogger and J.A. Robinson eds., Oxford University Press (1998)
7. Kowalski, R., and Satoh, K., "Goals in Information Seeking", Research Note, Meme Media laboratory, Hokkaido University (2000).
8. Lau, R., ter Hofstede, A.H.M., and Bruza, P.D., A Study of Belief Revision in the Context of Adaptive Information Filtering, *Proc. of the 5th International Computer Science Conference ICSC'99 on Internet Applications*, LNCS 1749, pp. 1 – 10 (1999).
9. Lifschitz, V., Computing Circumscription, *Proc. of IJCAI-85*, pp. 121 – 127 (1985).
10. McCarthy, J., "Application of Circumscription to Formalizing Common-sense Knowledge", Artificial Intelligence, Vol.28, pp.89 – 116 (1986).
11. Sakama, C., and Inoue, K., "Representing Priorities in Logic Programs", *Proceedings of JICSLP96*, pp. 82 – 96 (1996).
12. Satoh, K. and Iwayama, N., "A Query Evaluation Method for Abductive Logic Programming", *Proceedings of JICSLP92*, pp. 671 – 685 (1992).
13. Satoh, K., "Formalizing Retrieval Goal Change by Prioritized Circumscription - Preliminary Report", *Proceedings of CIA 2003*, LNCS 2782, pp. 324 – 335 (2003).
14. Shoji, H., Mori, M., and Hori, K., "Concept Articulation as Chance Discovery by Shoppers", *Proc. of PRICAI Workshop on Chance Discovery*, pp. 103 – 114 (2002).

---

[5] The idea of this prioritization is similar to the one in more general prioritization [11]. However, in this paper, we use a simpler prioritization since it is enough for our purpose.

Similarity of Documents
Based on the Vector Sequence Model*

Akihiro Yamamoto[1] and Akira Ogiso[2]

[1] Graduate School of Informatics
Kyoto University
Yoshida-Honmachi, Sakyo-ku, 606-8501 Kyoto, Japan
akihiro@i.kyoto-u.ac.jp
[2] Mitsubishi Motors Corporation

Abstract. In this paper we propose a new method for searching natural language documents. The method is based on the vector-sequence model where every document is transformed into a sequence of document vectors. The model is intended to clarify the dynamism of the usage of keywords in every document. In order to find similar documents in the model, we formalize the *Length-Based Refinement* (*LBR*, for short) of sequence of documents. The document management system based on LBRs requires users to give a query in the form of a document, but would support them to search documents in a quite different way of the keyword-based search. By developing the system we try to show that the search mechanism based on LBRs could be regarded as a type of intuitive access to documents.

1 Introduction

Although the Internet has made it easy for us to use various types of media, such as images, music, and videos, we are still depending on natural language documents (*documents*, for short in the present paper) for exchanging information. The growth of the Internet made the amount of documents that we can access explosively larger. As the consequence, we need mechanisms for searching appropriate documents from a large amount of documents in order to obtain useful information. Most of the popular search engine in the Internet are designed on the bases of using keywords in documents, but we often experience that such keyword-based search would not sufficiently support us to find documents that we want. The goal of our research is to develop new mechanisms to find documents that match our intuitive requirement as much as possible, and in this paper we propose one of such mechanisms.

Our mechanism is based on modeling every document with a *sequence of document vectors*. A *document vector* is in a Euclidean space and represents a document in the *vector-space model*. Since each element in a document vector is determined with the frequency of appearance of a keyword in the document, the vector-space model is useful for keyword-based search. Our idea is to represent

---

* Most of this work was accomplished when the authors were at Faculty of Technology and Meme Media Laboratory, Hokkaido University.

G. Grieser and Y. Tanaka (Eds.): Intuitive Human Interface 2004, LNAI 3359, pp. 233–242, 2004.

fragments of a document with a document vector, and whole of the document with a sequence of obtained document vectors. That is, our model represents the dynamism of usage of keywords in one document. We call it the *vector-sequence model*. We expect that the dynamism could be useful for searching documents, and explain in this paper how to realize our idea.

The vector-sequence model is originally invented with aiming at capturing narratives represented in documents. Narratives are very useful in managing information in our everyday life. When we read books, magazines, newspapers, or watch TV programs, we remember the contents as narratives. We may expect that narratives would help us in searching documents, though they are difficult for computers to recognize from raw documents. An important aspect of narratives is dynamism of events. Our idea is to approximate the dynamism of events with that of usage of keywords. More precisely, we start with an assumption that every event in the narrative corresponds to a part of the document. Then we put the second assumption that the dynamism of events would affect the usage of keywords (Fig. 1). If this assumption holds, we could use with the dynamism of usage of keywords as an approximation of narratives. Note that our aim is not to recognize the narrative from a given document. We are aiming at a new method of searching documents. Though neither of the assumptions above have theoretical witness, our experimental result reported in the present paper would show that they would be reliable in searching documents.

We represent our mechanism not only in a formal manner, but also as a document management system based on it. We think that explaining the system at first would help the readers to understand our goal and so give the overview of the system in the following section. In Section 3, we give formal explanation of our method based on Inductive Logic Programming [7], which is a branch of Machine Learning. In Section 4, we give the detail techniques for implementing the system. In Section 5, we report some experimental results and we conclude in Section 6.

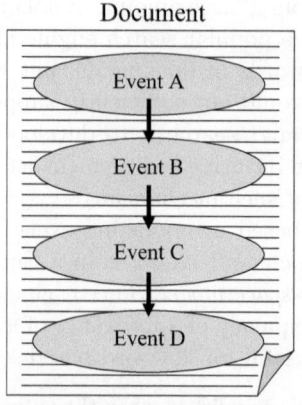

Fig. 1. Narrative in a document

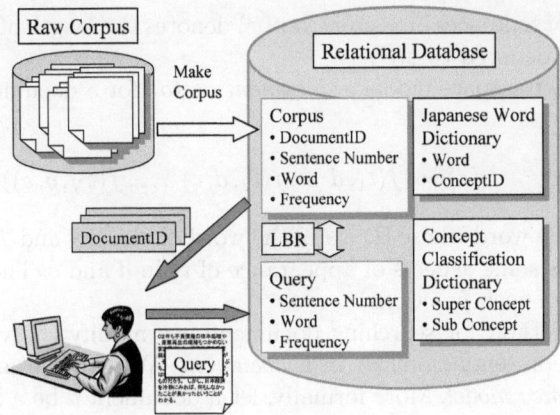

Fig. 2. Overview of the document management system

2   The Overview of the Document Management System

In Fig. 2 we illustrate the overview of our document management system. We developed the system on a relational database management system (RDBMS) so that it contains a corpora transformed into relations appropriate for the query processing. We also store two dictionaries, which we call a *word dictionary* and a *concept dictionary*. The two dictionaries are assumed to share indices of concepts. The word dictionary defines a relation between words in a language and concepts, and the concept dictionary gives a hierarchical structure of the set of concepts. In the current status of research we treat documents written in Japanese, and so use the Japanese Word Dictionary and the Concept Classification Dictionary developed and distributed by Japan Electronic Dictionary Research Institute (EDR) [5]. Our method could be applied to documents written in any other languages if the pair of a word dictionary and a concept dictionary for the language were provided.

In the system every document in a corpus is transformed into a sequence of document vectors and stored in the form of a relation in RDBMS. A user gives a query in the form of a document, which is also transformed into a sequence of document vectors. The system searches documents similar to the query in the corpus by applying the mechanism called *Length-Based Refinement* (*LBR*, for short) to pairs of document vector sequences. Before applying LBR, users can generalize words by using the concept dictionary. All of these processes are executed with SQL queries in the RDBMS.

3   Finding Similar Documents

3.1   Sequences of Document Vectors and LBR

We regard a *document* as a sequence of sentences and a *corpus* as a set of documents. A sub-sequence of a document is called a *sub-document* or a *window*. In order to make our explanation strict, we introduce some notations. For a sequence σ of sentences or vectors, $len(\sigma)$ denotes the length of σ. The cardinality of a set S is denoted by $\sharp(S)$.

In the vector-space model a *document vector* for a document d in a corpus c is a vector

$$v(d) = (f(t_1, d, c), f(t_2, d, c), \ldots, f(t_N, d, c)),$$

where t_i is the word whose ID is i in the word dictionary and f is a function. The function uses some aspects of appearance of t_j in d and c. The *tf-idf* function is well-known in such functions.

In our method for searching documents we modify the vector-space model so that it represents *windows* in a *document*. We call the modified model the *vector-sequence model*. More formally, let a document d be a sequence $s_1, s_2, \ldots$ of sentences, and the window $s_i, s_{i+1}, \ldots, s_{i+m-1}$ be denoted by w_i^m. We define the *document vector* for w_i^m as a tuple

$$v(w_i^m) = (f(t_1, w_i^m, d), f(t_2, w_i^m, d), \ldots, f(t_N, w_i^m, d)).$$

We also define a sequence $\rho_m(d)$ of document vectors as

$$\rho_m(d) = v(w_1^m), v(w_2^m), \ldots, v(w_{len(d)-m+1}^m).$$

Note that $\rho_1(d)$ is a sequence of document vectors each of which is made from a sentence in d. For $m > 1$ we regard $\rho_m(d)$ as approximation or generalization of $\rho_1(d)$ and call it a *length-based refinement* (*LBR*) of $\rho_1(d)$. We use the term refinement because generalization is sometimes called *refinement* in Inductive Logic Programming. The parameter m is called the *width* of the LBR.

For the function f we adopt the tf-idf function for windows defined as

$$tf\text{-}idf(t_j, w_i^m, d) = tf(t_j, w_i^m) \cdot idf(t_j, d), \text{ where}$$
$$tf(t_j, w_i^m) = \text{the frequency of the appearance of the word } t_j$$
$$\text{in the window } w, \text{ and}$$
$$idf(t_j, d) = \log \frac{len(d)}{\sharp(\{i \mid t_j \text{ appears in } s_i\})}.$$

3.2   Definiton of Similarity

We define the similarity of two documents by using their LBRs. For the definition we assume a function *sim* of two document vectors whose codomain is the set of positive real numbers. The function is called a *similarity function*. A popular similarity function is

$$c(u, v) = \frac{u \cdot v}{\|u\| \, \|v\|},$$

where $\cdot$ indicates the inner product of two vectors, and $\| \ \|$ indicates the size of a vector, respectively.

Let d and e be documents, and assume a parameter r $(0 < r \leq 1)$. We determine the window sizes I for the LBR of d and J for the LBR of e so that

$$\left\lfloor \frac{I}{len(d)} \right\rfloor = \left\lfloor \frac{J}{len(e)} \right\rfloor = r.$$

Without loss of generality we can assume that $len(\rho_I(d)) \geq len(\rho_J(e))$. For every vector in v_i in $\rho_I(d)$, we make a pair (v_i, w_{i_k}) where

$$i_k = \left\lfloor i \times \frac{len(\rho_I(d))}{len(\rho_J(e))} \right\rfloor,$$

and we put

$$\rho_r(d, e) = (v_1, w_{i_1}), (v_2, w_{i_2}), \ldots, (v_n, w_{i_n}).$$

We define two documents d and e are *simlar* w.r.t. real numbers δ $(\delta > 0)$ and ε $(0 \leq \varepsilon \leq 1)$ if

$$\frac{\sharp(\{k \mid (v_k, w_{i_k}) \text{ is in } \rho_r(d, e) \text{ and } sim(v_k, w_{i_k}) > \delta\})}{len(\rho_r(d, e))} > 1 - \varepsilon.$$

By introducing a random variable S for $sim(v_k, w_{i_k})$, the condition of the similarity can be represented as

$$Pr(S > \delta) > 1 - \varepsilon.$$

3.3   Estimating the Width for LBRs

The parameter r $(0 < r \leq 1)$ must be fixed so that we can detect the similarity of the documents. In case that r were too small, the width for the LBRs would be too narrow, there would be almost no word which appears in common in the pair (v_k, w_{i_k}), and the similarity $sim(v_k, w_{i_k})$ would be very small even though the two documents were similar. On the contrary, in case that r is too large size, the width for the LBRs were too large, and so words appearing in common would affect $sim(v_k, w_{i_k})$, without depending on where they occur in the documents.

We determined the value r by experiment. We used some various books on narratives fairy tales like "Issun-boushi", "Momotarou" and so on. We choose several different books for one tale. We prepared pairs of documents of the following types:

E1 two documents for a same tale
E2 a document and the document obtained by shuffling the order of the sentences in it
E3 two documents for different tales

We expected that an appropriate value of r should derive both of the following conclusions:

C1 The documents in any pair of Type **E1** are similar to each other.
C2 No pair of Type **E2** or Type **E3** consists of similar documents.

In the terminology of Machine Learning, pairs of Type **E1** are positive examples while pairs of Type **E2** and **E3** are negative examples. For better estimation of the parameter, we prepared the pairs of **E2** which are counters for the data structure, *sequences* of vectors. After repeating experiments with changing the value of the parameter, we eventually found a proper one.

4   Details of the Imprementation

4.1   Preprocessing

In order to transform every sentence in a document into a document vector we need to turn inflecting words into their original forms (stemming), decide the parts of speech of words (part-of-speech tagging), and so on. For languages, such as Japanese, in which no space is inserted between two words in a document, it is necessary to divide a sentence into morphemes (segmentation). Morphological analysis for such languages consists of all of these activities. In our development we adopted Chasen [4], a well-known morphological analysis system for Japanese documents.

After the activities, we had better remove *stop words*, which are hardly helpful for characterizing the contents of documents. We treat all words except nouns, verbs, and adjectives as stop words. We also add some abstract nouns to the stop words. The list of the stop words is shown in Fig 3.

ある, いる, お, く, げ, こと, ご, さ, す, する, とき,
ところ, なる, の, ほう, め, もの, る, れる, ん

Fig. 3. The stop word list

4.2   The EDR Electronic Dictionary

We adopted the Japanese Word Dictionary (JWD) for the word dictionary and the Concept Classification Dictionary (CCD) for the concept dictionary. Both are in the EDR Electronic Dictionary[5].

The JWD consists of the Japanese word records arranged alphabetically according to the Japanese syllabary. Each record in the dictionary consists of the record number (the ID for the word), headword information, grammatical information, semantic information, pragmatic and supplementary information and management information. The dictionary is designed for expressing the correspondence between a Japanese word and the concepts represented by the word and to provide the grammatical information for the word. A hexadecimal number is given to each concept for distinguishing it with others.

The CCD contains the classification of concepts that has a super-sub relation with allowing multiple inheritances, that is, allowing one concept to have more than two super-concepts. So the concepts constitute a lattice. In the CCD the pair of concepts that have an immediate super and sub-concept relation is registered in one record.

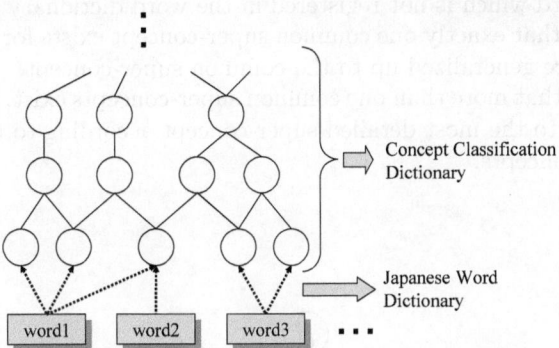

Fig. 4. Relation between words and concepts

4.3   Generalization with the Concept Dictionary

By using a pair of a word dictionary and a concept dictionary, such as the JWD and the CCD, we can define a *generalization* of a word as a concept corresponding to it or a super-concept of the concept. We also define a *common generalization* of two different words as a concept or a super-concept common to them. In our experiment we observed that replacing two different words with a common generalization sometimes helps us to find similar documents by using LBRs. However, it is clear that over-generalization of words is harmful, and we need some control mechanism for finding generalization. For the purpose we introduce the *fineness* of a concept and the *level* for generalization.

The fineness of a concept c is defined as

$$F(c) = d(c) + \frac{1}{w(c)},$$

where $d(c)$ is the *depth* of c and $w(c)$ is its *width*. Both of the depth and the width are determined based on the fact that the concept dictionary stores concepts in the structure of a lattice. The depth of the concept c is the *maximum* distance from the top to c. That is, we consider that the larger $d(c)$ is, c is more detailed, and the smaller $d(c)$ is, c is more abstract. We define the width of c as the number of super-concept of c. For two concepts c and d, if the super-concepts of c are less than those of d, we consider that c is more concrete than d and d is more general than c.

The level of the generalization is defined in the direction from the bottoms to the top. More precisely, generalization of a word w up to level 0 means no replacement is applied to w, generalization up to level 1 means that w can be replaced with the concept corresponding to w, and generalization up to level l

($l \geq 2$) means that w can be replaced to its super-concepts in at most $l-1$ steps up to the concept corresponds to w.

By using the fineness and level, we define appropriate generalization of words according to the following rules.

R1 The word which is not registered in the word dictionary is not generalized.
R2 In case that exactly one common super-concept exists for several words, the words are generalized up to the common super-concept.
R3 In case that more than one common super-concepts exist, the words are generalized to the most detailed super-concept according to the fineness values of the concepts.

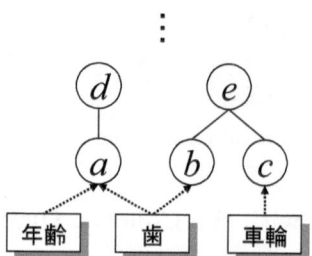

Fig. 5. An example of generalization

For example, consider the generalization of the words in Fig 5. Here, "年齢", "歯", and "車輪" represent "age", "tooth", and "wheel", respectively in English. Consider first the generalization up to level 0. Since the word "年齢" and the word "歯" have a common super-concept a, they are generalized to a. However, since the word "車輪" do not share any concept, it is not generalized. Next, consider the generalization up to level 1. The word "年齢" and the word "歯" have a common concept a, and the word "歯" and the word "車輪" have a common super-concept e. In the case, the concept fineness values of a and e are compared, and the words are generalized to the concept whose value is largest.

4.4   Documents as Queries

In the document management system a user gives a query in the form of a document. The query document is stored as a relation in the RDBMS in the same way as documents in corpora, without its document ID. The SQL query which a query document is stored as a relation in the RDBMS is the following:

```
insert into QUERY_TABLE
values (sentence_number, word, frequency);.
```

The similarity detection based on LBRs is applied to the documents in the corpora and a query document, and as the result return the document ID's which are judged to be similar.

5   Experiment

In order to check that our method based on LBRs find similarity of documents as we expected, we made an experiment.

We adopted the tf-idf function for the function for document vectors, and the function $c(u, v)$ for the similarity function of two document vectors. In some preparatory experiments using the fairy tale documents, we set $r = 0.3$, $\delta = 0.4$, and $\varepsilon = 0.35$.

In the practice of the experiment, we found the generalization of words up to level 2 causes over-generalization, and the generalization of words up to level 0 made us miss many pairs of similar documents. So we adopted the generalization of words up to level 1. In order to reduce the search space, we first select candidate documents from the corpus by using some keywords appearing in given query documents, and then we apply our method of finding similar documents.

We asked several persons to read all documents selected by the keyword search, and asked "Which documents do you feel similar to the query document?". As the result, when we select "near-miss" and "accident" as keywords, seven of eight persons answered the same result as our system. When choosing "individual", "information", and "ledger" as keywords, six of seven persons answered in the same manner of the system. Although these are subjectivity evaluation, we can conclude that the documents considered by people to be similar have been retrieved by our system.

6   Conclusion

In this paper we formalized a new similarity of documents based on the vector-sequence model. We also developed the system searching documents based on the similarity. The system is different from others on the point every query is given as a document, but as far as the result of our experiment, it looks supporting a type of intuitive access to documents.

References

1. K. Kita, K. Tsuda, and M. Shishibori: *Information Retrieval Algorithms*, Kyouritsu Press (in Japanese), 2002.
2. M. Haraguchi, S. Nakano, and M. Yoshioka: Discovery of Maximal Analogies between Stories, *Proceedings of the 5th International Conference on Discovery Science (LNCS 2534)*, pp.324–331, 2002.
3. M. Hearst: TextTiling: Segmenting Text into Multi-Paragraph Subtopic Passages, *Computational Linguistics*, 23 (1), pp.33-64, 1997.
4. Y. Matsumoto, A. Kitauchi, T. Yamashita, Y. Hirano, H. Matsuda, K. Takaoka, M. Asahara: *Morphological Analysis System ChaSen version 2.2.1 Manual*, 2000. http://chasen.aist-nara.ac.jp/
5. The EDR Electronic Dictionary, Japan Electronic Dictionary Research Institute, Ltd. http://www.jsa.co.jp/EDR/

6. W. B. Frakes and R. Baeza-Yates: *Information Retrieval: Data Structures and Algorithms*, Prentice Hall, 1992.
7. S.-H. Nienhuys-Cheng and R. de Wolf: *Foundations of Inductive Logic Programming (LNAI 1228)*, Springer, 1997.
8. G. Salton and M. J. McGill: *Introduction to Modern Information Retrieval*, McGraw-Hill, 1983.
9. T. Tokunaga: *Information Retrieval and Natural Language Processing*, University of Tokyo Press (in Japanese), 1999.

Towards Constructing Story Databases Using Maximal Analogies Between Stories

Masaharu Yoshioka, Makoto Haraguchi, and Akihito Mizoe

Graduate School of Information Science and Technology
Hokkaido University
N-14 W-9, Sapporo 060-0814, Japan
{yoshioka,makoto,amring}@db-ei.eng.hokudai.ac.jp

Abstract. In order to construct story databases, it is crucial to have an effective index that represents the plot and event sequences in a document. For this purpose, we have already proposed a method using the concept of maximal analogy to represent a generalized event sequence of documents with a maximal set of events. However, it is expensive to calculate a maximal analogy from documents with a large number of sentences. Therefore, in this paper, we propose an efficient algorithm to generate a maximal analogy, based on graph theory, and we confirm its effectiveness experimentally. We also discuss how to use a maximal analogy as an index for a story database, and outline our future plans.

1 Introduction

Since many documents can now be accessed through the Internet, various methodologies for retrieving, organizing and accessing documents have been developed. Information retrieval and document classification are examples of such techniques. As the number of documents to be processed is generally very large, most of these systems use a "bag of words" approach, and use an index based on words in each document. A "bag of words" approach works efficiently, but cannot discriminate between two or more documents that have same word sets in different order. For instance, any "bag of words" indexing system does not distinguish between "a dog bit a man" and "a man bit a dog", despite their different meanings. Thus, there is a need for an extended indexing system that can handle differences such as this, and is not based on index terms alone.

In addition, most of standard document databases handle document by using indices that represent facts in the document (e.g. existence of terms and sentences). Because of this, these systems cannot discriminate between two or more documents that have same sentences in different order (plot). We call a document database that can retrieve documents by using a plot as a story database.

In order to construct a story database, it is crucial to have an effective index that represents the plot and event sequences in a document. Since a single document can have various aspects, we need to add multiple indices even for a single document. Text summarization is one of the techniques to extract a plot from

G. Grieser and Y. Tanaka (Eds.): Intuitive Human Interface 2004, LNAI 3359, pp. 243–255, 2004.

a story [1]. However, most of these techniques mainly focus on extracting main plots from a story and are not sufficient to create indices for a story database. Research on topic focused summarization [2] aims to construct different summaries from a single document, but it requires pre-defined topic sets that are also difficult to extract automatically.

To address this problem, we have already proposed the concept of maximal analogy (MA) between stories, which represents a generalized event sequence of documents with a maximal set of events [3]. We have also proposed a method for constructing this index from a set of provided documents. However, the computational cost of this method is too high to apply to pairs of large documents.

In this paper, we propose an efficient method for enumerating MAs from given document pairs based on graph theory. We also discuss how to use the MA as an index for story databases.

This paper is divided into four sections. In Section 2, we briefly review the concept of maximal analogy between stories (MA). In Section 3, we propose a new method to enumerate MAs from two given documents. In Section 4, we demonstrate experimental results and, based on these, we discuss how to use the MA as an index for a story database. Section 5 concludes this paper.

2   Maximal Analogies Between Stories

2.1   Requirement for the Indices of Story Databases

In this paper, we use the term "story" to mean a plot or event sequence in a document. An "event" is a basic unit that represents facts in a story. In this paper, we use a simplex sentence that has one verb and dependent words for this unit. In order to handle a complex sentence, we decompose it into a sequence of simplex sentences. As each single sentence in a document corresponds to an event, a given document is itself a story, and includes various sub-stories that are sub-sequences of the entire event sequence. Since it is difficult to define meaningful sub-stories a priori, we do not restrict to use any sub-sequences of the event as indices for a story.

To handle documents containing story information, indices of story databases should satisfy the following criteria.

(R1) Since a document can have various aspects and each of which can be represented as a story, an index should contain story information.

(R2) Such indices are automatically extracted from documents.

(R3) The determination of what constitutes a significant story in a document is subjective, so the indexing varies according to individuals.

(R4) Once such indices are discovered and constructed, documents should be quickly accessible by their indices.

The most significant requirement is to determine the most important event (sub-)sequence that characterizes the document. One possible standard approach is to evaluate the significance of events using their frequencies and the co-occurrences of words within them [4]. Although such a scheme is quite effective, some important words or sentences may be missed from a particular story extracted from the document. The basic argument of this paper is stated as follows.

> The problem of what constitute important events in a document cannot be determined by examining only one document. If some event sequence is regarded as significant from a particular point of view, then we will find another similar document in which a similar event sequence also appears. Conversely, when we find a generalized event sequence common to all the documents, that a user or a group of users consider similar, it may be a candidate for becoming an important sequence, and may therefore be used as a possible index for documents.

More precisely, we say that an event sequence is common to a set of documents whenever the sequence is a generalization of some sequence in every document. As the act of generalizing event sequences depends on the subsumption of relationships between words, we use the EDR dictionary [5]. Furthermore, we consider the concept tree representation of events in Section 2.2. A concept tree is a special case of a concept graph [6], and can be used to represent the case structures of document sentences.

Given two documents judged to be similar (R3), the concept of maximal analogy between the two is introduced in Section 2.3 to formalize the common generalization of event sequences with a maximal set of events. As an MA is itself an event sequence, it can provide a solution for (R1).

Although we have not yet designed a query-answering system for documents indexed by MAs, their subsumption-checking never involves any combinatorial computations. Testing whether a document meets an MA may therefore be performed quickly (R4).

2.2   Minimal Common Subsumer of Concept Trees

After morphological analysis and parsing, each sentence in a document is represented as a rooted tree, with words as nodes and cases (or role symbols) as edges. A verb is chosen as the root, as in Fig. 2. As verbs are first-class entities of events, the tree of words will be simply called an event in Definition 1. Although such a word tree is normally formalized as a semantic network [7], we consider it as a type of concept graph [6], allowing us to define an ordering for trees by restricting a similar ordering for graphs.

To examine the semantic relationship between concept graphs, we use EDR [5], a machine-readable dictionary. As a word may have more than two possible meanings, the dictionary must provide the concepts involved in words together with the relationships between these concepts. The EDR dictionary supports both types of information for Japanese and English words and concepts. Each concept is designated by a unique identifier, called a concept ID. Let $Terms$ be the set of all words and concept IDs in the EDR dictionary. Then a partial ordering $\prec$ over $Terms$ can be given by

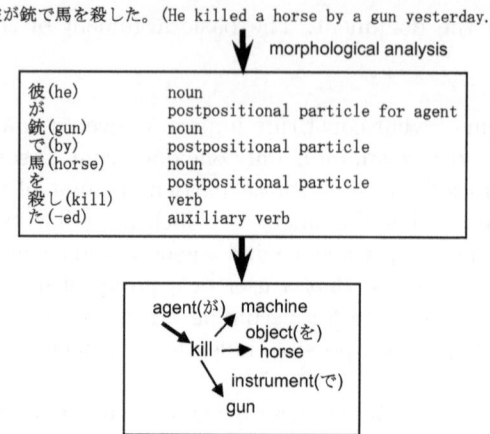

Fig. 1. Construction of a Concept Tree

$t_1 \prec t_2$ iff (1) t_1 and t_2 are both concept IDs and t_1 is more specialized one
                    than t_2 in the concept dictionary, or
                (2) t_1 is a word and t_2 is a concept ID that is more general one
                    than any concept ID associated with t_1 in the word dictionary.

Based on this partial ordering for terms, we now have the following definition of concept trees and their ordering.

Definition 1.
(Concept trees and their paths) *Given a set $\mathcal{L}$ of role or case symbols, a path of length n is a sequence of roles $p = (\ell_1, ..., \ell_n)$, where $\ell_j \in \mathcal{L}$. The empty path, $\lambda = ()$, of length 0 is always regarded as a path denoting the root of a tree . A concept tree is then defined as a pair $g = (Path(g), term_g)$, also called an event, where $Path(g)$ is a finite and prefix-complete set of paths including the empty path, and $term_g$ is a term labeling function, where $term_g : Path(g) \to Terms$.*
(Concept Tree Ordering) *We say that a concept tree g_s subsumes another concept tree g_i iff, for every rooted path $p \in Path(g_s)$, both $p \in Path(g_i)$ and $term_{g_i}(p) \preceq term_{g_s}(p)$ hold. In this case, we also say that g_s is a generalization of g_i, or that g_i is a specialization of g_s.* ∎

We use a morphological analyzer to construct a concept tree. We select noun and verb terms from a sentence and connect them according to the information of postpositional particle. Fig.1 shows an example of this process.

Intuitively, a concept tree g_s is more general than another concept tree g_i if every path in it is preserved in g_i and it uses more general terms than those used in g_i. For instance, both trees at the bottom of Fig. 2 are subsumed by the top tree. Now, the minimal common subsumer (MCS) of two concept trees is defined, similar to the case of the least common subsumers of concept graphs [6]. Formally, an MCS of g_1 and g_2 is defined as a tree consisting of the common

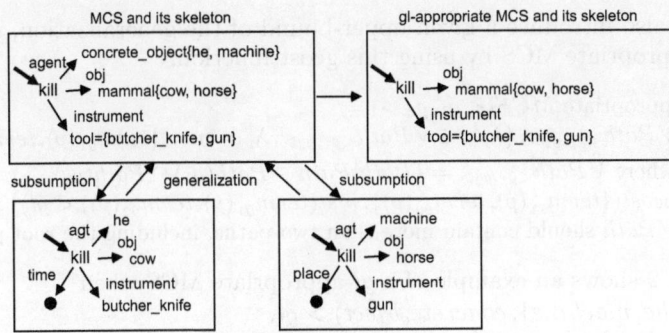

Fig. 2. Concept Trees, where the top example is an MCS of the bottom two

paths of g_j whose labels are some minimal upper bounds of the corresponding paired terms in g_j.

This may be formalized as follows:

$$MCS(< g_1, g_2 >) = (\; Path_{<g_1,g_2>}, \{\lambda_p | p \in Path_{<g_1,g_2>},$$
$$\lambda_p = mst(\{term_{g_1}(p), term_{g_2}(p)\})\}),$$
$$\text{where } Path_{<g_1,g_2>} = Path(g_1) \cap Path(g_2)$$

where $mst(A)$ is a chosen minimal upper bound of a set of terms A. In this sense, mst is called a choice function.

2.3   Maximal Analogy and Its Bottom-Up Construction

The maximal analogy between stories is a sequence of generalized events obtained from different stories. Therefore, we can represent a MA by using a sequence of MCS obtained from the paired events. In order to preserve the order of events in different stories, we define *op-selection* to be a sequence of paired events.

Definition 2.
(op-selection) *Each document* (D_i) *is defined as an ordered sequence* $g_1^{(i)}, ...,$ g_n *of events* $g_j^{(i)}$ *in their order of appearance in the story. We denote* $g_k^{(i)} < g_l^{(i)}$ *whenever* $g_k^{(i)}$ *precedes* $g_l^{(i)}$ *in document* D_i. *For two given stories* D_1, D_2, *an op-selection* θ *of these two stories is an order preserving one-to-one correspondence of events in* D_1 *and* D_2. *That is,* θ *is a sequence* $P_{i_1,j_1}, ..., P_{i_k,j_k}$, *where* $P_{i_n,j_n} =<$ $g_{i_n}^{(1)}, g_{j_n}^{(2)} >\in D_1 \times D_2$, $g_{i_n}^{(1)} < g_{i_{n+1}}^{(1)}$ *and* $g_{j_n}^{(2)} < g_{j_{n+1}}^{(2)}$.

In addition, in order to remove MCSs that are too abstract, we introduce the following cost function:

$$gcost(t, t') = \min\{length(p) \mid p \text{ is a path connecting } t \text{ and } t'\},$$
$$gcost(\{t_1, ..., t_n\}, t) = \max_j gcost(t_j, t), \text{ where we suppose } t_j \preceq t.$$

We also introduce a given upper-bound of the generalization, gl, and define a gl-appropriate MCS by using this gcost function.

gl-appropriate $MCS(< g_1, g_2 >) =$
   $(VPath_{<g_1,g_2>}, \{\lambda_p | p \in VPath_{<g_1,g_2>}, \lambda_p = mst(\{term_{g_1}(p), term_{g_2}(p)\})\})$,
   where $VPath_{<g_1,g_2>} = \{Path | Path \in Path(g_1) \cap Path(g_2)$,
   $gcost(\{term_{g_1}(p), term_{g_2}(p)\}, mst(term_{g_1}(p), term_{g_2}(p)) < gl)\}$
   $VPath$ should contain more than two paths, including the root path.

Fig. 2 shows an example of a gl-appropriate MCS when $gcost(\{he, machine\}, concrete_object) > gl$.

We also define $gcost(< g_1, g_2 >)$ and $gcost(\theta)$ as follows.

$gcost(< g_1, g_2 >) = \max\{gcost(\{term_{g_1}(p), term_{g_2}(p)\}, mst(term_{g_1}(p), term_{g_2}(p)))$
   $| p \in VPath_{<g_1,g_2>}\}$
$gcost(\theta) = \max\{gcost(P) \mid P \in \theta\}$

Definition 3.

(Maximal Analogy)   *Given two documents and an upper bound on the generalization level, gl, an op-selection θ is called gl-appropriate if all corresponding sentences have gl-appropriate MCSs. We then say that a gl-appropriate op-selection θ is maximal if there exists no gl-appropriate op-selection θ', such that it properly includes θ ($\theta' \supset \theta$).*   ∎

The construction of an MA is subject to the construction of maximal op-selections. In order to find maximal gl-appropriate op-selections efficiently, we use the following property corresponding only to the anti-monotonicity of support used in [8] .

(Monotonicity of Cost) $gcost(\theta) \leq gcost(\theta')$ if $\theta \subseteq \theta'$.

The construction is bottom-up to enumerate all possible op-selections without any duplication. For this purpose, we first introduce a partial ordering of the set of op-selections.

Let $D_j = g_1^{(j)}, ..., g_{n_1}^{(j)}$ be the entire sequence of events in this order. Then an op-selection θ is expressed as a sequence $P_{i_1,j_1}, ..., P_{i_k,j_k}$, where P_{i_ℓ,j_ℓ} is the ℓ-th pair of the i_ℓ-th event $g_{i_\ell}^{(1)}$ in D_1 and the j_ℓ-th event $g_{j_\ell}^{(2)}$ in D_2. P_{i_ℓ,j_ℓ} is called a singleton selection. The length k is called the level of θ. Then, the partial ordering $\prec$ among op-selections is defined by the transitive closure of the following direct successor relation:

$\theta_1 \prec \theta_2$ iff $\theta_1 = \theta P_{i,j}$ and $\theta_2 = \theta P_{i,j} P_{x,y}$ for some op-selection $\theta, P_{i,j}, x$ and y
   such that $i < x$ and $j < y$.

From this definition, it follows that any θ of level $k + 1$ has only one direct predecessor θ_1 of level k, a prefix of θ. So, by induction on the level k, all the op-selections are enumerated without any duplication according to the ordering $\prec$. Furthermore, we list only op-selections that satisfy the cost condition during the entire enumeration process.

Base step for level 1 op-selections: We list only singleton op-selections that satisfy the cost condition:

$$OPS(1) = \{P_{ij} \mid gcost(P_{i,j}) \leq gl\}.$$

Inductive step for level $k + 1$ op-selections: Suppose we have $OPS(k)$ holding all op-selections that satisfy the cost condition. We construct op-selections of the next level consistent with the condition as follows:

$$OPS(k+1) = \{\theta P_{i,j} P_{x,y} \mid \theta P_{i,j} \in OPS(k), P_{x,y} \in OPS(1),$$
$$i < x, \; j < y, \; gcost(\theta P_{i,j} P_{x,y}) \leq gl \; \}.$$

Note that, in the case of $k = 1$, θ is a null string.

Termination of construction: The generation of $OPS(k)$ terminates when we find a level ℓ such that $OPS(\ell) = \phi$, leaving ℓ to have a maximum $\min\{n_1, n_2\}$, where n_j is the number of events in the story D_j.

The number of selections generated and tested is minimized. To verify this, let $gcost(\theta)$ exceed the limit gl for an op-selection θ at level k. Then θ has its unique generation path $\theta_1 \prec \dots \prec \theta_k = \theta$ of length $k - 1$. As $gcost$ is monotonic, there exists a least j such that $gcost(\theta_j) > gl$. This θ_j is generated, tested and fails the condition, because $\theta_i \in OPS(i)$ for any $i < j$. However, as the predecessor θ_j is not listed in $OPS(j)$, none of its successors, including θ, are ever generated and tested.

The algorithm above shows a method for constructing the MA from two documents. For more than three documents, we iteratively apply the algorithm for two documents.

3 An Efficient Algorithm for Enumerating a Maximal Analogy

3.1 Enumerating MAs Using Directed Graphs

The algorithm discussed in the previous section works well for documents with few sentences, but it fails to enumerate MAs for larger documents. We thus require an efficient algorithm for this enumeration.

In the previous algorithm, the most significant problem is enumerating the many candidate op-selections that should be merged for generating MAs. Therefore, we need an algorithm that does not generate as many candidates. In this section, we propose a new algorithm based on graph theory.

Fig. 3 shows an example of a possible op-selection represented by a directed graph. Rounded nodes represent sentence pairs that have a gl-appropriate MCS. The two numbers in the node correspond to the number of sentences in the first and second document, respectively. Directed links show how connected nodes can be used as a sequence in op-selection.

By using this graph, the generation of op-selections can be formalized as the search for node sets that are connected by directed links. In this case, we have 11 (level 1), 17 (level 2), 7 (level 3), and 2 (level 4) op-selections, with

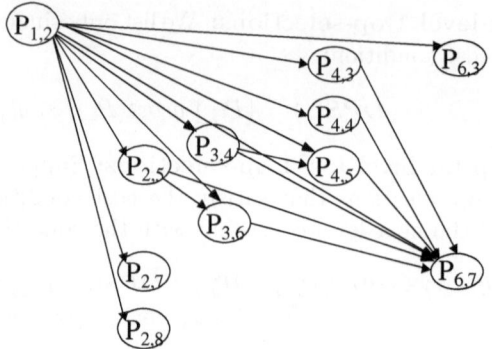

Fig. 3. Possible op-selections represented by a directed graph

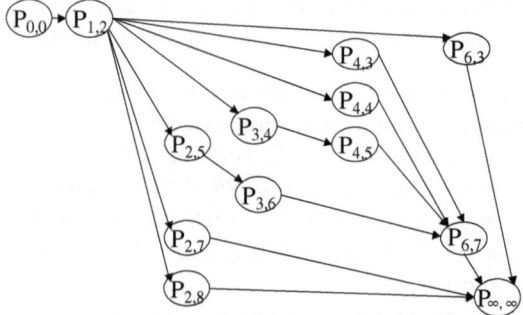

Fig. 4. Possible MAs represented by a directed graph

7 possible MAs (two from level 2, two from level 3 and two from level 4). By using the bottom-up approach, several subsets are generated for deriving one MA. For example, one level 4 op-selection MA $(P_{1,2}, P_{2,5}, P_{3,6}, P_{4,7})$ is generated from four level 3 op-selections, that is, as a subset of the MA $(P_{1,2}, P_{2,5}, P_{3,6})$, $(P_{1,2}, P_{2,5}, P_{4,7})$, $(P_{1,2}, P_{3,6}, P_{4,7})$, $(P_{2,5}, P_{3,6}, P_{4,7})$.

In order to reduce the number of these subset enumerations, we remove directed links that are ineffective in generating MAs. In the previous example, links between $P_{1,2}$ and $P_{3,6}$, $P_{2,5}$ and $P_{4,7}$ are ineffective because we can insert $P_{2,5}$ or $P_{3,6}$ between these nodes. In general, we can define ineffective links as follows:

Definition 4.
(Ineffective Link)   *A link between two nodes $(P_{i,j} P_{k,l})$ that can combine other gl-appropriate nodes $(P_{x,y} : i < x < k, j < y < l)$ is an ineffective link.* ∎

Since we can enumerate op-selections with ineffective links by using two or more links (e.g., links between $P_{i,j}$ and $P_{x,y}$, and $P_{x,y}$ and $P_{k,l}$), removal of these ineffective links does not affect the results for the enumeration of possible MAs.

In order to formalize this enumeration process, we introduce two virtual nodes $P_{0,0}$ and $P_{\infty,\infty}$ that we call start node and end node respectively. Fig. 4 shows a graph that removes ineffective links from the graph in Fig. 3 and adds $P_{0,0}$ and $P_{\infty,\infty}$. By using this graph, it is possible to enumerate MAs by following all paths between $P_{0,0}$ and $P_{\infty,\infty}$.

We can summarize the algorithm as follows.

1. **Base step for level 1 op-selections:** (Same as previous algorithm) We list only singleton op-selections satisfying the cost condition:

$$OPS(1) = \{P_{i,j} \mid gcost(P_{i,j}) \leq gl\}.$$

2. **Directed Link generation:** We represent singleton op-selections as a node. We also add $P_{0,0}$ and $P_{\infty,\infty}$, and generate links between nodes (from $P_{i,j}$ to $P_{x,y}$) that satisfy the following criteria.
   – $i < x$ and $j < y$.
   – The link is not an ineffective link.
3. **Enumeration of MAs:** All possible MAs are enumerated by enumerating all directed paths between $P_{0,0}$ and $P_{\infty,\infty}$.

The high computational cost of step 1 is inevitable when generating MAs. The computational complexity of this step is $O(n * m)$ (where n, m are the numbers of sentences in the two documents. In step 2, we generate links between each node, and the node size is of order $O(n * m)$. For each node, we must check the connectivity of the link from $P_{i,j}$ as follows:

a Check the connectivity for $P_{i+1,x}(x = j+1, \cdots, m)$.
b Check the connectivity for $P_{i+2,x}(x = j+1, \cdots, k)$, where k is the smallest number of $P_{i+1,k}$ connected from $P_{i,j}$. It is not necessary to check the connectivity for $P_{i+2,x}(x = k+1, \cdots, m)$, because $P_{i+1,k}$ exists between $P_{i,j}$ and $P_{i+2,x}$
c Iterate steps a and b until $P_{n,x}$.

Therefore, the computational complexity of link generation for each node is $O(n+m)$ and the total computational complexity is $O(n*m*((n+m))$. However, since each link generation process $(O(n+m))$ is negligible compared to the graph generation in Step 1, it takes negligible time compared to Step 1.

A higher computational cost is incurred for Step 3. However, one important feature of this algorithm is that we can control the order of enumeration. For example, the longest MAs, subject to the longest path between $P_{0,0}$ and $P_{\infty,\infty}$ in this directed graph, can be calculated by using the following algorithm.

a Set the path length of each node $(pl_{i,j})$ to 0 and a set of candidate longest paths $(clp_{i,j})$ to ϕ.
b Start from node $P_{0,0}$ and follow the connected links to check whether each connected link is a candidate for a part of the longest path.
   (1) Let $P_{k,l}$ is the start node and $P_{m,n}$ is a node connected by a link. When $pl_{k,l} + 1 \geq pl_{m,n}$, the connected link is a candidate link.
   (2) When $pl_{k,l}+1 = pl_{m,n}$, new $clp_{k,l}$ is computed by the following operation $clp_{k,l} \cup \{clp, \text{links between } P_{i,j} \text{ and } P_{k,l} | clp \in clp_{i,j}\}$. When $pl_{k,l} + 1 > pl_{m,n}$, new $clp_{k,l}$ is computed by the following operation
   $\{clp, \text{links between } P_{i,j} \text{ and } P_{k,l} | clp \in clp_{i,j}\}$.
c $clp_{\infty,\infty}$ is a set of longest paths of this graph.

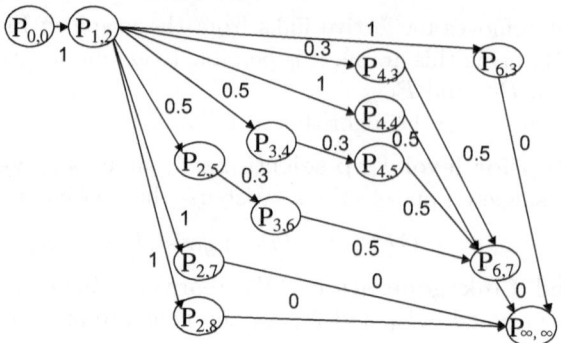

Fig. 5. Possible MAs represented by a weighted directed graph

3.2 Enumerating MAs by Using an Evaluation Function

In the previous algorithm, MAs were enumerated using the longest path. However, these longest MAs may not be appropriate. For example, each singleton op-selection has a gcost, and those with higher gcost may not be appropriate for inclusion if they are very abstract. Therefore, it is better to include a mechanism to order MAs by considering the gcost of each singleton op-selection.

In order to handle this, we formalize this problem with a weighted directed graph scheme. We define an evaluation function $eval(P_{i,j})$ to represent the suitability of including MAs based on their gcost function. This function increases for lower gcost values (i.e., 1 / (gcost + 1)). We also set the weights of links based on the nodes to which they are connected. For example, a link between $P_{i,j}$ and $P_{k,l}$ takes the weight $eval(P_{k,l})$. We also formalize the suitability of an MA by using the sum of the $eval(P_{i,j})$ values of all op-selections.

Since all MAs include $P_{\infty,\infty}$, the effect of $eval(P_{\infty,\infty})$ is canceled and the value of $eval(P_{\infty,\infty})$ does not have any influence. For convenience, we set $eval(P_{\infty,\infty}) = 0$.

Fig. 5 shows an example of the weighted directed graph of Fig. 4. In this case $eval(P_{2,5}) = eval(P_{3,4}) = eval(P_{6,7}) = 0.5$ and $eval(P_{3,6}) = eval(P_{4,3}) = eval(P_{4,5}) = 0.3$, and other nodes have $eval(P_{i,j}) = 1$. In this case MA $(P_{1,2}, P_{4,4}, P_{6,7})$ is the best MA based on this $eval$ function.

The longest paths between $P_{0,0}$ and $P_{\infty,\infty}$ indicate the most appropriate MAs in this weighted directed graph. We can find out these paths by modifying algorithm discussed in Section . We modify step b. of the algorithm as follows.

b Start from node $P_{0,0}$ and follows the connected links to check whether each connected link is a candidate for a part of the longest path.
  (1) Let $P_{k,l}$ is the start node and $P_{m,n}$ is a node connected by a link. When $pl_{k,l} + eval(P_{m,n}) \geq pl_{m,n}$, the connected link is a candidate.
  (2) When $pl_{k,l} + eval(P_{m,n}) = pl_{m,n}$,
      $clp_{k,l} = clp_{k,l} \cup \{clp, \text{links between } P_{i,j} \text{ and } P_{k,l} | clp \in clp_{i,j}\}$.
      When $pl_{k,l} + eval(P_{m,n}) > pl_{m,n}$,
      $clp_{k,l} = \{clp, \text{links between } P_{i,j} \text{ and } P_{k,l} | clp \in clp_{i,j}\}$.

4   Experimental Results
and Discussion for the Story Database

4.1   Experiments Generating Maximal Analogies

We have implemented this algorithm on a Linux-based PC (CPU: Dual Pentium III 1.0GHz, RAM: 4 GB). The basic procedure for obtaining MAs is:

1. Concept tree construction for each sentence
   We use the Cabocha parser [9] to obtain a case structure for each sentence, and convert this to a concept tree. The cases are therefore superficial.
2. Singleton gl-appropriate op-selection generation
   We compare pairs of concept trees created from two documents and generate a gl-appropriate op-selection. We use the EDR dictionary to calculate gcost.
3. Link generation
   We check the connectivity for each pair of gl-appropriate op-selections and generate links. We set the value of parameter gl to 4.
4. Generation of an appropriate MA
   We determine the highest appropriate MA using the evaluation function $eval(\theta) = \sum_{P \in \theta}(1/(1 + gcost(P)))$.
5. Enumeration of MAs
   We enumerate all possible MAs.

In order to analyze the computational cost of this algorithm and evaluate its efficiency, we use a children's story and a short folktale, as used in a previous paper [3] , as input for our algorithm.

Both of these two input stories contain 46 sentences, and have a common plot as follows.

(E1) There are two brothers.

(E2) The younger brother gains some property.

(E3) The elder brother kills the younger brother in order to steal the property.

(E4) The bone of the younger brother then sings a song that reveals the crime.

(E5) As a result, the older brother is caught and punished.

Table 1 shows the results obtained using these two input stories, and Table 2 shows the corresponding computational times for each step.

In some of the most appropriate MAs, (E1) and (E4) are correctly recognized and parts of (E3) and(E5) are also realized in the same MA. However, we find no generalized events corresponding to (E2). Since sentences in these documents have a finer granularity, our system can find more information than the results discussed in [3].

However, we still experience the same problem as the one discussed in [3]. Since the concept hierarchy of the EDR dictionary is constructed for general purposes, it does not classify terms into effective term groups that can perform the same role in different documents.

Table 1. Results obtained from two stories

gl-appropriate singleton op-selection	130
Number of links	715
Number of appropriate MAs	76
Maximum MA length	18
Number of possible MAs	905306

Table 2. Computational time for each step

Concept tree construction	17 s
Singleton *gl*-appropriate op-selection generation	3 s
Link generation	less than 1 s
Appropriate MA generation	1 s
Enumeration of MAs	672 s

4.2 Towards Constructing Story Databases Using MAs

From these results, we confirm that the number of possible MAs is very large, and that it is difficult to determine the most appropriate MA manually. Therefore, a good scoring function is required to select the appropriate indices.

We are planning two approaches to support this selection.

Definition of a better evaluation function. In order to improve the scoring function, we plan to apply the measure of importance or significance of terms [4] and use this for the evaluation function.

Usage of a base query. Since most MAs do not contain a common plot, which was assumed when extracting from a pair of stories, we introduce the concept of a base query to represent a simple skeleton of a common plot (that is, one described in few sentences) that should be included in MAs and used as a criterion for selecting meaningful MAs.

For future work, we also need a mechanism for retrieving a story based on the subsumed relationship between MAs and the query.

5 Conclusion

In this paper, we have proposed an efficient algorithm based on graph theory to generate maximal analogies (MAs), and confirmed the reduction in computation time. However, as the number of possible MAs is very large, we need a method to support selection of meaningful MAs for using MAs as effective indices of story databases. We also outline future work too.

References

1. Mani, I.: Automatic Summarization. John Benjamin Publishing Company (2001)
2. Firmin, T., Chrzanowski, M.J.: An evaluation of automatic text summarization systems. In Mani, I., Maybury, M.T., eds.: Advances in automatic text summarization, Cambridge, Massachusetts, The MIT Press (1999) 325–340
3. Haraguchi, M., Nakano, S., Yoshioka, M.: Discovery of maximal analogies between stories. In: Proc. of the 5th Int'l Conf. on Discovery Science - DS'02 LNCS 2534, Springer (2002) 324–331
4. Ohsawa, Y., Benson, N.E., Yachida, M.: Keygraph: Automatic indexing by cooccurrence graph based on building construction metaphor. In: Proceedings of the Advances in Digital Libraries Conference. (1998) 12–18
5. Japan Electronic Dictionary Research Institute, Ltd. (EDR): EDR ELECTRONIC DICTIONARY VERSION 2.0 TECHNICAL GUIDE TR2-007. (1998)
6. Cohen, W.W., Hirsh, H.: The learnability of description logics with equality constraints. Machine Learning **17** (1994) 169–199
7. Sowa, J.F., ed.: Principles of Semantic Networks. Morgan Kaufmann (1991)
8. Agrawal, R., Srikant, R.: Fast algorithms for mining association rules. In Bocca, J.B., Jarke, M., Zaniolo, C., eds.: Proc. 20th Int. Conf. Very Large Data Bases, VLDB, Morgan Kaufmann (1994) 487–499
9. Kudo, T., Matsumoto, Y.: Japanese dependency analysis using cascaded chunking. In: CoNLL 2002: Proceedings of the 6th Conference on Natural Language Learning 2002 (COLING 2002 Post-Conference Workshops). (2002) 63–69

Lecture Notes in Artificial Intelligence (LNAI)

Vol. 3155: P. Funk, P.A. González Calero (Eds.), Advances in Case-Based Reasoning. XIII, 822 pages. 2004.

Vol. 3139: F. Iida, R. Pfeifer, L. Steels, Y. Kuniyoshi (Eds.), Embodied Artificial Intelligence. IX, 331 pages. 2004.

Vol. 3131: V. Torra, Y. Narukawa (Eds.), Modeling Decisions for Artificial Intelligence. XI, 327 pages. 2004.

Vol. 3127: K.E. Wolff, H.D. Pfeiffer, H.S. Delugach (Eds.), Conceptual Structures at Work. XI, 403 pages. 2004.

Vol. 3123: A. Belz, R. Evans, P. Piwek (Eds.), Natural Language Generation. X, 219 pages. 2004.

Vol. 3120: J. Shawe-Taylor, Y. Singer (Eds.), Learning Theory. X, 648 pages. 2004.

Vol. 3097: D. Basin, M. Rusinowitch (Eds.), Automated Reasoning. XII, 493 pages. 2004.

Vol. 3071: A. Omicini, P. Petta, J. Pitt (Eds.), Engineering Societies in the Agents World. XIII, 409 pages. 2004.

Vol. 3070: L. Rutkowski, J. Siekmann, R. Tadeusiewicz, L.A. Zadeh (Eds.), Artificial Intelligence and Soft Computing - ICAISC 2004. XXV, 1208 pages. 2004.

Vol. 3068: E. André, L. Dybkjær, W. Minker, P. Heisterkamp (Eds.), Affective Dialogue Systems. XII, 324 pages. 2004.

Vol. 3067: M. Dastani, J. Dix, A. El Fallah-Seghrouchni (Eds.), Programming Multi-Agent Systems. X, 221 pages. 2004.

Vol. 3066: S. Tsumoto, R. Słowiński, J. Komorowski, J.W. Grzymała-Busse (Eds.), Rough Sets and Current Trends in Computing. XX, 853 pages. 2004.

Vol. 3065: A. Lomuscio, D. Nute (Eds.), Deontic Logic in Computer Science. X, 275 pages. 2004.

Vol. 3060: A.Y. Tawfik, S.D. Goodwin (Eds.), Advances in Artificial Intelligence. XIII, 582 pages. 2004.

Vol. 3056: H. Dai, R. Srikant, C. Zhang (Eds.), Advances in Knowledge Discovery and Data Mining. XIX, 713 pages. 2004.

Vol. 3055: H. Christiansen, M.-S. Hacid, T. Andreasen, H.L. Larsen (Eds.), Flexible Query Answering Systems. X, 500 pages. 2004.

Vol. 3048: P. Faratin, D.C. Parkes, J.A. Rodríguez-Aguilar, W.E. Walsh (Eds.), Agent-Mediated Electronic Commerce V. XI, 155 pages. 2004.

Vol. 3040: R. Conejo, M. Urretavizcaya, J.-L. Pérez-de-la-Cruz (Eds.), Current Topics in Artificial Intelligence. XIV, 689 pages. 2004.

Vol. 3035: M.A. Wimmer (Ed.), Knowledge Management in Electronic Government. XII, 326 pages. 2004.

Vol. 3034: J. Favela, E. Menasalvas, E. Chávez (Eds.), Advances in Web Intelligence. XIII, 227 pages. 2004.

Vol. 3030: P. Giorgini, B. Henderson-Sellers, M. Winikoff (Eds.), Agent-Oriented Information Systems. XIV, 207 pages. 2004.

Vol. 3029: B. Orchard, C. Yang, M. Ali (Eds.), Innovations in Applied Artificial Intelligence. XXI, 1272 pages. 2004.

Vol. 3025: G.A. Vouros, T. Panayiotopoulos (Eds.), Methods and Applications of Artificial Intelligence. XV, 546 pages. 2004.

Vol. 3020: D. Polani, B. Browning, A. Bonarini, K. Yoshida (Eds.), RoboCup 2003: Robot Soccer World Cup VII. XVI, 767 pages. 2004.

Vol. 3012: K. Kurumatani, S.-H. Chen, A. Ohuchi (Eds.), Multi-Agents for Mass User Support. X, 217 pages. 2004.

Vol. 3010: K.R. Apt, F. Fages, F. Rossi, P. Szeredi, J. Váncza (Eds.), Recent Advances in Constraints. VIII, 285 pages. 2004.

Vol. 2990: J. Leite, A. Omicini, L. Sterling, P. Torroni (Eds.), Declarative Agent Languages and Technologies. XII, 281 pages. 2004.

Vol. 2980: A. Blackwell, K. Marriott, A. Shimojima (Eds.), Diagrammatic Representation and Inference. XV, 448 pages. 2004.

Vol. 2977: G. Di Marzo Serugendo, A. Karageorgos, O.F. Rana, F. Zambonelli (Eds.), Engineering Self-Organising Systems. X, 299 pages. 2004.

Vol. 2972: R. Monroy, G. Arroyo-Figueroa, L.E. Sucar, H. Sossa (Eds.), MICAI 2004: Advances in Artificial Intelligence. XVII, 923 pages. 2004.

Vol. 2969: M. Nickles, M. Rovatsos, G. Weiss (Eds.), Agents and Computational Autonomy. X, 275 pages. 2004.

Vol. 2961: P. Eklund (Ed.), Concept Lattices. IX, 411 pages. 2004.

Vol. 2953: K. Konrad, Model Generation for Natural Language Interpretation and Analysis. XIII, 166 pages. 2004.

Vol. 2934: G. Lindemann, D. Moldt, M. Paolucci (Eds.), Regulated Agent-Based Social Systems. X, 301 pages. 2004.

Vol. 2930: F. Winkler (Ed.), Automated Deduction in Geometry. VII, 231 pages. 2004.

Vol. 2926: L. van Elst, V. Dignum, A. Abecker (Eds.), Agent-Mediated Knowledge Management. XI, 428 pages. 2004.

Vol. 2923: V. Lifschitz, I. Niemelä (Eds.), Logic Programming and Nonmonotonic Reasoning. IX, 365 pages. 2003.

Vol. 2915: A. Camurri, G. Volpe (Eds.), Gesture-Based Communication in Human-Computer Interaction. XIII, 558 pages. 2004.

Vol. 2913: T.M. Pinkston, V.K. Prasanna (Eds.), High Performance Computing - HiPC 2003. XX, 512 pages. 2003.

Vol. 2903: T.D. Gedeon, L.C.C. Fung (Eds.), AI 2003: Advances in Artificial Intelligence. XVI, 1075 pages. 2003.

Vol. 2902: F.M. Pires, S.P. Abreu (Eds.), Progress in Artificial Intelligence. XV, 504 pages. 2003.

Vol. 2892: F. Dau, The Logic System of Concept Graphs with Negation. XI, 213 pages. 2003.

Vol. 2891: J. Lee, M. Barley (Eds.), Intelligent Agents and Multi-Agent Systems. X, 215 pages. 2003.

Vol. 2882: D. Veit, Matchmaking in Electronic Markets. XV, 180 pages. 2003.

Vol. 2872: G. Moro, C. Sartori, M.P. Singh (Eds.), Agents and Peer-to-Peer Computing. XII, 205 pages. 2004.

Vol. 2871: N. Zhong, Z.W. Raś, S. Tsumoto, E. Suzuki (Eds.), Foundations of Intelligent Systems. XV, 697 pages. 2003.